Writing Architectural History

WRITING ARCHITECTURAL HISTORY

Evidence and Narrative in the Twenty-First Century

AGGREGATE

University of Pittsburgh Press

Published by the University of Pittsburgh Press, Pittsburgh, Pa., 15260
This paperback edition, Copyright © 2025, University of Pittsburgh Press
Copyright © 2021, University of Pittsburgh Press
All rights reserved
Manufactured in the United States of America
10 9 8 7 6 5 4 3 2 1

Cataloging-in-Publication Data is available from the Library of Congress

ISBN 13: 978-0-8229-6756-9

ISBN 10: 0-8229-6756-1

Cover art: a selection of images from the interior art and icons for
Aggregate's identity designed by Project Projects.

Cover design: Alex Wolfe

Publisher: University of Pittsburgh Press, 7500 Thomas Blvd., 4th floor, Pittsburgh, PA 15260,
United States, www.upittpress.org

EU Authorized Representative: Easy Access System Europe, Mustamäe tee 50, 10621 Tallinn,
Estonia, gpsr.requests@easproject.com

Contents

Acknowledgments ix

Introduction: Evidence, Narrative, and Writing Architectural History
Daniel M. Abramson, Zeynep Çelik Alexander, and Michael Osman 3

PART I Legends

Chapter 1 The Fires of Saint-Domingue, or, Landscapes of the Haitian Revolution
Peter Minosh 19

Chapter 2 Known Unknowns: The Documentary History of the Franklin Ghost House
Edward Eigen 33

Chapter 3 Vacuum Suction Conveyance, Part II
Meredith TenHoor 46

PART II Self-Evidence

Chapter 4 Talkative Timbers: A. E. Douglass, the Beam Expeditions, and the Construction of Architectural Evidence
Albert Narath 63

Chapter 5 Concrete Is One Hundred Years Old: The Carbonation Equation and Narratives of Anthropogenic Change
Lucia Allais and Forrest Meggers 75

Chapter 6 Medieval and Renaissance Money: On Trial, On Architecture
Lauren Jacobi 90

PART III Data

Chapter 7 From Truth to Proof: Friedrich Adler's *Medieval Brick Architecture of the Prussian States*
Laila Seewang   103

Chapter 8 The Banister Fletchers' Tabulations
Zeynep Çelik Alexander and Michael Osman   117

Chapter 9 Evidence and Narrative in Digital Art History: Exploratory Methods for Weimar Architecture
Paul B. Jaskot and Ivo van der Graaff   133

PART IV Pairings

Chapter 10 Comparative Architecture and Its Discontents
Roy Kozlovsky   147

Chapter 11 When Baghdad Was Like Warsaw: Comparison in the Cold War
Łukasz Stanek   162

Chapter 12 Forensic Architecture as Symptom
Andrew Herscher   177

Chapter 13 Architectural History after Sebald's *Austerlitz*: A Squirrel's Hoard, a Curved Road
Daniel M. Abramson   190

PART V Testimony

Chapter 14 Failing Memories and Forgotten Histories: The Dispute over the Venetian Church of San Giobbe
Janna Israel   203

Chapter 15 Settling Imaginations: Between Dust and Silt
Ijlal Muzaffar   214

Chapter 16 Dadaab Is a Place on Earth: Land and the Migrant Archive
Anooradha Iyer Siddiqi   227

Chapter 17 Learning from Johannesburg: Unpacking Denise Scott Brown's South African View of Las Vegas
Ayala Levin   235

PART VI Retrials

Chapter 18 Architectural Narratives of Habeas Corpus on the High Seas: Charles Frederick Lees versus the Crown
Lisa Haber-Thomson   249

Chapter 19 "This Whole Maze of Evidence": Revisiting Professionalism
and Property through *Hunt v. Parmly*
Erik Carver 260

Chapter 20 "Striking and Imposing Beauty": On the Evidence of
Aesthetic Valuation
Timothy Hyde 274

Notes 285
Selected Bibliography 333
Contributors 335
Index 341

Acknowledgments

The Aggregate Architectural History Collaborative is deeply grateful to several organizations for sponsoring opportunities for this project to be developed between 2017 and 2019 through a series of panels, symposia, workshops, conferences, and a preliminary publication. These include the Society of Architectural Historians 2017 Annual Conference and the Journal of the Society of Architectural Historians; the 2017 Chicago Architecture Biennial and the School of the Art Institute of Chicago; Boston University's Center for the Humanities and Department of the History of Art and Architecture; the Sterling and Francine Clark Art Institute's Research and Academic Program; the Taubman College of Architecture and Urban Planning, University of Michigan; and the Department of Art History, Northwestern University. Numerous individuals aided and participated in these activities and events. We are truly grateful for their contributions, insights, and generosity. We would especially like to acknowledge the efforts and support of Can Bilsel, Abby Collier, Jonathan Massey, Patricia A. Morton, Lisa Saltzman, Julián Serna Lancheros, Jonathan D. Solomon, and Claire Zimmerman. Aggregate is delighted to be working again with the University of Pittsburgh Press.

Writing Architectural History

Introduction
Evidence, Narrative, and Writing Architectural History

■

DANIEL M. ABRAMSON, ZEYNEP ÇELIK ALEXANDER, AND MICHAEL OSMAN

Writing Architectural History: Evidence and Narrative in the Twenty-First Century gathers together recent scholarship to explore the opportunities presented by rethinking issues of evidence and narrative in architectural history. Unifying the volume is a set of intertwined questions: What kinds of evidence does architectural history use? How is this evidence organized in different narratives and toward what ends? What might these concerns tell us about architectural historians' disciplinary and institutional positions in the past and present? And finally, how can consideration of evidence and narrative help us all reimagine the limits and the potentials of the field? These matters have not generally been addressed in architectural history.[1]

The twenty numbered chapters in Writing Architectural History represent a broad range of subjects, from medieval European coin trials and eighteenth-century Haitian revolutionary buildings, to Weimar German construction firms and present-day refugee camps in Kenya. This breadth, along with the volume's general thematic questions about history writing, opens it to readers beyond architectural history. The book's content, however, is not all-encompassing. It excludes the pre-medieval period and large swaths of the globe's built environment. Besides subject limits, the volume's perspectives and norms are also largely restricted to the writing of architectural history under North American conditions. Excluded are architectural histories produced under different situations—geographic and institutional (e.g., the heritage industry)—as well as in forms other than writing (e.g., exhibitions, teaching, design). While the volume's materials and methods thus reproduce established relations of authority and power, they also self-consciously take such conditions as a starting point from which disciplinary boundaries might be expanded and conventions rethought.

This volume examines some of architectural history writing's foundational practices, myths, struggles, and contradictions and, specifically, how historical evidence and narrative can or cannot represent a more liberated field of study for the future. This has particular resonance today. The book's formation took place during the presidency of Donald J. Trump, a period that surely registered in each contributor's life and work and in their thinking about evidence and narrative. Then, intensely, a global pandemic coincided with the resurgence of the Black Lives Matter movement, with these upheavals set against the background of climate catastrophe and migrant dislocations, thus laying bare and intensifying persistent, systematic inequalities and injustices. Overlapping crises and immediate emergencies often prompt practitioners in various disciplines to rethink entrenched concepts and practices, to seek analysis and restructuring. As is the case in most collaborations—and Aggregate is no exception—differences abound in how to respond. Some chapters in this book explicitly engage political goals. Others do so more indirectly. Some authors hold on to the "semistillness" of history's infrastructure, in the words of Fernand Braudel, identifying change in deep bedrock. Other authors might have reflected on the present in what Braudel called a "breathless rush of narrative," urgently applying historiography to the here and now.[2] These differences of approach—all critical in the end—vivify the volume's content and ambitions. The work as a whole is intended as a guide not only for students specializing in architectural history today but also for any scholar engaged in questions of history writing under the specificities of their time.

Given the exigencies of the moment, one might ask, Why rethink the field through themes of evidence and narrative? Wouldn't "climate" or "decolonization" be more productive categories with which to reexamine architectural history writing today? Our interest in evidence and narrative is informed by "historical epistemology," an approach that insists on asking questions about the historical conditions that make knowledge possible in the first place.[3] We adopt this approach strategically. We asked the contributors to detach themselves temporarily from the thick, focused descriptions in which they are so heavily invested as historians and to ask broad questions about their modus operandi—the kinds of evidence they rely on and the tactics that they use for weaving that evidence into narratives. For some authors, this approach has pushed them away from their explicit political priorities. However, we did so with the expectation that examining the implicit structural forces at work in history writing will allow us to return to those thematics with renewed vigor and focus. Historical epistemology in architectural history is offered here not to oppose contemporary relevance but rather as the necessary mooring both for the historical specificity of our descriptions of the past and for the criticality of our engagement in the present.[4]

Interdisciplinarity and reflexivity make this book an Aggregate project, along with sustained collective workshopping among the contributors.[5] Cooperative workshopping and open peer review are of course not unique to the Aggregate Architectural History Collaborative, but commitment to these activities defines Aggregate as a practice rather than an attachment to any specific theoretical approach. Accordingly, this volume is not a demand for methodological discipline but rather an open-ended exploration of various practicalities of writing histories. This introduction thus offers a working philosophy, not a hard method, formulated here as a soft set of questions, which are posed in the present tense because they are questions that the architectural historian may ask now. But the responses will mainly be historiographic, in the past tense, drawing from particular histories of architecture and other historical disciplines in the humanities.

1. How do uses of evidence and narrative in architectural history relate to the field's history and institutional settings?

In North America, architectural history traced a move from art history departments, where PhD candidates were once predominantly trained, to architecture schools, which have increasingly assumed that role since the 1960s. This shift altered how architectural history handled its evidence and narratives, as well as its relationships to other disciplines within the academy. From the primarily visual and sociopolitical evidence of art history, aligned with humanities subjects such as literature and its critical reception, evidence for architectural history drew from a wider field, including gender, race, and critical theory, plus philosophy, psychology, and economic history. More recently, a global turn further connected evidence in North American architectural history to revisionist currents in other fields producing histories of hitherto neglected geographies. Also produced were new narratives that side-stepped the universalizing notions often associated with traditional university disciplines such as art history. This "postmodern intellection," to use the term coined by Mark Jarzombek of MIT's History, Theory, and Criticism program, also sought alternatives to teleological, story-like narratives, which plotted the past in a straight line to the present and a desired future.[6] Querying traditional concepts of evidence and narrative, based in the inadequacies of the archive and the alternatives to narrative closure, is the function of the first section of this volume, the part titled "Legends."

Yet architectural history's disciplinary "dislocation," in Jarzombek's term, was not entirely by choice. The field's late twentieth-century "dissolution" from art history has been traced by Mark Crinson and Robert J. Williams, who cite in part architectural history being "vulnerable to other disciplinary interests."[7] At the same time, art history can be said to have pushed away architectural history. Fewer and fewer art historians concerned themselves with architecture, as notables such as Erwin Panofsky once did.

Architectural history's other position in professional schools of architecture gave it new opportunities for interdisciplinary sources of evidence and narrative beyond art history. Linking architectural history to histories of science, technology, and environment, as well as to business and legal studies, offered relevance to the technical and professional interests of architecture school colleagues and students. For example, numerous chapters in *Writing Architectural History*, especially those gathered in the final section, the part titled "Retrials," deploy legal evidence. Notwithstanding evidentiary and narrative innovations, however, few architectural historians would consider themselves and their work to have migrated from the margins to the center of professional education.

Such institutional arrangements have left North American architectural history unmoored among traditional university disciplines and without a defined methodology. This should be taken not as a negative consequence but as a context for the work of many architectural historians, like those contributing to this volume. They are necessarily left to their own devices to pursue an ad hoc interdisciplinarity, which asks questions, offers answers for the field, and sometimes poses problems to other disciplines and the world more broadly. Bridgeheads thus may be established in hospitable locations for an otherwise homeless field, not least by asking questions relevant across disciplines that require the critical use of both evidence and narrative.

2. How do certain kinds of evidence make a history "architectural"? What kinds of expertise and subjectivity are granted to the architectural historian?

The legitimacy of historical knowledge depends on the historian's claim to expertise over the subject matter. Architectural history has long fixated on evidence with an apparent internal coherence, especially buildings or architects. Both have been mobilized as material for historical narrative and have been the basis for the field's traditional monographic narrative form: the life story of a unified central subject, be it an architect or a building. Individuated "greatness" in subject matter has also been transferred to the subjectivity of architectural historians themselves, whose expertise and knowledge production are individualized because of institutional requirements. The contemporary university prizes first and foremost individual achievement for granting the PhD and for tenuring architectural historians in the humanities and in most architecture schools. But these are mythic, idealized coherences of evidence, narrative, and subjectivity, which may give way under pressure.

Such terms as "space," "form," "function," and "context" reinforce the choice to define an object of architecture primarily as a building. But the grouping of buildings into districts, towns, or cities, as well as acknowledging layers of revision over time, such as reconstructions, renovations, destruction, or technical retrofits, makes any assumption of a building's individuated coherence difficult to accept. Perhaps there is no more conspicuous example of a building's incoherence in the canon of Western architecture than the intermingling of designs for St. Peter's Basilica in Vatican City, a structure lavished with attention by generations of European and North American architectural historians.[8] Further troubles in centering the building in a narrative have arisen at the limits of formal analysis. As a tool for understanding the composition of ornament, mass, and figuration, formal analysis delivers clarity, even though it does not apply equally well to other aspects of architecture, such as plumbing, environmental controls, and legal restrictions.

There is also little stability in any definition of "the architect." Selecting an individuated protagonist has served to replace the assumption of a building's visual coherence with a focus on the position of the agent, one who accesses and organizes elements that resist formal interpretation. Understanding the variety of practical and institutional tasks required of an architect to produce buildings, in all their empirical disjunction, emerged more than a half century ago as a tool to define the boundaries of the architect's identity. Spiro Kostof's social history of the practice positioned historians to address the general "unease about the future of architecture" after challenges had been posed to traditional forms of architectural authority during the 1960s.[9] In the study of both buildings and architects, internal coherence has served as a practical myth for developing a claim to disciplinary expertise and an individuated professional subjectivity for the architectural historian.

It was also possible to take the two foci of building and architect as competing or reinforcing frames of reference. For instance, Stanford Anderson in the 1980s argued that the Viennese art historian Alois Riegl's concept of *Kunstwollen*, which centered on form as the primary source of evidence, was useful in creating a unified narrative for the visual coherence of everything from buckles to buildings. Alternatively, if one used, as Anderson did, the practicing architect Adolf Loos's words as primary evidence, written roughly around that time and in the same city, a more complex historical narrative released buildings designed by him from the overbearing influence of Riegl's conception of stylistic coherence.[10] The symmetry that Anderson brought between historical analysis (Riegl) and architectural practice (Loos) positioned architectural history against some of the well-worn methods of art history, toward defining architectural history's own disciplinary territory.

Against Anderson's search for a disciplinary semiautonomy for architectural history, more recent scholarship has revealed techniques for working without assumed disciplinary boundaries, thus diverging from the problematic of autonomy that preoccupied Anderson's generation coming of age in the 1960s. For example, historians who recently focused on infrastructure have expanded their scope from a building to a viaduct, a waste-treatment plant, and a system of standards. Such topics required incorporating expertise into histories of environmental, technical, and urban administration. This expansion offered an opportunity to understand the roles of architects and planners within networks of power.[11] Neither buildings nor architects centered these narratives. Instead, the evidence of infrastructure opened a broad scale of analysis and became a pretext for reflecting on a terrain of language that Michel Foucault called "discourse."[12] Take, for instance, Daniel Barber's notion of the "planetary interior," defined as "millions of interior spaces, all around the planet, [that] aggregate toward a collective impact on geophysical systems."[13] This vast terrain of discursive evidence is both real and metaphorical, designed by architects but also often merely abiding by a system of standards for environmental control. Set against the coherence of a building or an architect, Barber's proposal indicates an ad hoc attitude toward expertise. There is no preexisting method for representing the imbroglios through which those in power have constructed a "planetary politics." Instead, architectural historians are left to drift and diverge in their approach to "practical matters of induction, hypothesizing, causal theorizing, and the relating of matters of fact to their explanations," much like Steven Shapin and Simon Shaffer's characterization of the scientist Robert Boyle's working philosophy.[14]

A similar nonmethodical working philosophy may well be useful in characterizing the architectural historian's claim to expertise, as it moves away from a focus on individuated buildings and architects. But even as object, agency, and expertise are dispersed among architecture reconceived as discourse, media, and infrastructure, alternative subjectivities for the individuated architectural historian are harder to come by. Recent group work in architectural history—such as that of Aggregate, the Feminist Art and Architecture Collaborative, and the coauthored chapters in this collection—offer collaborative practices and subjectivities. But group work still usually redounds to the credit of individuals. The single-authored book remains the sine qua non for academic promotion for architectural historians in the humanities and most architecture schools.

3. What constitutes evidence in architectural history? What work does it do to build the historian's epistemological authority?

Yale University students of the 1970s have recalled scenes of Vincent Scully acting out the "buffalo dance" while lecturing about the architecture of Pueblo Indians (as conquering Spaniards had termed them). Scully's version of a minstrel show enacted a form of cultural colonialism while deploying a kind of evidence that has been ubiquitous in architectural history: the evidence of bodily experience.[15] Scully's performance exploited his audience's ignorance of Native American culture to convince them, in the service of architectural history, that the dancing body of the professor could transmit the elusive experience of Indigenous peoples in the American Southwest to the undergraduates crowded in a lecture hall. Scully's theatricality was also supposed to make buildings speak for themselves as if without any mediation. When Scully "beat his long wooden pointer at the slides on the screen," according to one student, "the buildings 'gestured,' 'thrust,' and 'thundered.'"[16] Another student recalled that Scully's whole body was "ultimately concentrated into the tip of his long bamboo pointer, a wizard's wand that coaxed, or jolted, the slides into their appointed roles."[17]

What "'gestured,' 'thrust,' and 'thundered'" under the authoritative wand of the architectural historian of course were not buildings themselves but their photographic reproductions on the screen in a lecture hall. Scully's dramatics, in fact, would have been impossible without the work of previous generations of art historians who had invented a formalism that harnessed technical media to create this peculiar effect of self-evidence. For most late nineteenth-century art historians in the German-speaking lands, the evidence of experience came first and foremost from photography. According to Anton Springer, who taught art history at the University of Leipzig, photographs were to art history what the microscope had been to the natural sciences. Just as the latter had made it possible for natural philosophers to proceed inductively from observed particulars to universal scientific laws, photography would offer art historians precise and concrete evidence that would elevate their analytic practices to those of a rigorous science. Hermann Grimm, who taught at the University of Berlin, explained that, practically speaking, this entailed "spread[ing] photographs out on the same table" so that they could be compared side by side and their formal characteristics observed.[18] Exceptionally, the art historian August Schmarsow was convinced that the essence of all architectural creation—spatial experience—could never be represented in images.[19] This produced the paradox that while photographic mediation was crucial to the rise of formalism in the late nineteenth century, knowledge gained from the evidence of direct experience—as defended by the likes of Schmarsow—persisted in an incipient field of knowledge that was at pains to distinguish itself from others.

Dismissing such "naïve" formalisms as nothing more than "appreciationism," Erwin Panofsky, too, urged a rigorous *Kunstwissenschaft* but suggested that science would now have to "bother about classical languages, boresome historical methods and dusty old documents."[20] In Panofsky's telling, no amount of projecting oneself experientially into and out of a cathedral (or photographs that captured one such instant of experience) could provide the historian with any reliable evidence. But one could understand the "habitus" shared by Gothic architecture and scholasticism by comparing *pilier cantonné* to the textual subdivisions of *Summa Theologiae*.[21] The historian's search for extra-experiential evidence, however, proved to be just as difficult. Such materials as wood and concrete, for example, have presented a seemingly obvious but nevertheless problematic form of evidence for architectural history, as explored in this volume's section titled "Self-Evidence." Moreover, some evidence was nowhere to be found, as explored in the section "Legends." At other times, the scale of evidence proved so overwhelming that historians had to invent new techniques to understand it, as historicized, demonstrated, and theorized in this volume's section titled "Data." And old formalist habits persisted even in the most document-minded historian. Manfredo Tafuri returned to deep archival research late in his career and ended up describing architecture in formalist terms, whose ideological dangers he had been wary of on other occasions.[22]

Postwar formalism in North America, however, was different from its earlier continental cousins. Unlike Scully, for whom form was the currency of emotional experience across incompatible temporalities, geographies, and subjectivities, Colin Rowe considered form a tool of detached, rational analysis.[23] As photography did not capture invisible formal relationships, it did not suffice as evidence. Rowe and his acolyte Peter Eisenman relied instead on analytic drawings that became mainstays of curricula in American architecture schools.[24] Like advocates of New Criticism, Rowe and those who followed in his footsteps insisted on close reading an increasingly narrow repertoire of buildings, an evidentiary technique used by Rowe and his detractors alike.

Against this kind of formal resurgence on North America's East Coast emerged an alternative spearheaded on the West Coast with the addition of "vernacular" and "non-Western" traditions to architectural history curriculum. At the University of California, Berkeley's College of Environmental Design, both faculty and students found new evidence of experience by tracing social bodies in their enactment of various cultural rituals.[25] Trained in that method, Diane Favro analyzed spectacles and festivals in ancient Rome, extending her earlier topographical analyses of Augustinian Rome into interactive and immersive models through computational methods.[26] Whether one favors experience or documents in architectural history depends, in part, on either the authority gained by the historian as a performer or the availability of archives for reanimating the textual past. This dichotomy in evidence may trace the unspoken and bidirectional influence of teaching and research in every scholar's career.

4. What counts as an archive, that is, the privileged site where evidence can be found? What kinds of histories result from reading along the grain of the archive versus against it? What are the implications of an archive that is too big or too small, inaccessible, or nonexistent?

In 1983, Francesco Passanti reviewed the first few books issued as part of the thirty-two-volume series that reproduced thirty-two thousand drawings from the archives of the Fondation Le Corbusier in Paris. He pointedly described the contents of this monumental publication project as "raw."[27] What he meant was that the published documentation followed the archive's order too closely, which made it difficult for the serious student to use the published series to make attributions correctly to Le Corbusier or someone else. Because Passanti assumed architectural history was organized primarily around the figure of the architect, he worried that the reproduction in print of an imperfectly organized archive would lead historians astray, preventing them from making accurate determinations of authorship.[28] As Passanti acknowledged, however, there was another sense in which the representation of the archive in print was "raw." Drawings constituted only approximately one-tenth of the entire Le Corbusier archive. The rest consisted of correspondence, books, magazines, mail-order catalogs, newspaper clippings, and every other scrap of paper that Le Corbusier had saved in anticipation of this would-be collection. These elements became the focus of Beatriz Colomina's attention a decade later.[29] Taking Le Corbusier's fabrication of his publicity as seriously as the architect himself did, Colomina demonstrated how the historian could shift her gaze from the one-tenth to the nine-tenths of the archive to understand the impact of mass media on that architect's polemics.[30]

While Colomina had shifted her historical attention *within* the archive from one small segment to the rest, others remade their own archives by forcing their historical gaze *beyond* the confines of an official archive. Consider Mabel Wilson's contribution to *Frank Lloyd Wright: Unpacking the Archive*, a 2017 publication that accompanied the exhibition organized by the Museum of Modern Art and the Avery Architectural and Fine Arts Library at Columbia University after jointly acquiring Wright's archive. Wilson based her arguments on the few pieces of correspondence and even fewer drawings for the unrealized Rosenwald School project for Black students in the segregated American South.[31] Because the organization of the official Wright archive around the figure of the architect elided the question of race, Wilson had to read the archive *against* the grain, making its absences visible by incorporating material she gathered from other sources. In this instance, remaining within the boundaries of the official archive would have amounted to reproducing the countless hagiographies of Wright and his purportedly reformist democratic agenda.

It takes political urgency, then, as well as historical imagination, to redraw the boundaries of an archive. When, in the 1940s, Sigfried Giedion turned to the US Patent Office as an archive in his newly adopted country, it was not just to produce a new "anonymous history" of modern architecture, akin to his teacher Heinrich Wölfflin's "art history without names."[32] That history by Giedion, *Mechanization Takes Command*, appeared in the wake of World War II. The parallels between anonymized and mechanized murder in the slaughterhouse and in concentration camps must have been all too obvious to a reader in 1948. Extending further the technological substrate of architecture in subsequent decades, Reyner Banham criticized the previous generation's attribution of architecture's modernity to tectonics by analyzing Wright's Larkin Administration Building among the archives of its *mechanical* systems. Banham argued that what made the building genuinely modern was its air-conditioning system, an attempt to reevaluate modern architecture's efficacy to change people's surroundings when worldwide change at that scale seemed imminent.[33] Against "space" (more precisely, *Raum*, in German-speaking lands), which had been the central concept of architectural discourses since the late nineteenth century, Banham's *Architecture of the Well-Tempered Environment* now imagined a discipline organized around the concept of "environment."[34]

Such reimaginings of the archive aspire to transformational disciplinary effects. Others move the focus of the field more slowly and cumulatively. Several historiographical interventions of the past few decades can be characterized as having expanded rather than transformed architectural history's jurisdiction by venturing beyond conventional sources—for example, by archaeologically documenting previously undocumented architecture, by using a previously neglected literature as a guide to sources, or by turning to institutional archives of various sorts.[35] Such archival moves have extended the focus of architectural history from individual designers to collectives, as well as to actors hitherto unacknowledged by architectural historians: from single buildings to entire cities, and from processes of design and construction to obsolescence and destruction.[36]

One kind of move to expand the archival imagination of architectural history has stood out among others: the project of readjusting the geographical focus of architectural history. A generation ago, the work of scholars studying what was called the "non-West" might have been presented as an addendum to a field still firmly focused on Europe and North America.[37] More recently, "global" histories building on this first-generation work have appeared, and they have demonstrated that these archives are not merely additions to the European canon but instead transform it completely, making any notion of canon increasingly untenable.[38] Read in conjunction with recent literature in the humanities, for example, the work of Louis P. Nelson on the architecture of plantations in Jamaica suggests that assuming the Industrial Revolution in England was a milestone for architectural modernity is mere provincialism.[39] In this sense, the cumulative expansion of architectural history's archival imagination beyond Europe and North America can be said to have transformed some of the most entrenched assumptions of a field essentially centered in these two continents.

In practical terms, such projects to reorient architectural history's archival imagination have had to tackle countless problems. Many scholars have pointed out the difficulties of writing architectural histories outside of Europe and North America with scant or nonexistent sources or with sources produced and maintained by institutions that are successors to colonial bureaucracies.[40] Others caution against the assumption of dichotomous, hierarchical relationships of influence or center-periphery, inherited from nineteenth-century colonialisms, when considering geographies outside of Europe and North America. In other cases, irrespective of geography, the expansion of archival sources, especially in digitized primary documents and text, has led scholars to suffer from information overload. When the archive is large and unwieldy, corollary digital techniques for "distant reading"—mapping, charting, graphing, quantification—offer potential clarity.[41] Such techniques may call not only for new technologies but, more importantly, for new forms of institutional and labor organization to make scholarship possible. Research visits by a lone scholar give way to multidisciplinary teams of researchers and experts building databases and visualizations. Redrawing the boundaries of an evidentiary archive, in short, requires not only historical imagination from the architectural historian but a fundamental rethinking and renegotiation of institutional, disciplinary, and working arrangements.

5. What kinds of narratives and counternarratives are produced in architectural history? What subjectivities and desires, individual and collective, are produced and pursued through narrative?

Nikolaus Pevsner's *Pioneers of the Modern Movement: From William Morris to Walter Gropius* (1936) features heroic agents of causality (especially the individuals of the book's subtitle) and design work as evidence, from wallpaper to buildings. This material Pevsner ordered into the particular narrative structure of a story. *Pioneers* possesses a strongly defined beginning (Morris) and a moralizing end, which calls upon readers and architects to choose Gropius's path of technology and anonymity over expressive individualism.[42] The decisive middle turn in the *Pioneers* story—when modernism's vanguard relocates from England to Germany—is attributed, however, not to a designer's agency but to a political economy. Pevsner contrasted English "private enterprise" in town planning with German "municipal initiative." "Directly this stage was reached, England dropped out and Germany took the lead," he wrote.[43] Social democracy, in other words, gained Pevsner's native land the architectural laurels over his adopted home. Implicitly, England would retake the lead in modern architecture only if it reformed. Thus, there is a political dynamic at the center of the *Pioneers* narrative.

Pioneers neatly illustrates "narrativity," the theory that philosopher of history Hayden White based on story-like historical narratives that satisfy desires both for political and subjective coherence.[44] The *Pioneers* narrative has a moralizing ending, a politico-social center, and, above all, a structuring of its evidence into the form of a story—a unitary version of events, from Morris to Gropius—which, White argued, "arises out of a desire to have real events display the coherence, integrity, fullness, and closure of an image of life that is and can only be imaginary."[45] A history story like *Pioneers* "displays to us a formal coherency to which we ourselves aspire."[46] The story's narrative wholeness soothes a need in both author and reader for a unified subjective identity.

Yet *Pioneers* in its story form can also be identified as a counternarrative to architectural histories differently organized, for example, by comparison and typology. Comparative narratives have been favored in art and architectural history since Heinrich Wölfflin's *Renaissance und Barock* (1888). This foundational technique is the theme of the section in this volume titled "Pairings." As for typology, it has an equally deep, privileged position in the field, exemplified by Pevsner's own monumental *A History of Building Types* (1976). *Pioneers* in its plot form and content was also a latent critique or counternarrative to other histories of modern architecture, for example, the Franco-American architect Paul Cret's long essay "Modern Architecture" (1923). The latter featured as evidence the constructed buildings of professional practitioners (versus Pevsner's more general design) and was organized narratively not as a story but by building type and national school. As such, Cret's essay lacked the *Pioneers* story's turns, termini, struggles, antagonists, morality, and politics.[47] *Pioneers* thus became a powerful *ur*-narrative for modern architecture, arguably because Pevsner harnessed storytelling's persuasive powers.

Historians write counternarratives to counternarratives as well. In the past generation, critique of *Pioneers*-style historical stories as elitist, determined, and determinate was encapsulated in a 2017 manifesto by the Feminist Art and Architecture Collaborative, which called for the study of noncanonical "diverse actors"; nonmonumental "vernaculars, interiors and social spaces"; and "narratives of contestation [that] foreground the contingent."[48] Revised theories of narrative since the 1980s have also supplemented White's emplotted-story analysis with concepts of narrative as performance and effect: narrative as intersubjective communication, as immersion in another's experience, however incomplete.[49] Digitalism, too, has potentially eroded the conventional historical narrative form.[50] The determinate, single-authored, and expensive physical book may be obsolesced by online publications, which can be produced more cheaply and disseminated more widely. Digital narratives lend themselves more easily to multiple collaborators, revision, and supplementation. Authorship may be dispersed among other voices more or less equalized. Sources, evidence, perspectives, and meanings multiply seemingly without end. Moreover, narratives based on digitized evidence, often in the form of data, lend themselves to discussions of the tools used to collect and analyze that data, a form of writing developed by authors of scientific papers. We may ask then, How might the linearity of historical narrative be affected or displaced when such an essay, following its scientific model, is divided into sections of "Methods," "Results," and "Discussion"?

As a manifestation of some of these recent developments, Esra Akcan's *Open Architecture: Migration, Citizenship, and the Urban Renewal of Berlin-Kreuzberg by IBA-1984/87* (2018) is billed by its author as an "alternative" to "established architectural history."[51] For its counternarrative structure—indeterminate, nonhierarchical, and collaborative—Akcan characterized *Open Architecture*'s "open architectural history" as a loose "interlacing" of "overlapped" and "intertwined" stories, which ends elliptically: "Other forms of open architecture might be . .

."[52] Its favored form of counternarrative evidence reflects, too, a recent turn in architectural history toward the oral histories of everyday inhabitants and coproducers of the built environment.[53] As one of the first book-length manifestations of this mode, *Open Architecture* attends to such stories as those told by the Turkish, noncitizen residents of Berlin social housing. "I entertain the idea of storytelling as a format for participatory architectural history," writes Akcan, who "acknowledges that the fabric of everyday life unfolding in an individual's experience of a space is also a part of the history of that space."[54] The highlighting of everyday voices, stories, and autobiography also undergirds the chapters in the present volume's fifth section, titled "Testimony."

Open Architecture, as a counternarrative, rejected turning evidence into a story, as *Pioneers* did. Instead, this mode of architectural history turns stories into evidence, to distribute agency from designers to inhabitants. In privileging stories, however, the oral history turn scratches the same itch as *Pioneers* for ideal coherency and meaning in events and subjectivity that the story form satisfies. What remains to be questioned, however, is oral history's category of experience as seemingly authoritative, direct, unambiguous evidence. Experience and subjectivity, as historian Joan Scott has written, should be considered not as foundational evidence but historically and "in terms of discursive or ideological fields, which are inherently contradictory and whose contradictions provide space for dissent and opposing points of view."[55] In other words, Scott argues, categories of identity and experience, such as citizen/noncitizen, man/woman, and black/white, are politically constructed, contingent binaries of power, which ought to be historicized, revisited, and resisted, not essentialized. Such critical analyses of experience and subjectivity would be applicable to the persons who people architectural history, as well as to the figures of architectural historians themselves. Thus are raised self-conscious questions about our subjectivities' ideological field and its contradictions. How, we might ask, do historically constructed power relations manifest themselves in architectural historians' professional, expert privilege of critical distance, gathering evidence and constructing narratives?

The account of architectural history writing in this introduction is particular and incomplete. The field's practices have always been shifting, not least in terms of evidence and narrative. And much has been excluded here, including a sense of finality to the analysis. Likewise, the collection of chapters that follows is disparate, contingent, and intersectional. They are neither unifiable, orderable, nor compartmentable by chronology, place, or subject matter. Instead, *Writing Architectural History* is organized into parts related by issues of evidence and narrative.

It starts with "Legends," in order to interrogate conventions of evidentiary and narrative certainty, not least the blurred boundaries between myth and history, presence and absence, fact and fiction. The next two parts revisit some familiar practices of architectural history, starting with types of material evidence—wood, concrete, and metal—traditionally accepted as unambiguous in their "Self-Evidence" (Part II). The section on "Data" (Part III), historicizes and critically theorizes that term. Part IV then elaborates a foundational technique of evidence and narration in architectural history—the practice of "Pairings"—exploring the comparative tactic's basis and then demonstrating its employment in a history of planning, in the attachment of the term "forensic" to architecture, and in a literary analysis. The final two parts feature chapters related to recent evidentiary and narrative turns in the field, starting with "Testimony" (Part V): memories and accounts by ordinary people as material for architectural history, and also an architect's own autobiographical statement. In the final part, "Retrials" (Part VI), the chapters feature evidence from the law as productive material for architectural history, used here to reevaluate icons of the field, as well as practices of evidence and narrative. Not just this final part but all the book's chapters in one way or another are counternarratives to prior practices of architectural history writing. As the cultural theorist Martin McQuillan has written, "every narrative is also a counternarrative" and, continuing the chain, "as a condition of its production a narrative will always initiate a counternarrative."[56]

The final question then is, How might today's counternarratives in architectural history writing lead to others? This volume was composed with the assumption that changing the politics of a field begins with reexamining its tools, in particular how practices of evidence and narrative intertwine with core concepts in history writing. How, for example, have concepts of environment, race, and migration—three current crises analyzed architecturally in this book by Albert Narath, Ayala Levin, and Anooradha Iyer Siddiqi, respectively—been produced in the field through certain evidential and narrative practices? How might such globally pressing matters be rethought architecturally with different practices, to account for and reconsider how knowledge is produced within today's unjust dynamics of social power? For instance, can practices of collective research and writing, which this volume's Aggregate editorship and several chapters exemplify, produce different kinds of knowledge? Do collaborative practices working within and across disciplines engage cross-cutting evidentiary and narrative possibilities that undermine presumptions of purity and rigor, in favor of hybridity and unorthodoxy? Might collaborative work also re-situate the field and its practitioners in relation to the liberal arts academy and professional architectural education, which still largely expects individuated achievement, reflecting the dominant values of capitalist democratic societies? What this volume ultimately offers is not so much answers as questions through consideration of evidence, narrative, and writing architectural history. The hard work of re-tuning the field addresses a complex past, an exigent present, and our opaque futures.

Part I
Legends

Writing Architectural History begins at the edges where evidence and narrative are most perplexed and least certain in architectural history. What if evidence is mythical, missing, or dreamed? What if narrative dissolves into skeins of memory, boundaries blurred between fact and fiction? These are the problems posed by the subjects and styles of the opening three chapters of *Writing Architectural History*. Rather than working from the field's firm foundations in evidence and narrative, and then toward experimentation, *Writing Architectural History* reverses the trajectory. Explorations with evidence and narrative are not saved for the end, the outgrowth of patient, incremental analysis. Why wait? To pose these questions at the outset puts the rest of the volume under self-critique.

1

The Fires of Saint-Domingue, or, Landscapes of the Haitian Revolution

■

PETER MINOSH

Historical sources agree that among the enslaved persons at the plantation of M. Lenormand de Mézy in Saint-Domingue's Plaine-du-Nord—the fertile plain that constituted the center of colonial agricultural production—was one who became a revolutionary leader. This rebel figure deployed *marronage*—autonomous rural settlements of escaped slaves—as the locus of insurrection against the white planters.

Mackandal, 1759

François Mackandal was one of the many one-armed enslaved persons of the Plaine-du-Nord. On occasion an enslaved person's hand would be caught in the heavy rollers of the mills built to crush sturdy sugarcane stalks. Efficiency was prized above all else, and mills were routinely equipped with an ax that could be used to sever the worker's limb rather than halt production.[1] Amputees were thus a common sight—markers of the shared experience of slavery under the violence of the plantation. According to some, Mackandal was a Muslim, perhaps from Senegal, Mali, or Guinea; to others he was a *bokor*, or sorcerer, born in the Kingdom of the Congo, who carried to Saint-Domingue the secrets of herbal medicines.[2] Whether Mackandal was burned at the stake in 1758 is also a matter for debate.

The Cuban-born magical realist novelist Alejo Carpentier recounted in *The Kingdom of This World* (1949) that Mackandal possessed the power of transmutation.[3] In this account Mackandal was a *houngon* of the Rada rite of Vodou. He could move freely across the plantations in various forms—a lizard, a moth, a large dog—to escape detection and spread his message of insurrection. For Carpentier, Mackandal was the unnatural lurking within the natural world, and his avatars were legible only to the revolutionary enslaved who were attuned to the power of the Loa—Vodou spirits—hiding in plain sight within plantation landscape. His power of transmutation allowed him to spread his revolutionary message by making direct contact with every worker on the Plaine-du-Nord. He could travel undetected and strike at any moment. He was a skilled poisoner, first attacking the cattle feed and felling entire herds, then moving into the plantation houses. Soon every arbitrary death was attributed to the work of Mackandal. Finally, nothing was considered safe—neither fruit taken directly from the trees nor goods off of foreign supply ships. Mackandal, in short, was the name given to the terror of slave revolt. The power to strike without warning and to hide in plain sight by melding into the commonplace is the power of a popular insurrection whose participants can be anyone, anywhere—indistinguishable from the plantation's normal operations.

The story of Mackandal originally comes to us from Médéric Louis Élie Moreau de Saint-Méry, who described the poisonings that terrorized the white population of Cap Français in his *Description topographique, physique, civile, politique et historique de la partie française de l'Isle Saint-Domingue* (1797), recounting the state of the colony in 1789.[4] Moreau de Saint-Méry was a Martinique-born Creole who served as a key member of the French revolutionary Assembleé Nationale. He was also a leader of the Club Massiac, the body representing the colonial planter class to the revolutionary assembly. He was both an active *philosophe* who backed the revolution's Enlightenment ideas (in 1789 he received the keys to the fallen Bastille, in his capacity as president of the electors of Paris, and delivered them to George Washington) and a key agent of the colonial planter elite, described by C. L. R. James as providing "the economic basis of the French Revolution."[5] He wholly rejected the principle of the natural rights of man, proposing instead *l'aristocratie de la peau*, in which skin color marked the inherent superiority of white people and justified the enslavement of Black people as plantation laborers.

At Mackandal's signal, according to Moreau de Saint-Méry, people would die, until Mackandal "conceived of the hellish project of eliminating everyone in Saint-Domingue who was not Black." The authorities captured Mackandal during a *rara*, or Saturday festival, at the Dufresne plantation (or the Lenormand de Mézy plantation, in Carpentier's telling) and brought him to the main square at Cap Français to face execution. Moreau de Saint-Méry recounts the legend of Mackandal in his description of the scene of execution:

> On 20 January 1758, the Cap Council condemned him to be burned alive. As he had several times boasted that, if the whites captured him, he would escape from them in different forms, he declared he would assume the form of a fly to escape the flames. As chance would have it, the stake to which he was chained was rotten, and his violent movements, provoked by the torture of the flames, pulled

out the metal ring and he tumbled out of the fire. The blacks cried out, "Mackandal saved!" There was an incredible panic and all the gates were closed. The detachment of guards around the place of execution cleared the square. . . . He was tied to a plank and thrown back into the fire. Although Mackandal's body was burned, many blacks believe, even today, that the execution did not kill him.[6]

Perhaps Moreau de Saint-Méry's version of events had been passed down from one set of eyewitnesses, just as the story of Mackandal's escape was passed down by another—a colonial myth and a revolutionary myth both springing from the same source. This immolation, then, either concluded or initiated a revolutionary movement—depending on which myth you prefer. Moreau de Saint-Méry offers an elaborate story of rotting stakes and conveniently produced planks to resolve the particularities of an event that occurred thirty years prior to his telling and that he had not witnessed, in order to prove that Mackandal did not in fact turn into a fly and escape the flames. Moreau de Saint-Méry assures the reader that with revolutionary ideas circulating around the Atlantic, white merchants need not fear: Mackandal was dead. But in his effort to dispel this myth he reveals an anxiety that this legend of revolutionary transmutation was not about to go away on its own. He unwittingly describes a second mythic register, one in which revolutionary action plays out. For the enslaved people of the Plaine-du-Nord, the revolution personified by Mackandal could not be extinguished upon his death. It necessitated his sublimation to a mythical plane.

In these two opposing myths that arise from the execution of Mackandal we can discern two discrete modes of the mythical, each with a distinct sphere of political action. In one arena the myth of the colonizer seeks to maintain a fixed order extending from the plantation regime to bourgeois notions of political sovereignty. This myth performs violence: Moreau de Saint-Mery's framing of the rights of humans possesses racial content and is built upon colonial violence.[7] The very nature of politics demands an epistemic ground—an *archē* (origin or first cause, as well as political authority)—from which to transform the political impetus into an apparatus of state. This *archē* is essentially mythic in that its foundation depends upon a social imaginary instituted by regimes of violence.[8] Opposed to this is the myth of the enslaved, a revolutionary praxis bent on destroying the colonial order. This violence performs myth: it has no articulate end, only the urgency of the present moment, creating indeterminate configurations that cannot yet be imagined. For Georges Sorel, the disruption of political regimes is immanently mythic, not because (as before) it relies on foundational myth as the basis of its legitimation but because it opens politics to the ineffable space of the unforeseeable. The proletarian strike, for Sorel, is the ultimate marker of the mythical in that it operates solely on the level of praxis; it maintains no telos or concrete projection yet nevertheless remakes the world.[9] Stathis Gourgouris explains that "myths are incommensurable to facts because they may exceed facts, much as revolutionary desire (or utopian vision) can never be exhausted in the fact/event of revolution. Yet myths are also not illusions; they are demonstrable historical forces: imagined alterities to society that make historical action possible."[10] This violence performs myth in that the mythic is that site that is both real and indeterminate. I offer a history of the Haitian Revolution told through a series of fires. Each fire marks a critical articulation of the revolutionary impetus; each enacts a mythical violence that opens the established political regimes to the realm of contingency; and each, I argue, has associated with it an architecture.

Uprising, 1791

On the evening of August 22, 1791, the colonial city of Cap Français burned at the hands of enslaved people excluded from the universality of rights on which the colonial metropole was ostensibly founded.

In 1791, Nicolas Ponce published his *Recueil de vues des lieux principaux de la colonie françoise de Saint-Domingue* as a compendium to Moreau de Saint-Méry's *Description topographique*.[11] While Moreau de Saint-Méry's writings described the smooth functioning of the colonial order, Ponce's folio put this order on display. Through maps of the eleven major ports of Saint-Domingue—each cartographic figure accompanied by harbor views showing great commercial frigates anchored, with pinnaces ferrying goods to shore—Ponce participates in colonial mythmaking through a picture of mercantile efficiency in which every route for plantation stock to reach the global marketplace is utilized. Drawings, maps, and architectural representations such as Ponce's that circulated across the Atlantic World in the years leading up to the Haitian Revolution served two main functions: to display colonial splendor through the image of wealth and to foster colonial investment through the image of efficacy. But by reading such images against the grain, perhaps we can discern another agency that these representations fail to fully dispel.

Two panoramas of Cap Français describe the main entrepôt of colonial extraction as it stood in 1789. A harbor view shows the bustling trade of global commerce, while a city view displays the splendor of commercial wealth built upon this trade. Ponce's map of Cap Français shows the neat arrangement of an urban grid with private dwellings and commercial spaces rendered in a uniform poché and with public spaces described in detail (fig. 1.1). It displays the civic life of Cap Français as well as the protection of its commercial arrangement from the competing powers of Atlantic mercantilism, with that protection provided by military barracks and exercise fields, military bastions, and an artillery park, arsenal, and powder magazine. Taken together, these features represent a territory militarized against threats both internal and external. The urban grid of Cap Français reaches its southernmost extent at the geographic low area of La Fossette, which contains the Bazar de la Vente des Nègres, the city's slave market. Cap Français is fortified

1.1. Nicolas Ponce, "Plan de la Ville du Cap François et de ses Environs dans l'Isle St. Domingue." From *Recueil de vues des lieux principaux de la colonie françoise de Saint-Domingue* (1791).

at the base of the Morne Lory hill by angled ramparts facing the slave market, behind which the École d'Artillerie is oriented to provide clear angles of fire.

Ponce's map provides a picture of the defensive systems of the city. The barracks located at the center of government provide civic order; the bastions on the shoreline adjacent to the docks protect commercial exchange; and the École d'Artillerie and Corps de Gardes at the city's southern boundary defend against slave insurrection. Taken together, these elements form a picture of the military-commercial enterprise of Cap Français. Yet this geographical knowledge is not limited to the bounds of the city itself—a full third of the page is given over to its extraterritorial reaches. La Fossette forms a mirror of Cap Français—essential to the city but necessarily separate. Slavery is required for the maintenance of colonial wealth, yet it must be partitioned from the civic life that cannot function without its presence. Ramparts are fashioned and guns are trained for clear angles of fire to enforce this distinction. To far-flung investors and absentee landlords unwilling or unable to see firsthand the enterprise of colonial extraction, Ponce's depictions of Saint-Domingue, its bustling ports, and its wealthy cities fully protected from internal or external threat operated as a security on investment in the colony. The slave market of La Fossette would be included in this depiction because ensuring the impossibility of slave insurrection was no small part of this guarantee.

With Ponce's 1791 publication date we know that the colonial order displayed in his renderings—which show civic and commercial structures framed by casernes, arsenals, and ramparts—was about to succumb to the terror rendered "impossible" by these plates. The origins of this revolution are obscure. In the narratives that privilege parliamentary procedures it was precipitated by a conflict over whether political representation would be determined according to race or property. This dispute pitted poor white farmhands—*petits blancs*—against racially mixed land-owning *mulâtres* and grew into a broader conflict between metropolitan oversight and colonial autonomy. In all of these transactions between the political institutions of the National Assembly and the Colonial Assemblies; lobbying organizations of the pro-slavery Club Massiac and the emancipationist Société des Amis des Noirs; and colonial interests of landed *mulâtres*, *petits blancs*, and the planter elite, the one key constituent entirely absent is the enslaved.

Popular myth, however, situates the revolution in a Vodou ceremony performed by Dutty Boukman at the *maroon* settlement of Bois Caïman—a forest refuge of those who escaped slavery, unmapped and out of reach of the colonial authorities. A ceremony, according to historian David Patrick Geggus, that was "successively elaborated over the years, as with the Mackandal story, so that few details can be considered authentic."[12] Boukman drank the blood of a suckling pig and called the gathered crowd to arms as they chanted "Eh eh Bombe! Heu heu"—translated by C. L. R. James as "We swear to destroy the whites." None of this can be confirmed.[13] We know this myth through reports by white planters to the Club Massiac intending to undermine the legitimacy of the revolution by marking it with superstition and primitivism.[14] These reports included accounts of bacchanalian violence: a carpenter bound between two planks and slowly sawn in half, and the body of a white infant impaled upon a pike that then served as the rebels' standard.

The archives of the colonial projects—maps, treatises, and official records—construct the mythologies that sustain colonial violence. These sources occlude those other mythic capacities that are inaccessible to historical knowledge but nevertheless remain fact. How can they give sense to historical events that, in the words of Michel-Rolph Trouillot, were unthinkable even as they occurred?[15] James took up colonial execrations against the uprising and transformed them into narratives of liberation—turning each charge levied against the uprising into a subversion of colonial violence. If the absences in the archive give rise to mythical production, an exegesis on architecture's mythic production might provide us with another kind of archive through which we can construct a revolutionary history.

Preserving the Revolution, 1793

On June 21, 1793, the revolutionary city of Cap Français burned when white planters sought to build in the colonies the last resort of the counterrevolution.

In that year, tensions between the republican commissioners and the wealthy planters of Saint-Domingue had erupted into open conflict. Léger-Félicité Sonthonax, the Girondist civil commissioner of the northern part of the island, had allied himself with the *mulâtre* population and supported equality for all free citizens, thus raising the ire of white planters and royalists. When François-Thomas Galbaud arrived in May 1793 to serve as the new colonial governor, he found the planters eager to rally around an opposing party, and he, having inherited land on Saint-Domingue, was immediately sympathetic to their cause. Sonthonax tried to have Galbaud removed from his post, but on June 20, with the aid of a French naval squadron in the harbor as well as a white militia force, Galbaud drove the commissioners and their Légion d'Egalité from Cap Français. Sonthonax appealed to *maroon* bands under the leaders Macaya and Pierrot in the hills around Cap Français, promising liberation in exchange for a military alliance, and together they defeated Galbaud and his supporters. This was only achieved with significant destruction to Cap Français and to the *maroon* fighters seizing much of the city's arsenal. Events precipitating a general emancipation of enslaved people unfolded quickly. On August 27, Étienne Polverel, the commissioner of the southern part of Saint-Domingue, declared a limited emancipation of enslaved people in the south who were not at the moment bound to a working plantation. Two days later Sonthonax issued a general emancipation in the north.[16]

This revolutionary uprising and the consequent abolitions of slavery have their architectural expression, I would argue, in a "Temple to Emancipation" described by Marcus Rainsford in an 1805 work, *An Historical Account of the Black Empire of Hayti*.[17] Rainsford had been a lieutenant in the British Third West India Regiment, stationed at Môle-Saint-Nicholas, during the British effort to wrest the colony from French control. In the early part of 1798 he sailed along the northern coast of Saint-Domingue aboard a schooner, the *Maria*, flying a Danish flag, to rejoin his regiment in Martinique.[18] A hurricane forced them ashore at Cap Français, which was by then under the command of Toussaint Louverture. To avoid capture as a prisoner of war, Rainsford dumped all of his military documents into the sea and fabricated the cover story of being an American merchant.

Free to roam Cap Français with his cover as an American, Rainsford describes with Romantic intensity the aftermath of the 1793 destruction, still very prevalent in the city, "where elegant luxury had exhausted its powers to delight the voluptuary" and "all was magnificent ruin!"[19] Wandering into a small public square, he discovers the Temple to Emancipation, dedicated to the memory of Sonthonax and Polverel. An engraving accompanying Rainsford's text shows a classical rotunda—a septastyle (seven column) tholos in the Doric order. This situates the temple in relation to two different landscapes (fig. 1.2). In the background, two hills are topped with military forts flying the Tricolore, between which are the cultivated fields of a sugar plantation—signified by a windmill, an essential component of sugar production, which utilized wind power to extract

1.2. Marcus Rainsford, "View of a Temple Erected by the Blacks to Commemorate Their Emancipation." From *An Historical Account of the Black Empire of Hayti* (1805).

the juice from sugarcane stalks. In the foreground the Temple to Emancipation is set within an uncultivated forest. A diminutive figure climbs the stairs to the temple as two sentinels wearing the military cockade of Toussaint's army invite the viewer to approach. Inside the temple a liberty cap is flanked by tablets enumerating the "Rights of Man and Citizen."

Rainsford's engraving, with the foreground of untrammeled nature opening up to the cultivated and manicured background, speaks to the conventions of the picturesque. In the landscape picturesque, the aesthetic transition from the sublime to the beautiful, standing in for the moral transition from the self-preserving drive of astonishment to societal passion of love, alludes to a dialectic of spiritual enlightenment (or salvation).[20] In this convention, a temple would be in the background—in the realm of the beautiful. The view of William Kent's Temple of Virtue from the River Styx at Stowe Gardens, for instance, might promise an escape from moral peril and a path to civic virtue.

We can draw a distinction between the conventions of the picturesque and Rainsford's deployment of it in his engraving. The "beautiful" background displays the military-agricultural complex of colonialism—the system of agricultural extraction built upon slavery and maintained through the French military apparatus. The stakes of this background are similar to those in Ponce's map of Cap Français. Rainsford's Temple to Emancipation is situated in the "sublime" foreground of an uncultivated overgrowth. In an extraction regime where every acre of arable land was slated for agricultural commodity production, such uncultivated spaces remained holdouts from colonial desire. The wooded hills surrounding the plantation landscapes of Saint-Domingue were in fact *maroon* settlements—the refuge of enslaved persons who had escaped the plantation and the sites from which they overthrew the colonial order.[21]

Through various descriptions and renderings of this Temple to Emancipation across Rainsford's writings it becomes clear that its imagery is almost entirely of his own making. In an earlier description it was "a structure in wood, forming a regular ascent of steps to a kind of canopy."[22] There may have been such a structure, but it was almost certainly nothing like the classical tholos depicted. The temple itself seems a specter. When Manfredo Tafuri described the eighteenth-century neoclassical style as architecture's "fatal autopsy" upon its own conventions, he was writing in terms of the sublimation of bourgeois values to the aesthetic plane in order to ward off anguish wrought by capitalist necessity.[23] Removal to the colonies shifts the terms of architecture's dismantlement of its signifiers. The classical tholos operates within the symbolic order of an absolute sovereignty; take, for instance, the temple of Venus at the Petit Trianon on the grounds of Versailles. The deployment of this classical representation toward a set of rights derived not from the *archē* of God but from the atomized sovereignty of democratic citizens, as in Rainsford's Temple to Emancipation, initiates a rupture between classical order and sovereign representation. Within this matrix, the enslaved figure is variously the absolute exclusion of sovereign representation and its privileged subject. Through the exclusion of enslaved people from the universal rights of humankind, the revolutionary republic determines the constitutive exterior of democratic sovereignty. A classical tholos enumerating the rights of humankind as pertaining to those formerly enslaved situates the classical precisely in that liminal space between divine legitimation and the right of nonright in which a *demos* is fashioned.²⁴ Rainsford's rendering of the Temple to Emancipation performs this placement. If the picturesque has a utopian telos of an enlightenment to be achieved, perhaps its inversion gives voice to a revolutionary condition situated in the immediacy of marronage.

National Potlatch, 1802

On February 4, 1802, Cap Français burned as an armada sent by Napoleon to retake the rebellious colony of Saint-Domingue made landfall. The accumulated wealth of an autonomous colony led by Black inhabitants in the name of the French Republic was destroyed. The enterprise of state was readily abandoned upon the necessity of revolution.

This final phase of the Haitian Revolution began in the French counterrevolution initiated by Napoleon's coup d'état of November 9, or the eighteenth of Brumaire, 1799. By this time Toussaint had installed himself as governor-for-life of an autonomous French colony. Napoleon sent his brother-in-law, Charles Leclerc, to retake to colony and provided him with secret instructions to depose the existing military order of Toussaint and reinstitute slavery. Saint-Domingue was to return to the prerevolutionary order, with Black inhabitants enslaved under white planters.²⁵

While the restoration of the plantation economy and the rebuilding of the Atlantic trade routes were priorities for Toussaint, a scorched-earth policy was in effect. At the threat of an overwhelming invasion, the people could immediately militarize by abandoning the cities and returning to the revolutionary condition of marronage. Ahead of Leclerc's invasion, Henri Christophe, as commander of the northern precinct, placed around Cap Français a number of garrisons, each ready to torch the city at his signal. Earlier in the day he had distributed barrels of tar throughout the rooms of his own mansion on Rue Royale. At the first report of attack he ordered his lieutenants to break the barrels open and spread the flammable contents throughout his home. He then set the fire himself; the order to burn the city was signaled by the sight of flames engulfing his home.²⁶ His troops destroyed Cap Français and its wealth and retreated to the hills of the Massif du Nord to engage in a guerrilla campaign.

The French forces, under the command of Rochambeau (after Leclerc's death from yellow fever), were defeated by the guerrilla army at Vertières on November 18, 1803. The nation of Haiti, the first independent nation in the Western Hemisphere led by Black citizens, was formally established on January 1, 1804. At its head was Jean-Jacques Dessalines, who took the title of emperor in October, with Henri Christophe and Alexandre Pétion as his top commanders. Christophe's act of torching Cap Français as a strategy of national potlatch was codified into law. The final article of Dessalines's 1805 constitution declared

1.3. View from upper plinth of Citadelle Laferrière overlooking Cap Haitien. Photograph by Peter Minosh, 2015.

that "at the first shot from the warning gun, the towns shall be destroyed and the nation shall rise in arms."[27] In the case of a foreign invasion, Haiti's entire population would retreat to the interior of the nation to wage a guerrilla campaign. Dessalines organized a series of inland fortresses as the architectural realization of this strategy. The most prominent of these installations was Fort Laferrière, defending the strategic corridors from Cap Français to the north and Gonaïves to the west. Under the subsequent rule of King Henri Christophe, Fort Laferrière would become the Citadelle Laferrière.

Covering ten thousand square meters and with sheer walls forty-five meters high, Citadelle Laferrière was the stronghold of the revolutionary state and could house five thousand people almost indefinitely. Christophe formalized this site of marronage into a fortress to hold the military order and the royal court. In times of war the state could exist autonomously, apart from the nation. The central plinth of the citadel is a sunken courtyard surrounded on three sides by defenses and open to the north (fig. 1.3). From the northernmost defensive feature of the plinth, Batterie du Pont-Levis, cannons once carried to Saint-Domingue to destroy the revolution—still bearing the insignia of the European kingdoms and empires that had abandoned them in retreat—were now turned outward. They had been deployed to maintain colonial order, but now they overlook the fields of battle: the Plaine-du-Nord, Cap Français, and the vast ocean whose mercantile powers sat just over the horizon.[28]

Sans-Souci, 1820

On the evening of October 8, 1820, Henri Christophe's Sans-Souci Palace was slated to burn. Although the nation was safe from invading armies, there remained the internal threat of the Haitian people and their refusal to tolerate their increasingly tyrannical king.

Christophe had built his court in a day, creating on April 5, 1811, a "hereditary" nobility that included an array of princes, dukes, counts, barons, and knights, all of whom took their titles from the plantations they owned—more often than not the same ones on which they had once been enslaved. On April 7, Christophe established a religious hierarchy, personally elevating Corneille Brelle to archbishop of Haiti (which precipitated the chaplain's excommunication by Rome), and on April 20 he founded the Royal Order of Chivalry and the Military Order of Saint-Henry. With the institutions of sovereign power set in place, Christophe had himself crowned king on June 2.[29]

Sans-Souci was the heart of his monarchy; it contained virtually all the major elements of the state within its precincts, combining royal, political, military, and religious functions within a single compound. At its center was the Sans-Souci Palace, set atop a berm with each of its elevations opening onto unique spaces, such that it became the fulcrum on which the multiple functions of the state operated (fig. 1.4). Adjoining the palace were the Council of State and Chamber of Ministers; the military command and exercise grounds were situated in the low valley to the north; and the Church of the Pantheon adjacent to the palace gates held the remains of Haiti's revolutionary heroes.

Each of the elevations of the Sans-Souci Palace addresses a unique landscape. The palace's north elevation, set atop a retaining wall, provided the ceremonial entrance from the town of Milot. A pair of monumental staircases leading to the palace flank a fountain set within two heavy buttresses and a rusticated triumphal arch—recalling the sheer walls of the Citadelle Laferrière. The courtyard in front of the palace, situated askew relative to the elevation, had no public function—it was to service the carriage house and stables of the king. This arrangement situates the entrance asymmetrically to the building such that one approaches it at an oblique angle, skirting the berm beneath the Council of State. The effect is that the north elevation atop the monumental staircase dominates every corner of the grounds, offering on its upper story panoptic surveillance from the balcony of the king.

While the north elevation was the palace's public face, the south elevation opened onto the terraced landscape of the Jardin du Roi, the private garden of the royal family. The scale of this south garden elevation is far more intimate than the north. A pair of curved staircases emerges from the concave walls of an austere three-bay portico. German geographer Carl Ritter was in Haiti at the time of Christophe's death and visited the palace just eighteen days later.[30]

1.4. Henri Christophe's Sans-Souci Palace, 1806–1813. Photograph by Peter Minosh, 2015.

He describes the Jardin du Roi as "neither in the old style nor the new" and plush with tropical plants and rows of mango trees. It seems to follow no European precedent (neither the "old" seventeenth-century baroque gardens nor the "new" eighteenth-century picturesque gardens) but replicates the natural growth of the uncultivated Haitian forest. Where the imposing scale of the north elevation was in emulation of the sheer walls of the citadel, the wild and overgrown Jardin du Roi—directly adjacent to the military exercise grounds—recalls the uncultivated sites of revolutionary marronage.

Between these two landscapes, atop the berm and adjacent to the palace, was the Patio de Caïmitier, a rectangular garden that functioned as Christophe's outdoor court. Christophe placed his mahogany throne at its center beneath the caïmitier (star apple) tree—still standing and said to have been planted by Christophe himself—that served as the "tree of liberty" of the Haitian state. This patio provides views over both the rear of the palace, with its Jardin du Roi and military yards, as well as the front, which overlooks the gatehouse, the Pantheon, and the town of Milot. It offered a panoramic view of the entirety of the compound, from which Christophe could surveil the armatures of state and the representations of revolution as he held court.

Christophe's draconian Code Rurale converted Haiti's plantations into operations of the state through a regime of *fermage*, or compulsory agricultural and architectural labor. After years of his tyrannical and increasingly erratic rule, a call to revolution had made the final article of the Dessalines constitution a fact and signaled the dissolution of the state. Rebellious troops faced off against the last of the royal guard while shouting, "Liberty! No slavery! No king!" and "Vive la liberté! Brissons les chaînes de l'esclavage!" This military group was led by the Duc de Marmelade, who had shed his noble title to reclaim the revolutionary rank of General Richard.[31] In his final hours, Christophe ordered his servants to escort him to the Citadelle Laferrière and set fire to the Sans-Souci Palace. They refused and, fearing that they would share his fate, fled the palace.[32] Christophe believed that only a silver bullet could kill the king, and as he had been incapacitated by a recent stroke, he shot himself in the heart as the rebellious army approached. Sans-Souci had fallen—the stronghold of state power whose gardens played out the revolution in miniature.

Two modes of the mythic have differing relationships to fact, which are revealed through their relationship to violence. Myth relies on violence in order to transform its ideologies into fact. The myth that performs violence has an architecture that is well known to us. Palaces, capitols, and statehouses transform political procedure into regime by giving symbolic substance to the imaginary of the state. These works depend upon forts, bastions, and armories to serve as guarantors of the stability of this order—to display the state's capacity for violence in order to maintain a regime of colonial extraction through slave labor. Conversely, violence becomes mythic when it claims no a priori truth and projects no concrete fact—only the imperative of transformation to an open horizon. The violence that performs myth also has an architecture: a classical tholos indeterminately situated between the foundation of sovereign legitimation and the groundlessness of revolutionary praxis, a citadel at the sites of marronage to give permanence to the revolutionary condition, and a palace striving to solidify the forms and spaces of these revolutionary configurations into an apparatus of state.

Politics organizes bodies; according to Jacques Rancière, politics is an intervention in the visible and the sayable.[33] Differently but relatedly, the political reflects critically upon that organization and exposes its gaps and aporia. The political capacity of architecture lies in its ability to become an announced site of experimentation for terms that are otherwise ineffable and mythic within the proper determinations of politics. The architectural utterances examined in this chapter are mythic, too. They are necessarily mapped upon and interlaced with unutterable violence, with its politics and symbolic orders.

2

Known Unknowns
The Documentary History of the Franklin Ghost House

■

EDWARD EIGEN

> *No pictorial evidence survived of [Benjamin] Franklin's house and many in the Park Service felt that the evidence that we do have is not solid enough. There are a lot of gaps in it and that reconstruction based on this . . . limited evidence would be conjectural. And so the decision there is not to reconstruct.* —Dennis Kurjack

It has become customary of late to begin essays with an anecdote, typically preceded by a semifeigned plea for the reader's tolerance ("Allow me to tell . . ."), as if this ostensibly self-indulgent bit of scene setting were getting in the way of more important matters. But what reader, in first encountering a text, would refuse such an undemanding request, especially when anecdotes, at least well-crafted ones, are by design brief and to the point? So here is an example, and what is an anecdote if not revealingly exemplary?

In October 1978, George A. Palmer, a researcher engaged in an oral history project on the design of Independence National Historical Park in Philadelphia (INHP), wrote to the architect Robert Venturi seeking "information" on the design of the Ghost House at Franklin Court (fig. 2.1). Palmer, who had already interviewed nearly seventy-five people on and off the National Park Service (NPS) staff, wished to confirm various "speculations" he had heard, including one that the Ghost House design had been "suggested" by Denise Scott Brown. In response to Palmer's request for a "written statement" on how he had arrived at the "three-dimensional concept for the frame," the Ghost House's most iconic feature, Venturi indicated that regrettably he had little to offer.[1] "I often vividly remember the moment of inception of a design and the associations which helped form it," the architect explained. In this instance, however, he could not "remember how we came to this approach to the design and I am sorry that I have no vivid anecdote to connect with it."[2] Apparently, there will be no anecdote for us to begin with after all.

2.1. Ghost House, Franklin Court, Philadelphia, Venturi, Scott Brown & Associates, 1976. "Ben Franklin's House" by elPadawan is licensed under CC BY-SA 2.0.

We need an anecdote? Then let that be our anecdote (apologies to Conrad Aiken). Allow me, then, to cite a definition from Frank Lentricchia's caring study of Wallace Stevens, if for no other reason than it was from that poet and insurance executive whom Venturi derived an epigrammatic prescription for how projects ought *not* to begin. Venturi was magpielike in his theoretical borrowings but had an affinity for T. S. Eliot, William Empson, and the New Critics, Cleanth Brooks in particular.[3] Complexity and contradiction indeed, to say nothing of the seeming paradox that what the New Critics considered "internal evidence" was in essence "public," discoverable through the semantics and syntax of a poem, while "external evidence" was "private or idiosyncratic," to be found, though not necessarily worth looking for, in sources "outside the poem."[4] As for the anecdote, which should be an instrument of vividness, Lentricchia defines it as a "small gossipy narrative generally of an amusing, biographical incident in the life of a famous person whose biography's broad outline has long been a matter of public record."[5] This narrative shard is hardly the autonomous "well wrought urn" of the internalist's critical imagination, but it still has the capacity, by its inclusion in the public record, to subtly reshape previously settled matters of fact and interpretation, not to separate the two species of knowing.

The focus in what follows will be on the formation of the record and how it produces a condition of inside and outside, on and off. For it to stand, the record must allow and indeed make provisions for a searching examination, including of those motes or mounds of evidence that may be missing from or otherwise kept out of it, by accident or by design. The process might unfold as described below.

Among the first questions encountered by Edward M. Riley, chief park historian at INHP, in preparing his 1950 preliminary historical report on Franklin Court was the direction the front door of Benjamin Franklin's house faced, north or south.[6] The underlying problem, as Riley wryly stated it, was that "meddling relatives saw to it that Franklin's home was to be seen no more by anyone." In 1812, twenty years after the founding father's death, these careless relatives "nonchalantly" tore the house down; without a thought for posterity, they ensured that, unlike for Washington (Mount Vernon) and Jefferson (Monticello), there was to be no homesite to commemorate Franklin's life and times.[7] As to the question of which way Franklin's house faced, Riley found one possible answer in the published reminiscences of Colonel Robert Carr, an apprentice in the on-site print shop erected by Franklin for his grandson, Benjamin Franklin Bache. Yet Riley judged Carr's "testimony" to be of "doubtful value" because of the period of time that had passed between when he had last seen the home and when his account of it was written.[8] The chief historian could only offer a probabilistic assessment: "A definite solution of the problem could not be made from the available information, but the weight of evidence appears to favor somewhat Colonel Carr's memory of the house."[9]

Whatever uncertainties appeared and remained in Riley's preliminary historical report, it nonetheless served as the basis for an actionable recommendation.[10] In evaluating the report, NPS historian Roy E. Appleman noted approvingly that Riley had gathered "what I imagine will be most of the material that will ever be assembled on the Franklin Court area, except what may be obtained later by archaeology." In exercising the Park Service's local control over history, Appleman concluded that Riley's "recommendations are for the most part sound."[11] The recommendations were as follows: "As shown in the historical narrative above, the available information regarding Franklin's house is too meager to justify its reconstruction. Even if more detailed information is discovered, it would probably be inadvisable to attempt a reconstruction."[12] A ghost house was to take its place, but that is getting ahead in our historical narrative.

The point at which the preliminary conclusions of Riley's report and the origin of Venturi's design converge is with an unlikely blinkering of documentary evidence, creating what might be called a pattern of retention. "Considering the widespread prominence of Benjamin Franklin, and the numerous visitors to his home," Riley notes, "it is odd that no contemporary sketch, drawing, or painting of his house on Market Street has been found."[13] And as Venturi writes, as if in response to Riley, "We like the idea of not trying to reconstruct something that would be inaccurate. It turned out there would seem to be no extant known illustration of the house. This seemed remarkable but was true."[14] Arguably the only thing odd and remarkable about this seeming lack of evidence was that it seemed odd and remarkable, as if historical prominence were some sort of apotropaic, warding off the losses visited by "meddling relatives" or by the impersonal or even ghostly effects of time and chance. What follows, then, is a tale, told by a historian, of excavated ground in Philly signifying something, the site of a "prototype" of semiotic architecture that marked the loss of Franklin's house, and the ghostly monument that was recommended in the absence of (sufficient) evidence of its former appearance.[15]

Documentary Discovery

Appleman's expectation that more archaeological evidence of Franklin's house would eventually be revealed was amply fulfilled. "Preliminary excavations" (1953–1955) supported by the American Philosophical Society and the more comprehensive "explorations" conducted by NPS archaeologist B. Bruce Powell beginning in 1958 led to the discovery of foundation walls, cellar-floor paving, and the innovative Franklin privy.[16] Powell saw his work as situated within a comprehensive investigative enterprise, including historical and architectural research, designed to provide "basic data" for the development of INHP and planning of its interpretive programming. "Archaeology," as he conceived it, "is concerned primarily with the recovery of physical remains and other evidence not available in documentary sources."[17] Yet documentary sources, especially when considered as physical remains, pose their own difficulties not unlike the "salvage" operation conducted by Powell while working on a dense, overbuilt urban site. The very evidence of a documentary source had to be detected within the thicknesses of archives, libraries, and manuscript collections, each subject to internal forms of disorder.

In his preliminary report, Riley noted the recent discovery of the "only document" in the Franklin Papers that may have been a plan of the house, "an intriguing outline of a plan in pencil on the back of a receipt for paper under date of May 17, 1764."[18] It is to anticipate things to come to note the prominence of the term "outline" in the eventual design of the Ghost House. For now, suffice it to mention that in John Platt's definitive 1969 historic structures report on the Franklin house he produced a speculative life history for this bit of planimetric evidence that "somehow managed to survive the vicissitudes of the Franklin papers."[19] And when he wrote of the scrap of paper that "such things do not lie around invitingly on desk tops forever," he was not referring to the particular aptness of receipts to become lost but rather suggesting that a further purpose for it was not long in being found. "An examination of the translucent sheet reveals that it was used as though it had been tracing paper, laid over a plan of the first floor."[20] The documentary medium bore material witness to the act of drawing upon it.

Following the discovery of the second-floor plan, NPS historian Martin Yoelson assembled a research team to take a second look through the Franklin Papers, which resulted in the identification of a plan of the first floor, drawn in Franklin's hand on the back of a letter, and also a possible framing plan. With this new information, the historians believed that they could establish the location of the front and rear doors of the house—the source of Riley's initial quandary—as well as of windows and fireplaces.[21] The voluminous correspondence between Franklin and his common-law wife, Deborah, provided further indications about room usages and furnishings.

Yet, as Constance M. Greiff indicates in *Independence: The Creation of a National Park* (1987), her exhaustively researched and documented administrative history of the complicated decades-long project, one crucial piece of evidence remained "elusive."[22] Yoelson's team became aware of a rumor that an exterior view of Franklin's house existed, a watercolor signed with the initials "JT," probably the engraver James Thackara (1767–1848). And while "a great deal about the building could be extrapolated from the documentation and the archaeological evidence, many details of its exterior appearance would remain unknown without such a view."[23] The Park Service began to query historical agencies and antiquarians about this crucial piece of visual evidence, and this process led to the antiques dealer Carl M. Williams.[24] These efforts were dubiously rewarded when Dennis Kurjack, chief park historian, received a letter from Williams offering delivery, on qualified terms, of what a Thackara specialist described as the missing "key to the reconstruction of one of the most important historical houses in the United States."[25]

Williams's letter, dated November 8, 1961, begins as so many letters do, with an expression of regret for his delay in replying to his correspondent. "This was due, of course," Williams casually explained, to his "inability to be of help at that time."[26] Williams had been completing a two-and-a-half-year sentence at Eastern State Penitentiary for the theft of historical documents from the Philadelphia city hall archives, most notably the will of the prominent Jewish American educator and philanthropist Rebecca Gratz.[27] This was not Williams's first run-in with the law. Back in 1936, the then curator of the Cumberland County (New Jersey) Historical Society had been held on charges of "obtaining money under false pretenses" in connection with the sale of antique silver pieces.[28] Several months later he appeared in court again on charges of larceny for stealing items from the historical society collections of which Williams himself was the former curator.[29] Two decades on, in its coverage of the even higher-profile city hall archives larceny, the *Philadelphia Inquirer* described the suspect—a bespectacled, "dignified-looking" Williams—as a "history fancier."[30]

In his 1961 letter to Kurjack, Williams explained how twelve years earlier he had acquired an album of Thackara's drawings and watercolors from the estate of Ellen Gordon Thackara, of Lancaster, Pennsylvania. He broke up the album and sold the pieces separately through dealers in New York and Philadelphia, with some items going directly to collectors. "Franklin's house off High-Street," the elusive bit of evidence, was first offered to Harry Stone of the Primitives Gallery, New York, who demurred at the price, and it was eventually sold to Stephen K. Nagy Jr., another Philadelphia antiques dealer.

Williams informed Kurjack that he was trying to "locate the original" but suggested that he might also have a photograph of the watercolor "somewhere in storage." He also had a written description he had drafted based on the original artwork. In any case, he made himself out to be a reliable witness. "Considering my recent unfortunate experience" (his time in prison), he wrote, "my memory is pretty sharp and I recall every detail of the original drawing." Referencing a Rube Goldberg version of the work of art in the age of mechanical reproduction, Williams explained that his wife, who went unnamed, "does art work" and was able to "reproduce" the view of the Franklin house from his description. "This will give a fairly accurate idea of the appearance of the house until I can obtain the photograph and perhaps find the original drawing," he assured Kurjack.[31] Evidence was merely something to be gathered and stored, sorted and described, but it also had to be, in some sense, developed.[32]

Documentary Review

Before pursuing the trail of the Thackara drawing any further (hint: it leads to a dead end), let us return to the context of Palmer's failed attempt to coax an anecdote from Venturi, if that in fact is what he had been seeking. On July 6, 1977, Palmer met with Penelope Hartshorne Batcheler, an architect-researcher in the National Park Service's Office of Archaeology and Historic Preservation, to discuss the decision not to reconstruct Franklin's house. "Let's start with the ghost," Palmer began, with less drama than similar words would likely have produced in another setting, explaining that he had already heard three different versions of how the design for the sculptural steel frame outline had been "conceived." Palmer thus asked Batcheler if Venturi was the "sort of person that I could write a letter to and he would tell me how it was conceived and who was . . ." Here Batcheler cut Palmer off, suggesting that he write to Venturi and ask him directly if he could remember "how it was conceived because frankly I think we'd get a lot of different ideas."[33] For her part, Batcheler was fairly certain that her own contribution to the design was in deciding against reconstruction. And then there was the idea—"I think it's our idea," Batcheler clarified—to have these "wells looking down on the old parts of the foundations that the archaeologists uncovered."[34] These semicircular *béton brut* viewing "portals," as they came to be known, reframed the original question of the house's north-south orientation, establishing a visual dialogue between the surface-level historical narrative and the subtextual archaeological footnotes. If we are looking beyond Franklin Court, *béton brut* might have been seen to express the then-present tense of Philadelphia architecture.

Our own backtracking to Palmer's interviews arguably fulfills the director's published admonition: "All Files should be returned promptly to the File Room." In March 1969, Ernest Allen Connally, chief of the Office of Archaeology and Historic Preservation, and Chester L. Brooks, superintendent of INHP, assembled a team to study Franklin Court and the question of reconstructing Franklin's house.[35] John Platt and Batcheler were as if the *Sic et Non* within this dialectical contest, their respective reports prefiguring Venturi's eventual design.

When Platt met with NPS chief historian Robert M. Utley that April to discuss research that was needed for the second part of the historic structures report on the Franklin House, Utley's directive was unambiguous: "Your first priority of work will be to make a determined effort to find the Thackara drawing or sketch of the Franklin House."[36] Utley correspondingly advised a mix of exhaustive effort and reasonable caution, "if possible, because it promises to be a vital piece of contemporary documentary value. However, if all leads end in blind alleys, you will stop this particular line of inquiry as offering minimum amount of value, and proceed with the report otherwise."[37] The committee met regularly during the spring and summer of 1969, with Platt providing updates on his bureaucratically heroic quest to secure the Thackara image. Yet during his negotiations with Williams, Platt later recalled, Williams's wife appeared and insisted that her husband had "never seen nor had the Thackara drawing in his possession."[38] Perhaps the Thackara watercolor was a ghost all along, the evidentiary ideal of which took possession of researchers desperate for an open-and-shut conclusion.

Batcheler's recommendation against reconstructing Franklin's house was advanced and carefully supported in her 1969 report titled "Architectural

Summary of Franklin Court and Benjamin Franklin's House." Her findings took the form of a balance sheet of all "available documentation and archaeological facts" bearing on the physical appearance of Franklin's house. "To present an objective architectural summary of what we *know* about Franklin Court," she writes, "I found it essential to also suggest what we *don't know*."[39] The exercise in skepticism might well have proved familiar to Franklin, who in his own writing sardonically echoed the Port-Royal logicians: "Some profess they know only this, that they know nothing; and there are others who assert, that even this cannot certainly be known."[40]

For Batcheler, who had internalized the cult of precision professed by Ludwig Mies van der Rohe when she was a student at the Illinois Institute of Technology, the available evidence failed to indicate the "very form of the architectural element."[41] Batcheler finally decided that the unknowns far outweighed the knowns, and in making a recommendation she "would not want to commit to three dimensional materials, and ostensibly a factual presentation, that which I knew was a selection of numerous conjectural alternatives."[42]

The report was reviewed by John L. Cotter, chief of archaeological research for the Philadelphia region, and, while praising its author's "scrupulous intellectual and professional honesty," he questioned whether the standards she adopted in producing "a reasonably accurate reconstruction" were appropriate. Like Platt, Cotter was a strong proponent of reconstructing Franklin's house and was accordingly comfortable with the idea that it was "impossible to recreate the literal Franklin House."[43] Conjecture would inevitably enter in, but a barrier could be maintained between a meaningful interpretation of the evidence and a "period house with no relevance to archaeological or historical documentation." As Cotter envisioned it, a careful reconstruction would provide the "most appropriate atmospheric housing" for a presentation of "Franklin memorabilia and paraphernalia which *are* authentic and literal."[44] The attempt to segregate orders of experience, to situate and limit reason and imagination, might be seen to correspond to the precepts offered by the Benjamin Franklin of *The Autobiography*: "Order: Let all your things have their places; let each part of your business have its time."[45] But according to one of Franklin's most incisive and unforgiving readers, D. H. Lawrence, the failure of this seer of the "perfectibility of man," the "pattern American," was his willed blindness to the "*wholeness* of a man," which encompassed "the unknown him, as well as the known."[46] Cotter was forced to conclude with respect to the reconstruction, "If literal accuracy were the objective, the answer would inevitably be, No."

Connally concurred with Cotter's decision, drawing attention to the particular character of the architectural evidence that was still missing: "From the general descriptions one must proceed to decisions regarding exact sizes and details, thus immediately resorting to conjecture. Conjecture then further builds on conjecture as further decisions have to be made."[47] The problem with Franklin's house was that it was "not a typical specimen" of eighteenth-century domestic architecture, incorporating as it did "vaguely described unusual features of Franklin's invention."[48] Prepared for this failure of description of already unusual forms, Batcheler arrived at the meeting with an architectural scheme, elaborated in an unmistakable Miesian idiom, for developing Franklin Court in the absence of an inevitably conjectural reconstruction. For the site where Franklin's house had stood she proposed a Miesian pavilion plainly derived from Crown Hall at the Illinois Institute of Technology, but far more modestly scaled. Within the pavilion, the plan of the house would be indicated in the flooring and by partial walls inscribed with descriptions of the house from Franklin's correspondence.[49]

When Venturi finally narrated the conception of his design, it could be read that it was the waningly relevant Mies (died 1969) who haunted the Ghost House and not a revenant or otherwise conjectured Franklin. The occasion was a public program entitled Architects in the Park (February 24, 1979), which brought together Romaldo Giurgola, who designed the Liberty Bell Pavilion, and Peter Chermayeff, who was responsible for the design of the INHP Visitor Center, and Venturi. "It had been decided, before we came on the scene," Venturi said, "that the original house would not be restored, would not be reconstructed because there was not enough evidence of how it looked." The approach, then, was to make do with the "least amount of architecture."[50] Regarding the idea to place the museum below ground (as conceived by Denise Scott Brown) and the Ghost House above, Venturi explained:

> We liked this idea because it would make it easier for us, in the sense that we would not have to produce any architecture and in this case the least amount of architecture that could be produced the better. If any had to be produced, I think everyone would agree it should be rather neutral in order not to intrude on the story which was being told, the late eighteenth-century story as it were. But we felt that we did not want to be entirely neutral and we felt that there should be some dramatic evidence of the house.[51]

The little stories we tell about projects—"For the Record." Venturi's "as it were" is as if to suggest that this unwalled "story" of the late eighteenth century was a monument in which internal and external evidence equally had a place, the taut outline of structural steel setting limits to the space of conjecture. There is an implied consensus, an anticipation of collective memory, in the form of "I think everyone would agree," precisely with respect to the neutrality of the architect's intentions, when it was the evidence of the (missing) house that required dramatization.

As we work toward a conclusion, allow me to present something approaching the anecdote that Venturi was unable or unwilling to provide. We turn one last time to the record, the commendably well-cataloged research files compiled by Constance Greiff, now deposited at the Independence National Park archives, and from within them a letter written by Cotter (who decided against reconstruction after reading Batcheler's summary) and addressed to Greiff's able research assistant, Robert Craig.

In response to a query from Craig about the origin of Venturi's design, Cotter sent a duplicate photographic slide of the speculative reconstruction of a seventeenth-century whaler's tavern on Great Island in Wellfleet Harbor, Cape Cod, produced by the NPS archaeologist James Deetz in 1970. In the image, as Cotter describes it, Deetz "drew the outline of the house structure above the foundation to indicate how the whaling station of the late 1600s may have looked in its essential dimensions."[52] While there was "little surface evidence to indicate what might be found there," Deetz and his colleague Eric Ekholm were attracted to the site by "vague" local traditions that the island had been the site of a Dutch trading post. Excavations at Wellfleet in the summer of 1970 uncovered the remains of a large two-story structure. "In all probability," Deetz and Ekholm wrote, "it had a shingled roof with a massive brick chimney projecting through its center."[53] The volumetric outline of the house, drawn by Deetz in white ink, certainly bears comparison to Venturi's Ghost House.

In establishing a significance for the image, Cotter then proceeded to draw attention to his own intermediary role in the design of the Ghost House, of which the slide was meant to serve as a form of evidence. In narrative theory his form of redirection is referred to as focalization, by which a "sort of information-conveying pipe" establishes what the reader can possibly know about a particular situation.[54] Again, by way of comparison, it was the diameter of the fragmentary clay pipe stems found at Wellfleet that allowed the archaeologists to date the period of occupation at the site. In Cotter's anecdotal recollection, "I showed this picture at a meeting of the INDP [now INHP] staff members conferring with Robert Venturi concerning schemes to interpret Franklin's house in the absence of a reconstruction. I recall his mentioning the concept I suggested of doing in steel framing what Deetz did in white ink was 'interesting—has possibilities.'"[55] Anything is possible, but only some things are historically probable.[56] What appears so, in any case, is an effect of (re)presentation.

Collapsing the difference between internal and external frames of reference in a sculptural outline lacking walls, the architecture functions in a manner very close to that articulated by Deetz when explaining his discoveries at Wellfleet. "The precise form of archaeological evidence of an architectural nature," he wrote, "can be thought of in terms of both its *focus* and its *visibility*. By focus is meant the degree to which archaeological features can be read clearly and unambiguously. The visibility of an archaeological feature is primarily a function of the quantity of material which is observed."[57] Franklin's house was a ghost-written architecture, one in which the survivability of documents determined a recommendation that was followed to the letter. The question, then, is, what is left to know?

When the Venturi firm received a 1984 Presidential Design Award for Franklin Court, the jury citation commended the manner in which the Ghost House "allowed archaeological remains of the building to be preserved for viewing *in situ*."[58] This approach was the outward expression of the intention for their architecture to remain "neutral in order not to intrude on the story which was being told."[59] But just as there are types of ambiguity, there are shades of neutrality. Venturi clarifies, "We did not want to be entirely neutral, and we felt that there should be some dramatic evidence of the house."[60] And the intention of making the "presence" of Benjamin Franklin felt evidently produced a great deal of feeling in Venturi. The story was the thing. The ghostly but unsepulchered museum without walls told a story about evidence and was shaped inside and out by a lack of evidence, or rather was designed to complicate what in architectural terms could be considered an internal or external reading. As with any worthwhile monument, it was subject to critical revision, in the sense suggested by Eliot and endorsed by Venturi, "of sifting, combining, constructing, expunging, correcting, testing," while the work of design was still being done.[61] Soon after the Venturi firm won the award, Batcheler saw fit to write a memorandum for the record documenting the "cooperative venture it was." There she reports that Cotter "says he showed Venturi a slide of an ink drawing," which in turn "gave Venturi the idea for the space frame."[62]

Filing Things Away

"What did Franklin's house look like?" That was the question posed by the headline of an October 25, 1972, article in the *Philadelphia Inquirer* describing the worldwide search the Park Service had initiated for the Thackara drawing.[63] At the same press conference where the search was announced, Venturi unveiled a model of a restored Franklin Court to be completed for the Park Service in time for the American Bicentennial. In its coverage, the *New York Times* made clear that a dead end had been reached: "Unless a picture is found, an open frame of stainless steel approximating the profile of the house will be erected over the still-existing foundation of the home to give a sense of the presence of the house."[64]

How we got there can be found on and off the record. At the end of her 1978 oral history interview by George Palmer, conducted at Franklin Park, Batcheler said of the conjectural plans she drew of Franklin's house, on which each graphic trace was accompanied by supporting historical documentation,

BATCHELER: I really believe that those drawings, with the weight of evidence on the side of what we didn't know being heavier, helped make the decision of whether we should try to restore this court or not. I presented those drawings at Connally's meeting. I don't know if the minutes are recorded that way or not, but that's my viewpoint that those drawings were important.

PALMER: Are those drawings extant?

BATCHELER: Yes, in the Denver Service Center Drawing Files.[65]

The drawings were on file, or so reads the interview transcript produced by Frances Stewart. But a different sort of conversation ensued when Craig (Greiff's assistant) interviewed Martin Yoelson on December 17, 1980. A set of handwritten notes, emphatically labeled "written *after* Conversation," reviewed the history of the Thackara drawing.[66] "We would love to find that missing Franklin print," Yoelson began. Craig asked Yoelson about the antiques dealer Carl Williams, and he responded that Williams was a thief. Craig's notes then reflect the tenor as well as the substance of the discussion. "It seems to be that more and more often, Marty [Yoelson] suggest[ed] to me that the substance of our conversation should not be published. I'm sure he wouldn't even appreciate it if he knew I were taking these notes. I have therefore written them down after our conversation ended." Yoelson finally warned Craig that anyone "who published this story could be sued. One would have to get affidavits from everyone involved, he says, before one could defend a libel suit."[67]

Such a suit would no doubt require the production of documents beyond the typical expertise of the architectural historian. Telling an anecdote up front might be an effective form of misdirection, especially when it promises to provide a shortcut to the beating heart of the story. But with respect to legal challenges, like the ones Williams himself faced, it is perhaps best to qualify the evidence presented. "To use a metaphor drawn from the law courts," writes Cleanth Brooks, "'evidence outside the poem' is always secondhand (or even hearsay) evidence as compared with evidence presented by the text itself."[68] In the absence of definitive proof of what Franklin's house looked like, the conjectural structure designed by Venturi was not so much an abandoned homestead as the materialized ghost of a chance of ever finding the Thackara watercolor promised, for a price, by Williams.

The case for Williams as a sort of public enemy (of history) was made explicit by his victim, the Philadelphia city archivist Charles E. Hughes Jr., who in a 1957 paper ruefully noted that Williams had written himself into the historical record by drawing unwanted attention to lapses in then-ongoing efforts to "modernize" the city's records management system. The president judge of the Orphans' Court had ordered Hughes to conduct a study of the Register of Wills, which was under the court's supervision. A check of security, housing, filing, atmosphere, and all factors considered essential in record administration disclosed that wills filed in the city, like the one stolen by Williams, were kept under "deplorable conditions."[69] And in this "chaotic" setting, the press speculated, there appeared "nothing odd in the fact that Williams could walk into the rooms with a briefcase and spirit away valuable documents."[70] *Spirited away*—that sounds like a perfect metaphoric pretext for considering narratives of evidence. For what is certain is that nothing about anything even so well known as a historical homestead can ever be surely known, especially when documentary proof of its very appearance remains "somewhere in storage," or not, and the rent on the storage space long overdue.

This is the sort of problem worked out not in the reading room of an archive or a hall of records but rather in a probate court. Yet probate, from the Latin word *probare*, "to test or prove," is precisely the kind of critical ordeal that all historical documents must undergo if they are to lend a sense of truth to the stories we tell. Some of the most interesting stories, of course, are about ordeal itself, with which Williams seems to have been intimately familiar, even if perhaps he learned nothing from it.

3

Vacuum Suction Conveyance, Part II

∎

MEREDITH TENHOOR

Editors' note: This chapter has a surprise ending. You are encouraged to read it without foreknowledge. However, readers who prefer their architectural history minus surprises may want to know the twist first; if so, please see our note at the end of the text.

2008

While exploring the recesses of Princeton University's Firestone Library one morning in 2006, I found a short article from 1970 in the journal *Technology Assessment Review*.[1] It described a set of rather surprising plans for a New Town called Etarea, designed during the 1960s. At first the plans seemed similar to many New Towns in Europe in that era.[2] Etarea, sited ten kilometers south of Prague, was to be a satellite town for accommodating an expanding urban population (fig. 3.1). What distinguished Etarea from any New Town plan I had previously seen was the fact that planners proposed to use vacuum suction conveyance—a network of pneumatic tubes—to deliver all household necessities from a central commissary, eliminating the need for most commercial spaces. Giant tubes, large enough to carry newspapers, mail, groceries, and small household objects, would run underneath the town. This tangle of conduits was drawn up at the behest of the Czechoslovakian State Commission for Technology by a group of architects and engineers at the Prague Institute of Architectural Design: Rako Cerny, Gorazd Čelechovský, Jaroslav Stehlik, and Vladimir Sýkora, who worked with a team of thirty-six other specialists to produce a highly detailed set of plans.[3]

These plans fascinated me (fig. 3.2). They seemed to be eerie antecedents of a world without material friction, the "cities of flows" dreamed of by internet pioneers I had known in the 1990s and interrogated by urban sociologists like Saskia Sassen and Manuel Castells in those same years. I continued my library research and discovered the following: the project represented Czechoslovakia

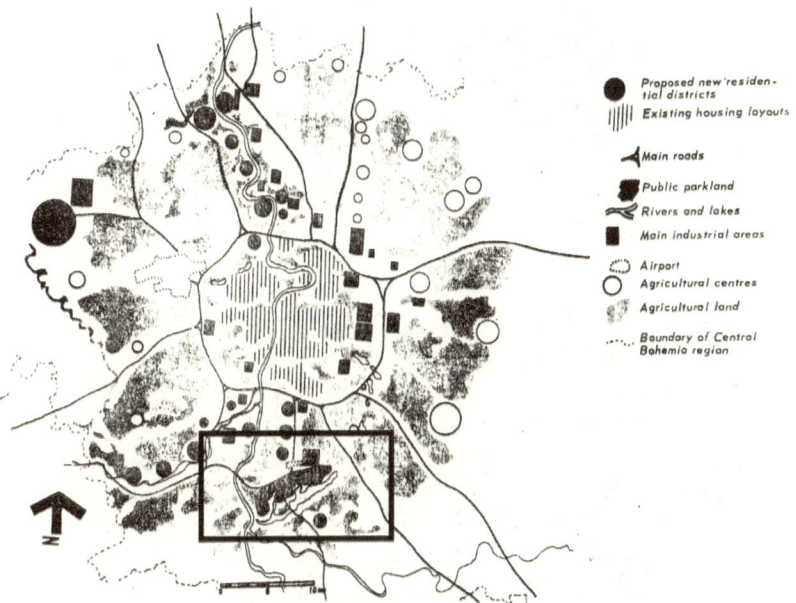

3.1. The location of Etarea (highlighted with a box added by the author), ten kilometers south of Prague. Source: Morris, "Urban Movement of Goods in Etarea," 205.

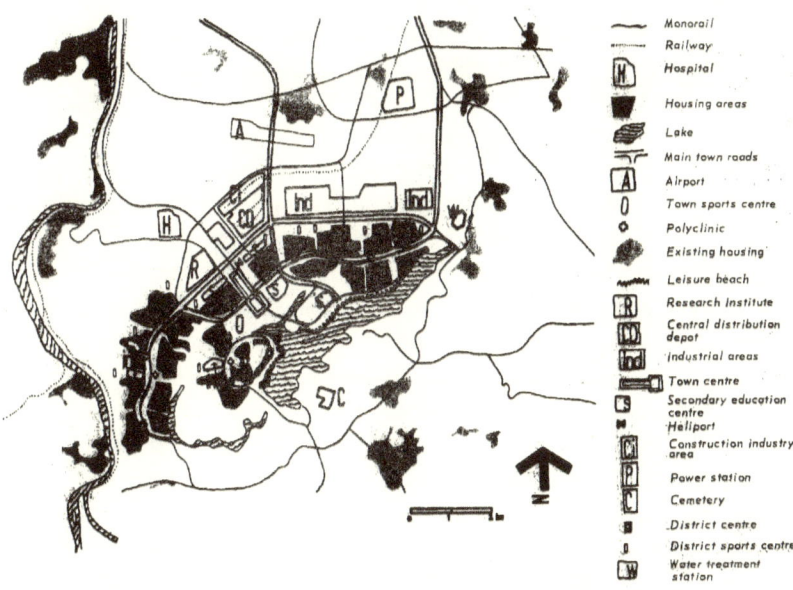

3.2. Town plan for Etarea. The town is arranged around an artificial lake to be made from damming a small tributary to the Vltava River. Source: Morris, "Urban Movement of Goods in Etarea," 206.

at Expo '67 in Montreal and attracted many visitors. A sixty-four-page folio about the town was translated into French and published as *Etarea: Étude du milieu humain dans la ville* the same year, likely for distribution at the exposition, and excerpts from this pamphlet were then republished in the magazine *Architecture Française*.[4] In 1970, a different set of excerpts from the original plans were translated into English and presented with a brief commentary by A. E. J. Morris, the British urbanist and historian of town planning, in *Technology Assessment Review* (this is what I had first found in Princeton's library). Translations of other parts of *Etarea: Étude du milieu humain dans la ville* were published in the United Kingdom in the journal *Official Architecture and Planning* in a special section on Czechoslovakian urbanization in 1970.[5]

In comparison to A. E. J. Morris's merely technical description of the town, the pamphlet for Expo '67 presented a compelling socialist vision for how pneumatic technology would transform everyday life. Instead of consolidating capital, as so many of today's Amazonian techno-capitalist infrastructures do, Etarea would redirect time saved by pneumatic household management to the town's inhabitants to be used for leisure. Etarea's planners, in spite of the fact that they were nearly all men, believed that women would be particular beneficiaries of this infrastructure. By not having to shop, women would be relieved from the drudgery, inconvenience, and inefficiencies of urban life and could instead enjoy semirural pleasures. What violence Morris had done, to excise that part of the architects' plans!

In spite of all the effort that went into designing Etarea, it seemed that no one in Czechoslovakia intended for the town to be built. The plans were simply supposed to sketch out a desired form of future urban development, one that represented socialist urban planning futures.[6] While such fulfillment was a Czechoslovakian socialist goal, it was not an implementable one, particularly after the Soviet crackdowns to bring about "normalization" after the Prague Spring in 1968. Discussion of Etarea seemed to have largely disappeared from the history of architecture and planning after 1972.[7]

Curious to know what had become of the plans and their architects, I made a few inquiries online in the spring of 2008. To my great surprise I soon received a message from a Dr. Věra Čelechovský. She told me she was a pneumatic engineer and the daughter of Gorazd Čelechovský, the town's main architect, who was also the poetic author of the text describing Etarea's social goals. We developed a virtual friendship, and she generously answered many questions I had about the town.

What follows is a transcript of two conversations with Věra about Etarea. The first was in July 2008 as part of an event organized by the artist Rey Akdogan to present Etarea to an audience of artists and architects at the Lower Manhattan art and architectural exhibition venue known as "common room." There, I sat in front of the audience, and Věra, who joined us via a contraption we invented, a kind of live satellite video phone, appeared on a projector screen to answer my questions. The subsequent conversation occurred in the summer of 2018. Where possible, I have added notes to corroborate Věra's quotations and claims and to suggest linkages to other relevant sources.

Conversation 1, July 27, 2008

MEREDITH TENHOOR (MT): Dr. Čelechovský, can you tell us a little about the plans for Etarea?

VĚRA ČELECHOVSKÝ (VC): Yes, but I want to make a correction for the audience first. When you introduced me you said I was a lifelong resident of Etarea, but actually I lived in San Francisco in the 1990s for the first few years of the dot-com boom. I was hired to be a network consultant.

MT: Thank you, I forgot to mention that in my introduction. That must be why your English is so great.

VC: Indeed. . . . So, Etarea. Originally the city was to have four ways to acquire the necessary goods for modern life. First and foremost there was a pneumatic tube delivery system, which would deliver small goods: groceries, beverages, newspapers, and the mail from a central distribution center. Everything that could fit into a nineteen centimeter by forty centimeter tube—up to four kilos of stuff! That is a lot. My father and his colleagues drew every detail of those tubes to be sure they would work. Then they would travel up a vertical chute and into the right apartment flat.

But this wasn't just done to be technically amazing. My father thought that cities were like organisms. He meant that if you could make a town that was biological, it would be self-supporting, a kind of perfect socialist town; he even thought this self-organizing biological system could survey everyone and just figure out by itself what everyone needed automatically.[8]

MT: Yes . . . this tradition was common in the urbanism of the Saint-Simonians, or even the Japanese Metabolists. Or later, with architect-ecologists in the 1970s. . . .

VC: Well, maybe he wasn't so original then . . . but that is your concern, not mine.

Anyway, you can imagine what these tubes did to grocery shopping. You only bought what you needed since anything could be delivered to you within three minutes.

MT: Wow! So Věra, what did the architecture of the town look like, given that you didn't need to have retail commerce? How did this impact its design and the layout?

VC: We had so much space! You wouldn't believe how much room and air you feel when there are not stores everywhere. . . . What's really important, though, is what the pneumatic tube systems did for us. With all of this space, and saved money, and saved time, you could do so many things that were impossible in Prague. They said leisure, but for us it was about making life.

MT: Thank you, Věra.... This is more or less what I imagined from reading the plans myself. It is good to have you confirm all of this! But I imagine that idea of liberation must have been hard to keep up after normalization, no? These are pretty radical ideas.

VC: They really were! But I tell you, Meredith, we lived this even after the crackdown. It wasn't quite as my father planned it, but we made marvelous lives out of the plans for Etarea.

MT: So Věra, I'm a bit confused about that, actually. Anthony Morris wrote that the town was just supposed to be a scheme, a theory, or a way of demonstrating how goods might ideally circulate—

VC: And you saw how Morris butchered all of the important ideas of my father!

MT: Yes, yes. He cut things out of the Etarea plans so they resembled his own visions.... But he didn't *invent* anything about the Etarea story, did he? He said very explicitly that Etarea was just a study plan, that it hadn't been built, so I'm kind of confused.

VC: Yes, the plan was that they would *not* build the town. But Meredith, as you know, we are talking because we *did* build it.

MT: Okay, then! So how did you do that? Maybe we can start with how you got the funds and permissions?

VC: As we discussed, normalization meant there was no enthusiasm for this project.... There was also the issue of whether the population of Prague demanded a new town; Etarea was only supposed to be built if there was a population boom. There *was* a housing shortage, but this was a town for 135,000 people, and women would only get their liberated town if they did a lot of reproductive labor....

MT: So women would both bring about and benefit from Etarea....

VC: Yes.... But really there didn't seem to be a political case for the town after 1969. That was not really a time for changing gender norms....

My father was of course disappointed, even though he had been told all along that the plans were merely to be "hypothetical." He had spent many years working on this project, and it felt like a real place to him. But he knew he had to let it go; he needed to keep working as an architect and not become some crank champion of a dead plan. But my aunt—I had an aunt who worked for the Prague Pneumatic Post—she had another idea. She wanted to live in Etarea.

MT: Did your father and his compatriots get the idea to build a pneumatic world from your aunt? I mean, I know pneumatic systems were all the rage in those days, internationally, too, but did her work have something to do with what happened in Etarea?[9]

VC: Prague had had a very extensive pneumatic tube–based post and telegraph system since the nineteenth century.[10] People were used to using pneumatic tubes, used to things just appearing. And yes, the technical infrastructure was there, there were already companies that made the parts. . . .

But I think, somehow, that ideas about conduits were just in the air. Do you know this film *Daisies* by Věra Chytilová?[11] There are two very funny girls, hungry girls, wandering around Prague, causing trouble. In one scene they decide to crawl in a dumbwaiter so that they can crash a banquet, and they have a food fight among the cream pastries. This was supposed to be a bit of a farce, but for my father it justified his project: why should they have to go in the dumbwaiter to have a feast? Technology should bring what people want *to* them. The city could be the dumbwaiter, everyone could have a feast. Women deserved to have their desires fulfilled and to have *conduits* for that fulfillment. . . .

You must also understand that Etarea was designed in the build-up to the Prague Spring. People were getting ambitious about how things might change. Věra Chytilová, my father and his friends, everyone.

MT: But let's get back to your aunt. You said she had something to do with this?

VC: Yes! She wanted to live in Etarea because of this feminist version of it. So my aunt told her colleagues—all of the other women who worked for the pneumatic post—about the plans for Etarea. This was a very tightly knit group of women. And you know, these women had been sneaking things around in the tubes for years. They knew how to use the system to their advantage, and they wanted to see it expand, to see what you could do with bigger tubes, more conveyance power. They decided Etarea *needed to be made*.

They did it by subterfuge and thanks to their mastery of networks.[12] The tube operators rerouted a few big checks destined for somewhere else. All of the official documents in Prague passed through the pneumatic post, and a quick operator could take one of these out of its canister, make a few changes, and boom, all of a sudden permission was obtained. The town planning authority had already authorized the transformation of a farm south of Prague into some sort of housing development. That fooled many agencies into believing that the plans were moving forward. Very quickly others forged documents authorizing the construction of the distribution center and a small hospital and school at Etarea. Then a research laboratory. We already had the promise of the tubes, but these *infrastructures* made Etarea into a town.

MT: Didn't anyone get wind of this? No one tried to stop your family?

VC: The government knew there were some forgeries, but they could not trace how they were occurring; they were embarrassed to admit this loss of control. We were not on Soviet radar either. I don't really know how we got away with it. . . .

Of course, Etarea could not be realized on the scale that my father originally planned. It was supposed to be for 135,000 people, and done in phases, with the infrastructure getting built first. We did get a smaller infrastructure in phase one, and we made it for 1,500 people. The automated department store, the small shops—those were just too much to do. But we made automats for farm products. . . .

MT: Did anyone know you were there, or write about you?

VC: Well, you know that the plans were very public, and later you historians rediscovered them. But the town we built was never described anywhere: we had to keep it a secret that we had stolen all these funds.

MT: Wow . . . that is amazing. Well. Can you tell me what life was like in Etarea?

VC: This is the best way I know to explain it. Imagine a city block, all of the space that is devoted to stores on the ground floor. You don't need any of it!

With no stores you have so much space—for me as a child it seemed like one big playground . . . trees, waterfalls, streams. . . . When I was older I used it to make sculptures! Hold parties! Do paintings! Start a rock band! No stores meant freedom back then. Why care when there were empty shelves, full shelves? Why not just get what you could from one central depot?

MT: It sounds like a world where all of your desires are instantaneously fulfilled. . . .

VC: Not really! I mean we still had to deal with each other. . . . But our desires around things sort of fell away. We did get what we needed instantly, and it freed up a lot of space, mental space, space in our houses, space not for things but for other desires. . . .

But look, this wasn't for everyone. Some people like looking for hat pins in old stores and find poetry in an empty shelf. But the people who went to Etarea, they went there because they wanted to spend their time doing something else.[13]

MT: You sound like Silicon Valley futurists. . . . Did things change in Etarea over time?

VC: Well, we started off using the tubes for things my father had planned . . . groceries and things like that. Then later someone had the idea to use the system for laundry and dirty dishes. With time everyone had all kinds of great ideas for what they could send in the tubes. Knitwear. Goldfish. Calculators. They got very sophisticated about packing them, comparing methods.

MT: And what happened after 1989?

VC: Well, like I said, before '89, official Czechoslovakia had forgotten about us. Our networks did not really link up with theirs. And over the years, on the surface, Etarea almost looked like any other area outside of a city, like a New Town village with some agriculture and things around it. We just had no stores. Nobody remembered or cared that we were there.

After '92 in Etarea, there was a sense that we needed to rethink how our tube network and our politics collided. Our equipment began to break down, and we had to do a lot of welding and soldering.... As I said, we had long ago realized that our tubes would not just get things to and from the central processing unit, but among one another. So we were more like a trading network. Less like consumers.

MT: It sounds great. And it looks like we are running out of time, so I will open it up to the audience. You all must be interested in pneumatic systems and their potential in architecture and urban planning. Do you have any questions for Dr. Čelechovský?

VC: Yes. I'd be happy to answer any of your que— [static—inaudible]

MT: Dr. Čelechovský? Are you still there?

Let's see... I think we may have lost the connection.... Well, I'll see if I can still get some audio through my earpiece. Yes. Okay. Dr. Čelechovský, can you hear me? Yes, good.

Well, feel free to ask Dr. Čelechovský questions and I'll convey the response. . . .

2018

In the years that followed this conversation I remained intrigued by the plans for Etarea. But writing about Etarea in a more scholarly context seemed full of perils: Věra's narrative was tantalizingly close to what I might have imagined the town to be like, but of course I could not cite or rely upon her words without corroboration. As I was neither an expert in Czech modernism nor a Czech speaker, I worried, too, about the ethical implications of indulging in projections about a place where I had no obligations. I turned my attention to other projects.

Yet I thought of returning to writing about Etarea many times. The "unbuilt" became part of ongoing conversations in the Aggregate Architectural History Collaborative through one of Daniel Abramson's essays, "Stakes of the Unbuilt."[14] Abramson argues that reading the projections of the unbuilt was a central practice of modernist architectural history, and he suggests that we release the unbuilt from its previous role as a manifestation and confirmation of a single architect's vision and instead orient it toward the generation of more contingent views of history. This resonated with my understanding of Etarea as the product of both a nation and an architectural discourse. And yet Etarea's unbuilt-ness seemed unstable. Perhaps it was a historical fact—I wasn't sure after Věra and I spoke—but perhaps the binaries of built and unbuilt could be set aside if we took seriously the labor done through design and if we filled in the forms of life that unfolded within it. The planners of Etarea thought about economies, labor systems, and material practices as central to architectural and urban design; their unbuilt was a world my fellow historians in Aggregate and I were trying to build within our discipline.

My thoughts returned to Etarea again in 2015, when a meme started to circulate in leftist circles angling for "fully automated luxury communism," or a redistribution of time, luxury, and benefits to all through the fruits of automation.[15] While deeply skeptical about the true time and resource benefits of late-capitalist automation, both the potentials and perils of Etarea seemed to be excellent precedents for interrogating this line of thought. As technocapitalist wealth aggregators started to make urban interventions (e.g., Amazon's assassination of main street retail, Google's "smart-city" Quayside project), I felt I was witnessing the negative mirror of the Etarean dream. I wanted to revive Etarea's socialist version of efficiency that could be recuperated for pleasure, not profit. On top of this, I found myself doing more and more oral history in my own research. In my book *Street Value*, I narrated historical events and decisions through interviews; this seemed the best way to expose the various forms of agency that transformers of urban space imagined and possessed. My book on architecture and political economy in France had also become filled with conversations, though this time, instead of featuring historical actors, these conversations were between fictional narrators and theorizers. What did that mean? Why this drive toward those voices instead of my own?

I decided to work on Etarea again but also to do more research as a way to appease my concerns about treating Etarea as if it were built on a *terra nullis*. Since my initial conversation with Věra ten years prior, a documentary had been shown on Czech television about the plans for the town; it clearly presented Etarea as an "unbuilt project." And other historians—Jan Dostalík, Kimberly Zarecor, Vladimir Kulić, and Maros Krivý—had started writing about the history of Etarea's planning, though none of these historians mentioned Věra, or the aunt at the pneumatic post, or the built version of Etarea that Věra had described to me.[16] Nonetheless, Věra's version of Etarea seemed quite real to me, and the only way to come to terms with this was to travel there, to see the place that had been so vivid in my imagination. I emailed Věra to see if she could show me around but unfortunately got an autoresponse that she was "off the grid" and on vacation in rural France. I had limited time in Europe—my trip was scheduled ten years to the day from my original conversation with Věra—so I went to Prague by myself. I called Věra immediately after my trip, and her phone somehow seemed to work again. This is a transcript of our conversation.

Conversation 2, July 28, 2018

MT: Hello, Věra. I hope you had a good vacation in France?

VC: Yes, it was very relaxing. Did you have a vacation too?

MT: Well . . . um, Věra, actually that's why I'm calling. I went to Etarea.

VC: You what??? Why didn't you tell me?!?

MT: I tried reaching you, but you were away . . .

3.3. Tubes International, July 27, 2018. Photograph by Meredith TenHoor.

VC: But how . . . well, how did you get there?

MT: The maps in your father's folio showed the location of the town quite clearly, between the bends in the river. I rented a Skoda and drove down.

VC: A Skoda?! But, where . . . where did you drive?

MT: I drove south, along the river. And Věra, it was pretty exciting: I passed a supplier of pneumatic tube parts on the way down—it was such a confirmation of the importance of that technology! Here, I'm texting you the photo [fig. 3.3]. And I think I saw remains of your settlements, though they weren't where I thought they were supposed to be. . . .

VC: Text me that image, too . . . [fig. 3.4]. I think those buildings were done by colleagues of my father's. . . .

MT: But Věra . . . when I got there, what I saw wasn't really what you described, or what your father had drawn. There were no lakes, no high-rises. . . .

VC: I told you we couldn't build the whole thing! It was supposed to be built in phases: the tubes first, then the landscaping, then the houses. We only got the tubes, and we made our own houses. What were you expecting to see anyway?

MT: Oh, I see . . . I didn't know what to expect. . . . I really . . . well, I saw some farms, a thriving electrical network, and some interesting modernist houses here and there. The countryside was quite beautiful . . . it was a perfect July day. And then I found this incredible glen filled with self-built off-the-grid chalets

3.4. Possible Etarean settlements, far in the distance, July 27, 2018. Photograph by Meredith TenHoor.

tucked into a mountain stream. I drove three kilometers along a rutted dirt road, trying to get right to the geographic center of the planned settlements. I just bounced and rumbled and then the road dead-ended in a stream in the forest. There was a mountain between me and that spot. . . . It was gorgeous. It felt like a secret world, though I nearly ruined the tires of the poor Skoda. Was that Etarea? [fig. 3.5]

VC: That is by the Davle, no? Yes, there are some Etareans that built houses there, but that is not the place I told you about.

MT: Oh . . . then perhaps Dolní Břežany? That looked a lot newer and had some buildings that looked like your father's plans. . . . Was that where you lived [fig. 3.6]?

VC: Meredith . . . I feel like you don't believe me.

MT: I'm sorry, Věra. We met on the internet. . . . I mean I know we've been talking for ten years, and I've been dreaming about life in Etarea all this time. But I wanted to write more about these plans, and I did need to *verify* what you've told me. . . .

VC: So you are struggling with your vision of this place after seeing my land?

MT: Well . . . a bit . . . I mean I knew you didn't, like, just build the plans as they were published, but still I imagined some kind of more definitive architec-

3.5. A road that dead-ends in a stream near Davle, a small village outside of Prague, near the site where Etarea would have been built, July 27, 2018. Photograph by Meredith TenHoor.

tural statement. Or just density. But then when I got to Zvole and Březová and Oleško and the other villages that would have been swallowed up by Etarea, I felt like it would have been a tragedy to build a new town in such gorgeous countryside; I was glad it wasn't there. . . .

I don't want to doubt you, Věra.

VC: What is the nature of your doubt, Meredith?

[long pause]

MT: Věra, I wanted to tell the story of Etarea. . . . But I'd rather tell this story with your way of bringing a plan to life. Your narrative enables what some have called thick description, but it's not at all a formal one, the kind we usually get in architectural histories. And it's not the efficient one I use to quickly make a

3.6. A possible Etarea, near Dolní Břežany, July 27, 2018. Photograph by Meredith TenHoor.

point when I write an article. Your narrative is the opposite of efficiency! Or it's what escapes efficiency.

VC: Ha! You make me sound just like Etarea then! Efficiency recuperated for pleasure and play!

MT: Well, I'm not so sure. . . . I mean we just discussed that there are some reasons to believe that you might not have—

VC: Will you stop?!?

[Pause]

MT: Věra, I always want to project myself into other times and places. It's why I want to work on plans, it's why I'm an architectural historian. I mean, this does tie into a lot of conversations about historiography that interest me. . . . Latour's engagement with subjectivities in *Aramis*. Or my colleague Danny Abramson, calling on architectural historians to *inhabit* plans, which you and I had been doing.[17] And Arlette Farge is in here, too, tasting the archive, getting lost in it. She articulates so beautifully this desire to shift one's subjectivity to another time—a key desire when writing history. The archive's materiality is a sign of its simultaneous alterity and closeness. . . .[18]

VC: I am not a historian, so I don't know. . . . Why are you telling me this? Don't you think you tried to encounter the material a bit too much?

MT: Věra, these plans were drawn on real grounds, and I had to see the land that would become your father's dream, and also yours and mine. . . .

VC: Maybe. That is kind of the trap of studying architecture maybe? That you can always go to the source, encounter the land under the building? Start sowing doubt? Have a referent?

MT: Yes, that's why this problem is not just Arlette Farge's encounter with the materiality of the archive but one specific to studying architectural plans. The unbuilt always unfolds onto a preexisting landscape; it can't write one anew even when it pretends, in that horribly colonial mind-set, to be able to.

But my interest in returning to our conversation is somewhat separate from this responsibility to land and people already inhabiting and using it, and in many ways also separate from the question of the unbuilt. Your father's plans are, first and foremost, conduits for desires about ways of living together.

VC: Conduits about conduits! It's gotten very meta, hasn't it!! This text is an infrastructure for thinking about an infrastructure for fulfillment?

MT: Ha! You're right.

VC: It was your slip. . . . But seriously: I think what you're saying is that you can't tell the story of that desire with my father's plans alone. You need my version of how we lived together.

MT: Exactly. Inhabitation histories, anthropology, oral history . . . the turn toward the user that is at the center of revisionist modernisms.[19] It happens in architectural history too, even in my own work.

VC: Huh?

MT: Never mind. Though if I were to follow that line of thought, then in this text I would just reproduce your father's plans (with your permission of course) and let people see what they make of them. They would surely see things you and I don't. We could defer history to all readers of plans. We could just publish them and lose the privilege that positions our own interpretations of things.

VC: But then you'd be a transcriber and not an intellectual! Not that I think transcribers *aren't* intellectuals. . . .

But I think that is the opposite of what you're doing. My father's voice is barely present here; we quoted him and maybe you will reproduce some plans, but you are not building him up as a heroic figure. His voice is a bit lost in this conversation.

I think what you are doing is actually quite different and somewhat like what I am doing, and my aunt and the other people who made the town. We have both hopped into my father's work and claimed it as our own. We are all acting like architects.

MT: Věra, I totally agree. I've long thought of architectural history as a form of architectural practice, or artistic practice. We tell stories to help architects

3.7. Věra Čelechovský (*on screen, left*) in conversation over "satellite video phone" with Meredith TenHoor (*right*), in the exhibition space known as "common room," New York, 2008. Photograph by Rey Akdogan. It is a bit difficult to see in this photograph, but an audience member commented that we seemed almost like long-lost twins; only our accents, our hairstyles, and the color of our dresses differed.

understand their history and work. We are not thwarted architects, but we create the architectures that construct the narratives of architectural practice . . . the narratives that hold it up.

VC: Historians are scaffolders then?? Maybe. But this is not about restoring the glory of my father's collective creation but about talking about what's been done with it, what could be done with it. You and I have shared his dream. We have tried to make it more real. Your methodology is central to that. But don't lose sight of why you're here: this is a political dream, and you still believe in the potential of radical imagination. And so do I.

Hey, I am texting you a picture that you once sent me. It's us, talking in 2008! Look at us, we were so young! But also: we complement each other [fig. 3.7].

Editors' note: To clarify, Etarea is an actual historical unbuilt project. But "Dr. Věra Čelechovský" was created and performed by the author, Meredith TenHoor (see fig. 3.7).

Part II
Self-Evidence

Self-evidence is understood in everyday parlance as evidence whose validity can be objectively verified, an apparently patent truth that requires neither proof nor reasoning. Despite their seeming obviousness, claims to self-evidence emerged historically in the early modern period, when it was believed that humans could not be trusted to vouch for truthfulness, when epistemic authority was deferred from ethics among humans to objects. The chapters in this section explore the mechanisms of this deferral for architectural history. Specifically, the chapters explore how material objects of wood, concrete, and metal were made to speak as evidence at moments when speech among humans was vexed. The self-evidence of things—buildings, cities, and landscapes—in architectural history is one of the field's most important modus operandi. But what questions of ethics do claims of self-evidence obscure?

4

Talkative Timbers
A. E. Douglass, the Beam Expeditions, and the Construction of Architectural Evidence

■

ALBERT NARATH

> *The desert was clairvoyant, this is what he'd always believed, that the landscape unravels and reveals, it knows future as well as past.*
> —Don DeLillo, *Point Omega*

In June 1923 the National Geographic Society sponsored the first of three "Beam Expeditions" through the American Southwest, going from Flagstaff, Arizona, to the Hopi village of Oraibi, to Canyon de Chelly, and then to the large-scale archaeological sites at Chaco Canyon and Mesa Verde. Although these sites were already long-established stops on expedition itineraries, the Beam Expeditions' mission was distinct: instead of securing artifacts for museum display, the campaigns were conceived for the purpose of creating a historical methodology. Under the direction of the astronomer-cum-archaeologist Andrew Ellicott Douglass, the most immediate goal of the program was to establish absolute dates for the construction of Pueblo Bonito, a monumental Ancestral Puebloan building complex then under excavation by the National Geographic Society. Across the different sites that they visited, ranging from abandoned building complexes to living communities, Douglass and his team extracted hundreds of core samples from structural beam timbers that had been preserved over centuries in the semiarid environment of the high desert. From this material, they attempted to derive temporal data points from the seasonal ring patterns that accumulated year after year, as indexes of precipitation levels, temperatures, and other natural forces, in the xylem tissue of the trees from which the beams were hewed. As Douglass himself described it, "the same dry country that has preserved these evidences of former habitation has produced this method of measuring the exact age of the ruins."[1]

At the conclusion of the expeditions, Douglass claimed to have dated the beginning of construction on the western half of the Pueblo Bonito site to 919

CE, the major period of construction to around 1060, and a second wave of building activity some twenty years later. It wasn't so much the dating of Pueblo Bonito itself, however, that he considered to be the expedition's most important contribution. In his reports on the Beam Expeditions, he emphasized the specific nature of the "evidences of former habitation" that his team uncovered. For Douglass, tree-ring analysis suggested that archaeological narratives could be anchored in the sure footing of science. In the 1920s, the qualities of absoluteness and precision that Douglass attributed to his data became central points of reference among archaeologists who sought to transform their discipline into a "New Archaeology," or what the American Museum of Natural History anthropologist Clark Wissler characterized as a shift from the mere collecting of "curious and expensive objects once used by man" to a "rigorous science of cultural history."[2] Dates established from the analysis of tree rings were celebrated for introducing rigor to historical arguments at particularly sensitive junctures, where the establishment of a construction chronology or other narrative datum might be compromised by the intrusion of judgment. In Douglass's investigation of beams, archaeologists found evidence posed as facts.

Almost immediately, these qualities led to the enthusiastic application of tree-ring analysis to historical problems across a wide range of other disciplines, from astronomy to climatology, ecology, and art history. Well beyond the context of southwestern archaeology, dendrochronology has also been a frequent source of evidence in the discipline of architectural history. In scholarship on Byzantine churches, medieval cathedrals, Palladian villas, and almost any other building type with datable timbers and a contested or unknown chronology, references to tree-ring data have served to bolster the credibility of a theory, to demonstrate the falsity of a competing claim or prevailing interpretive convention, or even to assess the relative accuracy of other interpretive techniques such as formal analysis or archival documentation. To take only one example, starting in the late 1960s the dendrochronologist Ernst Hollstein developed an expansive data set on oak specimens for buildings around western Germany, Luxembourg, Belgium, and the southern Netherlands. With it, he attempted to establish definitive construction chronologies for a range of monuments, including the Worms cathedral, the Roman bridge in Trier, and the Trier cathedral.[3] What is representative about Hollstein's data set is that it was perceived as evidence for architecture, similar to the way that tree-ring studies have served, in climatology, as evidence for paleoclimatic weather patterns.

To state it this way would be to acknowledge the role of absolute information in the discipline of architectural history, echoing the by now well-known assertion made by Lorraine Daston and Peter Galison that "scientific objectivity has a history."[4] My primary interest in tracing the history of dendrochronology here, however, lies elsewhere. In what follows, I explore a different way in which Douglass's preoccupation with the rings in beams might shed light on the role of evidence in architectural history. In the context of the Beam Expeditions, buildings were taken to be not only the subject of historical research as objects in need of dating but also, in and of themselves, primary sites of knowledge production. At stake in the expeditions was not simply the development of a precise chronology for Pueblo Bonito but the creation of broader narratives that set the history of construction in the Southwest within wider timescales of environmental change. I suggest that in assigning dates to ruins, Douglass's investigations offered more than a chapter in the history of scientific objectivity or in technical art history. The Beam Expeditions pose illuminating questions about what buildings are as objects of study and how historians of architecture might use them to trace the intimate and often fraught imbrications of human histories and natural histories.

Self-Evident

In order to situate the development of tree-ring analysis, it is useful to start with a biographical episode. When Douglass was commissioned to organize the Beam Expeditions, he was not an archaeologist but an astronomer. Beginning in 1894, when he first made his way to the desert Southwest, he played a formative role in establishing Lowell Observatory, founded by Percival Lowell at a site near Flagstaff, Arizona. One of Douglass's main responsibilities was to participate in Lowell's Mars research program. During the observatory's inaugural year alone, Lowell, Douglass, and fellow astronomer William Henry Pickering made more than one thousand hand drawings of Mars as seen through the observatory's powerful telescope. The team was particularly interested in recording a network of faint lines that seemed to crisscross the reddish surface of the planet. Because of their straightness and remarkable contrast with the rest of the planet's visible morphology, Lowell famously argued that the features must have been canals, or *canali*, constructed by a form of Martian life. In the 1906 book *Mars and Its Canals*, Lowell attempted to back up his controversial findings by citing the team's carefully controlled discipline of observation as well as the advantageous conditions under which those observations were made at the state-of-the-art high-altitude facility. He claimed, "Not everybody can see these delicate features at first sight, even when pointed out to them; and to perceive their more minute details takes a trained as well as an acute eye, observing under the best conditions."[5] Lowell referred to the drawings that resulted from this practice as "impersonal intercomparable representations" whose value was predicated on their being "scientific data" rather than "artistic delineations."[6]

For all of Lowell's concern with scientific rigor, the canal theory failed to garner any kind of professional consensus. This reception was due in no small measure to Douglass's dissatisfaction with the drawings of the features. In 1907 he published a long article in *Popular Science Monthly* that attributed the canals to a simple case of visual illusion. With a series of illustrations, Douglas demonstrated that what Lowell had described as deliberate constructions were, in fact, the products of optical tricks. No matter how skilled and impartial the observers may have been, residues of subjectivity still remained in their drawings. In the end, Douglass concluded that Lowell's findings were a product of the team's looking; they were a matter of aesthetic judgment and personal obsession rather than of irrefutably observed facts.

It was against the background of the Mars controversy—which resulted, not surprisingly, in Douglass's being asked to leave the observatory—that he then sought a more convincing form of evidence right in his own backyard. During the many hours that the team spent looking at Mars through the telescope, they were often struck by the uncanny visual parallels between the planet in their instrument's frame of view and the arid landscape that surrounded them directly outside the observatory's windows. "Even in its mottlings," Lowell mused, "the one expanse recalls the other."[7] For Douglass, the comparison between Mars and the high desert of Arizona was not simply a matter of visual resemblance. During the previous years, he had been developing a parallel research project on sunspot activity. His interest was in confirming the presence of a solar cycle that astronomers speculated to occur approximately every eleven years. Since solar phenomena were known to affect weather patterns on earth, Douglass reasoned that sunspot cycles might be decipherable in the growth markings of trees.

In 1904, Douglass began to assemble a collection of trunk sections from stumps in the Flagstaff area right after Arizona Lumber and Timber Company loggers had felled the trees. As his collection expanded to include specimens from yellow pine stands fifty miles away in Prescott, he noticed the repetition, across a wide geographic range, of specific ring sequences that arose from a set of common climatic variables. Based on these signatures, he attempted to create a bio-climatic chronology for the Colorado Plateau that would extend back in time far enough to show the periodicity of solar cycles. This was accomplished through a process called "cross-dating," in which, starting with a ring representing a known date, Douglass aligned complementary sections from different tree samples in order to create a continuous time line reaching back beyond the lifespan represented by the ring signatures of any single specimen.

The problem that Douglass faced, however, was that samples taken from living or recently felled trees provided only a limited chronological reach. After investigating—and then discounting—the potential of using old-growth trees from different climate zones to push his chronology further, he shifted his attention to the remarkably preserved wooden beams that remained in place at several Indigenous villages or were being uncovered by archaeologists at ancient sites around the Southwest. As he put it in one report, "Thus we would find a certain pattern in the central parts of a modern tree, and find the same pattern in the outer parts of a tree cut by the Indians three hundred years ago, whose central rings grew centuries before the earliest rings in modern trees."[8] As early as 1919, Douglass received six beam sections from a large-scale excavation at the site of Aztec Pueblo in northern New Mexico. By comparing the overlapping ring patterns in those samples to a group of other log sections from Pueblo Bonito that had been collected at the end of the nineteenth century by the famous Hyde Expedition, he was able to determine the construction sequence of the two sites.

These, however, were only relative dates; in Douglass's terms, they represented a "floating chronology." In order to secure absolute dates for Aztec Pueblo and Pueblo Bonito, Douglass would need to convincingly bridge the time gap between the tree-ring signatures of the archaeological material and the more recent specimens that he had taken from living trees and lumberyards. This was the main task of the Beam Expeditions. In the third season, at a site in the Mormon settlement of Show Low, Arizona, the team recovered specimen HH39, a partially buried fire-scarred beam whose ring patterns overlapped at each end with other specimens from the expeditions. From this "Rosetta Stone of American archaeology," as Douglass described it, he was able to assign absolute dates to Pueblo Bonito, Aztec Pueblo, and several other major sites across the region.

In contrast to the Mars sketches, tree-ring analysis seemed to succeed in generating what Lorraine Daston and Peter Galison have called "knowledge that bears no trace of the knower."[9] This was in part due to the rigor of Douglass's method. Originally, he made use of photographs and skeleton plot illustrations to visually align, one at a time, the ring sequences of his specimens. Over the course of many years, in an effort to minimize observational error and overcome the logistical difficulty of analyzing an avalanche of ring samples, Douglass developed a special device that he called an "optical periodograph" (other devices followed—the "cyclograph" and "cycloscope").[10] The optical periodograph, which facilitated a statistical method of representing mass results, was aimed at visualizing underlying cyclical patterns in his data. The periodograph promised to turn observation itself into a quasi-mechanical procedure that no amount of learned looking could equal. Through a complex process of visual translation, the device produced a type of image that Douglass called a "frequency periodogram." Looking at the periodogram, he argued, was an exercise in pattern recognition, where temporal data derived from thousands of tree-ring signatures would "strike the consciousness with the effect of repeated blows."[11]

The values of automatization and self-denial that Douglass attempted to incorporate into his technique were not limited to his own practice of observation. What made tree rings such a compelling form of evidence was that trees themselves appeared to tabulate environmental events with an almost mechanical sensitivity and dependability. Douglass explained, "Every year the trees in our forests show the swing of Time's pendulum and put down a mark." Trees, he declared, were "chronographs, recording clocks, by which the succeeding seasons are set down through definite imprints."[12] In equating the tree ring with the machine known as a chronograph, Douglass was referring to a piece of equipment often used in astronomical observation at the turn of the twentieth century. Chronographs of the period usually consisted of a revolving cylinder covered by a sheet of white paper. As the cylinder rotated, the astronomer tapped a telegraph key that created an electric signal. In this way, observable events were registered as a mark on the paper.

For Douglass, the rings in the trunk of a tree were like the lines traced around the surface of the cylinder. There was, however, an important difference between the two. Whereas the accuracy of the chronograph was ultimately dependent on the reliable input of the astronomer, the tree seemed to produce its marks in an automatic way, as if it was itself tapping the telegraph key. In Douglass's words, tree rings constituted a historical record that was "more accurate than if human hands had written down the major events as they occurred."[13] As a form of evidence, they collapsed the distance between the observer and the object of observation. In this way, they most closely approximated the evidential structure of diary entries. According to Douglass, "A tree is not a mechanical robot; it is a living thing, and its food supply and adventures through life all enter into its diary. A flash of lightning, a forest fire, insect pests or a falling neighbor may make strong impressions."[14]

In revealing their own physiological reactions to impinging forces, beams offered evidence that was not simply objective but apodictic. Echoing the original Greek *apodeiktikós* and its associations with "showing off," "demonstrating," or "pointing to," tree rings were envisioned as a body of evidence that pointed to itself. For Douglass, tree rings were *self-evident*. With this term, I am evoking a discourse outlined in the 1992 essay "Self Evidence," by science historian Simon Schaffer.[15] In it, Schaffer describes a strand of experimentation and debate in the eighteenth century wherein natural philosophers attempted to establish matters of fact through rigorous procedures of auto-investigation, proffering, as he puts it, "their own bodies in evidence" and "making evidence out of the person of the experimenter."[16] We might view Douglass's conception of dendrochronology as another chapter in this history of self-evidence. The crucial difference, however, is that instead of considering the body of the scientist as a site of knowledge production, tree-ring analysis envisioned beams as being endowed with the agency to produce evidence, or to be self-evidential. Tree rings, for Douglass, were "talkative"; they were "signs and glyphs" and "stories . . . written by Mother Nature."[17] It was the archaeologist's responsibility not to record or tabulate events, as was the case with the Mars sketches, but to translate the signs preserved in old timbers into meaningful historical narratives.

If we are to take Douglass's assertions to be more than rhetorical, it is useful to situate his conception of evidence within his own writings about the Beam Expeditions. In 1929, following the last of the three campaigns, *National Geographic Magazine* published a long celebratory article written by Douglass.

In "The Secret of the Southwest Solved by Talkative Tree Rings," he presented the team's travels through the Southwest as a heroic adventure narrative, a genre common to the publication. According to Douglass, the team's quest for data was beset at every stage with obstacles that needed to be overcome and cultural conflicts that required resolution. At the heart of this were the beams themselves. Douglass bemoaned the fact that such valuable material, as seen from a scientific perspective, was routinely used as firewood by local community members, sheepherders, prospectors, and even previous archaeologists. At the Hopi village of Walpi, for example, kiva beams that the community had originally recovered from the destruction of local Spanish mission churches following the 1680 Pueblo Rebellion were burned for fuel after the US government supplied new spruce logs from Black Mesa to replace the old timbers. "Many another log," Douglass reported elsewhere, "with its wonderful hidden story, perished at that time."[18]

For all its adherence to ideals of automatization and detachment, dendrochronology was clearly not formulated in a vacuum. Each beam's condition and position, whether chopped at the ends with stone axes, charred by fire, weathered, or relocated from another site, were the product of local sociopolitical events and cultural negotiations that in many cases reflected the larger crosscurrents of settler colonialism in the Southwest. The timbers were shaped not simply by weather but also by Spanish occupation, the Pueblo Rebellion, US government Indian policy, intercommunity rifts and tribal politics, and the impacts of archaeological campaigns like the Beam Expeditions. Indeed, Douglass's own field practices were often extremely intrusive. His method involved carrying away whole logs or crosscutting full sections out of beams. When this was not feasible, as in cases where large cuts would threaten the structural integrity of a building or irreparably damage a place of cultural importance, the team employed a specially designed tubular borer capable of extracting one-inch core samples from intact wooden beams.

Not surprisingly, these techniques were routinely met with resistance. At the village of Oraibi, where the team's quest for old wood led them directly to sacred kiva structures, they attempted to gain access to off-limits or strictly controlled spaces by offering gifts such as purple chiffon velvet, felt hats for making ceremonial masks, and turtles for making rattles, as well as sums of money and cigarettes. At Walpi, the expedition team "had to appease the spirits for the Indians by inserting a piece of turquoise at the base of the plug with which we filled the hole made by the extraction of a core." This ritual, he continued, "was to prevent the lodgment of the 'spirit of decay' in the timber."[19] Whether or not the gifts and turquoise were effective or sincerely conveyed, Douglass's aim in reporting these episodes was to mark the redefinition of a beam from its immersion in a matrix of geo-spiritual relations and deeply established cultural protocols to its reconceived status as a piece of scientific self-evidence.

Climatic Evidence

In Douglass's writings, the removal and processing of beam sections and core samples is portrayed as both a technical procedure aimed at physically preparing samples and an act of cultural—we might even say epistemological—transformation. This work, flowing from Indigenous building sites to the spaces of the Laboratory of Tree-Ring Research, which Douglass founded at the University of Arizona to analyze the material collected during the expeditions, served to translate the "diary entries" contained in tree-ring markings into far-reaching historical narratives. One of the primary goals of the Beam Expeditions was to make the time relations of southwestern sites conform to the linear span of the Christian calendar. Throughout Douglass's writings, the construction histories of Oraibi, Walpi, and ancient complexes such as Pueblo Bonito were compared not only to each other but also to distant, largely European and American monuments and historical events. In the *National Geographic* article alone, Douglass related the dates of the ruins they encountered to "the conquest of Spain by the Moors," to the time when "William the Conqueror faced Harold the Saxon at the Battle of Hastings," to "the rise of Charles Martel or the Mohammedan invasion of India," and, on multiple occasions, to the moment when "Columbus reached the shores of the New World."[20] Through this kind of historical superimposition, Indigenous architecture was claimed as part of a wider, America-centered, global history. Well before the Beam Expeditions, such rhetorical devices were already a familiar trope. In the 1850s, visual representations and physical parts of trees from the American West circulated widely in publications and international exhibitions where they were cast as the fruits of American territorial expansion, simultaneously symbolizing the great antiquity of the North American landscape and the "naturalness" of the country's history of colonial impositions.

Perhaps the most pressing narrative that emerged from the Beam Expeditions, however, related to the connection between architecture and natural systems. This connection was embedded in the materiality of tree rings themselves, which notate the beginning of construction at the very moment when the growth of a tree, represented in the expansion of its rings, is put to an end. The act of architecture, we could say, is the tree's final diary entry. As his work at Pueblo Bonito progressed, Douglass observed that the enormous use of pine timber in the building of communal houses at Chaco Canyon contrasted with the almost complete absence of local pine trees across the present-day landscape. Owing to the fact that the beams he uncovered were predominantly smooth and unweathered, meaning that they were not scarred from transportation from a distant location, he reasoned that there must have been a substantial forest in the immediate area of the ruins at the time of the construction. This was substantiated by a small number of trees, stumps, and logs that he managed to locate in dispersed spots around the canyon. Douglass further speculated that an ancient forest at Chaco Canyon would have played a key role in the conservation of the local water supply by helping to hold soil and moisture. Cutting down the forest would have directly influenced the aridification of the surrounding landscape, decreasing its capacity for supporting human life. This thinking was compounded by Douglass's realization that the "gap" in his tree-ring record that was eventually filled during the third Beam Expedition coincided with a critical period of drought in the Southwest—one of several that he and his team established through the periodographs—that stretched from the year 1276 to 1299. Anticipating a major strand of speculation in academic and popular writings about population collapse in Chaco Canyon, he concluded that the period represented a "great crisis in the history of the Pueblo people" and a "break in the continuity of Pueblo history."[21]

With this kind of observation, Douglass's research was readily incorporated into an emerging ecological discourse in the United States. He was an active member of the Ecological Society of America, founded by Henry Cowles in 1917 with the twin objectives of advancing ecological ideas and advocating for environmental protection. Douglass contributed an essay on tree rings and climate cycles to the inaugural 1920 issue of the society's journal, *Ecology*.[22] In it, Douglass summarized his methods and argued for the power of tree rings as a source of "climatic evidence" capable of aiding in the reconstruction of paleoclimatic conditions that could not be accurately assessed through written weather records and other methods. In this context, his research was sometimes put in the service of overly simplistic environmental determinist narratives, such as the geographer Ellsworth Huntington's attempt to directly equate the development of Indigenous cultures in North America with the influence of climatic factors.[23]

For Douglass, ring signatures did much more than provide a window onto historical patterns of human adaptation. His expedition teams' pursuit of beams (and before that, Lowell's search for irrigation canals on the desiccated surface of Mars) took place against the background of an unfolding environmental crisis across the American West. In contemplating the interruption in Chaco civilization that he observed in the tree-ring record, Douglass was also posing the critical question of whether the severe droughts of the 1930s might portend a similar deviation in future ring signatures. As he put it, "Drouths [sic] are working havoc today, just as they did in the days of the old Pueblo people. When times are good we forget the discouragement of 'dry spells,' believing naively that we can do nothing about it."[24] Douglass's concern for present-day human-caused environmental degradation pulsed through his thinking about tree rings. In a vignette from his *National Geographic* article, he relates an experience viewing a rehearsal for a "bean dance" at Oraibi. Twenty men formed a semicircle in a large kiva structure and recited prayers directed at stimulating the coming of rain. "As I sat watching the dance," he recalled, "I realized that I was one of three terms in a human series: First, the Indians of a neighboring village, who believe that rain is actually controlled by proper magic, performed by their powerful priests; then those before me, who were praying to the more powerful spirits that rule the rain; and, lastly, I, myself, who was there to study the rainfall history in pine timbers and learn the great natural laws which govern the coming of the rain."[25]

In distinguishing his study of the kiva beams to expose natural laws from the inhabitants' use of the ceremonial space to connect with natural forces, Douglass emphasized his self-consciously detached positionality as a scientific observer. At the same time, he implied that the answer to environmental crisis was not in summoning nature spirits or attending to the health of a building (in the sense of the turquoise episode mentioned above) but in instrumental actions that used the "diary entries" legible in beams to inform large-scale infrastructural and landscape preservation programs. He noted, "True, we cannot change nature's great laws that govern the movement of the earth's atmosphere, but perhaps we can protect our cities and farms to some extent by the wise reclamation projects and preservation of the forest cover."[26]

Throughout the 1930s and 1940s, Douglass argued for the practical value of the architectural evidence derived from the Beam Expeditions for landscape preservation, weather forecasting for agriculture, and large-scale land reclamation projects. In the early 1940s, for example, the dendrochronologist Edmund Schulman, originally an assistant to Douglass at the Laboratory of Tree-Ring Research, conducted a landmark study of water flow through the Colorado River basin. Schulman used ring data from Douglas fir trees in the region as a form of proxy evidence for measuring long-term streamflow levels. In a 1942 report for the Los Angeles Bureau of Power and Light entitled "A Tree-Ring History of Runoff of the Colorado River, 1366–1941," Schulman argued that his centuries-long reconstruction could be used to assess the reliability of long-term power production in the region, especially with respect to the construction and expansion of hydroelectric power at Boulder Dam. For Douglass, the outcomes of research like Schulman's constituted a "gift to the future that emerges from our prolonged, but finally successful, effort to learn the age of prehistoric Pueblo Bonito."[27]

Epilogue

In recent years, the capacity of tree rings to reveal human impacts on the environment has become a highly publicized and sometimes politically charged flashpoint in academic research, popular writing, and government debate. In the same way that beam timbers at southwestern sites such as Oraibi, Walpi, Aztec Pueblo, and Pueblo Bonito preserved signatures of historic droughts, deforestation, and population collapse, scientists have recently found distinct anthropogenic signatures in trees around the world resulting from a spike in carbon-14 levels created by atomic bomb testing.[28] One could also cite an episode like the Climate Research Unit email hacking of 2009, which, in the lead-up

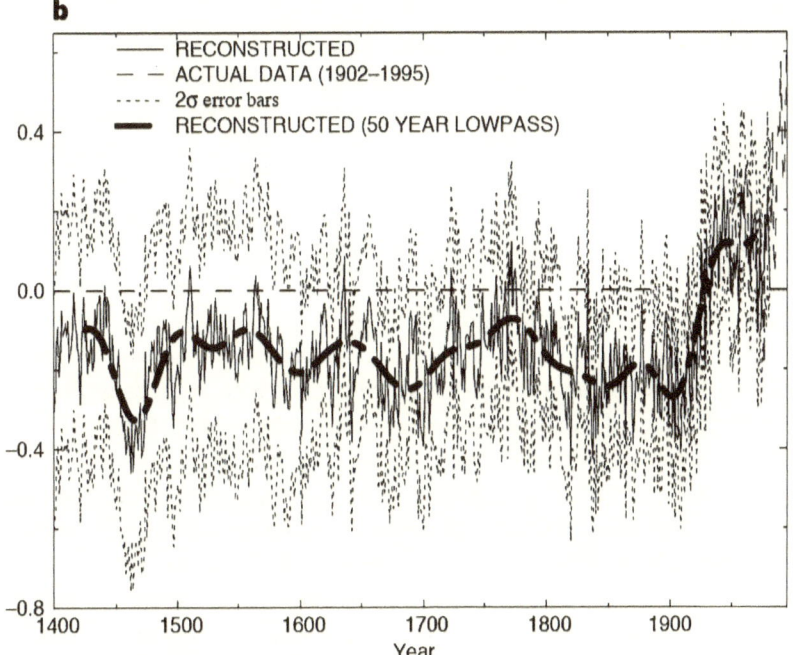

4.1. Michael Mann, Raymond S. Bradley, and Malcolm K. Hughes, "Hockey Stick Graph." Published in *Geophysical Research Letters* 26, no. 6 (1999).

to the United Nations Climate Change Conference held at Copenhagen that year, directly fed what many media outlets referred to as the "Climategate" controversy. At the center of this episode was an iconic image—the so-called "hockey stick graph"—created by a team of scientists. This graph clearly illustrated a rise in global temperature levels corresponding to, and resulting from, increases in industrialization and the use of fossil fuels. Of all of the "proxy data" that the team employed in reconstructing paleoclimatic climate conditions, including glacier ice, lake sediment, coral material, pollen, and speleothems, it was the veracity of tree-ring readings that became a central target of critique among self-proclaimed "climate change skeptics" hoping to cast doubt on scientific consensus regarding human-caused global warming.

In the domain of architectural history, narratives based on tree-ring analysis have not occupied a similarly visible or controversial place on the stage. Tree-ring data sit in the footnotes; they are the inert, stable substance of more visible arguments. In most cases, the architectural historian maintains a self-consciously distanced relationship to dendrochronology, not to mention other specialized techniques such as radiocarbon dating, luminescence analysis, or archaeomagnetic dating. These techniques impact but are seldom taken to be the proper subjects of architectural history.

One result of this situation is that while the technical precision that Douglass and his lab carefully endowed in tree-ring analysis survives, its robust apodictic narrativity has been cast aside. By situating the history of dendrochronology with respect to Douglass's involvement in the Beam Expeditions, my intention has been to sketch one way in which the materiality of buildings has stimulated particular historical narratives concerning the connection between architecture and ecological issues. Rather than calling for the revival of the environmental-determinist, imperialist, or techno-reclamationist narratives outlined above, however, my interest is ultimately in suggesting that architectural evidence—manifest in the substance not only of beam timbers but also of countless other building materials such as the plant fragments embedded in adobe walls or the rare earth materials contained in photovoltaic panels—might open the way for new histories, expanded histories, and counterhistories of architecture. Historians of art and architecture are increasingly probing the effectiveness and implications of their methodologies in order to reflect a general feeling that, in the face of the large-scale cultural and environmental implications of the Anthropocene, "our models for how to think, write, and teach about history are no longer adequate," according to photograph historian Robin Kelsey.[29] Tracing the place of techniques such as dendrochronology in the history of architectural history points to expansive stories behind what is taken to be self-evident.

5

Concrete Is One Hundred Years Old
The Carbonation Equation and Narratives of Anthropogenic Change

■

LUCIA ALLAIS AND FORREST MEGGERS

What good is an equation for writing architectural history? As a historian and an engineer, we have different answers. Historians relativize equations, situating their truth claims in context and narrating how they emerge over time.[1] For engineers, equations serve as glue for research communities, as conveyors of the general principles of "basic science" used to communicate across subfields.[2] Yet climate change is palpably affecting how historians and engineers talk and write. Scientists and humanists alike are feeling the urge to make legible a new era in the earth's history, named the Anthropocene in geological fashion: an age in which natural phenomena are not just a backdrop for human action but in which human and nonhuman events profoundly affect each other. As they account for this dynamic, historians are increasingly interrupting their narratives to defer to science with a capital S. "Not being a scientist myself," explains Dipesh Chakrabarty, "I assume the science to be right in its broad outlines."[3] Architectural scholars are among those who have adopted the present tense to cite scientific consensus (and have also disclaimed the caveat "I am not a scientist") and delivered cogent explanations of the phenomena that drive global warming.[4] Laboratory researchers, for their part, are increasingly resorting to historical storytelling when they describe the motivations for their work, usually before adopting a drier voice in which to intone their findings. Research about the science of reinforced concrete is a case in point: it is not unusual for technical papers to begin by stating that concrete has been "a building material for over two millennia" and calling it "the most abundant anthropogenic sedimentary rock on the planet."[5] Two different modes of periodization are thereby mixed: one, the geological image of the earth being sedimented with rock; the other, a dynamic picture of human inventions being perfected daily by technicians. Juxtaposing them is supposed to ensure that even highly detailed and incremental experimental results are factored into a global and millennial balance of energy, but, as with the historian's nod to science, a gap remains between the evidence and the narrative.

In this chapter, we take up the challenge to the traditional division between historical and scientific writing to address one equation and its impact (or lack thereof) in the architecture, engineering, and science of reinforced concrete. The equation was published internationally in 1968. With little fanfare, its formulation marked a major transition in the scientific understanding of common reinforced concrete: from being a permanent material—as permanent as stone—to being explicitly impermanent, an assemblage that inevitably decomposes into its constituent parts. Concrete is an ideal case study for exploring how climate change forces new modes of writing about architecture, because concrete is both a resource and a technology, and, at the intersection of those two timescales, it is also an architectural material.

The equation we are concerned with is one that predicts the number of years, t, that any reinforced concrete structure "under conditions of natural exposure" will take to fail through carbonation.[6] That is,

$$t = kx^2$$

where k is a constant defined by the variable material and environmental parameters:

$$k = \frac{1}{2D} * \frac{[Ca(OH)_2]}{[CO_2]}$$

And chemically:

$$Ca(OH)_2 + CO_2 \rightarrow CaCO_3 + H_2O$$

What the equation says is that all reinforced concrete structures have a finite life (because all concrete is in contact with the atmosphere) and that this finality is triggered by the ongoing environmental process of carbonation. Carbonation is driven by atmospheric CO_2, which slowly permeates the concrete and reacts with the $Ca(OH)_2$ within. Since there is universally CO_2 in the atmosphere, this process occurs universally across design, use, climate, or structural behavior of a concrete structure. The equation also tells us that there are two variables affecting the rate of carbonation: D, a measure of the porosity of the cement, which corresponds to the holes and pores that make up its cavernous interior, and x, a measure of the concrete "cover," which is the distance of the steel reinforcing bar from the edge. Thus, the simple formula $t = kx^2$ correlates the dying "age" of a concrete structure to the distance between the steel and the outside air.

On its face, the equation describes only one phenomenon: how any reinforced concrete structure "passivates"—how it comes to a chemical equilibrium with its environment. This "becoming passive" is essential to concrete's nature as a human-made thing, originating from the extraction of energy from the earth and eventually sedimenting to become one with the earth again. But the equation also describes failure of an *architectural* kind: carbonation transforms the chemical balance of the concrete that surrounds its steel reinforcement, enabling reinforcement to rust, expand, and crack the concrete. Once cracked, the steel and concrete can no longer perform together as a single building material; any part of a structure may fall down. Concrete's initial purpose, its anthropogenic raison d'être, disappears, but its agency on the earth is not entirely forestalled: it continues to passivate and contribute to the energetic accounting of humans' presence on the globe.

By plugging into our equation the standard specifications for concrete construction today, we can estimate that it will take about one hundred years for most reinforced concrete structures around the world to fail through carbonation. Add to this the fact of the material's invention at the turn of the last century, and we arrive at a notable coincidence: reinforced concrete is about one hundred years old, and it takes about one hundred years for reinforced concrete to die its architectural death. Neither figure is an exact number, as this chapter will show, and most reinforced concrete today is demolished, maintained, or replaced long before this failure occurs. But carbonation generates a surprisingly reliable and determinant outcome: most concrete structures built using globally standard dimensions and processes today can be expected to last about one century. Putting these two findings together, then, yields a remarkable image: a moving wall of physical failure has begun to rake through the built environment, ensuring that much of what is built on the globe today—not just buildings but also roads, as well as infrastructure for water and electricity—can be predicted to fail in about a century.

This fundamental problem with the finite material life of reinforced concrete has only very recently been brought into public discourse, and it barely appears in conversations about future concrete research.[7] This is not because "the science" is new. The carbonation equation was first proposed in 1928 by a team from the University of Tokyo, based on experiments begun in 1907. The formula was refined and verified over the decades, then published in English by Minoru Hamada in 1968, leading to a germinal review of the formula's literature by a Swedish researcher, Kyösti Tuutti, in 1982.[8] Since then, Hamada's mathematical model has given rise to an entire subfield of materials science. These researchers have described, with specificity and nuance, the many rapid failure processes to which concrete is exposed: localized freeze-thaw cracking, salt on roads causing chloride attack, and others, including climatological extremes. But the more important subsequent debate, about the long-term dynamics of reinforced concrete as "the world's most common building material," as well as the necessary rethinking of its lifespan in the culture at large, never followed suit.[9]

This chapter, then, describes the carbonation of reinforced concrete and investigates its history in order to spur this debate and help rethink technical causality in the Anthropocene more broadly. The challenge, as we understand it, is to attend equally to historical and technical explanations, doing justice to science "in its broad outlines" but also breaking the habit of keeping those outlines out of reach of humanistic inquiry.

We follow the equation as it has traversed the twentieth century, in three distinct settings of knowledge production: on-site experimental work, institutional norm-making, and the birth of a new discipline. We address how different lifespans of importance have been defined in each realm: in the patronage and patenting of concrete, through cultural and legal rationales; in engineering research, through empirical refinement; and in materials science, through an analytical framework we call a "productive ontology." We conclude with questions about anthropogenic dynamics more broadly, as well as architecture's role in establishing relationships between equations that embody the energetic view of human history. By taking an equation as our historical actor, we depart from the usual architectural histories of reinforced concrete that take buildings, persons, institutions, standards, and practices as their objects of study. While architectural historians have cogently described the hybrid human and nonhuman work involved in concrete construction, we are concerned with how the material performs this blurring of natural and cultural history not only in its initial making but, in a radically different way, after it has set and begins its life *as made*.

Liquid Stone and Centennial Fever

The carbonation equation challenges a century's worth of architectural discourse about concrete being a quintessentially modernist material, homogeneous yet human-made, as permanent as stone, and emblematic of the way modern scientific rationality dominates the forces of nature.[10] Architectural historians tend to agree that the most important feature in the history of reinforced concrete is that making it required little exactitude.[11] The early history of reinforced concrete is filled with approximation, trial and error, and theories that trail behind empirical findings. Thus, reinforced concrete was not invented once, by one person, in one place, but rather emerged from a widespread experimental network of amateurs and, later, engineers. Gradually standards emerged, and around 1910 an industry was born.

Of course, concrete had existed since Roman times. The "invention" that concerns us—the one that dramatically expanded the influence of concrete, making it the second most abundantly used material in the world, second only to water, and completely redefining how old it could be—was to have systematically

5.1. An experiment on the Hennebique system in Frankfurt, 1900. From Cyrille Simmonet, *Le béton: Histoire d'un matériau* (2005).

introduced *steel* into it. By putting metal reinforcement on the lower part of a concrete beam, engineers and architects designed a building system of unprecedented versatility, removing the mass that had apparently characterized older academic architecture. More than a new material, reinforced concrete was perceived as a veritable kind of liquid stone, which therefore *competed* with nature itself. Here is how the architectural historian Sigfried Giedion promoted the material he called "Ferroconcrete" (*Eisenbeton* in German) in 1928: "From slender iron rods, cement, sand, and gravel, from an 'aggregate body,' vast building complexes can suddenly crystallize into a single stone monolith that like no previously known natural material is able to resist fire and a maximum load."[12] As Giedion's rhetoric shows, concrete's novelty was proclaimed with incredible historical hubris.

This hubris, it turns out, was measured in centuries. Developments in the industry were entirely bound up with the centennial fever that motivated international events like the colonial expositions and world's fairs, which showcased the progress of humanity in many ways, including by displaying and marketing reinforced concrete as a quintessential secular product for a new age.[13] The obsession with the century as a historical unit (the idea that history progresses in numbered multiples of one hundred) had begun earlier, in the wake of the French Revolution. As Reinhardt Koselleck has argued, revolutionaries wanted to eliminate older modes of periodizing human history, such as kingdoms and, later, generations.[14] For them, quantifying time was a way to free up the writing of history, to secularize it. And the one-hundred-year figure was especially useful because it seemed metrical.

Paradoxically, however, and precisely because concrete was perceived as an authorless material, its engineers operated in a kind of perpetual "now." In the United States and Europe, early advances in concrete technology were measured in extremely short increments, spurred by a competition for patents. The first patent (for the Hennebique system, which won the prize for innovation at the 1900 Paris Exposition) expired in seven years. Other measures of longevity were also capped by social and financial rules. For example, the French architect Auguste Perret was allegedly refused a mortgage for his now-canonical Rue Franklin Apartments because bankers took its *visual* thinness as sufficient evidence that the building would collapse before the end of the mortgage—a forty-year period.[15] This principle of performance ensured that any standards intended to guarantee concrete's lifespan would do so by locating its failure beyond a more reasonable temporal deadline. A 1911 American source put the lifespan of reinforced concrete at seventy-five to ninety years. In Italy, a lifespan of seventy years was used as early as 1935 for legal purposes. In 1953, Britain's Building Research Station estimated that concrete was a "permanent" material, which meant seventy years.[16] Once reinforced concrete became the material of choice for infrastructure, one hundred years became the more standard figure, not because it was acceptable for structures to fail after a century but because it was assumed that any maintenance and replacement could be achieved before this deadline. In 1979 Indian engineers surveyed the carbonated structures built during British rule and still in use after fifty years, but they recommended a minimum of thirty years for design lifespan.[17] Once concrete had expanded to become a global technology, temporal predictions barely changed, in part because national competition discouraged any radical rethinking of building specifications.[18] In South Africa, British standards continued to be used until 1982.[19] As late as 1986 one American textbook said reinforced concrete could last "indefinitely."[20] Looking retrospectively at this history of reinforced concrete's emergence and global spread, nothing seems more short-sighted than the persistence of its promoters in tying longevity either to the span of a single human life or to perpetual care and survival. What none of these standard setters explained or realized is that even with maintenance, all reinforced concrete structures are subject to failure through carbonation.

From Law to Phenomenon

The systematic failure of reinforcement did appear in the logbooks of early reinforced concrete researchers, in the 1910s. The earliest observations were that concrete cracked and failed faster where the steel reinforcing bar was placed close to the surface of the concrete. In 1917 researchers in Italy correctly described this process and its relationship to depth.[21] It was also noted that proximity to seawater would increase the rate of failure due to the chloride from salt.[22] This evidence was quickly translated to imply, correctly, that the *oxidation* of steel into rust causes it to delaminate from the surrounding concrete. The structure fails, it was noted, as it loses the tensile resistance provided by steel. But while these experimenters knew that rust was a mechanical culprit for failure, they had no analytical models of the physical processes occurring inside the material. Even if their estimates for rates of failure were correct, diagnostics pointed elsewhere; failures were thought to be failures of design, or maintenance.

Environmental factors were at play in early research as well. Chemists had good intuition about the "square root" relationship between time and the diffusion of chemicals through solids, and the image of chemicals diffusing into concrete was central to the earliest discussions of reinforced concrete failure.[23] In that sense, failure was understood to be related to Fick's 1855 law of diffusion, one of several formulas that scientists used to produce a new, atomic-level description of the world at the turn of the twentieth century.[24] According to Fick's law, any medium (say, air) that has a high concentration of a particular substance wants to equilibrate with another adjoining medium (say, concrete) with a lower concentration of that same substance.

What Minoru Hamada and Yoshikazu Uchida finally described in 1928 is *what exactly was diffusing* in reinforced concrete. Since the cause of failure was the oxidation of the reinforcement, one logical thought had been that oxygen was being transported from the outside air, via rainwater, toward the steel reinforcing bar. In fact, as Hamada and Uchida described, the driving force was the oxygen *already inside* the concrete. It turns out the cement binder in concrete, that apparently magical component whose reaction with water had been turning liquid to solid since Roman times, had been given a new task when reinforcement was introduced: protecting steel from oxidation. It is the high pH of the binder that "passivates" the oxidation reaction—a reaction that would need a low pH environment to unfold. The fact that the binder had a high pH was observed in the 1950s by applying electrical potentials—essentially treating a reinforced concrete sample like a battery and checking to see if it had a charge. In 1957, German researcher Von A. Baümel wrote that if this layer of "high pH cement gel" around the steel were to break down, rust would be able to form.[25] But when he hypothesized what possible factors threatened to end the protective process of passivation, he still imagined exposure to chlorides or other reactants. His research continued to align with the view that proper maintenance and avoidance of "bad" chemical influences would make reinforced concrete a permanent material.

What Hamada and his colleagues understood before all the others was that *another* reaction—carbonation—eventually lowered the pH level and canceled out this passivation.[26] To visualize this low pH, they used a phenolphthalein re-

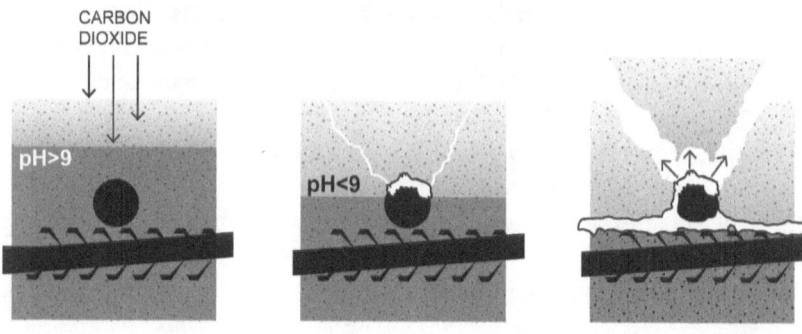

5.2. Visualizations of carbonation using phenolphthalein reagent to show the change in pH.

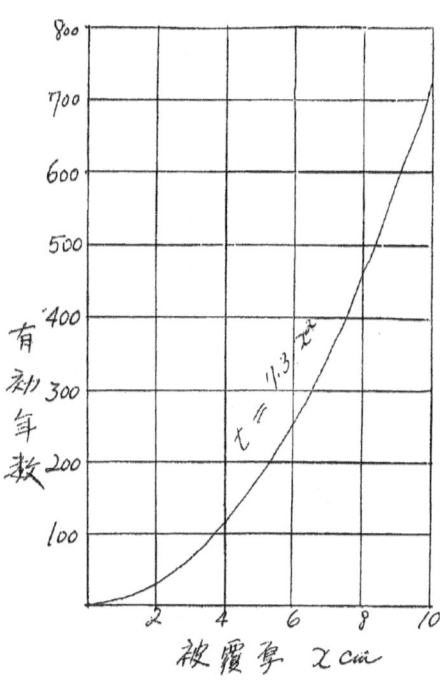

5.3. Curve indicating the "root of time" equation. From Minoru Hamada and Uchikazu Uchida, "Durability Test of Concrete," *Journal of Architecture and Building Science* 12, no. 516 (1928).

agent with a characteristic purple color, which remains to this day how carbonation is traced physically and graphically. It was by correlating his observations with the depth of carbonation of various concrete samples during different time periods that Hamada produced his initial equation in its original form, $t = kx^2$.

By 1968, Hamada also recognized that k was not a constant but varied significantly. A concrete sample with 10 cm depth of cover, he calculated, could fail in *either* ten years *or* after more than one hundred years. Looking at the curve Hamada first published in 1928 (where the depth of the carbonation is shown on the x axis), it is easy to see why, once k became variable, observed carbonation lifespans began to range so widely on either side of the estimate of one hundred years: because the deeper the carbonation, the slower it is. The bending of the curve means that with each centimeter of concrete it takes significantly longer for carbon to penetrate than the preceding centimeter. In Hamada's first analysis, k had a value of 7.3. Today this value has been updated and k has been mathematically modeled, but the curve retains its shape, and indeed 7.3 was a good starting estimate.[27] Using standard dimensions for a concrete cover today (1.5 inches for a floor or wall), Hamada's 1928 equation still predicts that a beam lasts about one hundred years.

The breakthrough of Hamada's equation, in other words, is that it *registered a limit*. Carbonated concrete does not fail instantly, as in a spectacular bridge collapse; instead, carbonation enables a mode of failure, which then has its own dynamics. In fact, Hamada's curve describes a first "initiation phase," after which comes a second phase, when the steel oxidizes and the crack grows and propagates, resulting in further cracks. Much of the research into carbonation today is devoted to "extending longevity," or manufacturing solutions that are offered to clients for "deferring maintenance," merely by pushing off the onset of the second phase.[28] Yet even with many more inputs, standards informed by materials science's further refinements of Hamada's equation still allow us to say with confidence that concrete can last about one hundred years. Why, then, does the carbonation equation remain a marginal finding in the concrete industry?

The Historical Pivot That Wasn't

It may seem especially surprising that no big revelation followed the publication of the carbonation equation in 1969, since it came at a moment of rising environmental awareness.

The term "carbonation" should set off bells among climate-conscious readers, given its association with climate change. The CO_2 in the atmosphere that is diffusing into the pores of every concrete structure is the same CO_2 whose concentration in the atmosphere has risen to just above 0.04 percent, from 0.03 percent a century ago. These two phenomena, concrete carbonation and the rise in the earth's temperature, influence each other reciprocally. Today, the concrete construction industry contributes approximately 5 to 8 percent of anthropogenic CO_2 emissions. Thus, the factor k is dynamic in part because it is affected by the change in the nature of the atmosphere, including the change provoked by all of the accumulated concrete production around the world since 1900. In that sense, concrete propagates its own failure. The feedback loop between the carbon emitted in concrete production and absorbed during passivation has been quantified, with one hundred years as the temporal unit.[29] One way to visualize this feedback loop more broadly is to juxtapose Hamada's curve with another set of curves: the dashboard of "hockey sticks" that indexes climate change in the Anthropocene. Hamada's curve is driven by these indices: increased CO_2 in the atmosphere generates the risks of climate change, and this same CO_2 accelerates the inevitable risk of the failure of concrete.

But if these hockey sticks and Hamada's curve are related mathematically, connecting them historically and conceptually is not so simple. Take the way the Anthropocene is typically periodized, in three phases: beginning around 1800

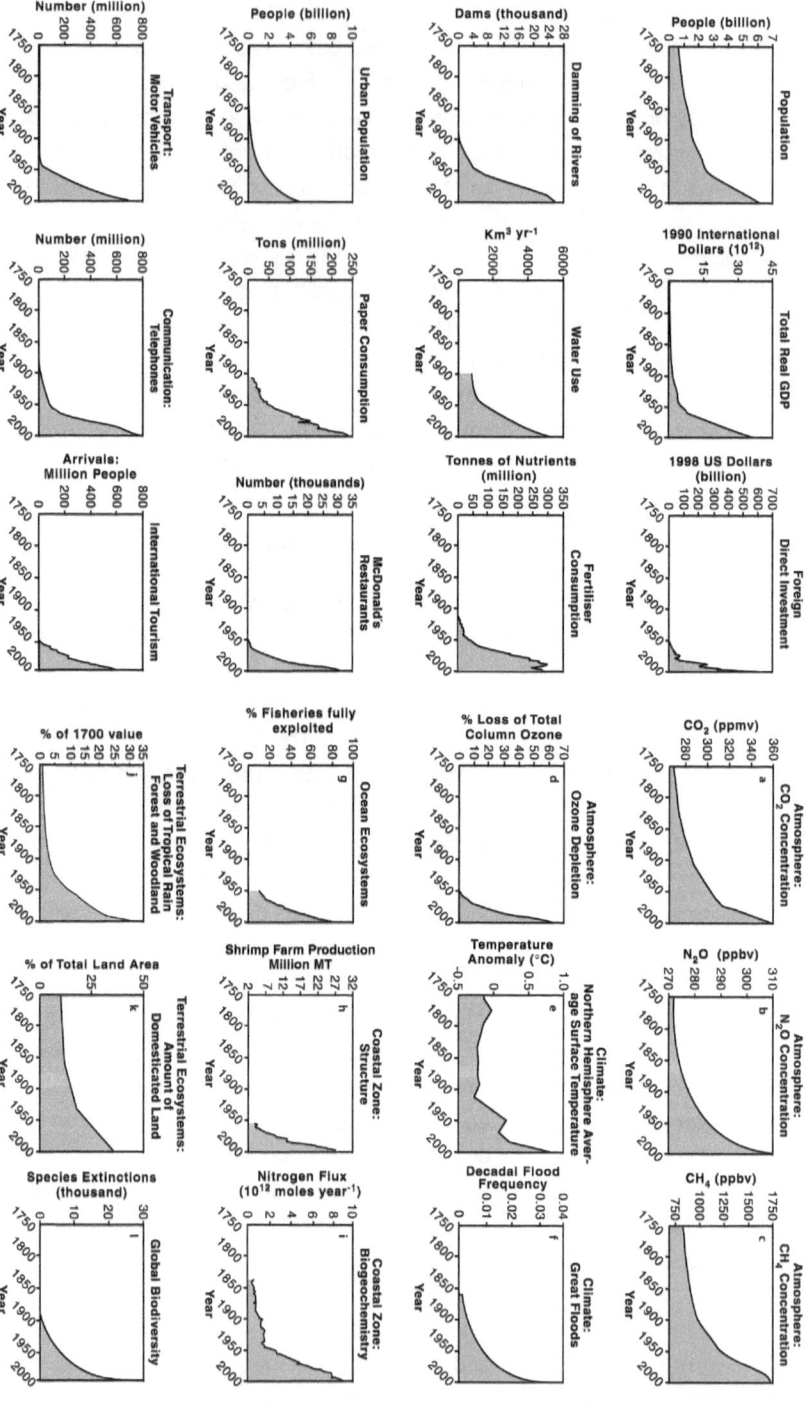

5.4 "Dashboard" of cultural and earth system indicators used to describe the Anthropocene. Christophe Bonneuil and Jean-Baptiste Fressoz, *The Shock of the Anthropocene* (2016).

with the Industrial Revolution, then experiencing a "great acceleration" after 1945, and entering a third phase of "no return" after 2000.[30] In the middle of this accelerated phase there is a specific moment in the history of construction when the design, production, and consumption of concrete underwent significant changes under pressure to find new sources of energy. In the 1970s, the US Army Corps of Engineers experimented with substituting bamboo for steel reinforcement in the American South and in US-held territories with tropical climates.[31] Across Europe and North America, concrete designers reduced material use through form-making with lightweight construction. In the Persian Gulf, large-scale use of concrete decreased significantly in the 1980s, based on a review of buildings from the previous two decades.[32] But all of these changes were driven by market forces, the perception of material scarcity, and the ideology of energy "transition"—not by any "awareness" of carbonation as an environmental factor leading to eventual failure.

Indeed, by looking at where knowledge of carbonation emerged and how it circulated, we find no single satisfying story line of a great realization about concrete's mortality. For scholars of the Anthropocene, this is nothing new. The historian Christophe Bonneuil, who has cautioned against mapping elegant narrative arcs onto the history of the earth, is especially skeptical of the "awareness" narrative—the argument that simply *knowing* about climate change will necessarily lead to action.[33] This narrative casts engineers as shepherds of the earth and feeds philosophically into theories of reflexive postmodernity, which celebrate humanity's presumably recent self-awareness and entrust this self-knowledge to provoke change. But as Bonneuil reminds us, the act of interpreting the earth's transformations has *always* been of a piece with anthropogenic change and has helped to direct the adoption of technologies.

This cautionary tale certainly applies to carbonation research. By correlating the history of scientific findings about concrete carbonation to the history of the ecological self-knowledge that accompanied it, as we do below, we find that the research provoked no fundamental transformation of global building practices, no challenge to concrete's global dominance, and—most to the point—no effort to put a dent in the global image of reinforced concrete as a uniform building material, homogeneous as stone, and more or less related to the older, Roman, metal-less precursor. Three phases can be provisionally established in this history.

In the first phase, research dynamics went exclusively from site to laboratory. Hamada's work in Japan began when he was a research assistant to Toshikata Sano, an architect-engineer who traveled to San Francisco to witness the widespread structural failure of buildings after the 1906 earthquake and fire. Returning to Tokyo, Sano produced material samples for testing reinforced concrete, immersing them in a number of environments—inside, outside, buried in dirt, submerged in a lake, and surrounded by bricks—and reporting on these experiments as early as 1911.³⁴ It was these samples that Hamada used to write his 1928 paper. Hamada was undeniably one of the most versatile, internationally connected, and accomplished concrete researchers of the midcentury.³⁵ At Tokyo University he tested samples of concrete on the roof of the faculty of architecture and later built a chamber devoted entirely to pumping CO_2 onto concrete samples to accelerate aging. But he was involved in many other kinds of testing as well: to ensure concrete's safety in earthquakes, fires, and wars; to study ways to protect concrete against salinity; to specify national building standards; *and* to encourage its trade and commercial export. When he finally published his findings about carbonation in English in 1969, he was at the end of a long career whose goal was not to define the temporal essence of the material but to help create a monopoly institutionalizing and industrializing reinforced concrete production in Japan.

The second phase began in 1977, when Hamada's findings were picked up in Sweden, as Kyösti Tuutti took the 1968 equation as the basis for his doctoral dissertation. Tuutti conducted no new experiments.³⁶ Instead, he verified and refined the mathematical model by using results of experiments that were already being conducted in Sweden's institutes of design, construction, and/or research. Crucially, this means that he fed the carbonation equation with data from a very specific set of decaying buildings: modern architecture, from traffic facilities to housing façades, that had been erected across Sweden partly to promote modernism as a national idiom, beginning in the 1930s and greatly accelerating after 1945. For example, he studied the balconies of estates built in the 1960s for the "Million Housing Program."³⁷ (In contrast, Hamada's empirical data had come from an eclectic mix of buildings: an imperial bank, an American military base, seven chimneys that had collapsed during a typhoon, industrial equipment, the basement of an apartment building, and the Takao lighthouse near Taipei.) The Swedish industrial research complex into which Tuutti imported the carbonation equation was shaping not only safety standards and commercial interests but also the cultural and energy policy of a welfare state. This was a moment when the Swedish state worried about a "crisis" in the public welfare model and was working to reduce its oil dependence in part by asking households to attain energy savings by modifying the insides of their homes.³⁸ Although Tuutti's work confirmed the fragility of concrete and disseminated Hamada's findings, then, it also associated the viability of concrete with a new ideology of conservation compatible with modernism's survival and continuation.

The third phase in the awareness of carbonation began in the 1980s, when research was isolated in the field of materials science. Having grown out of mining and metallurgy in the late 1960s and 1970s, the field was experiencing a golden age. Before 1950, chemistry had been the main discipline exploring materials, with cementitious reactions playing an important role in the elaboration of basic principles. In contrast, materials science was a discipline created to host and develop equations such as Hamada's—to mathematically describe and predict molecular behaviors, often by transferring the properties of one material onto another.[39] The goal was to design new materials, not to deal with existing ones. Within this productive ontology, researchers focused on fixing properties in design, not over time.[40]

Even today, advanced carbonation research resides entirely in the field of materials science, which typically isolates one component of reinforced concrete's performance for testing. What if the cement paste were made denser? (This would slow down carbonation).[41] What if the steel were encased, or made stainless? (This would make it immune to oxidation, but writ large this solution would make concrete a rarefied, bespoke material.) Mathematically, the main challenge of this laboratory work is how to model the factors that affect porosity over time. Here are four: pore-level geometry of the interior of the concrete; water/cement ratios used in the setting; environmental conditions such as humidity (since CO_2 diffuses more quickly through pores that have remained saturated with water) and temperature (since dry climates render air more mobile, including inside the pores, thus convecting CO_2 more rapidly); and cracks, including microcracks and voids (which dramatically increase carbonation). Add to this the fact that concrete, on its own, is actually strengthened by carbonation and that steel might dissolve, rather than expand, if it chlorinates before carbonation reaches it—and materials scientists have a nearly endless source of dynamic complexity to model. While they undeniably pay attention to the carbonation equation, and often cite fighting climate change as a research goal (for example, by reducing the CO_2 emitted in the production of cementitious materials), their research remains siloed.[42] In their hands, the carbonation equation is only asked to produce predictions or results.

The Earth as Record

It may have surprised the reader to learn that Japanese scientists were conducting experiments on rusting reinforcement as early as 1907 and that the period between 1907 and 1982 saw a gradual accumulation of discoveries about carbonation, verified with numerous empirical findings drawn from failing buildings across several nations, to confirm that reinforced concrete was mortal as soon as it was invented. The carbonation equation, it turns out, *did* play an important role in expanding the small reinforced concrete community into the multinational industrial sector it is today. But today materials scientists look at carbonated reinforced concrete through electron microscopes and see a highly messy, complex, unpredictable material environment. Elsewhere, architects and historians squint at cracks in aging infrastructures and imagine utopias deferred by ecology or perpetual maintenance. Both sides imagine dynamic processes. Neither imagines a dynamics of dynamics, an alliance.

A new narrative is needed, one to accompany the history of carbonation into the evidentiary cabinet of anthropogenic data. One such narrative could begin in the late eighteenth century, when the earth began to be deforested and its capacity to capture carbon was increasingly depleted. Much of the ground exposed by this deforestation began to be covered in concrete a century later, a process itself requiring immense amounts of energy extracted from earthly material. Over the next hundred years human settlement spread out, striating the globe with reinforced concrete ribbons of roads, infrastructure, public buildings, and homes. Today, many of these have reached a replacement age. Many of the trees that were removed have been replaced, and many of the buildings have been demolished or repaired, but a new layer of the earth has been formed regardless. It transforms the air that is breathed by humans and absorbed by trees, accelerating the warming of the earth but also potentially offering a vast, decentralized source of carbon absorption.[43]

Telling this narrative will require giving up, or radically repurposing, the old organicism that lingers in the language of architecture and its allied fields. In engineering research, terms such as "lifespan" and "mortality" are used to describe and regulate building materials as if they were biological products. In architectural history, cities continue to have a "life and death" and architectural styles a "rise and fall."[44] A new narrative will also require changing what architectural historians expect from science's laws and equations. Thermodynamics —the study of energy—is a case in point. The first law of thermodynamics, according to which nothing is lost and nothing is gained in an energy transfer, has almost exclusively been studied by scholars who associate it with the design experiments of postwar avant-garde architects: buildings designed to be closed systems, metaphors for a zero-sum life on earth. Yet as the history of the carbonation equation shows, such a zero-sum operation is not limited to a single space or to one period in time; it is a highly dynamic relation between divergent fields of human activity and study, pushing and pulling values, persons, and energy across all sorts of built environments. Similarly, the second law of thermodynamics, according to which things tend toward equilibrium, is too often called upon to support the argument that humans are fundamentally passive against the deeper forces of ecology or economy. But as a case study of the process of equilibration, our carbonation history shows that "passivation" is an eminently human-scaled transformation, measured every day with pink dye that progresses visibly, millimeter by millimeter, into a concrete wall, while the air around it gets more and more carbonated.

The ultimate record of this energetic transformation is the earth itself. The earth is an anthropogenic document of carbonation if there ever was one, and insofar as science has long been a part of human decision-making, the earth is also a record of all accumulated human interpretations of the agnostic output of equations, which have produced narratives of significance, whether measured in centuries, lifespans, or hockey sticks. To return to the question we began with, What good can an equation do when writing about the Anthropocene? Equations, in addition to being objective translators of dynamics and products of the history of objectivity, are also ways of transforming invisible change into tangible evidence. Architects have a preeminent role to play in this work, given architecture's own productive ontology. As the primary consumers of knowledge about concrete, they should be as educated about the energetic provenance of concrete as an average consumer is about the provenance of a plastic bag. Architects who know that concrete is "like rock" in its external appearance should also know that concrete is also "like air" in the energetic sense: a pervasive environmental product, which partakes in the earth system's servicing of life. In our ubiquitous CO_2-laden atmosphere, carbonation history demonstrates that reinforced concrete is an architectural material, an energy agent, and, at the same time, a globally failing technical system.

6

Medieval and Renaissance Money
On Trial, On Architecture

■

LAUREN JACOBI

In Dante's *Inferno*, dropsy is the punishment that eternally haunts a certain Maestro Adamo, morphing his body into a grotesque shape like a lute, immobilizing it with the exception of one arm, which the "shade" uses to strike his foes.[1] Maestro Adamo states that, burned for his crime, he has been banished beyond redemption to the tenth *bolgia*, or trench, of the eighth ring of hell for counterfeiting the gold Florentine florin. Rather than coining florins at their standard twenty-four carats, the fabricator made coins containing only twenty-one-carat gold. Virgil reprimands Dante for being transfixed by the interactions between Maestro Adamo and others—impersonators, putrid prevaricators, and leprous alchemists—who are darting around in the tenth *bolgia*. Dante stares as Maestro Adamo craves water, damned to be riddled by perpetual dehydration, "the sickness that has dried [Maestro Adamo's] shriveled face."[2] Of the thirty-four cantos that comprise the *Inferno*, canto 30 is unusual in that the shades that Dante and Virgil encounter suffer from internalized disease—either mental or physical—rather than something external in their spatial environment that causes suffering.[3] Maestro Adamo himself, as a shade associated with alchemy, paradoxically gestures to fluidity: the "watery *prima materia*" that the alchemist allegedly transmuted into gold from base metals, which medieval alchemists believed were generated from moist exhalations arising in the substrates of the earth.[4] Dante addresses Maestro Adamo directly, querying about shades close to the counterfeiter: "Who are those two poor souls | lying to the right, *close to your body's boundary?*"[5] In this description, Maestro Adamo is more deteriorated land mass than whole being, doomed to occupy a winding ditch—a ring of hell without architecture. Dante's text reveals the acute medieval and Renaissance concerns about the potentially spurious nature of coins. Deception troubled medieval money, as did the issue of passing off contemporary medals as ancient ones, and it is therefore not surprising that the first Renaissance treatise on art forgery, the medalist Enea Vico's *Discorsi sopra le medaglie degli antichi* (1555), explicitly addressed numismatics.

This chapter explores the mixed medieval and Renaissance worlds of money and medals, forgery and mimicry, ornament and architecture. Counterfeiting coinage, the play of material and meaning, may have been a sin and a crime, as Dante dramatizes it. But other modes of transformation, when applied to coins and their imagery, could be a means of aesthetic exploration and social representation in the hands of designers and patrons. The truth and use of coinage was more flexible than Dante's morality play allows. Coins and buildings stood at a nexus of concerns and innovations in matters of economy and symbolism, authenticity and authority, material and meaning.

On the one hand, architecture was the setting for enforcing the material authenticity of coinage. In the late fifteenth century, Munich's city officials—or perhaps the town's wealthy merchants and bankers—hung a print on one of the main doors of the city's town hall. The woodcut is a single-leaf broadsheet that was issued in several Upper German cities of the Holy Roman Empire, including Augsburg, Basel, Magdeburg, Munich, Nuremburg, Reutlingen, and Ulm, to depict copper coins cloaked with gold—counterfeit money, or in the words of Carlo Ginzburg, false documents.[6] With the exception of the Magdeburg version, the prints, produced in the workshop of Hans (or Johann) Schaur, include text that warns locals about the coins. A chronicle from the sixteenth century conveys the evident success of the broadsheets: "In the year of our Lord 1481, here in Göttingen, a man was captured on Saint James's day, he had minted false coins with the foreknowledge of Dukes Wilhelm and Heinrich van Hardenberge; and they were used very widely."[7] The woodcut thematizes ever-present late medieval and Renaissance economic anxiety about how to discern the quality and caliber of coins—and other commodities.

Specific buildings were sites, too, for materially testing money's authenticity. One such example hails from Florence, where those engaged in monetary trade could go to have coins tested for their fineness and therefore for their legitimacy. Located at a busy corner of one of Florence's main markets, Mercato Nuovo, the house of the assayer was a substantive building that by the fourteenth century was the location of Florence's primary site for testing coins (fig. 6.1). The material truth of money did not merely concern relations between individual merchants but involved the state as well in adjudicating authenticity. In the middle of the thirteenth century in England, Henry III and the Westminster Cathedral's abbot rebuilt the important Benedictine abbey church, which included, adjacent to the eastern cloister, a vaulted undercroft—an architectural space that would soon come to house a monastic and royal treasury, as well as

6.1. The house of the assayer, Florence, fourteenth century. Courtesy of Ralph Lieberman.

metal trial plates used in a ceremony known as the Trial of the Pyx (fig. 6.2).[8] In a practice still followed today, coins were chosen at random from collections of each denomination struck and secured in small, wooden boxes. Members of a jury then randomly selected coins from the pyx boxes; the coins were tested and later weighed.[9] The clerk of the Goldsmiths' Company several weeks later pronounced the verdict of the national Assay Office. The Trial of the Pyx demonstrates how architecture and materiality—coinage and banking—were interlaced in testing and testifying to money's veracity. The trial demonstrates how the Crown, too, was keen to make the process of legitimizing its money transparent. Rather than a mere local check on the quality of money, as in Florence, the London trial in its sacred, royal setting was designed to prove to the kingdom that the actual composition of various monetary denominations

6.2. Chapel of the Pyx, Westminster Abbey, London. © The Dean and Chapter of Westminster.

met standards of fineness set by the Crown, in effect validating the latter's own authority and rulership.

Coins were tested within an architectural setting to ensure their veracity. In contrast, coins were also *set into* architecture in ways, transgressing their materiality and meaning. To follow this neither venal nor illegal form of counterfeiting, we begin with noting the homology between coins and medals. In early modern Europe the word used for medals and coins—*medaglie*—indicated both types of object, blurring the lines of the antique and the contemporary.[10] While medals and coins were ontologically distinct in some ways, conceptions of them overlapped in a double logic that was not contradictory. Renaissance inventories indicate how polyvalent the term was. A *medaglia* could mean either a medal or a coin—the objects were conflated linguistically. Early modern inventories lumped together medals of different size, by different artists, and sometimes by type of metal. The inventory of Cardinal Francesco Gonzaga's possessions, taken after his death, indicated he had 414 *medaglie* in a chest; 47 gold ones in a silver clock case; 281 silver ones in a wooden box; 11 such objects, possibly lead or bronze, in a paper bag or folder; what were probably medals in a damask bag; and a small *busoleto* of medals.[11] The Renaissance medal united an intense study of the past with an interest in promoting individual fame. Antiquarians evaluated objects that originated in past cultures.

Like money, medals were exchangeable objects of value. Due to their small size and the fact that they were reproduced serially, portrait medals were easily transferable, and they were among the most prized items collected.[12] The size of medals was and is key to their appeal, and it enabled their easy circulation. Medals, like prints and coins, could be cast or struck in multiples, which eased their dissemination to a wide audience. During the Renaissance, medals meant mimetically to evoke classical antique coins often were distributed broadly to send a calculated message about one's public persona and to commemorate achievements. Medals circulated among networks of friends. They were even used to solicit marriage. As Stephen Scher has written, a medal, "commemorate[s], memorializes, glorifies, criticizes, or even satirizes its subject."[13] When not stored, medals were held, turned over in the hand, and talked about.[14]

Medals were mobile in other ways, too. Their migration took many different forms, including working their way literally into the material of other media. Medals were inserted into artworks, perhaps evoking a long practice of setting into objects coins from historically remote periods, as seen in a drinking bowl from the late fifteenth century set with a coin of Alexander the Great surrounded by twenty-five Roman denarii of the consular period, which in more recent times was given to the Danubian Literary Society by the chancellor of the Kingdom of Hungary.[15] Likewise, there is a vibrant and probably related tradition of setting medals or casts of them into book bindings. For example, a presentation copy of a Latin version of *Dio Chrysostomus* composed by Andrea Brenta and given to Pope Sixtus IV has an impression taken from a matrix of the obverse of Sixtus's medal celebrating a bridge, the Ponte Sisto, that was constructed in Rome during his papacy.[16]

Architecture, too, was the recipient of medal implants. In 1962, conservators set about cleaning the central door of Rome's major basilica church, St. Peter's. As the conservators removed layers of dirt, matter out of place, and accretions marking the passage of time, they found that an object resembling a small portrait medal measuring fifty-nine millimeters in width had been cast into the middle of the bottom rail of the left door (fig. 6.3).[17] Held by mythical hoofed centaurs, the medal depicts a man shown in profile. Cherubs present a similar object in the equivalent position on the right door. A punched inscription identifies the figure shown on what is either a medal or a quasi medal as Antonio Filarete, the architect, theorist, and sculptor responsible for designing the door.[18] The depiction and the inscribed roundel conform to an eighteenth-century account of the door in which the author noted that "he who had them [the doors] made and he who made them could be known through their names and portraits," referring to Pope Eugenius IV, to the patron who can be seen in the middle panel of the door on the right side, and to Filarete.[19] We have seen already how architecture provided sites for authenticating the coinage. Now we see how coinage, conversely, could provide validation of architecture's authorship.

6.3. An image of Antonio Filarete on the central portal of St. Peter's Basilica, Rome. Artwork in the public domain; photograph courtesy of Robert Glass, © Fabbrica di San Pietro in Vaticano.

Medals and coins were not only collectible and exchangeable authenticating devices in the Renaissance. Like money, they could also be transfigured—in effect counterfeited—into objects of architectural ornamentation. Representations of medals were transposed onto other media at a scale that was more expansive than the original object, a practice tied to a Renaissance understanding of medals as objects intimately related to antique coins and engraved stones. When medals—and related material objects—were magnified and placed in architectural settings, there was the potential for mimicry, in effect a form of authorized reproduction. At the Palazzo degli Scaligeri in Verona, frescoes with figures from the Flavian dynasty associated with the town were commissioned from Altichiero da Verona by Cansignorio della Scala after he chose to modernize the building in 1364. A loggia adjacent to the *sala grande* had a series of grisaille paintings of Roman emperors, set in quatrefoil frames. All of the depictions were based on portraits from ancient coins. Four Roman emperors were depicted on each of the underarches. Depictions of female figures interrupt the chronology; for example, between Elagabalus (r. 218–222 CE) and the last of the Severans who ruled after him, Severus Alexander (222–235 CE), there was a representation of Faustina the Elder, who lived a century earlier. The first published systematic classification of Roman coins is Vico's *Discorsi sopra le medaglie degli antichi*, though this came well before manuscripts were illuminated with portraits, derived from coins, of famous Romans.[20] Others have suggested that such a text possibly was the inspiration for the use of numismatic imagery on the Palazzo degli Scaligeri. During Cangrande della Scala's lifetime, a scribe penned a volume that included the biographies of Roman emperors and medieval kings from Julius Caesar through Charlemagne, and two copies of it contain illustrations of Roman coins. Regardless of their origination, the images on the palace pictorialized and announced qualities the family saw in itself or wanted to have others envision about it; they were a way of managing, curating, and giving evidentiary information about the familial self-image.

Two other revealing examples of coins and medals being scaled up in reproduction are found in northern Italy. One is on Bartolomeo Colleoni's funerary chapel in Bergamo, which he commissioned from Giovanni Antonio Amadeo. The second is Amadeo's work at the Certosa in Pavia (fig. 6.4). In each case, what emerges is a dynamic in which medals and coins were thought of relationally to history though architectural ornamentation. The Certosa, one of the most impressive buildings to deploy *all'antica* decoration that referenced coinage and sculpture from the ancient world, was begun in 1472 and finished four years later. As Andrew Burnett and Richard Schofield have noted, the façade displays motifs that were taken from small antique objects in northern Italy or that were available through drawings.[21] The Colleoni chapel's façade is the first sacred building in Lombardy to bear figural depictions based on antique coins.[22] The four pilasters that grace the façade each have a number of *tondi*, with sculptures of celebrated Romans alternating with a total of twelve lozenges depicting male saints, probably apostles.[23] Depictions on the pilasters on the left side of the building include images of Diva Faustina and Tullus Hostilius. On the lowest register of the building, portraits of Nero, Galba, and Hadrian can be found among other Roman emperors. The authenticity of the images with respect to antique coinages varies: whereas Nero's profile and inscription are derived directly from coins, Galba's and Hadrian's portraits are based on coins, but the inscriptions in the roundels are not antique. For Diva Faustina, the opposite occurred—the inscriptions are antique, but the imagery is either not based on coins or it is highly abstracted. The image and inscription of Tullus Hostilius appears to be invented, with great liberties taken.[24]

Begun slightly later than the Colleoni chapel, the Certosa of Pavia was meant to house the tombs of the Visconti dukes of Milan. Its elaborate façade was initiated in the mid-1470s by Giovanni Antonio Amadeo and others, but it was left incomplete in the middle of the sixteenth century. The Certosa has a number of stone medallions with profile heads of figures from antiquity, all of which are situated underneath scenes from the New Testament.[25] Some of them were installed as early as 1480 and others finished in the 1490s under the patronage of Lodovico Il Moro. As Burnett and Schofield have suggested, the program in all likelihood was meant to demonstrate that the ancient world served as a building block upon which the New Testament sat. Several aspects of the portraits were

6.4. Giovanni Scolari, Guinforte Scolari, and Giovanni Antonio Amadeo, Certosa of Pavia, 1396–1495. Courtesy of Sergio D'Afflitto, licensed under CCA 4.0.

taken from Roman and Greek coins and Renaissance medals.[26] The portraits fall into several categories. The first group comprises medallions in which the portrait relates explicitly to representations on coins or medals, and there are ten examples, including the medallion of Claudius. Second, the portrait of Octavian is a good example of the five roundels wherein the portraits were derived from numismatic prototypes but in which the inscriptions are deliberately inaccurate. The third group, including the roundel of Judas, consists of examples in which the head was copied from a coin or medal but then misidentified. Fourth and final are portraits that were either invented or else have not yet been traced to coins or medals, like the depiction of Pompey.[27] Several of the images appear to have been derived from medals or drawings of them. The head of Caracalla appears to have been taken from a medal produced in 1466, attributed to Giovanni Boldù.[28] The reverse of Boldù's medal also provided inspiration for an adjacent roundel. An image of Constantine was taken from the previously discussed French medal of him. A different portrait of the emperor was gleaned from the French medal that depicts Heraclius, metamorphosed into the famous Roman emperor. There are several striking aspects about the series of roundels. One wonders if, when medals were used as a source, it was because they were mistaken for ancient objects or if the source objects were esteemed enough on their own merits to be magnified.[29] Perhaps more interesting, though, is that the sculptors or whoever inset the roundels appear to have grouped the objects according to type (Roman emperors, Persian kings, etc.), but then they ignored the internal chronology of that group even though successions were known through sources such as Sutonius or the *Historia Augustus*. Accurate lineages were depicted through coins in contemporaneous books, although those texts appear not to have been accessible at Pavia or in the ducal libraries.[30] Tracing a precise lineage appears not to have been as important as generically referencing the past. In other words, the large-scale representations of coins and medals seem to have been valued not because they designated a singular moment in time that could be ordered chronologically but because they referenced a distant world, however old. The roundels made explicit a sense of collapsing time, pulling the past into the present.

Representations of coinage in architecture pull the past into the present in order to enhance patrons' status. In his biography of the life of Donatello, Giorgio Vasari reported that "in Palazzo Medici, in the first courtyard, there are eight marble *tondi*, where there are portraits from antique cameos and reverses of *medaglie*, and very beautiful stories made by him, which are placed in the frieze in between the windows and the architrave above the arches of the loggia."[31] Those scholars have connected the figural imagery in the roundels to seven ancient gems and hardstones and, in one instance, a sarcophagus relief. Knowledge about the gems on which the *tondi* were based might have been indirect, the product of drawings, casts, or plaquettes.[32] These small precious, collectible objects—gems and coins—are at the Palazzo Medici, reproduced and enlarged into architectural ornament. It is as if the architecture of the Palazzo Medici becomes a display case for an ornamental, re-presented collection of small valuable material objects: gems and coins. The roundels and their subject matter instantiate a dynamic in which Lorenzo de' Medici and his clan become known though small objects celebrated for their collection value. In a sense, a coveted collection, including coins long out of economic circulation, was placed on exhibition—put back into circulation—with the gaze of those who enter the courtyard directed to the coined ornament, so as to enrich the patron's social and cultural—and not just economic—status.

In closing, it is productive to turn to Georg Simmel's comment that money has no intrinsic value. Perhaps another way to say that is that medieval and Renaissance coins, to borrow from Catherine Gallagher and Stephen Greenblatt, are "fictions in the sense of things made . . . [and] shaped by the imagination and by the available resources of narration and description."[33] Medieval society used various "proofs"—including coin trials and architectural structures—to construct money and to make coins serve as trusted objects of value, representation, and exchange. Those in the late medieval world shared an interest in establishing not just facts but evidence that coins were the material objects they claimed to be. There was a need to see money not as an abstract container that could index equivalence but as a material reality that could be trusted to be physically what it claimed. Coins had to be *made* to act as money. Perhaps another way of thinking of this is that coinage had to be woven into a narrative of social relations involving merchants, bankers, and the state. This is not to suggest that I am making a claim to a singular narrative about the history of money and its intersection with architectural and art history. Rather, I see my reading as a counternarrative that questions the modern tendency to see money as a purely economic abstraction, as disembodied paper and account books, and now immaterial bytes. The stories told here are of money as disputed material coinage and negotiated cultural artifact. In both cases, architecture was a crucial framing device to help to establish authenticity, meaning, and social relations. In coin trials, architecture helped validate the material legitimacy of coinage. And, reciprocally, coinage counterfeited as ornament, materially reproduced and represented in buildings, helped architecture validate authorship and patronage. Even as Dante damned counterfeiters, architects acted as authorized alchemists of money, demonstrating its fluidity in meaning, scale, and setting.

Part III

Data

Three chapters are placed together in this section to historicize interest in the use of data as another kind of self-evidence in architectural history. Data, and assumptions of data's abundance, have found recent entry into architectural historical narratives through the so-called digital humanities. But the category "data" is historically not new, and it is not essentially connected to digital technologies. The term "data" constitutes the epistemic unit of any statistical, numerically represented assembly: a survey, an estimate, a map, a table, or an Excel spreadsheet. To bring data into evidence, some have translated numbers into graphic form, including maps. The shared assumption among users and interpreters of data is that the meaning produced by visualizing information is transparent or self-evident to its observer. At some level, the very idea that images can be compared through formal analysis to produce meaning is also based on the assumption of interpretive transparency. Recognizing and historicizing data's self-evidence amount to casting a critical eye on the capacity of numbers and images to make meaning and generate narrative.

7

From Truth to Proof
Friedrich Adler's *Medieval Brick Architecture of the Prussian States*

■

LAILA SEEWANG

Between Art History and Infrastructure

In 1858, the Prussian Ministry for Trade, Industry, and Public Works agreed to fund an architectural history project to identify and document all medieval brick architecture across the kingdom. In appealing for the ministry's support, the effort's lead historian, Friedrich Adler, claimed the project vital not only for "advancing the study of the art history of the Fatherland" but also for "improving contemporary construction techniques."[1] Positioned between the infrastructure of the public works department and the disciplinary beginnings of art history, the project expanded the state's interest in its architectural heritage. Its scope made it a unique undertaking for a department whose main responsibility was the design and construction of public works in a kingdom that stretched from the Rhine in the west to Russia in the east, with projects including Berlin's legislative and administrative buildings, railways, mining infrastructure, waterways, churches, and schools, as well as oversight for building security and the training of civil servants. But it was also original in terms of Berlin's art history.[2] While previous scholarship on medieval Prussian architecture had addressed a handful of the more notable monuments, Adler intended this project to be a complete survey of the kingdom's medieval structures, detailing all ruins, monasteries, churches, town halls, and military facilities scattered across the entire territory.[3]

Adler was clear that the distinction between his research and other scholarship was empirical accuracy; he attacked a recent architectural history that highlighted "'the masterful medieval characteristics'" of a renowned Gothic town hall by (falsely) highlighting its eighteenth-century addition.[4] It was this type of scholastic inaccuracy that Adler was hoping to rectify by employing what he called an "objective standpoint."[5] For him, objectivity fell somewhere between "an exact survey" (extensively collected information), "historical accuracy" (archival research from church, town hall, and personal records), "reliable details" (as he himself discerned), and the "representation of entire structures under consideration in a consistent manner" (rather than just the most impressive details). Art-historical inaccuracies accompanied a generally dismal state of boom-time construction as Berlin's population and industrial activities mushroomed after midcentury. The public works ministry faced criticism for its public buildings as well as its inadequately trained architects, which likely made it more amenable to funding a study that might rectify both problems simultaneously.[6]

Data Collection

Collecting all the necessary information on the kingdom's medieval structures was an impossible undertaking for an individual, which meant it would be an unprecedented collaborative effort within the public works ministry. The project began when the minister sent questionnaires to the thirty-seven provincial administrations asking *Baubeamte* (state-employed architects) to survey and document their regions for potential candidates. Gathering information in the form of a survey or census had been in use for more than a century by the city's police department, particularly to assist in shaping urban and health management policies. The establishment of the Berlin Statistics Bureau in 1862, as well as an increase in the number of scientists involved in public works projects, cemented this recourse to quantitative knowledge. Statistics were used to paint a picture of the city that eluded the human eye: its population, health, weather, and the invisible relationships between them. With this new effort, the survey was transformed into a tool to locate and assess historical artifacts across a wide area.

The use of a large-scale survey was in itself not such an uncommon approach among scholars of Gothic architecture, who had been working at a frenetic pace since the rediscovery of medieval architecture in the eighteenth century. Topographical studies, inventories, and national collections were from the beginning aimed at capturing as much data as possible to make up for a seeming lack of evidence compared to what was available on classical architecture.[7] Already in 1830 the Cambridge Camden Ecclesiological Society had introduced its "Church Scheme," whereby budding archaeologists would travel to medieval churches with a "blank, mass-produced form on which were printed by category headings such as window, pier, roof, font, etc. Information was to be filled in during the actual visit, using a specially-developed coding system which encouraged uniformity, to enable effective comparative analysis."[8] But Adler, a civil servant as well as respected archaeologist and architect, had recourse to a state apparatus already geared toward collecting data on a vast scale, which made executing and operationalizing a comprehensive set of art-historical findings much more effective.

The survey was a substitute for direct observation by the expert. Although the categories in the survey were supposed to regulate the input of the regional data—name, location, original function of the building, presumed date of construction, layout, main dimensions, building style, surviving archival material—Adler was not the one seeing these structures with his own eyes. Observation had been outsourced to regional *Baubeamte*, who were now acting as a corps of de facto archaeologists, compiling information on all structures of possible aesthetic and technical merit built of red brick between the eleventh and sixteenth centuries. This was a decisive methodological shift from an earlier generation, when the legitimacy of claims about German architectural history rested on the authority of an expert's direct observation to unveil the truth of that artifact to a lay public. This did not extend only to art historians: Wolfgang von Goethe was one of the earliest to embrace the "Germanness" of Gothic architecture when he stood in front of the Strasbourg cathedral.[9]

The project's shifting of legitimacy from observer to data was not necessarily unique: Leopold von Ranke would upend the way in which legitimacy was established. It was he who introduced an art-historical method based on the collection of empirical data to act as proof for historical claims and to distance the author's subjectivity from the data obtained. Generations of professional historians would begin to pay attention to particulars. Ranke would insist that the aim of history was to present a "unity" of events but that this unity would only come from "a perception of the particular" and never by working backward from a presumed romantic narrative toward the identification of particulars.[10] Adler was socially active within the group of Friedrich-Wilhelm University historians around Ranke who were uncovering the evidence for, and writing narratives of, Brandenburg's history in the second half of the nineteenth century.[11] Thanks to the nature of the public works department, the surveys would document an exhaustive set of particulars that were safely removed from the bias of the initiating author. Both the scale of data and the data's distance from the author formed a significant part of Adler's "objective standpoint." But with so many particulars to take note of—every medieval brick structure in Prussia—the direct experience of empirical facts was necessarily mediated by Adler's survey categories and their interpretation by the *Baubeamte*.

It is clear that the guiding questions had an impact on what data would be returned; in a way, they designed the historical field itself. The coupling of inexperienced eyes with a certain openness in Adler's categories certainly muddied any intended accuracy. Two categories in particular highlight the interpretive task the surveyors faced in using this mediated form of art-historical research: "distinguishing between the un-tampered original remains and later alterations" and "commenting on any remarkable aesthetic or technical aspects of the structures."[12] If architectural remains were going to become "the evidence of history," as Adler claimed, he had nonetheless broadened the relevant data to include archival documentation and individual assessments of the *Baubeamte*. To some degree it was irrelevant if the survey was more or less accurate than traditional methods of direct observation. The type of broad historical claims that the project aimed to address—to write the history of the art of the fatherland and to learn about medieval construction techniques—demanded a systematic method and a large quantity of evidence in the face of an increasingly scientific discipline. The expertise of art historians was still demanded, but their eyes had now been tasked with the editing and arrangement of the collected data instead of its observation.

Translation into Evidence

At least twenty-one districts sent back bound dossiers labeled "Evidence" (*Nachweisung*), some of which were practically research projects in themselves, with sketches, dimensions, and written historical and structural interpretations (figs. 7.1 and 7.2).[13] In the hands of regional *Baubeamte* the assessment of potential cultural monuments had become distinctly varied and uneven and their dossiers enormous and difficult to interpret. This resulted in much information being returned and later discarded during the editing process; for example, all forty pages of data from Cologne ultimately went unused. Consequently, the project ran thirty-four years behind schedule as Adler rechecked evidence and judged the data collectors' interpretations. In explaining the delay to the public works minister, he invoked diligence: had he wanted to "compose an [inaccurate] history in the tradition of Lübke, Schnaase, and Woltman, he would have already been finished . . . [but] enduring fruit ripens only slowly."[14] Enduring fruit meant, as he had explained in lectures on architectural history, a "scientific handling" of evidence: "painstakingly taking historical archival material as a basis for each structure, then comparing it to related monuments, overlooking neither the technical specificities nor the artistic particularities in order to arrive at a secure vision of the inner arrangement as well as the outer composition of different epochs."[15]

Medieval Brick Architecture of the Prussian States was published serially between 1859 and 1898 as a supplement to the journal *Zeitschrift für Bauwesen*, the official publication arm of the public works ministry. It was also published as two volumes, with attendant atlases of copper engravings, in 1862 and 1896. In these publications the collected data had been translated and separated into two parts: the text, which was a historical narrative interspersed with smaller details and views, and the atlases of technical drawings. Of the two parts, it was the drawings that received far and away the most attention.[16] For the first time in Prussia, a study on medieval architecture included elevations, sections, plans, and details drawn consistently to the same scale, making a wide variety of individual structures comparable. The drawings marked a shift in representative techniques from earlier studies of medieval brick architecture of Prussia, the most notable of which were the well-circulated etchings produced by Friedrich Frick after Friedrich Gilly's survey of the Teutonic fortress of Marienburg in

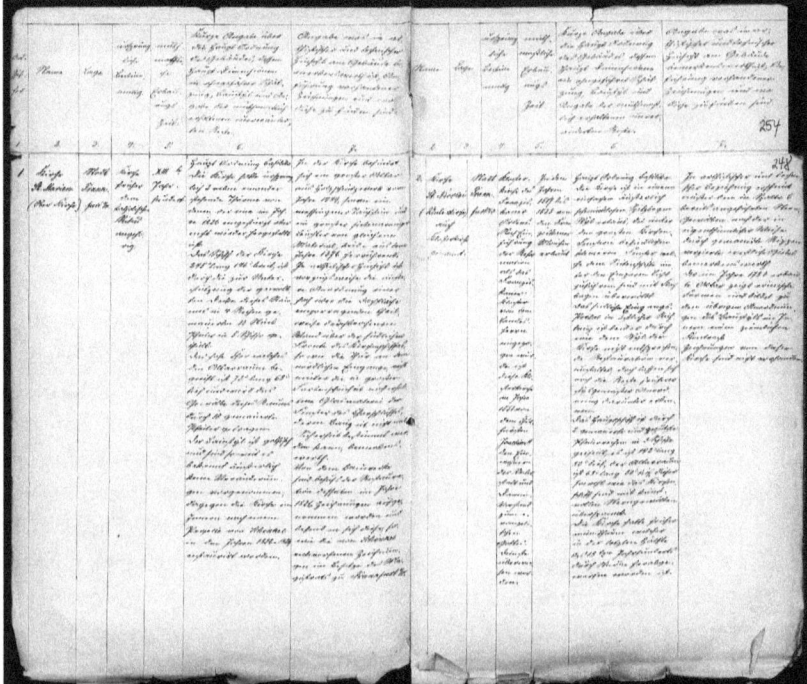

7.1 (*above*). "Evidence" submitted by the town of Frankfurt an der Oder answering Adler's categories of (1) name and location of structure; (2) siting and function; (3) assumed date of construction; (4) layout, including dimensions and style; (5) existing archival documentation and drawings; and (6) comments. Geheimes Staatsarchiv Berlin Preußischer Kulturbesitz I. HA Rep. 93B, Nr. 1004, 248.

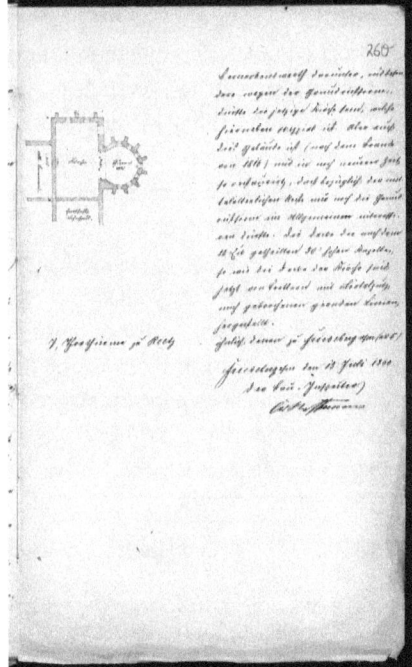

7.2 (*right*) "Evidence" submitted by the Prussian town of Friedeberg (now Strzelce Krajeńskie in Poland) detailing the city gates at Reetz (now Recz, Poland). Dated July 13, 1860. Geheimes Staatsarchiv Preußischer Kulturbesitz Berlin I. HA Rep. 93B, Nr. 1004, 260.

1794. Frick's aquatints were instrumental in making the structure one of the first protected historical monuments in the state and in providing momentum for its restoration. They showed the fortress in perspective as exaggerated and isolated ruins, with all evidence of neo-baroque alterations removed. With dramatic lighting and Teutonic medieval knights reinserted in the scenes, they resembled grand tour representations of ancient Greece or Rome typical of the Romantic period, when architectural accuracy was subordinate to historic symbolism and nuanced construction details were narratively insignificant.[17]

The drawings produced for the project did not try to restore the medieval scene; their composition was didactic and offered a clear explanation of both architectural form and the relationship among its various components. Bearing almost no resemblance to Frick's sublime images, these drawings strove to show monuments in their entirety by highlighting the structures' orthographic entirety, rather than the unique or exemplary details and impressionistic views of more well-known monuments presented in the "expensive works of splendour" of more recent scholarship on red-brick medieval monuments in Prussia.[18] If Gilly and Goethe had attempted to articulate the truth of a monument's character—a true nature that evaded the layperson's eye and that included a monument's symbolic value and emotive power—then these drawings would have functioned as working objects; standardizing of the way the viewer encountered the artifacts and not focusing on design idiosyncrasies, they were made available as a didactic and comparative tool.[19]

The text was organized geographically, broken up by town and region into individual chronicles complete in themselves and then supplemented with numerous smaller sketches. As such, it was difficult for the text as a whole to work cumulatively toward any territory-wide typological conclusions concerning medieval architecture, a typical motivation for early Gothic research. Comparison was employed as a way of exposing the impact that geographical and historical context had on architecture, not as an opportunity to look beyond the individual objects in order to make larger claims. Placed side by side, region after region, the sketches accompanying the text highlighted the local variations of brick-making, coursing, sizes, color, construction details, ornament, and arching capabilities—differences that were all rigorously documented. Efforts were made to show a region in its entirety: structures from towns of archaeological renown such as Brandenburg an der Havel were shown on equal footing with those from seemingly insignificant villages, lending a kind of democratization of significance.[20]

The Middle to an Existing Narrative

Petering out in 1896 due to Adler's significant archaeological distractions, the unfinished project "d[id] not so much conclude as simply terminate," according to philosopher of history Hayden White's characterization of the narrative element of the chronicle.[21] The work produced may—in its separation of text and drawings, its descriptive tone, and lack of narrative conclusion—be more accurately considered an architectural ordering project rather than a treatise; a catalog of materially alike medieval structures that, through sheer quantity of technical drawings, mapped a territorial inheritance. The gap between the extensive graphic evidence and the descriptive text, coupled with a lack of drawn conclusions between the two parts, meant that drawings and text ultimately operated separately. Unable to provide closure within itself, the project, its drawings in particular, now provided a body of empirical evidence that could be deployed as ready evidence for larger historical and contemporary narratives.

The idea that the surveyed architecture was deployed as the evidence of history at large—and not in order to make a statement about historical architectural styles—was embedded in the structure of the resulting publications. Adler used the survey to show how architecture—when scientifically revealed—could fulfill its real purpose as the "evidence of historical events," "a true testimony of its epoch," and the "monumental illustration of world history" or, in this case, Prussian history. *Medieval Brick Architecture of the Prussian States* established a continuous sequence of red-brick medieval architecture from the twelfth century to the nineteenth, concretizing—architecturalizing—a popular political-historical narrative of Prussian history that had been until that moment rather lacking in what White terms transitional motifs.[22] Architectural and dynastic narratives converge in the project's text for the town of Brandenburg, which constitutes the first chapter of the report's first volume. The capture and reconstruction of the early Slavic village on the site of the present-day town of Brandenburg mark the beginning of the German eastward colonization of Slavic territories in the twelfth century. The mythic founding of Prussia thus begins with Brandenburg's first German ruler, Albrecht the Bear—a Saxon. Because the town was handed over to the Hohenzollern dynasty only in the fifteenth century, nineteenth-century Brandenburg was thus not genealogically connected to the mythical founding of its own territory. Its rulers wrested land away from other German states, most importantly Saxony, but also Poland, Silesia, Lithuania, Swedish Pomerania, and Denmark, and over the centuries the Hohenzollerns expanded their domain into the Kingdom of Prussia. Where dynasty could not establish territory, architecture could. The monasteries, churches, and fortresses constructed of red brick in a simple, early Gothic style tied this region together; an architectural legacy established by force in the twelfth century helped legitimize the territorial occupations of the nineteenth. In making this architectural lineage visible and tangible, the volumes assisted in the efforts to define an authentic historical culture for Prussia beyond its infamous militarism—a Prussia "hatched from a cannonball."[23] In the multitome opus, geography trumped bloodline as a dynastic narrative: the legitimate unit whereby the Hohenzollern empire could be connected to its territory was not the DNA of a family dynasty but the red brick of its buildings.[24]

This material legacy also helped to legitimize the claim that early Gothic architecture was the most appropriate style for a new German architecture.[25] Once printed, 410 copies of the report were sent back to the regional *Baubeamte* in 1888 to bring their attention not only to local medieval monuments and the value of their cultural history but also to "offer significant lessons about the techniques of medieval exposed-brick construction."[26] Studying the extensive drawings of brick construction, compared to brick construction disguised behind a layer of plaster (a practice that had become typical well before the nineteenth century), would then "naturally lead to better quality fabrication and masonry work in contemporary production, and reduce costs for this building art."[27] The territory-wide distribution of *Medieval Brick Architecture of the Prussian States* was enough to signal a change in building policy. The strictly hierarchical structure of Prussian administration practically ensured that exposed-brick, neo-Gothic architecture would play a role in future public works. Therefore, even the commissioners of public works in the few regions that possessed stone reserves (and thus had no need to manufacture bricks) replied that they "would be happy to learn about brick construction and use it in public buildings."[28] The final work, once back in the hands of the regional *Baubeamte*, was transformed from a history of architectural inheritance into an early type of handbook to improve the construction quality of new buildings, which in all likelihood had been Adler's primary motivation for undertaking the project.

Unexpected Trajectories and New Narratives

During the course of the long survey project, a shift in power had occurred in urban governance. When Prussia emerged victorious from the Franco-Prussian War in 1871, Berlin became the capital of a nation-state and its king became emperor. An increase in immigration, a surge in administrative activities, and a financial boom in the wake of French reparations combined to facilitate urban development on an unprecedented scale. In the face of increasingly powerful and wealthy bourgeois governance, the history project now (likely unintentionally) provided Berlin's municipal institutions with their own historical legacy reaching back to the Middle Ages. The surveys uncovered a tradition of strong municipal *civitas* represented by imposing monuments, particularly in the larger Hanseatic free towns but also in smaller towns in Brandenburg. The documentation of defensive towers in Stendal, Tangermünde, or Prenzlau or the town halls in Brandenburg, Frankfurt (Oder), Königsberg (Neumark), or Jüterborg provided the increasingly powerful municipality with both architectural as well as legal precedent.[29] Berlin's municipal architecture from the last quarter of the nineteenth century, epitomized by the Red Town Hall (Rotes Rathaus) and by the later police headquarters building (known as the Rote Burg), as well as the city's vast array of schools, gas works, electric power plants, hospitals, and

7.3. Towers of the Middle and Schwedter Gates in Prenzlau. Friedrich Adler, *Mittelalterliche Backstein-Bauwerke des Preussischen Staates*, vol. 2 (1898), 50.

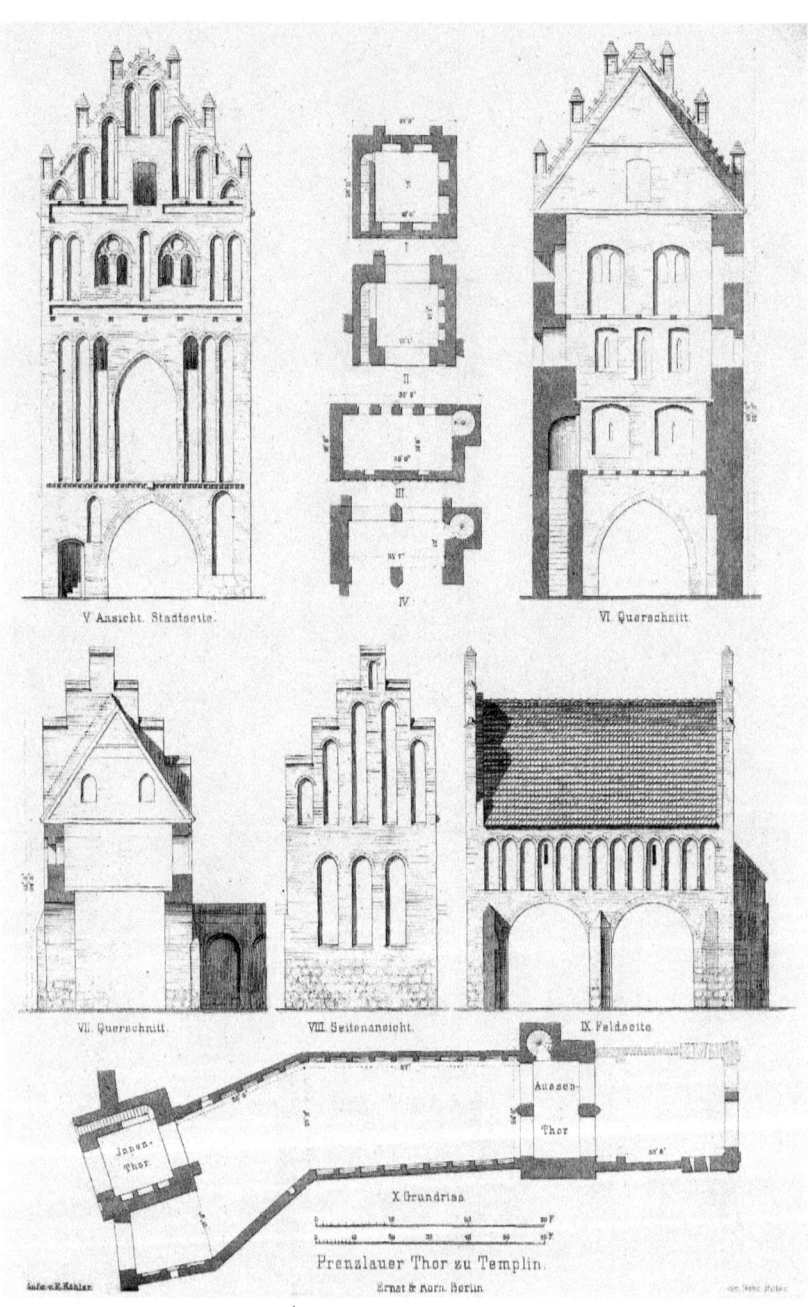

7.4. Prenzlau Gate in Templin. Friedrich Adler, *Mittelalterliche Backstein-Bauwerke des Preussischen Staates*, vol. 2 (1898), 52.

churches, speaks to the perhaps unintended operationalization of the project's evidence.³⁰

The impact of the published volumes, beyond the material and stylistic change in Berlin's new buildings, extended to institutional and educational reform, particularly at the Bauakademie, by emphasizing improved *Technik* based on medieval precedents. The *Handbuch der Architektur* that appeared in 1888, of which Adler's project can be seen as a forerunner, became the model for establishing once and for all the optimal ways of building and of interpreting history, making it "a work like no other nation owns and perhaps no other nation will be called on to create."³¹

Legitimacy, New Narratives, and Observation

Medieval Brick Architecture of the Prussian States represented a change in the relationship between evidence and narrative in architectural history because of its status as a public works project. What changed revolved around three key moments in art-historical methodology. First, the method of outsourcing observation of relevant data from an expert witness to a kind of technological and bureaucratic consortium broadened the research questions and distanced architectural historians from the empirical artifact, directing them instead to the data derived from that artifact. Second, assumptions about what legitimized something as evidence elevated the measured drawing to a form of proof of its function in revealing an inner truth. Last, as a result of the first two changes, there arose a method of yielding narratives that could not otherwise have been produced.

The diminished control over observation during the project successfully turned art history into an infrastructural backbone for public works. It was a collaborative infrastructural project funded by a public works department, managed by its survey system, its research carried out by civil servants, and the final work dispatched across the kingdom as a kind of architectural handbook. Not only did architectural history provide evidence for a history of the Prussian state, but medieval construction techniques had been operationalized for state production of contemporary architecture. This method separated art historians from the activity of observation and shifted them to one small part of a systematic bureaucratic process. Whereas a gap might have opened up between the historian and the artifact, there was now no gap between the historian and the institution operationalizing the results of the historical research. In this light, Gottfried Semper's critique that historians of the Berlin school were little more than bureaucrats has some value.³² With the art historian no longer physically present at historical sites to reveal the truth about the artifacts, an epistemological shift in historical methods proceeded to align the repositioning of the historian's body from the field to the office, with the transfer of legitimization from an individual expert to a scientific method. During the course of the project, the basis upon which legitimacy was founded had shifted not only for the discipline of art history but also in public works. Hegel referred to the state as necessarily both the subject of a historical chronology and the producer of historical fact; objective facts were established because of the legitimacy provided by the state's framework and the assumed universal relevance of the resulting narrative. Hegel's concept of the state as an external ideal for, rather than a representation of, its subjects provides a relevant model for the period when the survey project started. When the king ordered public works built and organized through his ministries, objective data were usually not called upon to act as evidence: a commissioner of works, as the state's representative, was typically relied upon to observe relevant regional and international examples and then reach an informed conclusion. The legitimacy of the claim was derived from the authority invested in a network of educated and aristocratic men—state representatives who had risen to the top of an established and hierarchical system. This system was key to the functioning of not only the Prussian ministries but the state itself. Legitimacy lent by a person rather than data had been typically true for predisciplinary historical narratives such as Goethe's.[33]

When Hegel claimed that no events had proper historical import without the legal context of the state, then a transition in state power would necessarily affect the state's historical methodology, content, and narratives. Methodologies employed in Berlin's public works departments, strengthened by an increasingly powerful municipal framework during the 1870s, certainly affected the way in which art history was produced. Suddenly the state was, at least legally and financially, not only an ideal for but also responsible and answerable to its citizens. This was especially true in terms of expensive public works: research methodologies ensured that proof was firmly established and evidence circulated to an involved public before works proceeded. The expansion of public works to include specialists was not only informed by but also contributed to a greater demand for scientific evidence in decision-making. These changes to the public works departments reverberated in the cultural sphere at large: the shift affected the architects producing work as civil servants (like Adler), the institutions founded to train them (like the Bauakademie), and the archaeologists and art historians of the entire Berlin school of art history (who were also employed by, and thus representatives for, the state).

The success of *Medieval Brick Architecture of the Prussian States* may be one of method, rather than model. Being initiated by two broad guiding motivations rather than precise research questions, this survey method produced unexpected conclusions. The generality of the first result, "advancing the study of the art history of the Fatherland," was rather unproblematic, since all evidence found could potentially further this aim. However, the result of the work was that the particulars of red-brick medieval architecture became not just one chapter advancing the art history of the fatherland but came to stand in for the history of the fatherland, as physical evidence. The imprecision of the second result, "improving contemporary construction techniques," was countered by unexpected and precise discoveries. A methodology arising from broad motivations and requiring large quantities of data to be collected somewhat parallels recent digital research methods. One major benefit of a large set of data seems to be that it can open up a productive field for new questions to be asked rather than suggesting that the answers to research questions are in any way more objective.[34] If the building department in Berlin wanted to improve the construction methods of the present by looking at the past, there were certainly no specific parameters for how to do so. But thanks to the huge amount of data collected under broad categories and from a wide geographical area, details emerged about architectural history that could not have been discovered with more precisely defined research aims.

First, geographical context mattered. Construction types, architectural form, coursework, detailing, stone manufacture, and colors had all varied according to geographical (and geological) environment, and a smaller sampling would not have proffered this information. This not only affected the structure of the volumes but also the importance of geographical context for the historical narrative. Second was a more specific understanding of "truth to materials" (*Materialgerechtigkeit*). Architects like Adler, as well as other advocates of Karl Friedrich Schinkel's Berlin school, generally believed that ornament should be derived from structure and specifically that brickwork should not be covered in stucco. In reality, this meant that brick not only had to become aesthetically pleasing but also needed to be waterproof, strong, and durable. Only then might it have a chance of succeeding against a building tradition that separated structural work from decorative finishing and generally preferred stucco as a waterproofing method. What the data were able to show was that *Materialgerechtigkeit* was based on essential specific details repeated across the different Prussian regions, even if implemented differently; the variations depended on the quality of the mortar, the density achieved by hand-finished bricks as opposed to machine-formed bricks, the structure of the coursework, the quality of artisanship, and the fashioning details—cornices, decorative framework, and other ornamentation—out of whole pieces of brick, rather than the forming of special bricks. Natural variation between the clays and firing processes of different regions could appear as ornamentation on brick façades, tying a building even closer to its place. These were now specific construction problems that could be tackled.

The results of this research reverberated throughout the boom years of municipal construction in Berlin. Alongside the gas works, hospitals, schools, and churches, the city's first municipal waterworks (1874–1896) in particular embodied the influence of these historical findings. The architect of the waterworks, the *Baumeister* Richard Schultze, claimed, "On *märkisch* ground, only [Gothic] brick buildings could be considered, which follow their native medieval precedents."[35] The complete lack of further explanation for stylistic and material choices in any contemporary articles about these works, or countless others produced by the public works department in the same period, shows the degree to which historical precedence established by Adler's volumes acted something like a kind of legal precedent for justifying architectural style. Schultze went to great lengths to employ medieval techniques at the waterworks, specifying handmade and specially fired bricks in order to achieve superior performance. These bricks replicated the size of the regional medieval cloister format (*Klosterformat*)—long and narrow, with a deep red-brown color—and were assembled using a more intensive, medieval technique in which Schultze had to instruct his builders. This was not normal practice. In fact, the newly normed brick in Germany, the *Normalformat* (or *Reichsformat*, later to become DIN 105), established in 1869 and mandated for all public works, was intentionally not used in Schultze's work. This striking defiance of governmental mandate was in the service of a contemporary understanding of *Materialgerechtigkeit*. In substituting the normal *Verblendstein* (exterior-grade brick) for a handmade brick without a ceramic or "unnaturally" smooth, glazed surface that exterior wall bricks usually featured (for waterproofing), Schultze selected clay of a better, less porous quality to provide weatherproofing. This labor-intensive process did have advantages: it meant that the bricks could be worked by hand into arch pieces or three-quarter pieces without shattering the brick and without requiring additional finishing. In addition, no specially formed terracotta ornamental pieces had to be fabricated. Naturally, this also assumed that the bricklayers—who may have received their training by working on walls to be covered with stucco or may have been accustomed to facing buildings with glazed bricks—would be able to perform this kind of craftwork.

Medieval Brick Architecture of the Prussian States contributed to Berlin's urban identity through built works. In light of its bureaucratic entanglements, the project may not have proved a respected model for writing architectural history, within which it faded into obscurity. But as it became part of the Prussian state infrastructure, its art-historical methods cast a long shadow, contributing to central tenets of the Berlin school of art history. It represents a moment in Berlin when the aim of art-historical research—to locate and narrativize the truth lying beyond the visible artifact—was complemented by another desire—to provide the data to prove that narrative. Despite its shortcomings, the project now sheds considerable light on the changing relationship between evidence and narrative in architectural history.

8

The Banister Fletchers' Tabulations

∎

ZEYNEP ÇELIK ALEXANDER AND MICHAEL OSMAN

The so-called Banister Fletcher, the architectural history textbook that was used around the world for most of the twentieth century, was written by not one but two Banister Fletchers, a father and a son. The elder Fletcher (Fletcher Sr., 1833–1899) began his career as an architect in Newcastle-upon-Tyne before moving to London, where he developed a practice with numerous services, including surveying, arbitration, and sanitation. He wrote several books on these practical matters.[1] In 1890, he was appointed a professor of building construction and architecture at King's College, London, a position that he held until his death. While he taught there, he was assisted by his son, Banister Flight Fletcher (Fletcher Jr., 1866–1953), who, apart from practicing architecture, offered lectures at University College, London.[2] In 1896, in a joint effort, the father and son published the first edition of *A History of Architecture on the Comparative Method for the Student, Craftsman, and Amateur*, a volume that came to be known as the "Banister Fletcher."[3] Intended for specialized students as well as a general public, the book went through numerous editions and covered an increasing geographical expanse. The twenty-first edition, consisting of two volumes, seven sections, and 102 chapters written by dozens of experts appeared in 2020 under a revised title—one with an additional adjective: *Sir Banister Fletcher's Global History of Architecture*.[4]

The book's "global" aspirations have not escaped critical scrutiny. One of the earlier critiques came from the architectural historian Gülsüm Baydar Nalbantoğlu, who in 1998 attacked the book's separation of history from nonhistory. It was starting with the fourth edition, published in 1901, that the Fletchers added the so-called nonhistorical styles (Saracenic, Indian, Chinese,

8.1. "Tree of Architecture." Frontispiece in Banister Fletcher and Banister F. Fletcher, *A History of Architecture on the Comparative Method for the Student, Craftsmen, and Amateur*, 7th ed. (London: B. T. Batsford, 1924).

Japanese, and ancient American architectures) to a more predictable genealogy of European architecture that started in ancient Egypt and ended in the United States. Nalbantoğlu provocatively questioned the boundary she viewed as constructed by these two categories: "What are the mechanisms that define the inside and the outside of architecture and how do they operate?"[5] She found the answer hauntingly illustrated in the "Tree of Architecture" drawing that served as the frontispiece to several editions. In one version, the tree, fed by six roots that represented "influences," grew into Greek, Roman, Romanesque, Gothic, and ultimately Renaissance architectures in the West. In other versions the trunk would be topped by American architecture. The continuous transmission of influence (roots) into outcome (upper branches) was how Nalbantoğlu's notion of an "inside" of architecture was constituted. By contrast, lower branches, reserved for "nonhistorical" styles, led nowhere and therefore belonged to architecture's "outside" (fig. 8.1). More recently, in response to the repackaging of the volume as a "global history of architecture," Kathleen James-Chakraborty has continued this line of critique by rightly calling out the "patent racism" and the "egregious Orientalism" of the authors and institutions that produced the original editions, while also meditating on how they cast a long shadow on the subsequent rewritings of the text.[6]

In what follows, we seek a different path of critique, one focusing on the political economy of the Fletchers' *A History of Architecture* and its implications for writing global histories. Following a little-known aspect of Fletcher Sr.'s career—his successful business as a quantity surveyor—we consider the consequences of surveying practices on the history that he wrote jointly with his son. Apart from the homonymic resonance of two kinds of *survey*—on the one hand, conducted to document or estimate the amount of labor and material required to realize a building project and, on the other, taught with the goal of providing students with an overview of architecture's past—what emerges from an examination of the continuum between these seemingly distinct practices is the potential transferability of their concept of *value*. While the quantity surveyor's primary goal was the arbitration of one kind of value in buildings—whether those that already existed or those that were yet to come—the architectural historian's task was to pass judgment on something that the Fletchers called "architectural value"—an elusive relationship between "artistic motive" and the material and labor required for its realization.[7] As outdated as we think "architectural value" may sound today, it persists in a category of objects referred to as the "historical canon," a category that inherently relies on the distinction made by the Fletchers between works deemed historical and others nonhistorical—even in histories that claim to leave that distinction behind. We ask in this chapter what aspects of the concept of value found in quantity surveying carried over into a survey of architecture's history. Can aligning these forms of valuation reveal epistemological assumptions in writing surveys in general and "global" surveys in particular? What might the "Banister Fletcher" illuminate about the practice of writing global architectural histories today?

What was quantity surveying? In early modern Britain up through the end of the eighteenth century, a group of semiprofessionals known as measurers, who often also practiced as architects, quantified the labor and materials for construction. Usually two measurers made these calculations: one employed by a builder and the other by the client who was having something built, with the measurers representing the interests of their respective employer. The quantities commissioned by the builder and the client were then used to negotiate the final price of some aspect of the project. Each measurer accounted for construction costs as "after-measurement" values—that is, values calculated after each task of construction had been completed.[8] General contractors, who managed the building trades, gradually replaced this system by supervising and coordinating different types of labor as well as the supply of materials for each type. The contractor could thereby speculate and bid on the total cost of a construction project by offering an estimate in advance of breaking ground. If contractors could develop new forms of efficiency to save time or labor, they could generate profit. Thus, the "all-trades contract," in contrast to the system of two competing measurers, established an opportunity to produce capital through construction.[9] This contract and the estimate given by the contractor relied on the work of an emerging professional called a "quantity surveyor."

For a survey to make claims to objectivity—that is, one that did not favor either the client or the contractor—it would require that a surveyor measure the distribution of value in a would-be building based on data tabulated from the architect's working drawings. Banister Fletcher Sr. was among the first to systematize and standardize the surveyor's tabulation practices; it was in his book *Quantities* (1877) where he developed an analytic framework for a survey.[10] Fletcher's system brought architectural elements—column, wall, arch, vault, foundation, and the labor required for their assembly—into comparison with other similar elements and labors. One goal of standardizing this system was to achieve compatibility of one tabulation to the next. Thus, with each survey, the surveyor produced a continuity of value, linking projects through this quantitative method. The value of any new construction project could be related to others back through time.

To tabulate the value of would-be buildings, Fletcher Sr. proposed that measurements should be "taken off" from the drawings starting on the left and then moving to right, as though they were being read like a text. The surveyor recorded these dimensions in a measuring book, entering them into columns, drawn with parallel vertical lines, to organize the different kinds of recordings. Dimensions were tabulated in the left-most column, labeled D; calculations of area were recorded in column A; and the final column included other descriptive information regarding each element, such as particularities about its assembly. In several rows, B was used to signify brick, and in one instance two and one-half bricks would be used for footings (fig. 8.2). In this tally of materials and dimensions, a building's size and shape could thus be represented numerically and therefore algebraically. That is, in cases in which a dimension for an element was repeated—for example, columns of the same height—the surveyor would note its multiplier to the left of the first column. In other words, the surveyor's tabular representation was not merely a list; it sought to condense dimensional data into an efficient form for calculating value.

Fletcher Sr. summarized the surveyor's process as three steps: "*taking off*, by which we mean the measurement ... from the drawings; *abstracting*, that is, arranging or apportioning the several works from the dimensions, so as to arrive at the totals of each; and *billing*, that is, bringing the quantities with their descriptions from the abstract and arranging them in the form of a bill, and it is only the bills that are supplied to the various builders to enable them to prepare their estimates."[11] Once the surveyor converted measurements recorded in the measuring book into bills of quantities, the contractor's calculations were fully separated from the architect's drawings, producing a distance between the conception and execution of a project from which a contractor could derive profit. This profit differed from a simple difference—an

QUANTITIES.   7
SPECIMEN.

	D	A		
	32·2 22·2 1·6	1070·0	Dig wheel and deposit to surface 20·0 (width of building) 2/1·2 = 2·4 (thickness of outside walls) 17·8 (net length of end walls) 30·0 front wall (gross) 17·8 end wall (net) 2/ 47·8 95·4 total length of four walls	
	95·4 4·0 2·6	953·4	Ditto to trenches part return wheel fill in and ram (walls collected)	
	95·4 4·0 1·6	572·0	Concrete as described	
	95·4 9	71·6	2½ B. footings	
	95·4 12·0	1144·0	1½ B. wall to top of plate (ground floor)	
	95·4 18·0	1716·0	1 B. add to roof plate	
	8 6 7·0	24·6	1 B. ddt. entrance door	
	4·3 7·3	31·0	½ " "	
3	3·0 6·0	54·0	½ B. ddt. windows (ground floor)	
3	3·9 6·3	70·4	1 " " "	
2/3	2·6 5·6	82·6	½ " " (1st and 2nd floor)	
2/3	3·3 5 9	112·2	½ " " " "	

8.2. Tabulation for valuing prospective building projects. Banister Fletcher [Sr.], *Quantities: A Textbook for Surveyors, in Tabulated Form, Explanatory of the Best Methods Adopted in the Measurement of Builder's Work* . . . (London: B. T. Batsford, 1877), 7.

operation of subtraction—between income and expense that previous builders had relied upon. Profit in the hands of general contractors could be speculative in that it was projected as a ratio of their capital into the future.[12] While "abstracting" translated the measure of the drawing into a set of multiplicative formulas, "billing" allowed these formulas to be set into the emerging political economy of construction under general contracting.

Any discrepancy between the quantities tabulated from drawings and the actual building, once realized, would lead to an estimate that either overvalued or undervalued the materials and labors of a building's construction. If left unaddressed, as in the case of an inexperienced builder or an impractical architect, discrepancies could lead to the kinds of costly legal proceedings discussed by Fletcher Sr. in his earlier book *Arbitrations*, also organized in tabular form.[13] Masonry was particularly problematic in Fletcher Sr.'s view: "Many surveyors take out the labour on stonework somewhat excessively, so as to cover any omission in quantity or error of description, which through their incapacity might arise. ... The more elaborately the work is measured the greater will be the builder's estimate."[14] As the surveyor's measurement of labor became more precise, the builder needed to avoid the errors of over- or undervaluation and thus responded by exploiting the unknown through an overestimation of its value. The value of rubble walls, held together with mortar, could thus be more precisely predicted than windowsills and ornamental string courses. The exposure of stonework to the process of tabulation revealed that valuation deviated from a norm *as a result of* the surveyor's meticulous representation of labor tasks. As labor became distant from the brute form of a material and associated unskilled labor, it aligned with the unknowable cost of design, thus producing the greatest potential error in estimation, as well as the greatest potential profit for the contractor.

It was for this reason that the quantity surveyor's arbitration was necessary. To Fletcher Sr.'s mind, the surveyor brought a unique quantitative expertise to bear in controlling the many possible divergent forms of valuation and the corresponding exploitation of the unknown.[15] Experts' authority grew as they expanded their tabular logic to encompass more aspects of the building process. Over time, this power would rein in, for example, builders' tendency to expand their profits, thereby positioning the surveyor as the regulator of such base capitalist motivations. This expertise also solidified the surveyor's standing as a professional in future legal proceedings. Fletcher Sr.'s reasoning depended on one critical correlation: the more specific the calculation of a building's quantities of materials and labors, the more the assessment of its value would be wrested away from the profit motives of a contractor. By estimating a building's value with a uniform method and using this method consistently from one project to the next, the surveyor's technique would be secured as the center of legitimate valuation. There were now two competing views of the would-be building's potential value: first, the contractor's treatment of the building process as a generator of profit, and second, the surveyor's rhetorically objective tabulation of data that reconstituted the building through the arbitration of value.

The Fletchers tabulated as historians as well. After the death of his father, Banister Fletcher Jr. edited and revised various editions of *A History of Architecture* that he had jointly written with him. This work also gave him the opportunity to teach courses at University College, London, among them "a course of 24 lectures on the history of architecture." Lecture notes from 1909—that is, between the fifth and sixth editions of the textbook—demonstrate that the historian's methods of organizing information were not dissimilar from those of the quantity surveyor. Fletcher Jr. neatly organized pages of his twenty-four lectures into two columns. In the left-hand column were generalizations about a particular style, sometimes handwritten but more frequently cut and pasted from the pages of the fifth edition of *A History of Architecture*; in the right-hand column were particular buildings that exemplified the style, as well as references to numbered glass lantern slides (fig. 8.3). Fletcher Jr. recommended that students follow a similar method of tabulation when they took notes; he even encouraged them to buy the special notebook that he had designed for this purpose so that they could keep their lecture notes and sketches in two columns, on the left and right sides of a spread, just as he kept his. He promised his students that following his method would help them save study time. The twenty-four hours of his course would amount to studying architecture for twenty-four months.[16]

In these notes, in fact, Fletcher Jr. was simply translating the analytic logic of *A History of Architecture* into the format of a lecture. The systematics of tabulation found in the lectures were fundamental to the organization of the book. First, the book was punctuated at crucial moments with "comparative" sections that developed relations between one style and another by juxtaposing their attributes in two columns carefully arranged on a page. After a general introduction to Renaissance architecture, for example, the reader could use this tabulated arrangement to compare plans, walls, openings, roofs, columns, and moldings in Renaissance architecture to the same elements found in Gothic architecture. This reader would learn from the "A. Plans" row of the left column that Renaissance plans were distinguished by "symmetry and proportion of part to part carefully studied"; sliding across the same row to the right column, the reader would discover that plans of Gothic buildings were marked, by contrast, by "picturesqueness and beauty of individual features more particularly sought after" (fig. 8.4).[17] Fletcher Jr. added throughout the book ample illustrations (usually line drawings), frequently presented in a grid, to serve a similar tabular purpose.[18]

Prehistoric.
Sir Banister-Fletcher, 1, King's Bench Walk, E.C.4

D. Syllabus of Course
'An illustrated review of the History of architecture'

PREHISTORIC ARCHITECTURE.

"Study mere shelter, now for him, and him ;
Nay, even the worst—just house them ! Any cave
Suffices ; throw out earth ! A loop hole ? Brave !
. . . But here's our son excels
At hurdle weaving any Scythian ; fells
Oak and devises rafters ; dreams and shapes
His dream into a door post, just escapes
The mystery of hinges. . . .
The goodly growth
Of brick and stone ! Our building-pelt was rough,
But that descendants' garb suits well enough
A portico-contriver.
* * *
The work marched : step by step—a workman fit
Took each, nor too fit—to one task, one time—
No leaping o'er the petty to the prime,
When just the substituting osier lithe
For brittle bulrush, sound wood for soft withe,
To further loam-and-rough-cast work a stage,
Exacts an architect, exacts an age."—BROWNING.

THE origins of architecture, although lost in the mists of antiquity, must have been connected intimately with the endeavours of man to provide for his physical wants. It has been truly said that protection from the inclemency of the seasons was the mother of architecture. According to Vitruvius, man in his primitive savage state began to imitate the nests of birds and the lairs of beasts, commencing with arbours of twigs covered with mud, then huts formed of branches of trees and covered with turf (No. 2 C). Other writers indicate three types of primitive dwellings—the *caves* (No. 2 H) or rocks or those occupied in hunting or fishing, the *hut* (No. 2 A, D, E) for the agriculturist, and the *tent* (No. 2 J) for those such as shepherds leading a pastoral or nomadic life.

Structures of the prehistoric period, although interesting for archæological reasons, have little or no architectural value, and will only be lightly touched upon.

The remains may be classified under :—

i. **Monoliths**, or single upright stones, also known as *menhirs*, a well-known example 63 feet high, 14 feet in diameter, and weighing 260 tons, being at Carnac, Brittany. Another example is at Locmariaker, also in Brittany (No. 2 B).

ii. **Dolmens** (Daul, a table, and maen, a stone), consisting of one large flat stone supported by upright stones. Examples are to be found near Maidstone and other places in England, also in Ireland, Northern France, the Channel Islands, Italy (No. 2 F), and India.

iii. **Cromlechs**, or circles of stone, as at Stonehenge (No. 2 G), Avebury (Wilts), and elsewhere, consisting of a series of upright stones arranged in a circle and supporting horizontal slabs.

iv. **Tumuli**, or burial mounds, were probably prototypes of the Pyramids of Egypt (No. 4), and the beehive huts found in Wales, Cornwall, Ireland (No. 2 D, E) and elsewhere. That at New Grange (Ireland) resembles somewhat the Treasury of Atreus at Mycenæ (No. 15).

v. **Lake Dwellings**, as discovered in the lakes of Switzerland, Italy and Ireland consisted of wooden huts supported on piles, and were so placed for protection against hostile attacks of all kinds.

These foregoing primitive or prehistoric remains have little constructive sequence, and are merely mentioned here to show from what simple beginnings the noble art of architecture was evolved, although unfortunately the stages of the evolution cannot be traced, owing to the fact that the oldest existing monuments of any pretension, as in Egypt, belong to a high state of civilisation.

Prehistoric Architecture has no architectural value.

Buildings in prehistoric times consisted of :—

a. The Cave or rocks, occupied by hunters and fishermen.

b. The Hut for the agriculturist.

c. The Tent (easily moved) for Shepherds and those following a nomadic life.

8.3. Lecture notes prepared by Banister Fletcher [Jr.] in 1909 for General Course 1, London University. University College London, Special Collections, 6B-B0990-S03.

4. COMPARATIVE.

RENAISSANCE.

A. **Plans.**—Symmetry and proportion of part to part carefully studied (Nos. 198, 203, 213, 223, 252).

Grandeur gained by simplicity (Nos. 200, 201, 254). Fewness and largeness of parts have a tendency to make the building appear less in size than it really is.

Towers are sparingly used, and when they occur are symmetrically placed. In England those at S. Paul (No. 254), and Bow Church (No. 255), are exceedingly fine. The dome is a predominant feature (Nos. 181, 205, 212, 223 and 254).

Interiors of churches were planned on Roman principles (Nos. 193, 199 and 203), and covered with domes and pendentives. The parts are few, the nave being divided into three or four compartments (No. 253), by which a general effect of grandeur is produced.

Compare S. Paul, London (No. 213).

B. **Walls.**—These were constructed in ashlar masonry of smooth-faced walling, which, in the lower stories, was occasionally heavily rusticated (No. 192). Materials are large, and carry out the Classic idea of fewness of parts. Stucco or plaster were often used as a facing material where stone was unobtainable. The use of the material according to its nature was lost, the design being paramount.

Angles of buildings often rusticated, *i.e.*, built in blocks of unsmoothed stone, as in Florence, or carefully indented with patterns (No. 197).

GOTHIC.

A. **Plans.**—Picturesqueness and beauty of individual features more particularly sought after (Nos. 117, 155, 159 and 187).

Grandeur gained by multiplicity (Nos. 162, 175 and 189). In consequence of the large number of parts, the building appears larger than it really is.

Towers are a general feature, and are often crowned with a spire (Nos. 110, 114, 115, 116, 121, 140 and 154). Small towers, turrets, and finials help to emphasize the vertical tendency (Nos. 125, 128 and 173). The tower and spire are predominant features.

Interiors are more irregular, and are covered with stone vaulting (Nos. 112, 123), or open-timbered roofs (No. 113). The parts are many, a nave of the same length as a Renaissance church probably divided into twice as many compartments.

Compare Cologne Cathedral (No. 213).

B. **Walls.**—These were often constructed of uncoursed rubble or small stones (No. 136), not built in horizontal layers; also of brick and rough flint work. Materials are small in size, and carry out the Gothic idea of multiplicity. Masonry was worked according to the nature of the material to a new and significant extent. It is not too much to say that, as in a mosaic, each piece in a wall has its value in this style.

Angles of buildings often of ashlar masonry or smooth-faced stone, the rest of the walling being of rough materials, as rubble or flint.

8.4. Tabulation comparing Renaissance with Gothic buildings. Banister Fletcher and Banister F. Fletcher, *A History of Architecture on the Comparative Method for the Student, Craftsmen, and Amateur*, 5th ed. (London: B. T. Batsford, 1905), 442.

Second, the entire corpus of *A History of Architecture* was the result of a tabulation whose principles were summarized in the opening pages of the volume in a "diagram table." This "System of Classification for Each Style" consisted of the following:

1. INFLUENCES
    i. Geographical
    ii. Geological
    iii. Climate
    iv. Religion
    v. Social and Political
    vi. Historical
2. ARCHITECTURAL CHARACTER
3. EXAMPLES OF BUILDINGS
4. COMPARATIVE
    A. *Plan*, or general distribution of the building
    B. *Walls*, their construction and treatment
    C. *Roofs*, their treatment and development
    D. *Openings*, their character and shape
    E. *Columns*, their position, structure, and decoration
    F. *Mouldings*, their form and decoration
    G. *Ornament*, as applied in general to any building
5. REFERENCE BOOKS

The Fletchers applied the structure of the "diagram table" to every style discussed in their book. This meant that despite its chronological structure (at least in the section dedicated to "historical styles"), the book was not intended be read in a linear fashion as a continuous narrative. Rather, the reader could go back and forth to form a mental tabulation of how, for example, climate might have played a role in Italian, French, or German Romanesque architectures or how roofs of the Florentine, Roman, or Venetian schools of Italian Renaissance architecture might compare. Frequent cross-referencing in the book's prose made this kind of nonsequential reading necessary at times. In the section for the nonhistorical styles, the tabular logic was even more blatantly on display. Having forgone chronology altogether for these styles, the Fletchers divided up a section on architectural character into subsections for China and Japan. Under Saracenic ornament they listed Arabian, Syrian, Egyptian, Spanish, Persian, Turkish, and Indian types. While the tabular structure of the diagram table disrupted the narrative for the historical styles, the nonhistorical styles lent themselves to tabulation even more readily.

Finally, the logic of quantity surveying appeared in *A History of Architecture* in a less obvious manner but one that might be more relevant to our understanding of the transferability of the Fletchers' concept of value. They traced "influences" through the architecture of the past as methodically as the quantity surveyor, who followed how labor and materials would be used in future buildings. These "influences," listed at the bottom of the Tree of Architecture as the roots of the tree (the "structural" influences of geography, geology, and climate on one side and the "external" influences of religion, social and political, and history on the other), were meant both literally and figuratively. As the etymology of the word suggests, an "influence" is a fluid force in motion; the root influences of the Tree of Architecture fed the system and flowed through it, manifesting themselves as styles on the branches. For the Fletchers, these "influences" were also primary analytic categories through which to follow an elusive thing that they called "architectural value." Consider their discussion of Roman construction:

> The Greek method of building with large blocks of stone, unconnected with mortar, was employed in the buildings of the Republic. The practical spirit of the Romans, however, urged them to make a more economical use of materials, and instead of composing the walls of their monuments of squared-blocks of stone produced by skilled masons, they inaugurated the use of concrete, a material consisting of small fragments of stone or quarry *debris* mixed with lime or mortar. These materials, not being special to any country, were used with success in every part of the Empire, and gave a similarity to all Roman buildings. The craftsmanship required, under the direction of the central authority, was perfectly simple; for only rough labour, both plentiful and cheap, was required for mixing the materials of which the concrete was made, and spreading it to form the walls. The structures could be erected by hands quite unused to the art of building; thus the Romans employed the slaves of the district, subjects liable to statute labour, or even the Roman armies; while the legal punishment of condemnation to work on public buildings was largely enforced.[19]

The Fletchers did not provide an explicit definition of "architectural value" in *A History of Architecture*, but they did write that "the more [artistic motive] is developed, the greater being the value of the result."[20] Roman architecture had "value" precisely because it successfully employed available material and human resources to maximum effect. It would have been valueless if its builders had disregarded the scale of the empire and its provision of abundant free but unskilled labor and if they had continued to use the mortarless building techniques that required the precision found in ancient Greek temples. "The style of the Romans tended to become everywhere uniform and generally above the influence of local conditions," they wrote in a passage eerily resonant with imperial ambitions in their own time, adding that "new methods penetrated to the extremities of the empire . . . and cities could be improvised, which became in their turn centres whence radiated the architectural ideas as well as the manners and customs of Rome."[21] In other words, Romans knew how to direct "influences" properly; instead of succumbing to local frictions, they turned to concrete, a material and technique that surpassed those frictions, thus expanding their empire with a construction system that made their style of architecture replicable in any colony.

Architectural value, then, was not simply a matter of aesthetic effect; for architecture to have value, this effect had to be commensurate with the labor and material expended in its construction. For example, according to the Fletchers, while "prehistoric architecture" (huts, caves, etc.) required hardly any labor or none at all, it also had no value. On ancient Egyptian architecture they wrote that "the relative return in impressiveness and the higher beauties of art is small when compared with the amount of expense and material used in their erection."[22] However grand pyramids might be in stature, their beauty did not justify the massive expenditure in material and labor. Likewise, nonhistorical styles required too much labor in their ornamentation, often unequally distributed, and therefore offered value that did not produce influence beyond their own spheres. To put it differently, architectural value for the Fletchers was not absolute. It was a relative value to be figured out by the historian who appraised the aesthetic merits of an architectural style in relation to the costs incurred during its construction. The historian had to imagine architectural value as a *ratio*: the proportion of aesthetic effect relative to material and labor outlay, as well as its extension through time. The calculation of this ratio required an operation akin to accounting—except this accounting was now performed by the historian rather than by the quantity surveyor.

In an essay that historicizes "profit," that seemingly immutable goal of capitalism, the historian Jonathan Levy argues that around 1850 the meaning of the term changed from a simple *difference* between income and expense to a *ratio*—whether operating ratio or its later iterations, rate of return on capital invested and rate of return on equity.[23] This was historically necessary to turn static wealth into dynamic, productive capital. "Wealth, taking the form of capital or not, demands an *adding up calculation*, a momentary capture," Levy writes. "Profit, however, always concerns a 'flow,' a process, and *rate over time*."[24] Circa 1850, capitalists no longer simply subtracted the output of their commercial activity from the input to evaluate their ventures; they calculated their capital's distribution over time as a ratio. Levy then paraphrases: "profit also quantitatively organizes capital's temporal motion."[25]

This was precisely the task that the Fletchers took upon themselves in *A History of Architecture*. The book, then, is a relative of the quantity survey, a survey whose temporal frame is not weeks and months but rather centuries and millennia. The architectural styles to which the Fletchers devoted most of their energy did not deviate from the well-established norms of nineteenth-century architectural theory; the text abounds with elements of the writings of Laugier, Semper, Viollet-le-Duc, and Ruskin. What distinguished their work was its focus on value: not absolute value (they did not favor one style or one national manifestation of a style over another, for example) but rather how value flowed through time. Steps in the process of quantity surveying—taking off and abstracting—might as well apply to surveying the history of architecture. *A History of Architecture* "took off" from countless other nineteenth-century accounts of architecture's past but "abstracted" those for the reader through the repetitive structure of the book and the line drawings with which the Fletchers illustrated the work. While the Tree of Architecture schematized value's temporal flow, the reader could decipher its movement through time and space only by engaging with the book's tabular logic.

This point is further illustrated by the Fletchers' interest in materials. In his prize-winning essay *The Influence of Material on Architecture* (1897), Fletcher Jr. redeployed the nineteenth-century concept of style but now privileged materials above all other factors in its determination: "style is created," he wrote, "by the discoveries of experience or genius out of the qualities of the materials employed."[26] Rehearsing a familiar argument of nineteenth-century architectural theory—elaborated, among others, by Gottfried Semper—Fletcher Jr. argued that architectural forms were nothing more than traces left behind as one material was transformed into another. For example, reeds vertically bound together to build temples in ancient Egypt changed into granite columns over time.[27] But Fletcher Jr.'s materialism was different from Semper's. Among the midcentury materialists, Semper in particular took up scientific theories about *Stoffwechsel* (metabolism, literally a changing of matter) with revolutionary zeal: because those theories showed how force could be redistributed in the universe, they proved that existing structures of power could be dismantled and rebuilt again.[28] Fletcher Jr., by contrast, tracked the movement of force from one material to another in architecture's past with an eye on value. In contrast to the surplus value the Roman architecture created, the late nineteenth century appeared to be producing a deficit. He explained: starting in the Renaissance, when materials no longer determined "design" but were instead determined by it, the figure of the architect became preoccupied unjustifiably with "form," forgetting the core source for producing architectural value—the materials used. As the division between designer and builder deepened, Fletcher wrote, nineteenth-century architecture was hastening to its decay, with engineering securing its dominance over the production of new value.[29] In other words, the modern architect's preoccupation with design dislocated the materials of the age from the governing internal order of valuation. The task of reasserting architectural value to avoid the entropic hole of decay fell to the historian: with the historian's help, nineteenth-century architects could invent forms and techniques of assembly that harnessed the value-making potential of such materials as wrought iron and reinforced concrete. This way, "not only do we take advantage of their infinite resources and open up a vast field for variety in design," Fletcher Jr. wrote, "but we also extend the boundaries of artistic expression by this constant endeavour to give to every object the form that befits its nature."[30] In other words, the historian, like the quantity surveyor, was an expert who knew how to account for the ratio of a material's value over time so that moments of potential profit—as well as loss—could be identified with increasing precision. The history survey revealed overvalued historical styles and the undervalued nonhistorical styles, thus flagging potential instabilities as well as potentials in the Tree of Architecture.

Yet the question remains: On whose behalf did the Fletchers perform this accounting in *A History of Architecture*? If the quantity surveyor's tabulation was crucial to both revealing and regulating potential profits for the general contractor and the client through the extraction of value (always for capital and never for labor) in an increasingly organized building industry, what purpose did the Fletchers' historical evaluation serve? Who profited, in other words, from the architectural value arbitrated by the historian?

In the preface to the first edition of *A History of Architecture*, the Fletchers wrote that the book was intended not only for students in their artistic and professional education and others engaged in the arts but also for a general public, who would read the book as "a result and record of *civilization*."[31] In his lecture notes, Fletcher Jr. provided a list of who might constitute this general public: "architectural value" mattered, he wrote, to the antiquarian, photographer, literary person, and the journalist, in addition to the architect, the craftsman (builder, bricklayer, mason, carpenter, joiner, plasterer, etc.), designer (of carpets, metalwork, woodwork, pottery, etc.), and the art student.[32] If, as the epigraph that would appear in later editions of *A History of Architecture* declared, architecture was "the printing press of all ages," then "the study of Architectural History [would] soon take its proper place as part of a liberal education."[33] According to the 1905 edition, the book was adopted at various educational institutions beyond Great Britain—in the United States and Australia. By 1928, this more geographically dispersed definition of civilization appeared to be consuming its own history as new editions of the book were translated into Japanese, Russian, and Spanish, among other languages.[34] As Fletcher Jr. wrote in his lecture notes, "the history of architecture is the history of civilization"—in the lands not only of historical styles but of nonhistorical styles as well.[35]

However similar their techniques might have been, the quantity surveyor's arbitration of value in the construction process was at some level fundamentally different from the historian's evaluation of historical styles. If the surveyor's tabulation of value opened architecture up to the possibility of profit through construction, the historian's accountancy sublimated value into the realm of *civilization*. The resulting history was not absorbed by the capitalist motives of the construction industry but by the civilizing institutions of liberal education. What was thereby accrued was capital of the cultural kind. And the architectural historian was the central agent of this process of sublimation. This, then, might be where the hidden ideological work of *A History of Architecture* resides: instituting a political economy that employed techniques of tabulation for the transformation of value for the sake of capital into the evaluation of culture for the sake of civilization.

Understanding this political economy might be crucial to writing architectural histories today. We return, in conclusion, to Nalbantoğlu's argument that the Fletchers' distinction between historical and nonhistorical styles constructed a core "inside" (or, as it is sometimes called, the "historical canon") and a marginalized "outside" for architectural history. Global histories that have been written since then have taken this line of critique and its topology seriously: the twenty-first edition of the "Banister Fletcher," for example, has supplemented the chapters on Europe with a proliferating number of chapters on regions around the world. It is likely that more chapters will be added to subsequent editions. The implicit assumption is this: the addition of more styles, especially those the Fletchers might have viewed as nonhistorical, will overcome the topology of "inside" and "outside" civilization found in such concepts as "the canon."

Yet, if our argument in this chapter has any validity, the entrenched topology of the architectural history survey, illustrated by the Fletchers' Tree of Architecture, may not be fundamentally challenged by such operations. The Fletchers' survey, we have argued, was developed by the logic of the ratio. That is to say, *A History of Architecture* created an ecumenical tabular system in which that elusive thing called "architectural value" could be produced over and over again—not simply by adding new nonhistorical styles to compare to the historical ones (so that the difference would prove the superiority of the latter) but rather by the possibility of placing every element into new comparative permutations. The Fletchers therefore did not force the development of a disciplinary topology that separates an inside from an outside; there is neither an inside nor an outside in a world of ratios. They did, however, create an epistemology in which the historian borrowed concepts and techniques from the production of capital through the evaluation of labor, material, cost, time, and value. No amount of adding to the corpus of the architectural history survey, we therefore suggest, will change its basic ideological foundations. To change this foundation, what is needed is a critique of a now-naturalized transformation of the evaluative function of the architectural historian, who—whether wittingly or unwittingly—produces new value through the continued expansion of the global survey. Without that kind of critique, the institutional allegiance of liberal education to the Fletchers' civilizational claim persists, revivifying the Tree of Architecture through the architectural historian's habituated evaluation of a ratio between material and value.

9

Evidence and Narrative in Digital Art History
Exploratory Methods for Weimar Architecture

■

PAUL B. JASKOT AND IVO VAN DER GRAAFF

Digital art historians founder on the rocks of the Scylla of positivism or the Charybdis of an inflated reliance on visualization's bells and whistles, or so its critics say. In both cases, scholars find wanting the synthetic analysis that distinguishes a strong contribution to humanities debates. At its heart, this perception of the distinction between digital and "analog" scholarship is a conflict between an art history that, on the one hand, emphasizes vast quantities of evidence as well as its computational organization and, on the other, produces a narrative, that is, an evaluation of information in a rigorous form. Digital art historians are prone to fall into the trap of emphasizing evidence at the expense of narrative. Even within their community, digital humanists have warned that scholarship often lapses into mere data-driven methodological innovation instead of contributing analytic substance to our disciplines. The digital historian Cameron Blevins has perhaps expressed such concerns best: "In terms of argument-driven scholarship, digital [humanities] has over-promised and under-delivered.... The digital wave has crashed headlong into many corners of the discipline. Argument-driven scholarship has largely not been one of them.... The argumentative payoffs of these methodologies are always just over the horizon, floating in the tantalizing ether of potential and possibility."[1]

Such doubts point to the fact that so much of a subfield like digital art history seems to be about digital tools and their application, rather than direct art-historical analysis.[2] In this context, digital art history remains incomplete, an example of methods that never get to the main art-historical question concerning the object(s) under investigation. The digital approach constantly defers art-historical answers as ever more complex data and visualizations flood forth. This sense of promise without fulfillment is a result of digital methods that often require above all else a systematic scholarly attention to evidence, its completeness, and its organization. Terms like "metadata," "structuring a database," "visualizing a dataset," and so on, proliferate in digital art history and point to the importance of the gathered source material as the core of any analysis in this particular subfield. Yet the danger of treating evidence-as-data is that such a slippage between terms conjures up a positivist faith in facts, that is, of analyzing art-historical evidence as though it were mere "neutral" computational data. Such an insidious accentuation of quantifiable information comes at the expense of the subjective and the interpretive practices in the humanities. For its critics and in relation to the theme of this volume, the narrative argument is too often missing from the digital art-historical text. Scholars of digital art history can focus on process to such a degree that any real addition to an art-historical debate ends up being just another promise to be fulfilled in some future utopic time when all possible data have been magically gathered and digitally visualized. Although there are exceptions to this pattern, much digital art history nevertheless seems to sacrifice narrative on the altar of evidence, to the detriment of each.[3]

This characterization of digital art history, however, fails to take into account the analytical and critical potential of its process-oriented method. Conversely, it places a false hope on individual works by scholars who construct compelling but nevertheless closed narratives on a specific aspect of an art-historical subject. Such narratives simply cannot answer particular art-historical questions that, for example, rely on evidence at a vast scale—at the level of, say, ten thousand buildings instead of one hundred. Digital art history privileges the scale of the evidence. In this regard, what if the *process* of research central to digital art history—that is, central to grappling with the very different challenge of an ever-expanding basis of evidence—is itself the critical aspect of the analysis that brings forth new interpretations in specific lines of art-historical inquiry? Put bluntly, instead of an art history that privileges the two-step method of first gathering evidence and then turning it into a narrative analysis, a focus on process means that the gathering and (crucially) organizing of art-historical data is itself an analytical result. Digital art history offers a more dialectical way of thinking about data and its analysis as core constituents of the broader categories of evidence and narrative. As the digital humanist Willard McCarty put it, "'evidence' is what argument does to data to make it meaningful."[4]

The key to accrediting digital methods in art history is emphasizing the research process, which in digital terms means both evidence gathering and analysis. Process mediates between evidence and analysis and gives that relationship form. A focus on process avoids the reductive narrative that abstracts from an overly selective sample of sources as much as it denies the false promise of a positivist claim for completeness. In social art-historical terms, this focus puts an emphasis on the relational and thus irreducible historical connection between cultural production and political economic systems.[5]

This chapter argues for an emphasis on process as a way of addressing such big questions of art history, especially those involving art's relationship to society. With the example of a dataset from the Weimar Republic of the German construction firm of Dyckerhoff & Widmann, an evaluation of the structuring and querying of the data leads to specific analytical points that challenge the established narrative for the architectural development of Weimar Germany. At the same time, grappling with large bodies of data necessarily opens up the scale of the research itself in a manner that demands further—and collaborative—work if big questions of art history are to be addressed. Thus, while the evidence and its digital visualization help point to a different narrative of architecture and the building industry in Weimar, understanding the political economic goals of the period demands more data and further complexity. That is to say, embracing the critical concept of the art-historical process is a way of demanding attention for a wider field of evidence as well as calling for a more collective and exploratory approach to answering disciplinary questions at scale. This approach is exactly what a critical digital art history can provide.

Digital Mapping and the Analysis of the Construction Industry in the Early Weimar Republic

Method, in the strictest sense of the term, speaks to how we find and identify evidence, how we organize it, how it is structured and becomes part of a scholarly argument. Method in art history—an interpretive discipline at heart—is neither entirely about the evidence that it uses nor completely transparent to the analytical and theoretical results of the argument. Rather, it points to the relationship between the two, between dead history and allegory, as it were.[6] In social art history, method is crucial for mediating between the unstructured facts of the past and our attempts to derive from them critical meaning for works of art. A similar focus on research methods in digital art history points to both the foundation of social art history in a broad evidential base as well as the potential for a radical analytical expansion of the discipline.[7] An emphasis on method is to point to the promise of a digital art history that derives its power from an extended source base and demands an ever more complete accounting of the function of art in human society.

A case derived from the construction industry in Weimar Germany (1918–1933) helps to clarify the dynamic between evidence and (narrative) analysis in the social history of art. Architecture and the building economy expanded by leaps and bounds in Weimar, especially after the stabilization of currency in 1924 and before the destructive results of the Great Depression after the US stock market crash of 1929. However, even before 1924, much more building activity and architectural innovation occurred than many art historians have assumed.[8] Much of this activity emerges when looking toward the vast sites of operation of the construction industry rather than following the art-historical penchant to look at limited samples of buildings designed by a handful of avant-garde architects. While there are peaks and troughs in this activity (and in the data), large construction enterprises like the Philipp Holzmann and Hochtief firms continued to expand their production even in the most dire economic and political circumstances of the early Weimar Republic.[9] With revolution on the right and left a constant threat and occasional reality, in addition to the catastrophe of hyperinflation, construction's priority in this period seems unfathomable. But from vernacular to high design, these firms found patrons and contracts that require a broader study of architectural evidence than usual if we want a more convincing account of what construction did and what it meant. Extending the data to incorporate the building activity of construction firms means highlighting different questions rather than focusing narrowly on standard accounts of architecture, especially with regard to those historical questions in which building intersects with political and economic struggles. Digital methods—particularly digital mapping—help to organize and typologize the evidence in new ways that lead to different and more critical conclusions about this period, its architecture, and its building activity.

Here the focus falls on the construction firm of Dyckerhoff & Widmann (or Dywidag), which has a particularly rich base of evidence because the largest part of its archive survives and is available at the Deutsches Museum in Munich. The firm engaged a variety of builders during the period and undertook a wide range of building activity, from vernacular industrial structures to "high design" architects like Erich Mendelsohn, among others. Mapping the building sites of an actual construction firm like Dywidag shows how construction knowledge spread in specific ways, the typological developments of construction activity, and the disruptions to predictable patterns that point to other social-historical problems.

Dywidag began its activity in Karlsruhe in 1865, with a subsequent headquarters in Biebrich and affiliates in Nuremberg, Dresden, and other cities. They specialized in the use of both pressed cement and reinforced concrete construction, such as the Nonnenbrücke in Bamberg (1903–1904), designed by Theodor Fischer. By World War I, the firm had extended its expertise to a wide range of buildings—train stations, industrial facilities, religious structures, office buildings, exhibition pavilions, and more. Dywidag's most famous projects, like Max Berg's Jahrhunderthalle (1911–1912), focused attention not only on the firm's technological know-how but also on its introduction of labor rationalization processes and the movement of materials on site. In these examples and others, the construction firm is equally as important as the architect for understanding the social significance of building.[10]

Digitally mapping evidence from Dywidag helps to analyze the firm's contributions to the built environment during World War I and its aftermath in

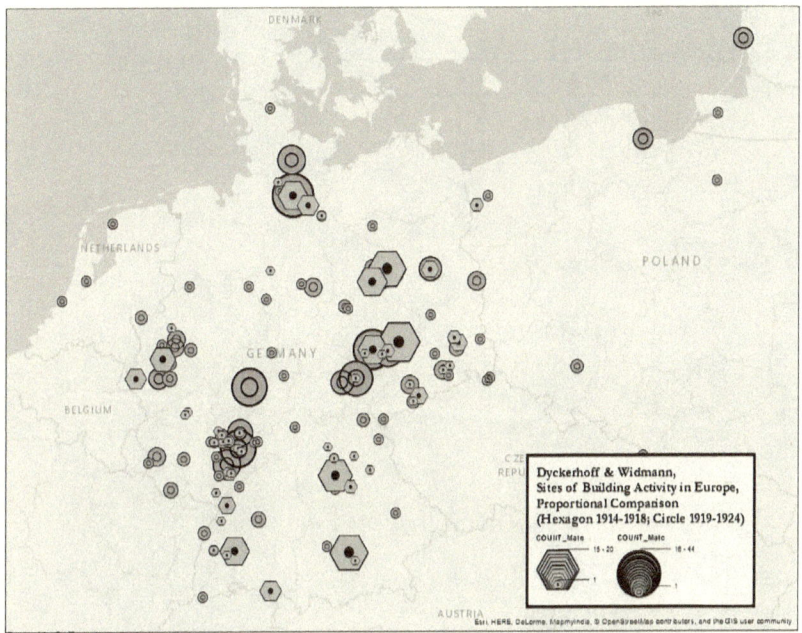

9.1. Sites of construction activity by Dyckerhoff & Widmann, during and after World War I. Draft map by Paul Jaskot.

Germany. An internal index recovered in the archives of Dyckerhoff & Widmann detailing all the projects it conducted between 1914 and 1930 begins to help give shape to the construction activity of this firm. Such a seemingly neutral bureaucratic list proved interesting in its possibilities (and problems, as we shall see) when reentered as data for digital visualization.[11] Following modern bookkeeping practices, the index was already structured as data organized by discrete fields of building type, location, patron, and date.[12] As we in turn entered the data into our database, one initial question came up as to whether the evidence would support an argument for a distinction between wartime and postwar construction. Figure 9.1 shows some initial results that divide the building activity into wartime and postwar sites, displayed proportionally in terms of the number of buildings at a particular location. Some obvious and predictable patterns emerge, such as a concentration of activity in Baden, Württemberg, and Hessen, that is, areas in relative proximity to the firm's main headquarters and affiliates. Note as well the concentrations of activity, such as around the Ruhr and Lower Rhine. Other trends are less obvious, such as a move out of southern Germany to sites in the north and into East Prussia. In contrast to the usual narrative of architectural history that posits a contraction of construction activity, it appears that the firm expanded and diversified, particularly in the immediate postwar years.

9.2. All sites of construction activity by Dyckerhoff & Widmann, 1914–1930. Draft map by Paul Jaskot.

Visualizing the Dywidag index also points to areas of geographic activity and typological interests that indicate a more complex relationship between the firm and the changing architectural and economic environment of wartime and postwar Germany.[13] Most obvious is the global reach of Dywidag, with a concentration in South America (fig. 9.2). Looked at proportionally over the whole period of the index, Dywidag was notably active after World War I in Chile, Uruguay, and Argentina. These clusters are interesting because they suggest how Dywidag survived the postwar period relatively easily: the firm diversified its client base and expanded its reach not only in Germany but also in German-friendly countries in South America. Thus, Dywidag could survive a wave of economic chaos and social turmoil by building factories, housing, and some of South America's first reinforced-concrete skyscrapers, including notable structures such as Mario Palanti's Roccatagliata Building in Buenos Aires (1921).

From this larger map, the digital process allows us to create innumerable smaller and iterative versions as a means of querying the evidence to highlight new art-historical problems. For example, a further revelation comes from a small but nevertheless geographically widespread number of clients who turned to the firm for cultural buildings, such as theaters, in the immediate postwar period. This comes as another surprise given that we tend to associate firms like

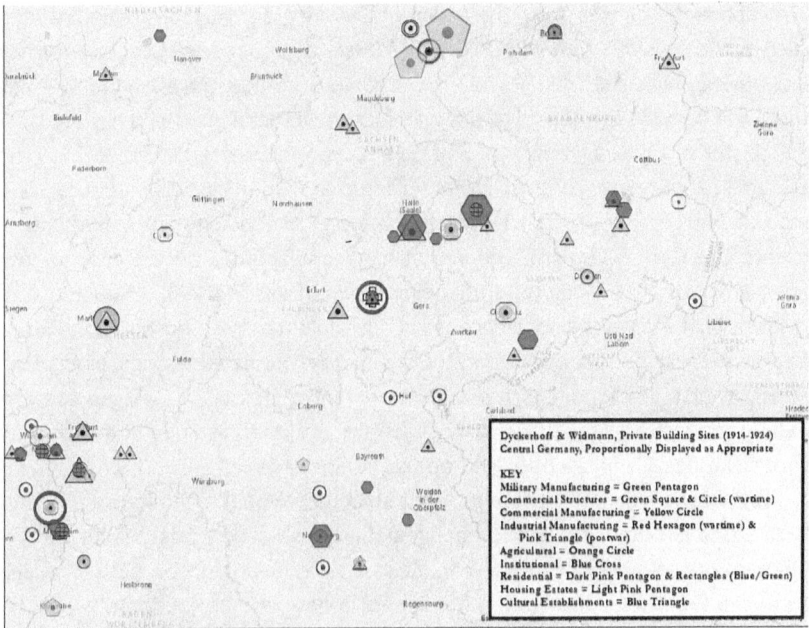

9.3. Postwar sites of construction activity by Dyckerhoff & Widmann, central Germany (Jena is in the center of the map with the overlapping triangle, circles, and cross). Draft map by Paul Jaskot.

Dywidag with industrial and vernacular structures. With the exception of a few examples, like Hans Poelzig's Grosses Schauspielhaus in Berlin (1919), scholars conceive of cultural construction activity as relatively unimportant during the years of revolution and inflation. Instead, Dywidag's expansion of its client base to include theater construction could help account for the firm's ability to overcome tight restrictions on materials or manage labor disputes.

But the larger point is that the Dywidag dataset gives shape to unseen patterns of actual building activity through the iterative process of mapping. It thus raises new art-historical questions in ways that research at the scale of the individual building or even a regional case study could have. Such an expansion of the evidence base requires the application of digital methods that can make analytic sense of this morass of "data," and it produces a critical intervention in standard accounts of Weimar architecture as a result. Indeed, it makes us question the accepted narrative.

Mapping Dywidag not only gives us new geographies and temporalities but also highlights the spread of architectural technologies in new ways. It shows both general patterns as well as new and specific problems that would otherwise remain undetected. Figure 9.3 is a draft map displaying the firm's construction projects for private patrons in central Germany. There are prominent clusters in Baden and Württemberg, the home of Dywidag, and notably industrial sites such as those to the west of Berlin or in Merseburg, outside of Leipzig. Another less obvious highlight is Jena, which was a town of slightly more than forty-eight thousand persons at the end of the war. Despite its small size, Jena has the largest cluster of Dywidag buildings of different types compared to any other city: commercial business, commercial manufacturing, institutional, and cultural. The map unambiguously points to what became one of Dywidag's most important clients: the Carl Zeiss firm in Jena that has manufactured optical instruments for many years. Dywidag began building for the Zeiss works in 1906 and was responsible for almost all of the construction at its massive industrial complex.[14] During the war Zeiss specialized in the production of rifle telescopes, binoculars, photographic lenses, and other war-important materials. As is so often the case in modern society, its war industries and profiteering aided in its postwar success, especially in scientific and optical equipment.

Dywidag's help on a postwar 1922 structure would make its partnership with Zeiss famous, and it also changed the construction possibilities for architects of the period. In that year, Zeiss was following up on a 1913 order from the Deutsches Museum in Munich for a new star projection device, one designed to surpass Chicago's Atwood Celestial Sphere from 1912. Atwood's design used a rotating sphere made of sheet metal pierced with small holes that passively allowed light to shine into the interior chamber to mimic the night sky. In contrast, Walter Bauersfeld, a Zeiss engineer and leader of the project, came up with a very different idea. Bauersfeld envisioned using lens technologies developed for the military to create the first mechanism actively to project stars onto a flat surface from within the chamber itself, as is now common in a modern planetarium. For the flat surface, Bauersfeld worked with Dywidag to construct a geodesic dome on the roof of the factory, and for its construction the firm developed an innovative method of spraying concrete to create a light and thin but strong shell (fig. 9.4).[15]

Bauersfeld's mechanism needed a structure that was wide enough to receive the light spread from his projector. Furthermore, such a structure had to be light in weight, since Zeiss wanted the initial "test" dome to be constructed on the roof of the factory. In order to avoid doing damage to the building, Dywidag used the newly developed spray concrete method to create the extremely thin shell that had no need for columnar support. In order to achieve a self-supporting dome, the firm also developed the monocoque technique, in which the skin bears the load of the structure. Once completed, the trial dome proved to be a huge sensation, which resulted in pressure to allow public access to the test site in 1924. In 1925, the Zeiss-Dywidag System, as it came to be known, was premiered outside the factory with the opening of two public planetaria, first in Munich and then Jena, both to great acclaim. Among other architects, Adolf Meyer, Walter Gropius's colleague, immediately took note of the innova-

9.4. Dyckerhoff & Widmann, Jena planetarium showing spray concrete dome method, 1924. Construction photograph. Courtesy of Deutsches Museum.

tive construction in the pages of the avant-garde journal *die form*, calling out the pure tectonic expressiveness of the building.[16]

The mapping process—which included gathering, organizing, and cleaning the evidence in a database structure—pointed to Jena. From there, we could continue to point to other subsequent planetaria that lead to the use of this influential new construction method in a large number of buildings for much more than a single public exhibition of astronomy. The 1929 Dywidag index lists thirteen planetaria that used the Zeiss-Dywidag System, including the planetarium in Moscow. The Adler Planetarium in Chicago and then the Hayden Planetarium in New York, among others, would follow in the 1930s. The index lists another forty-three buildings that Dywidag had constructed using the same technique in that period; they included garages, festival and market halls, train stations, and many other building types.[17] The patented system led to a knowledge exchange among the construction firm, the clients, and the architects, who could now experiment with these new techniques, adding to the active interest in concrete construction that continually expanded in the period.[18]

This last observation drives home the point. Scholars of the history of architecture too often have emphasized in their narrative accounts how the publication of photographs of single buildings, such as the image of an American grain silo reproduced by Gropius in 1913, are fundamental to German architects' interest in concrete construction and vernacular structures. But such a narrow interpretation ignores the day-to-day experience of architects on the building site and in ever-changing built environments that the digital map makes explicit through the visualization of large-scale evidence. Instead, such assessments overlook the important work that construction firms like Dywidag contributed to architectural developments.[19] In sum, and as our examples show, the digital process not only represents archival results but allows us to conceptualize analytically the archival evidence in new and critical ways.

The example from Jena illustrates how digital mapping draws attention to historically significant aspects of the construction industry that may otherwise be ignored or marginalized. This dome was built at a particular moment of public fascination with planetaria and the rapid increase in scientific knowledge of the stars. The Zeiss-Dywidag planetarium at Jena might be a minor planet in the recognized cosmos of architectural history.[20] However, probably the biggest star of the era is oddly absent from the map: Erich Mendelsohn's Einstein Tower in Potsdam (1921). The purpose of the tower was to prove Einstein's theory of relativity by measuring spectral light from the universe. Mendelsohn designed the shell and the layout of the rooms, Zeiss provided the scientific equipment, and none other than Dyckerhoff & Widmann constructed the exterior.[21] Yet for all of its prominence in today's narrative accounts of Weimar architectural history, the Einstein Tower went unlisted in the archival construction index of Dywidag. The reason remains unclear. It may have been left out due to construction problems resulting from the unusual shape of the building—issues that the concrete firm would rather not have emphasized. Instead of a star, it seems, one of Mendelsohn's most famous works is a black hole in the database. It points to the limitations of sources but also emphasizes what absences in the historical record might reveal in terms of other concerns and alternative trajectories. The lacuna also reminds us of an important point with which we started: digital processes are relational to cultural production and social systems. That means that our digital maps do not promise to show a complete account of Weimar architecture any more than they reveal the exact nature of the political economy of construction. Instead, they point indexically to analytical problems that relate the two.

Still, our conclusions also allude to another fundamental art-historical issue: the development of concrete technologies is perhaps more important to gaining an understanding of the relationship between building and society than the scholarly emphasis on the Einstein Tower as a high-profile and singular example. The Zeiss-Dywidag System, for instance, resulted from decades of previous innovations nationally and internationally, and it then began to appear in a wide variety of structures.[22] These buildings would have specific political and social relevance, such as the subsequent use of the system at the 1936 Berlin Olympics sponsored by the National Socialist state or the participation of Dywidag in forced-labor construction activity in World War II. Shell construction has since contributed to military building in the United States as well as some dramatic Cold War monuments, notably in the work of Eero Saarinen. These longer-lasting and more complex connections to patrons, to aesthetic tastes, and thus to society are harder to observe in a single building or even by a single scholar. Mapping the construction industry perhaps rightly dims Mendelsohn's star, not to dismiss it but to enable a view of the other matter of the universe of which it was merely one part. These exploratory methods tell us of something important but also leave the promise of a more complete analysis. They demand ongoing and collaborative work to advance a critical agenda of a social history of art.

Digital Art History and the Social History of Art

The balance between historical evidence and narrative analysis is a challenge methodologically familiar to those engaged in the long chronicle of the social history of art. With its roots in Marxist concepts of history, social art history regards the gap between evidence of production conditions and public reception and artistic meaning as the central conundrum of the field.[23] This move connects to a politics and a way of understanding the complexity of the world by focusing on the struggle within human society made evident in art and its history. Marxist art historians must constantly refine the interpretation of the world as the material complexity of it is increasingly exposed. In this regard, the social history of art—like digital art history—is both a dynamic and an ongoing process of discovery at the same time as it produces analytical and critical results that claim a historical validity.[24]

In our specific analysis here, the visualization of the database of the Dywidag construction firm indicates important analytical points about the reality of the architectural history of early Weimar. It demands in this case the inclusion of a broader field of architectural and vernacular building activity otherwise almost entirely expunged from the art-historical record. Yet, mapping establishes new challenges in relation not only to the evidence but also to the art-historical analytic narrative. The digital maps here point to individual structures, like the planetarium at Jena, that are more important than previously assumed for explaining the adoption of specific materials and new technologies. However, the visualizations are also cautionary tales: they are incomplete and, as we all know, maps "lie."[25] The process of digital mapping—a core method of digital art history—helps to examine and explain evidentiary sources just as it points to the potential for new but not as yet definitive conclusions, such as the role of labor in concrete construction.[26] Thus, mapping mediates between evidence and the social art-historical narrative. As a point of mediation, mapping speaks to the limitations of the former as well as the narrowness of the latter. That is to say, the digital map has the critical function of pushing for a more complex and rigorous understanding of art and society.

Digital art history can embrace the process that characterizes its work not as a critique of its utopic promise but as an essential part of an analytic art-historical project. If social art history has a drive for a total analysis, one that achieves a critical understanding of art deriving from the overwhelming complexity of human experience, it must by definition search for ever greater bodies of evidence, ever more granular sources on class, race, gender, and the struggles that define histories. At the same time, its scholars must constantly refine interpretations and make a critical intervention into the political conditions of the moment. Digital art history is uniquely situated to help expand the evidence of social art history and refine the rigor of its narrative. This can be achieved, however, only by embracing the scale of the project and in turn calling for more scholarly collaboration, which tackling such grand challenges demands. Art history at such a scale has great promise for new critical questions that include, for example, architecture's role in the fundamental human struggle over resources. A collective of scholars is needed, as well as a shared agenda, but also the individual contributions to the whole. It requires more than what one lecture, one article, or one monograph can contain. It requires having confidence in the art-historical process and, simultaneously, de-naturalizing this process as an uncritical daily practice.

Part IV

Pairings

In the nineteenth century, when the comparative method emerged simultaneously in various disciplines, pairing became a primary heuristic technique. Even its most adamant advocates recognized that this was a flawed epistemic operation at best. Especially when pairs were compared, just the mere act of juxtaposing—whether two phonemes, animal skulls, buildings, or entire cultures—forced similarities and differences that would otherwise have been inconsequential. Even while comparing pairs reduced all complexity to background noise, however, it offered an irresistible cognitive advantage. In a world flattened by comparisons, making judgments was easier and the road to action shorter. The chapters in this section put the opportunities, outcomes, and dilemmas of comparing pairs on display. The four chapters analyze first the technique in architectural historiography and urban planning, and then they deploy the practice to uncover ways in which law and literature are relevant to architectural history.

10

Comparative Architecture and Its Discontents

■

ROY KOZLOVSKY

Dominick LaCapra characterized historiography as a conflicted linguistic field in which objectivist, documentary modes of historical knowledge that apply scientific procedures for observing and evaluating evidence interact with the rhetorical dimension of history as a form of writing that reconstructs the past into a living memory.[1] This productive tension is especially relevant to the critique of comparative history. In fields of knowledge such as economics, biology, or sociology, comparison is ordered according to the logic of deduction. It is used for testing a hypothesis and establishing general patterns and laws out of the plurality and heterogeneity of phenomena. Yet the operation is to some degree arbitrary and creative, as "everything more or less resembles or differs from everything else in accordance with the disposition or ingenuity of the observer."[2] Comparativists have the freedom to combine discrete objects and produce relationships where none existed before.[3] In antiquity, comparison was classified as part of *inventio*, not logic, and considered alongside metaphor as a literary trope—the analogy.[4] Plutarch commenced his *Parallel Lives*—a work of comparison that pioneered the integration of biography with history—with a quote from Aeschylus to explain his criteria for comparing Greek and Roman statesmen: "'Whom shall I set so great a man to face? / Or whom oppose? Who's equal the place?'"[5]

Plutarch's moralistic reconstruction of the past as a symmetrical, dramatic pairing of historical and mythical characters leads us to the topic at hand: comparative history.

Comparison and Historical Reconstruction

Beginning with the work of Hayden White, the relation between history as an objective account of the past and a literary form has undergone scrutiny. White argued that in order to render the plurality of facts and events meaningful, historians organize them into narratives—stories that display "coherence, integrity, fullness and closure of an image of life."[6] To expose the constructed nature of historical accounts, he contrasted them with non-narrative forms of historical writing, such as the annals and the anatomy. His example of the anatomy was *Democracy in America*, still regarded as an exemplary work of comparative history. Tocqueville is singled out as one of the few historians who "refused narrative in certain of their historiographical works, presumably on the assumption that the meaning of the events with which they wished to deal did not lend itself to representation in the narrative mode."[7] Beyond this comment, White did not elaborate on the metahistorical status of the comparative mode of history. The contrast he made with narration suggests that comparison may be utilized as an antinaturalistic and de-familiarizing mode of historical reflection.

If we invert White's mode of analysis and consider comparison by its differential with narrative, it can be said to differ in two fundamental ways. First, it does not permit a detailed exposition of facts necessary for a comprehensive representation of objects and events, nor does it account for the possible interrelation between them. Instead, only those features that may be discussed through a common denominator may enter the discussion. Consequently, the unity of the plot gives way to the transcendence of the set of terms by which discrete objects or events are made comparable. As Edward Carr stated, "the historian, in virtue of his urge to understand the past, is simultaneously compelled, like the scientist, to simplify the multiplicity of his answers, to subordinate one answer to another, and to introduce some order and unity into the chaos of happenings and the chaos of specific causes."[8] Comparison, as a mind-shaping mechanism, reorders reality into an easily perceived, rule-governed unity. This effect of language problematizes the evidentiary status of comparative facts. Historians working through differences and similarities must decide which are relevant to their aims; otherwise, as Stanislaus von Moos remarked in his comparison of Loos and Le Corbusier, "it would be a Sisyphean task, and one with little sense, to identify every similarity."[9] To paraphrase Carr, differences and resemblances that do not advance the comparison are "from the point of view of the historian dead and barren."[10] Therefore, comparative history entails the selection and accentuation of differences and similarities so they may fit into the historian's conceptual explanatory system.

Second, while narrative naturalizes the account by aspiring to present things as they really happened to constitute the reader as a moral witness, comparison foregrounds its segmented, additive working mechanism to constitute the reader as a detached observer of a world in which unique things become equivalent and exchangeable according to a common measure. As Chaïm Perelman suggested, it has a "discrediting" effect: "To treat *my* country, *my* family, as *a* country, *a* family is to deprive it of part of its prestige."[11] Since a comparison defines an object relative to another, its claim for certainty is constantly eroded. It is therefore not uncommon for a comparative work of history to conclude with a reflection on the agency of the form: the authors enter a dialogue with the text that problematizes the universality of the method's reasoning.

The contrast with narration provides a convenient starting point for inquiring into its historiographical role, if we keep in mind that the relationship between comparative and narrative modes of historical representation is more complex than suggested by the initial comparison. One consideration is that these forms are rarely found in their pure state and are often intermixed by writers who negotiate the structural constraints and potentialities latent in comparative structures of thought. In another consideration, as suggested by Hayden White's summation of comparison, the relation between comparing and narrating should be examined in relation to the specific historical context in which the comparative act is activated. And in light of LaCapra's assertion that the writing of history entails a "conversation" with other inquirers seeking to understand it, it establishes a dialogue with previous comparative acts.[12] Therefore, a comparative text is not as self-contained as its tight structure suggests.

These initial thoughts on comparative history and its relation to narrative will be brought to bear on the practice of comparing buildings as a means for writing architectural history. What are the implications of comparison to the study of architecture? What are the blind spots of this approach, those aspects of architecture that slip through the comparative gaze or become distorted by it? These questions will be treated historically. Comparative architectural histories emerged in the nineteenth century as the dominant method for inferring the principles that govern the development of architectural styles. After it was usurped by historiographical methods that interpreted the production and reception of works of architecture within a dense network of social forces and cultural formations, the use of comparison continued to crop up at moments of disciplinary crisis as a minor rhetorical practice aimed at destabilizing established narratives of architectural history. This rough historical synopsis would guide analysis of the agency of comparing for architectural history. Special attention would be given to an issue that is specific to art and architectural history—the evidentiary status of visual representations such as plans, drawings, or photographs once they are brought into a comparative relationship.

Systematic Comparisons

The introduction of systematic comparisons into the field of architecture in the middle of the nineteenth century transformed the discipline's historical self-understanding and its relation with other arts. Historians as diverse as Gottfried Semper, Alois Riegl, Heinrich Wölfflin, and Paul Frankl developed their interpretive systems by comparing sets of objects accessible to them in museums and libraries in order to deduce the general principles governing their variations. Their main category of analysis was style, itself a relational concept that can be articulated only by way of comparison. Their aim was both to assemble a series of buildings—and generalize from their common traits the principles of a style—and to discover the rules governing stylistic development by comparing a series in relation to what came before and after it. Two preconditions for this comparative stylistic enterprise are the rise of the comparative method in the natural sciences and the philosophy of history that ascribes to art an ideal toward which it develops through history.[13] The intersection of deductive and teleological modes of interpretation yielded two distinct historiographical models: the empirical and the dialectical. Not without trepidation, the work of Semper and Wölfflin will be treated as exemplars of this development, therefore forcing them into a comparative relationship.

Semper's opus, *Style in the Technical and Tectonic Arts* (1860–1863), transposed to the study of art and architecture methods drawn from two comparative fields of knowledge. The first is comparative anatomy, which examines "plans" of living organisms as a relation between form (morphology) and function (organization). It uses historical records such as fossils to reconstruct the logic of their transformation. The second is philology, which traced common roots and structures across families of languages to chart their separate, historical course of development.[14] Both were predicated upon an epistemic shift in how things are connected to the eye and to discourse. According to François Jacob and Michel Foucault, the Renaissance era organized knowledge in terms of similitude and resemblances. The trope of analogy shaped the literary genre of the comparison of the arts, a theoretical discussion that is generated through the successive comparative treatment of painting and poetry (*ut pictura poesis*), painting and sculpture (two and three dimensions of visual imitation), and architecture with all of the above.[15] Classical thought in turn operated through the synchronic ordering of the diversity of beings into descriptive classification systems composed of independent linguistic terms (organs, structures, types)—as in Durand's theory of architectural types, which parallels Linnaeus's ordering of nature into the homogeneous space of the table. In what Foucault defines as modern thought, objects are both abstracted according to their invisible, interrelated living functions that tie them to the environment and also historicized into separate, discontinuous lineages of development.[16] In its ordering of the plurality of artifacts according to the principle of taxonomy, Semper's *Style* belongs to the emerging modern episteme.[17] It is divided into four sections following the basic techniques of textiles, pottery, carpentry, and masonry, echoing Georges Cuvier's four distinct categories of living organisms. Borrowing from comparative philology, Semper concentrated on architectural motifs and charted their adaptation and reapplication in new cultural or material contexts, where they acquire symbolic meaning as metaphors. The object is finally stylized according to universal aesthetic laws and integrated with other, similarly evolved objects to form a unified style.

Semper's chapter on ceramics will serve as a case study for discussing the tensions generated by the comparative treatment of cultural artifacts. He likens the historical inquiry into the evolution of ceramic vessels to that of reconstructing the transformation of living organisms out of an incomplete record of fossils: "Fossil pots are as interesting for the history of art (and of humanity in general) as the prehistoric remains of plants and animals are for natural history. Pots are the oldest and most eloquent of historical documents. If one examines the pots produced by a given group of people, it is usually possible to say what they were like and what stage of development they had reached!"[18] In associating a taxonomic arrangement of objects according to their function and form with the people who made them, Semper strays from the empiricist logic of scientific comparison. This will be demonstrated in the much-discussed comparison of an Egyptian situla with a Greek hydria (fig. 10.1). The comparison commences with the constants of geography and the laws of physics. Their different forms are associated with their fitness to collect water and transport it. The situla was designed to scoop water from the Nile and to be carried on a yoke, hence its low center of gravity; the hydria was intended for collecting water flowing from a spring and then carrying it on the head, hence its high center of gravity. The ornamental treatment of the situla is shown to have retained the memory of the folds of the older, leather-tube vessel for transporting water. In the next stage of reasoning, the comparison is used to relate the "soaring, spiritual and lucid essence" of the spring-worshiping Hellenes with the Egyptian adherence to the "physical law of gravity and balance" and to position them as "embryos" of each nation's monumental architectural style, which reflects "the respective natures of these people."[19] The comparison rests on Herder's idealist interpretation of art as an organic expression of the inner life of a collective. However, the logic of reasoning in *Style* is to argue for the historicity of the art form, its discontinuous translation, repurposing, and resignification as a metaphor. How then could a single artifact transcend this discontinuous, temporal dynamics to provide an unmediated expression of an entire people? This is possible only by activating comparison as a figure of thought that generates a symmetrical, analogical relation between two forms, two geographies, and two races. Semper's own mode of comparison undergoes a similar transformation to the one he attri-

Situla. Hydria.

10.1. Comparison of Egyptian situla and Greek hydria. From Gottfried Semper, *Style in the Technical and Tectonic Arts* (1860–1863).

butes to cultural objects: he borrows from scientific disciplines the procedure of comparison and adapts it to the field of architecture, while retaining traces of comparison's Renaissance-era epistemic status as similitude—with the result that his comparison becomes metaphorical.

Opposite Semper's empiricism is Wölfflin's dialectical comparative method. As Alina Payne has noted, his comparative endeavor explored the question of why styles change and what the fact that they do change reveals about art and the times in which it is created.[20] The problem of stylistic transition (*Stilwandlung*) is treated philosophically, through a system of polar concepts such as the painterly and the linear, unity and multiplicity, close and open—terms that allow Wölfflin to organize differences and similarities into a meaningful order. The analytical categories for defining a style already presuppose that it emerges in contrast to and in mutual dependence with the preceding style: "We should therefore do better to deduce the characteristics of the baroque style by comparing it with what went before, that is, with the Renaissance."[21] This comparative system draws upon the Hegelian dialectics of identity. Each style necessarily implies the antithetical style as a negative self-image.[22] Wölfflin's conclusion to *The Sense of Form in Art* (1931) hints at this reflexive property, which is the by-product of the comparative operation: "perfection must always permit 'the other' to show through as a perpetually opposing background."[23] As media historians have pointed out, his bipolar art history relied on the technology of slide projectors for placing images of works of art side by side, and Wölfflin voiced his "well-grounded misgiving" of the "one-sidedness" of "pictorial demonstration" and its tendency to exaggerate "for the purpose of clarification (and entertainment)."[24] To explore the relation between the analytical and rhetorical affordances of paired comparisons, I shall concentrate on *Principles of Art History* (1915), in which the comparative treatment is accompanied with photographic diptychs of works of art and architecture.

Principles of Art History is organized in five chapters according to the five polar terms of comparison, a design that allows the work, at great cost, to interpret architecture, sculpture, and painting as obeying the same rules of historical development. The point is to show how Wölfflin negotiates the constraint of the static, symmetrical spatial structure of paired comparisons. In the chapter devoted to multiplicity and unity, Wölfflin matches the street façades of Palazzo Rucellai and Palazzo della Cancelleria and, on the next page, Palazzo Odescalchi (fig. 10.2). Type is compared with type to neutralize other forces acting on a work of architecture, such as symbolism, materiality, urban context, or historical circumstances, to bring into sharp relief the visible differences in their treatment of the façade. The three buildings stand for a three-stage development from the leveled equality of the quattrocento, in which there is no accent of particular interest and the windows, columns, and floors are independent, to the "multiple unity" of the cinquecento, in which the elements are harmonized and fused, and finally to the "unified unity" of the baroque, when the colossal order subordinates the ground floor as its plinth. The series is analyzed in analogy to a comparison made in an earlier section on painting: "A building like the Cancelleria is the architectonic pendant to the form of Titian's *Venus*. . . . And if we have contrasted it with this Velasquez's *Venus* as the type of the living form drawn into absolute unity, we should have no difficulty in producing architectonic parallels to that too. . . . The pure baroque pendant to the Cancelleria is given in Rome in the Palazzo Odescalchi."[25] The Cancelleria thus has the same necessary transitional position relative to Titian's *Venus* in the development of the desire for unity out of the prior experience of the beauty of multiplicity.

Why then did Wölfflin pair a photo of the Cancelleria with the Rucellai rather than the Odescalchi, as was done for Titian and Velázquez? Is it because of later alterations to the building that Bernini's original design could not be photographed in a manner that makes it equal to the Cancelleria, the photograph of which was cropped to resemble in its proportions the Rucellai? Or perhaps architecture must be distorted to fit the pattern deduced from painting? In *Renaissance and Baroque* (1888), Wölfflin compared Bramante's cloister at Santa that even the narrow bays are still independent proportional values, and the ground floor, for all its subordination, remains an element that has a beauty of its own.

Composed, as it is, merely of beautiful separate elements, a building like the Cancelleria is the architectonic pendant to the form of Titian's *Venus*, reproduced above (p. 170). And if we have contrasted with this Velasquez' *Venus* as the type of the living form drawn into absolute unity, we should have no difficulty in producing architectonic parallels for that too.

Hardly is the renaissance type developed when the desire becomes manifest to overcome multiplicity by greater general motives. Then, no doubt, we speak of the "larger outlook" which determined the more comprehensive form. That is wrong. Who could not be convinced from the outset that the patrons of building in the Renaissance—a Pope Julius was among them—sought the highest that human will could reach? But not everything is possible at all times. The form of multiple beauty had to be experienced before unified arrangements became imaginable. Michelangelo, Palladio are transitional. The pure baroque pendant to the Cancelleria is given in Rome in the Palazzo Odescalchi,* which shows in the two upper storeys that colossal order which

Florence, Palazzo Rucellai

Rome, Palazzo della Cancelleria

Rome, Palazzo Odescalchi

from now on becomes the standard for the occident. The ground floor thereby receives the definite character of a plinth, that is, it becomes a dependent member. While in the Cancelleria every bay, every window, even every pilaster has a clearly expressive beauty of its own, the forms here are all handled in such a way that they are more or less fused in a mass effect. The separate sections between the pilasters present no value which could have a meaning outside of the whole. The windows are meant to blend with the pilasters and the pilasters themselves take hardly any further effect as separate forms, but only in the mass. The Palazzo Odescalchi was a beginning. Later architecture continued on the lines here indicated. The Palais Holstein* (to-day the Archiepiscopal Palace) in Munich, a particularly distinguished building by the elder Cuvilliés, is only effective as a moving surface: no bay can be separately apprehended; the windows are blended with the pilasters, which have almost entirely lost their tectonic significance.

It is a natural result of the facts here given that the baroque façade will tend to emphasise individual parts, at first in the sense of a dominating central motive. Indeed, even in the Palazzo Odescalchi, the relation of middle block and wings (invisible in the photograph) already plays a part. Before we go into this, we must make ourselves clear as to whether the schema with the colossal order of pilasters or columns was the only one or the prevailing one.

Even in façades without any vertical combination of the storeys the desire for unity could be satisfied. We reproduce the Palazzo Madama in Rome*— the present Palace of the Senate. The superficial spectator may think that the building does not look essentially different from what was current in the Renaissance. The decisive factor is how far we feel the part as an independent and integral element and how far the detail is swamped in the whole. It is characteristic here that in the striking effect of the total movement, the separate storey retreats, and that beside the lively speech of the window pediments, which co-operate as one mass, the separate window can hardly be felt as a constituent part of the whole. On this line lie the manifold effects which northern baroque achieved even without plastic exuberance. By the mere rhythm of the subordinated windows, a strong impression of mass-movement was imparted to the wall.

But, as we have said, the tendency to the salient point is always present in the baroque: the effect tends to be gathered into a main motive which holds the

10.2. Comparative photographs of the Palazzo Rucellai, Palazzo della Cancelleria, and Palazzo Odescalchi. From Heinrich Wölfflin, *Principles of Art History* (1950). With permission of Dover Press.

Maria della Pace to Michelangelo's Campidoglio, which introduced the colossal order. Michelangelo's disharmonious composition of architectural elements contradicts the "logical" progression in the emergence of a unified sense of beauty out of multiple, harmonized unity, and therefore Wölfflin did not reiterate this comparison in *Principles of Art History*. The architectural sequence of development and the visual evidence to support it are shaped to fit the symmetry of the argument. Yet the situation is more complex. What Wölfflin attributes to the object of representation—that "form has the power to awaken vision"—also applies to his writing of history. This is implied in the discussion of Dürer's *Virgin's Death* in the same chapter: "The picture is an excellent example of a tectonic composition—the whole reduced to clear geometric oppositions ... the principle of multiple unity." In the comparable work by Rembrandt, "the arrangement of obvious side-by-side and clear opposite are replaced by a single weft. Pure oppositions are broken. The finite, the isolable, disappear."[26] What then would be the status of Wölfflin's own method of comparing? Does it organize art and architectural history like a Dürer, constructing multiple polarities to create a balanced whole? Or do the individual comparisons get swallowed up in the whole to create an illusion of one great movement, by which the observer fills the gaps left open by the painterly historian?[27] In the same discussion, Wölfflin associated the independence of the details (multiple unity) in tectonic works of art with the capacity to tell a story, while the baroque is said to be invested in the moment, "but only in this way does the historical picture really speak."[28] To make art "speak," one must charge comparison—itself a "clear," "tectonic," and "multiple" form—with its opposite, the dynamic expressive force of the baroque.

Wölfflin's dialogical system analyzes the past according to the philosophical schema of relational identity and makes it memorable by dramatizing the oscillation between order and movement. The limit of his system is that it stipulates a circular, repetitive historical structure that cannot progress beyond the bipolar terms of comparison. This presented a problem to his modernist successors who were ideologically compelled to portray the modern movement as a rift with past traditions. To establish the legitimacy and historical inevitability of modernism, its early historians constructed genealogical studies of its conceptual origins.[29] Semper's emphasis on the impersonal, rule-governed transformation of technical processes into works of culture did not fit the modernist valorization of originality, which compelled its historians to reactivate Vasari's biographical approach to narrate the rise of modern architecture as the achievement of individual masters.[30]

Comparing Modern Architecture

During the second half of the twentieth century, overreaching rule-governed explanatory systems of architectural development were replaced with historiographical methods that interpret the production and reception of works of architecture within a dense, interrelated network of social forces and cultural formations. The shift to contextual analysis altered the status of comparison, transforming it from a method for deducing general principles into a rhetorical framing device. An exception that proves the rule is *Form Follows Finance* (1995), by Carol Willis. It is one of the few works of comparative architectural history that dares to apply the rules of deductive logic for establishing causal relations between antecedent conditions and outcomes. Willis compares the Chicago and New York skyscrapers like a social scientist: "the aim is to describe the broad principles that affect all skyscrapers and to explain how these universal factors, adapted to the historical land patterns and codes of a particular city, generated typical formal solutions, widely applied for similar sites."[31] However, when discussing the postwar evolution of the American skyscraper, Willis is compelled to abandon the comparative method to account for the rise of the International-style skyscraper. This presents a paradox, since the process of deduction that was essential for constructing the category of style can no longer be used to account for its historical agency.

Comparisons do have an important role in historicizing modernism, but they tend to assume what sociologists call the "mirror-import" form, in which the phenomenon under investigation is relativized by contrasting it with another.[32] Since the result of a comparison depends on the selection of the counter case, it is especially susceptible to selection bias.[33] But as a rhetorical strategy, it affords memorability by countering the reader's expectations in suggesting parallels where none have been observed before. A comparison that repeats Wölfflin's method and at the same time invalidates it is Colin Rowe's 1947 essay "The Mathematics of the Ideal Villa." As this essay has been analyzed by countless scholars, I will focus only on how it negotiates the trappings of mirroring comparisons. The section that compares the rhythmic spacing of Palladio's Malcontenta and Le Corbusier's Villa Garches plan is typical of Rowe's writing style (fig. 10.3). It initially draws a contrast or similarity, states the relationship in terms of inverted symmetry, and concludes with an ambiguous, unresolved observation: "Each house exhibits (and conceals) an alternating rhythm of double and single spatial intervals; . . . the one scheme is, therefore[,] potentially dispersed and possibly equalitarian and the other is concentric and certainly hierarchical; but, with this difference observed, it might simply be added that, in both cases, a projecting element—extruded terrace or attached portico—occupies 1½ units in depth."[34] The effect is to set the text in motion and establish a dialogue between the two buildings, despite the half millennium separating them. In Palladio's villas, the mathematical order is manifested in the plan, while the elevation allows for incidental irregularity. For Le Corbusier, the freedom of the open plan cannot be extended to the façade due to the horizontal slab system, and therefore it is regulated by mathematical relations: "Free plan is exchanged for free section; but the limitations of the new system are quite as exacting as those of the old."[35]

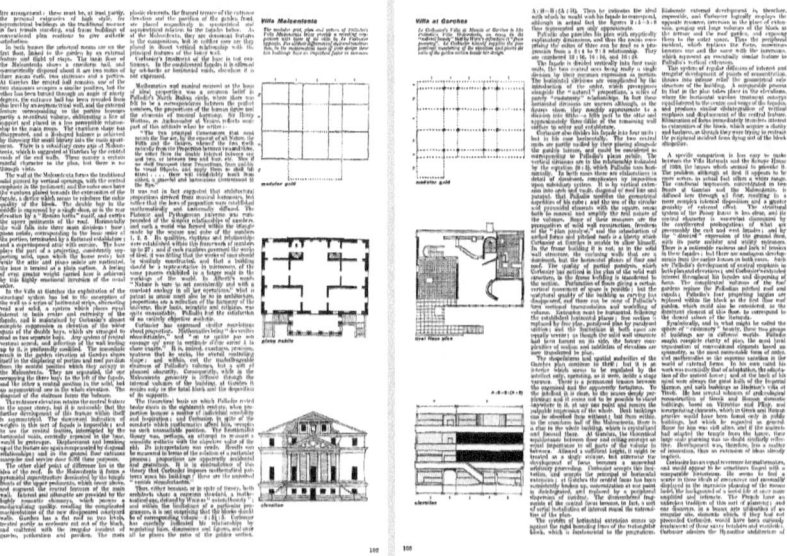

10.3. Original publication of "The Mathematics of the Ideal Villa" in *Architectural Review*, March 1947. Courtesy of Architectural Review.

This argument is reiterated in the rhythmic ordering of the text. As Francis Goyet explains, a comparison is not only an intellectual tool but also an aesthetic form that modulates repetition "by a general schema in which everything tends toward symmetry . . . with the pure fact of counterpoint, of setting two elements beside one another, of comparing."[36] Rowe's essay is structured like a musical fugue with three concentric thematic rings that correspond with the basic ABCBA alternation of the bays in the Malcontenta. It commences with a comparison of Villa Rotonda with Villa Savoye; it then pairs Malcontenta with Garches. Located in the middle is a historiographical discussion of the symbolism of mathematics. The essay then retraces its steps in crab-like motion, revisiting the Malcontenta and Garches pair, as well as the Rotonda and Savoye, and concludes with a statement on the nature of architecture that ties it back to the introductory quote from Christopher Wren. The layout of the illustrations on the printed page accentuates this tripartite structure, bringing closure to an otherwise additive literary operation.

Therefore, it is of major significance that when the essay was republished in 1976 Rowe unsettled its concentric structure by attaching an addendum that comments on the method of comparison: "A criticism which begins with approximate configurations and which then proceeds to identify differences, which seeks to establish how the same general motif can be transformed according to the logic (or the compulsion) of specific analytical (or stylistic) strategies, is presumably Wölfflinian in origin; and its limitations should be obvious. It cannot seriously deal with questions of iconography and content; it is perhaps over symmetrical; . . . [but it] might still possess the merit of appealing primarily to what is visible."[37] None of Rowe's claims can be seen in the visual evidence without the supporting artifice of words. The ambivalent comment establishes a comparative symmetry between the historian and the modernist architect. In the text, Rowe argued that while for Palladio it was ideologically possible to draw upon the Platonic belief in proportions as representing a divine order, for a modern architect such an engagement with antiquity has the ironic status of a "quotation within a quotation." Likewise, Rowe cannot reiterate Wölfflin's deductive method. The work's addendum is therefore analogous in structure to the asymmetric porch that Le Corbusier was "obliged" to project from the rectangular block of Villa Garches (see fig. 10.3).

Rowe's essay became canonical for its suspension of the moment of closure of comparison and for interpreting modernism through an untimely comparable other. Yet to make the buildings comparable, the drawings were purged of scale, furnishing, and surrounding context. Plans other than the *piano nobile* were left out, as were the side elevations. As noted before, to transform facts into evidence, the comparativist selects and abstracts the documentary material—and architectural drawings are especially susceptible to such treatment—in order that the specific cases may verify, through induction, a universal argument about the essence of architecture.

In one of the first works of historical scholarship in which Rowe's comparison is cited, the method is implicitly criticized. Stanislaus von Moos's *Le Corbusier: Elements of a Synthesis* restaged the pairing of Garches with Villa Malcontenta, including Rowe's original set of comparative drawings, while complementing it with two additional comparisons. First, von Moos paired a photograph of the front façade of the Moller House (1928) with an image of Le Corbusier's Planeix House (1927) to establish their uncanny likeness (fig. 10.4). The visual comparison provides evidence of his claim that Planeix was influenced by Loos's Tzara House, while the Moller House was Loos's retort to Planeix, "this time, however, in cold, funereal marble."[38] The paired images support von Moos's claim that in the late 1920s the two architects were engaged in a conscious dialogue as they faced the similar problem of establishing a synthesis between the "severe classical order" and the "intricate and picturesque requirements of the 'functional' plan."[39] Later research suggests that the resemblance was accidental: the original design of Planeix House was elevated on pilotis. The ground level was filled with commercial functions after the client ran into financial difficulties, making Planeix visually similar to Moller House."[40] The second comparison of Le Corbusier's houses, at Weissenhof (1927), with Theo van Doesburg and Cornelis van Esteren's theoretical study of a villa (1920–1922) makes a similar argument regarding the direct influence

10.4. Comparison of Adolf Loos's Moller House (1928) and Le Corbusier's Planeix House (1927). From Stanislaus von Moos, *Le Corbusier: Elements of a Synthesis* (1979). Photographs © Albertina, Vienna; ADAGP, Paris 2015; © G. Thiriet.

of De Stijl on Le Corbusier, while observing that "any comparison with the free and dynamic unfolding of volumes in space, which is typical of the efforts of the Dutch neoplasticists, makes Corbusier's formal vocabulary look closed."[41] As a series, these three comparisons triangulate Le Corbusier's design approach to the house while tracing the influence of other architects on his development. This composite method acknowledges the structural limitation of comparison in accounting for the interaction between the studied units, since the operation treats them as autonomous entities.[42]

The match between Loos and Le Corbusier was canonized in *Raumplan versus Plan Libre*, a comparative study commemorating the latter's 1987 centennial. A well-known offshoot of this project is Beatriz Colomina's *Privacy and Publicity* (1994), a comparative history that works around the tendency of visual comparisons to support formalist interpretations of architectural objects. Following Walter Benjamin's statement that "to live is to leave traces," she draws attention to the placement of items and human figures in photographs of interiors—minor details that are normally excluded from architectural analysis as accidental. The legal scholar Günter Frankenberg defined comparisons that draw attention to "marginal stuff that is normally skipped for lack of relevance" as *deviant comparisons* whose aim is to deconstruct the "lego-centric" conception of the law.[43] Colomina's comparison is critical in the sense that it works against "archi-centric" accounts of domestic environments such as the one developed by Rowe.

The series of comparisons of Le Corbusier with other architects suggests that the form became a medium for theorizing architecture through its relation with history.⁴⁴ Here it is pertinent to quote Max Risselada's introduction to *Raumplan versus Plan Libre*: "The comparison is one of the means through which design can be discussed, of vital importance in a situation in which an educational program can no longer be built up around one, all-encompassing architectural theory."⁴⁵ The justification for comparing resides in a crisis it cannot resolve. Does comparison have a future beyond its pedagogical usefulness?

Panayotis Tournikiotis's *The Historiography of Modern Architecture* (1999), a work that initiated a wave of historiographical research into the histories of modern architecture, including this chapter, suggests that the comparative method may still be relevant if its disassembling, structuring gaze is cast upon historical texts rather than on architectural works.⁴⁶ Tournikiotis "compares and contrasts" nine influential histories of modernism from the 1930s to the 1960s. The large sample is organized into three typologies in terms of their démarche: the "operative," "derogative," and "objective" positions toward their subject matter. The comparative gaze allows Tournikiotis to identify a shared historiographical project: each historian recounted the past in order to trace the roots of modernism and endow it with historical necessity and a stable, unified conceptual foundation, one that could guide the course that architectural practice ought to take. Tournikiotis proposes a cyclic narrative of these architectural histories that is synchronized with the evolving fortunes of modern architectural practice: the first interwar German art historians, who were influenced by Wölfflin's emphasis on visual perception, operated at a time when the movement was in the process of vying for influence; the architect-historians of the middle postwar period addressed the more constructional aspects of structure and function when modernism was already an established movement; and the late phase of the 1960s confronted the modern movement's buildings with its rhetoric at a time when the unity of modernism had begun to dissolve. Tournikiotis claims that underneath this surface division there is a "common denominator," a historicist discursive formation that binds cultural phenomena with a specific historical reality, one that also shapes his own interpretation.⁴⁷ The implicit aim of this temporal model is to position historians and their readers outside this discourse and, through this distancing operation, "to make peace with the past."⁴⁸ To achieve that aim, his account constructs a causality that the method of comparison cannot validate by itself—as Foucault noted in *The Order of Things*, a comparative work that informs Tournikiotis's historiographic project: "It is not always easy to determine what has caused a specific change . . . [it is] highly embarrassing because there are no definite methodological principles on which to base such an analysis."⁴⁹ This leads us back to the initial problem of assessing comparative history in relation to narrative. Is comparison by its structure a counternarrative mode of historical representation, or does it dress it in a different costume that conceals the author's complicity in homogenizing the irreducibility of facts and events by structuring them in a legible conceptual matrix?

To answer that objection we can do no better than to quote Wölfflin's conclusion to *Principles of Art History*, which ended the additive, open-ended format of comparison with a confession of comparative guilt: "Another question is how far we have the right to speak of two types at all. Everything is transition and it is hard to answer the man who regards history as an endless flow. For us, intellectual self-preservation demands that we should classify the infinity of events with reference to a few results."[50] Can comparison overcome its incompleteness? Perhaps the question ought to be reframed, not to challenge the validity of the comparative method for historicizing architecture but rather to ask how comparison, as a relational mode of writing and reading, interacts with and is shaped by the ecology of visual and textual architectural representations—plans, sections, photographs, visual and spatial concepts—that offer themselves as a common ground for comparing.

11

When Baghdad Was Like Warsaw
Comparison in the Cold War

■

ŁUKASZ STANEK

"Baghdad was like Warsaw"—this is how Polish architect Lech Robaczyński recalled his work in Iraq in the 1960s.[1] Robaczyński was part of a group of architects who traveled to Baghdad from socialist Poland after the pro-Western monarchy in Iraq was toppled in the coup led by Colonel Abd al-Karim Qasim in 1958, followed by a rapprochement with the Soviet Union and its Eastern European satellites.[2] This rapprochement initiated three decades of exchanges between Iraq and the socialist bloc motivated by various, and evolving, objectives. Iraqi governments from Qasim's to Saddam Hussein's mobilized Soviet and Eastern European expertise and resources in programs of state-building, economic modernization, and regional diplomacy. In turn, while the opening of the "second" world toward the "third" world since the mid-1950s was informed by visions of socialist internationalism and geopolitical aims, in the wake of the 1973 oil embargo it was economic objectives that became dominant for the debt-stricken Soviet satellite states, which badly needed convertible currency revenues and access to Iraqi crude oil.[3]

When Robaczyński compared Baghdad with Warsaw, he had something quite specific in mind. "Everything we produced was showcased and people flocked to see the plans," he said, likening the huge popular interest in the work of local and foreign architects and planners in Baghdad to the febrile atmosphere during the reconstruction of Warsaw after World War II.[4] In particular, he recalled two master plans of Baghdad, delivered by the Polish design institute Miastoprojekt-Kraków in 1967 and 1973, and presented to Baghdadi professionals and the public at large by means of exhibitions, seminars, and debates.[5]

Yet, at the same time, Robaczyński's statement points to a more general phenomenon: a new comparative environment that emerged in Iraq, and throughout the postcolonial world, during the Cold War. When the untangling of Western European empires opened up Africa and Asia to architectural and planning expertise beyond the former colonial metropolises, the Soviet Union and its satellite countries, later joined by the Non-Aligned Movement and China, offered new sources of knowledge and new candidates for comparison. Within this environment it became possible to juxtapose sites that had never before been thought of together, among them Warsaw and Baghdad.

In the wake of the coup of 1958, professionals from socialist countries challenged the hegemony of Western European knowledge and technology in Iraq. Eastern Europeans argued that not only was their expertise useful for Iraq but also that their position toward the West was similar to that of the Iraqis, given both regions' history of political subordination, economic exploitation, and cultural devalorization by Western Europe. Architects and planners from socialist countries offered to Iraqis architectural tools and planning instruments that had been introduced in Eastern Europe since the late nineteenth century in programs of economic development and cultural emancipation. In this context, comparison became an opportunity and an obligation for Iraqi decision-makers, who compared the proposals of the newcomers with those already in place, including a master plan for Baghdad that British planners had delivered in 1956. When faced with the demand to substantiate their claims, Miastoprojekt planners, too, turned to comparison. They did so in order to demonstrate their professional competence, to provide evidence of the relevance of their earlier experiences for their work in Baghdad, to gain knowledge about the city, to build trust with Iraqi decision-makers, and to construct and maintain a professional community.

This chapter highlights how comparative practices in Baghdad were entangled with Cold War geopolitics in Iraq and its political economy. I argue that this "politics of comparison" needs to be understood beyond questions of ideological representation, which is primarily how comparison across Cold War antagonisms has been addressed by architectural historians, with the Hansaviertel and the Stalinallee in divided Berlin being one paradigmatic pairing. Instead, I show how the comparative urban knowledge produced in Baghdad was part of a broad political, economic, and cultural restructuring of Cold War Iraq and how the involvement of Eastern Europeans in these procedures came with emancipatory potential and dangers for Iraqi decision-makers.

The comparative practice performed by Miastoprojekt planners and their Iraqi counterparts required them to work across fragmented and heterogeneous cartographic documents. They practiced comparison by means of material operations performed on images and extended this approach to a study of Baghdad's urban development. In this chapter I test the ways in which comparison within digital environments, including geographic information system (GIS) software, opens a possibility for a more active, dexterous, and transformative way of producing historiographic evidence—much in the way that the Polish planners conducted comparison. While coming with epistemic risks, such environments provide opportunities for a historian to reflect upon the politics of comparison in Cold War Iraq and beyond.

A Comparative Agency

Even before its occupation by Britain during World War I, Iraq was a destination for architectural and technological expertise from European imperial centers.[6] In the wake of the Ottoman Empire's collapse, Iraq in its mandate status and later the Britain-dependent Kingdom of Iraq became part of the globe-straddling British space of imperial knowledge production and circulation.[7] The eternal day of an "empire where the sun never sets" illuminated Britain's colonies, dominions, and protectorates, juxtaposing them with each other in a fictitious simultaneity and allowing for comparisons between them.

This approach differed from the tradition of collecting prestigious precedents in urban design, whether southern European public squares, revisited by Camillo Sitte in his *Art of Building Cities* (1889), or Athens, Rome, and Haussmann's Paris, referenced by Daniel Burnham in his *Plan of Chicago* (1909).[8] The latter publication included Burnham's own designs for Manila and Baguio in the US-occupied Philippines, thus showing that imperialism widened both commission opportunities for metropolitan planners and their comparative spectra.[9] This was confirmed by first comparative urban studies across multiple continents, including the Town Planning Conference in London (1910), which discussed cities in Europe, North America, and the British colonies, and the International Congress on Urbanism in the Colonies and Countries in the Intertropical Latitude in Paris (1931), which covered cities in Africa, Asia, and Latin America.[10] Colonial urbanism also appeared during the Fourth International Congress of Modern Architecture (CIAM), in 1933, which featured, besides cities in Europe and North America, the cities of Dalat in French Indochina and Bandung in the Dutch East Indies.[11] The congress testified to the double effects of imperialism: the extension of candidates for comparison beyond Europe, as well as the inadequacy of categories developed in the European context for the urban realities in other parts of the world, notably the racially segregated cities in the colonies and the United States.[12]

Comparative practices were conceptualized, developed, and reproduced in the training of architects and planners for service in European empires. At Britain's first full-time course in architecture at the University of Liverpool, for example, architecture was regarded as an international culture of professionals trained both in rationalist, universally applicable methods of design, as well as in empirical methodologies of accounting for regional conditions and solutions.[13]

This training emphasized the adaptation of British architectural and urban typologies to the climatic conditions, construction materials, building technologies, and craftsmanship traditions across the empire.

In the wake of World War II, this pedagogy informed the practice of several prominent Iraqi architects, among them Mohamed Makiya, a graduate of the Liverpool school and the future dean of the Department of Architecture at the University of Baghdad (established in 1959). But after the 1958 coup, the new government embarked on a fundamental restructuring of design and construction industries in Iraq to be facilitated by technical assistance and cheap credits offered by the Soviet Union and its satellites. This restructuring was inspired by Soviet modernization, featuring examples from Eastern Europe and Central Asia, including Tashkent, Samarkand, Dushanbe, Bishkek, and Ashkhabad. These became candidates for comparison for Iraqi cities, with which they shared some climatic conditions and Islamic heritage.[14] Such comparisons were further encouraged by Moscow's argument that the Soviet "liberation" of Central Asia from the "colonial oppression" of tsarist Russia was a precedent of a political, economic, social, and cultural emancipation to which the newly independent countries in Africa and Asia aspired.

Historians of imperial planning mapped its mobilities within the spectrum ranging from "authoritarian imposition" to "synthetic borrowing" of professional knowledge.[15] The colonial metropoles were centers of this expertise, even if it was also exchanged across colonial borders, notably in Ottoman Iraq. Qasim's coup complicated the dynamics of these mobilities, as it opened Iraq to alternative sources of knowledge beyond Western Europe and the United States. What from the imperial archives in Western Europe often appears as a closure of the former colonial markets, conveniently attributed to "nationalism" or "Soviet propaganda," many Iraqi architects and planners experienced as a multiplication of flows of knowledge and a widening of horizons of choice.[16] This was the case because the new candidates for comparison from Eastern Europe did not replace the previous ones, and British and Western urban regulations, knowhow, technologies, and teaching curricula continued to have an impact in Iraq.

Iraqi decision-makers made an effort to diversify the candidates for collaboration. For example, they distributed the competition brief for the Baghdad Electricity Board Building (1961) in Western and Eastern Europe, as well as in the Arab world.[17] They also invited Eastern Europeans to Baghdad's International Trade Fair, where machinery, prefabrication systems, industrial facilities, and building typologies were displayed and compared across and within Cold War geopolitical divisions.[18] For Iraqi architects, planners, and administrators, however, comparison was often a frustrating experience, as it confronted them with incommensurable standards and diverging professional traditions. But it was also emancipatory, because it challenged the hierarchy of power and prestige inherited from the colonial period, and it put Iraqis into the position of appraisers of metropolitan knowledge.[19] It also questioned the presumed coherence of Western expertise by dismantling its components and combining them with knowledge from other sources.

Both empowerment and frustration are readily visible in the reports about Miastoprojekt's master plans written by Iraqi and foreign professionals. After their arrival in Iraq, the Poles soon learned that the comparative environment in Baghdad was not just an opportunity for them to assert themselves in competition with more established actors. It also meant a high level of scrutiny of their own work by Iraqi decision-makers, who were often educated in the United Kingdom, and increasingly in the United States, and who were sometimes skeptical about Eastern Europeans. At every stage of the work on the master plans, Miastoprojekt planners needed to substantiate their decisions vis-à-vis the Consulting Board for the Affairs of the Master Plan, a body that included architects, administrators, and professors from the University of Baghdad's Department of Architecture. Beirut-based UN experts who visited Baghdad were also involved in the assessment of the plan. Consultants on the plan included professionals at the Department of Architecture, the Association of Iraqi Architects, and the Union of Iraqi Engineers.[20] In parallel to the work on the plans, Miastoprojekt planners participated in the municipality's planning committee, which decided where to place new buildings in the city.[21] As UN advisor Sayed Shafi recalled, this practice provided training for the municipality's planning staff and officials and accustomed them to the master plan before its official acceptance.[22] It resulted in an increasing professionalization of the planning culture in Baghdad and elsewhere in the country, which Iraqi historians counted among the biggest impacts of the master plan.[23]

The Poles' way of working differed from that of other foreign planners in Baghdad, including the British firm Minoprio, Spencely, Macfarlane, which produced the previous master plan of Baghdad (1956), and Doxiadis Associates, a Greek firm that produced an outline for the city plan (1958).[24] The most obvious difference was the bulk of the plans and their accompanying documentation: twenty-three pages for the British plan versus four volumes for the final plan prepared by Miastoprojekt. This documentation was produced by a large, interdisciplinary team of Polish professionals based both in Baghdad and at numerous universities in Poland. That team's size, composition, and the length of its stay in Iraq were facilitated by Polish trade agencies, which exploited the differences between the political economy of socialist foreign trade and that of Western actors. Notably, by manipulating the exchange rate of the Polish currency (inconvertible on international markets), decision-makers in Warsaw secured resources for an extensive urban survey of Baghdad.[25]

But this large amount of material also stemmed from the plan's mode of presentation. Rather than being a set of definitive decisions, Miastoprojekt's plan documented the planning process itself. The presentation of each functional

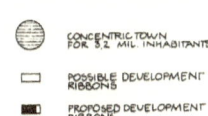

11.1. "Master Plan of Baghdad: Variants of Town Development." Town Planning Office, "Master Plan of Baghdad," 1967, vol. 1B, 4/III. Private archive, Kraków, Poland.

component of the master plan, such as housing, followed the same pattern: quantification of existing housing conditions in Baghdad, estimation of future housing needs as a function of increases in population and employment, and the spatial distribution of housing in the city. Since at every stage of the design process the planners were working with uncertain and incomplete data, conclusions were presented as alternative scenarios. This included, in particular, several models of physical development of the city and their variants (fig 11.1).[26]

Planning by means of alternative variants, complemented by the comparison of their methodological assumptions, data requirements, risks, and advantages, was a way for Miastoprojekt planners to support the conclusions of their work. When suggesting urban standards (e.g., number of hospital beds needed per thousand inhabitants) the planners estimated Iraq's capacities and goals in reference to standards applied in India, the Middle East, and Western and Eastern Europe.[27] They validated the proposed increases in certain amenities, such as theaters and concert halls, by the experience of Nowa Huta, the new industrial town in Poland designed by Miastoprojekt, since the late 1940s.[28] References to socialist countries, newly independent countries in Central Asia and the Middle East, nations in Western and northern Europe, and the United States showed that old paradigms were not simply replaced by new ones.[29] Rather, foreign planners in Iraq were expected to substantiate and validate their proposals in view of competing bodies of expertise from across professional cultures and practices.

Models and Simulations

Substantiating Miastoprojekt's decisions was just one among many reasons for the Polish planners' use of comparison in Baghdad. They also compared historical maps, studies, and aerial photographs of the city in order to understand Baghdad's historical development since the Ottoman period and its water management, transportation network, and housing needs. These data often included widely diverging estimates of Baghdad's urbanization processes, for example its population growth, provided by various Iraqi ministries, UN experts, and the master plans prepared by Minoprio and Doxiadis.[30] Miastoprojekt planners used those prior plans not only as sources of data about Baghdad but also in order to assess the impact of earlier planning decisions on the city's urbanization and to distinguish their own plans from those of their predecessors.

Some of the British planners' decisions were upheld by Miastoprojekt, including the green belt, the general ovoid shape of the city, and the principle of the neighborhood units.[31] By contrast, Polish planners took issue with Minoprio's proposal of a threefold expansion of the urbanized area without proper phasing. They argued that it would lead to a "scattered city," resulting in excessive costs for infrastructure and public transport.[32] In particular, Miastoprojekt planners contrasted the large-scale demolitions of the Ottoman-era urban fabric recommended by the British plan with their own proposal for the extensive preservation of the historical districts of Baghdad, including the district of Kadhemiya, built around a revered Shia mosque.[33] Polish planners stressed that this proposal reflected the experience of the reconstruction of Warsaw's Old Town, which negotiated the re-creation of its historical image with the requirements of mass mobility. In line with the Iraqi regimes' instrumentalization of Baghdad's history as part of the nation-building process, the planners compared both cities in terms of the pedagogical roles played by their monuments and the urban fabric. They argued that as a "school for educating the Iraqi nation in the spirit of studying and appreciating their great national heritage," Baghdad was indeed like Warsaw.[34]

These comparative practices in Miastoprojekt's field office in Baghdad often centered on cartographic documents: maps, plans, and diagrams. Miastoprojekt planners often accessed these images, which had been part of earlier urban surveys or planning documentation, in isolation from the texts, drawings, and references that originally had accompanied them. Their appearance of immedi-

11.2. Architect Władysław Leonowicz in Miastoprojekt's field office in Baghdad, no date. Private archive, Kraków, Poland.

ate accessibility was as much an illusion as it was an opportunity. The planners took that opportunity by producing maps that represented Baghdad with varying degrees of speculation, sometimes as hypothetical as the master plans that followed. This blurring of borders between a map and a plan was reinforced by their similar ways of production, based on the layering of images and their tracing.

This procedure was captured in a photograph taken in Miastoprojekt's field office in Baghdad (fig 11.2). The photograph shows architect Władysław Leonowicz, a member of the Miastoprojekt team, in front of a large-format plan for Kadhemiya. Clipped to this plan is a smaller drawing, probably an alternative land-use scheme for the area around an existing wharf. By pinning this drawing to the larger plan, the architects were able to compare and assess both designs. To produce such a composite drawing one can assume that the architects first cut a piece of paper that fit the area in question in the same scale as the Kadhemiya plan. They pinned the paper onto the district plan and traced the outline of the riverbank and the boundaries of the area. They probably then moved the traced drawing to a drawing board and drew a new layout starting with a grid. Then they would have pinned the smaller drawing back onto the larger one and created a composite image. They could flip the smaller drawing up and down to examine both versions of the layout in the context of the district plan.

If any of this is true, one can begin to see comparison of images not as their juxtaposition, which was how comparison was practiced in Central European art history by the late nineteenth century.[35] Rather, comparison appears as a series of material operations: layering, framing, folding, trimming, rescaling, aligning, and tracing.

The tracing, trimming, and folding of documents seem far away from the conventional practices of historians. Yet their professional habitus is changing in view of the digitization of archival materials that produce new ontologies of historical data. The availability of digital photographs and scans of archival documents facilitates ways of historiographic work that are similar to Miastoprojekt's transformative, dexterous, and experimental operations. They may be particularly useful for researching Baghdad's urbanization during the Cold War and the impact of Miastoprojekt's planners on these processes, as such research requires coming back to the sources used by these planners themselves: dispersed and fragmented, heterogeneous and incongruous, detached from their accompanying commentary, and often accessible only as poor-quality monochromatic copies.

Such study may begin with layering cartographic images in order to compare them, whether in an editor of raster graphics (bitmaps) or by georeferencing them within a GIS environment. The latter procedure includes rescaling, rotating, and skewing maps and plans so that they fit the real-life geographical coordinates. Each of these steps, however, results in some loss of information. For example, enlarging a land-use map from a smaller scale to overlay it with one in a larger scale points at scale as an index of precision and not just of size. When these steps are actively logged rather than just glossed over, they document the diversity and sometimes incommensurability of the compared maps, including their scale, orientation, or projection system.

Opportunities for registering such differences grow exponentially when raster images are translated into vector graphics, or "shapefiles" in a GIS environment. Each shapefile is an object-oriented database consisting of discrete objects grouped into three parent classes of points, lines, and polygons. Objects in each class branch into more specific ones, characterized by attributes (graphic, textual, or numerical) and functionalities, including the ability for some classes to be clustered together.[36] Far from being a purely technical procedure, the translation from raster into objects populating shapefiles is an interpretive one. This includes not only interpreting partially preserved or discolored material but also negotiating the frequent inconsistencies in the symbology of a map. Variations among categories, such as "housing" or "social facilities," and their subdivisions become an opportunity for a historian to record and reflect upon the specificity of scientific, technological, and professional regimes within and across which the planners worked, as well as their assumptions and omissions. The latter include, for example, the fact that Miastoprojekt planned the distribution of mosques in

- ▨ Residential use in the 1973 master plan
- ■ Gross residential land use in 1985
- ▧ Tigris belt (1973 plan)
- ☐ Planned area of Baghdad (including the Green Belt)

11.3. Comparison between residential areas in Baghdad surveyed in 1985 (by the Japanese Consortium of Consulting Firms) and the housing layouts foreseen by the 1973 master plan (Miastoprojekt-Kraków). Drawing by Ł. Stanek; postproduction by Kacper Kępiński.

Baghdad without differentiating between their denominations, thus avoiding a political controversy but also obscuring the social reality of the city.

Shapefiles lend themselves to manipulations that can be differentiated into "models" and "simulations," a distinction introduced by historians of cybernetic and nuclear weapons research, climatology, and biology in the Cold War.[37] Modeling is a recursive process of manipulating a digital representation, or their series. This may include comparing maps of Baghdad from the late 1950s with plans produced by Miastoprojekt in the course of the two following decades, and with surveys from the 1980s, when Japanese planners plotted the city's land uses, among them housing (fig 11.3). Yet the comparison between the Japanese survey and Miastoprojekt's master plan requires a series of translations between their categories, in particular the merging of the seven categories of housing from the master plan into the single one presented by the survey ("gross residential land use").[38] Another form of modeling would be a study of the urban standards that underlay the designs of Baghdad's neighborhoods in the 1980s. The reconstruction of indicators of habitation density, catchment areas of public amenities, number of parking places, and square meters of green space per inhabitant as implemented in specific designs, when compared with urban standards introduced by Miastoprojekt, provides clues for assessing the regulatory impact of the master plan on Baghdad's urbanization.[39]

At the same time, a model can be expanded toward a "simulation," or an inquiry that tests hypotheses and rules out competing explanations.[40] While comparison of planning documents is often concerned with numbers—habitation densities, catchment areas, radii of social facilities, traffic indicators—simulations allow historians to read these data in view of their technopolitical conditions and consequences. This approach leaves behind the concept of a container-space, which, as scholars have pointed out, is the ontological assumption of a GIS database, and it promises to open that database toward an understanding of Baghdad as produced and reproduced by practices that are not only material but also representational, imaginary, and lived.[41] For example, doing a comparison of housing densities in both Miastoprojekt plans helps to unpack the controversies about the introduction of multifamily housing in Baghdad, which straddled concerns about welfare distribution, political loyalties, and cultural and national identities. The comparison of traffic flows planned in and around Kadhemiya challenges the discourse of heritage preservation and its vagaries, from the celebration of Baghdad's history under Qasim to the politics of preservation under Saddam Hussein during the Iran-Iraq War. A study of urban standards regulating catchment areas of education, health, cultural, and religious facilities draws attention to visions and realities of everyday life in Baghdad and their relationship to the program of Arab socialism as advocated by the Baath Party. Each of these inquiries builds upon the GIS database and interrogates it in view of an expanded range of historical sources.

Models and simulations are means for approximating the knowledge of Baghdad produced by Miastoprojekt planners based on the cartographic materials available to them, for estimating their horizons of choices, and for evidencing the impact of the master plans on the development of the city. But these procedures come with considerable epistemic costs. Besides the reductive ontologies of space presupposed by most GIS-based studies, as critics of historical GIS have pointed out, there is also the incommensurability between the often ambiguous and enigmatic character of historical sources and the quantitative nature of databases.[42] Others objected more fundamentally to a historiography that privileges cartographic sources and thus tends to favor the view of the producers of these documents, which are often entangled with state and military surveillance, normalization, policing, correction, and racialization.[43] In addition to these concerns, GIS-based studies of cartographic documents from Cold War Baghdad may result in yet another type of obfuscation. Such studies are unable to register antagonisms around the legitimacy, reliability, and prestige attributed to cartographic materials, as well as the negotiations that resulted from their confrontation by actors on the ground. In other words, when read in isolation from a broad range of historical sources, digital models and simulations risk obscuring what I have called the politics of comparison. This politics included, in particular, the high stakes and dangers for Iraqi decision-makers and professionals that resulted from extending the candidates, terms, and positionalities of comparison beyond those derived from Western centers.

Unforgetting the Cold War

Cold War politics of comparison made a surprising reappearance in August 1982 at a conference on the adaptive reuse of historical cities that was organized in Cambridge, Massachusetts, by the Aga Khan Program for Islamic Architecture at MIT. Among the speakers were John Warren and Roy Worskett, the British architects commissioned to deliver a new plan for Kadhemiya. In the published proceedings, they summarized Miastoprojekt's recommendation to "demoli[sh] the slums around the shrine of Kadhimiyeh [sic]."[44] After the proceedings of this conference reached Poland, they caused fury among those who had been in charge of the planning of Kadhemiya. Among them was Andrzej Basista, an architect, scholar, and educator who had published two substantial reports about Kadhemiya in 1976.[45] In a letter to the British designers and in his later book published in Polish (1995), he pointed out that Miastoprojekt's plans from 1972 and 1973 did not recommend the demolition of the urban fabric in Kadhemiya. Rather, they only accommodated the illegal demolitions of that fabric that were taking place in parallel with the planning process. Like his colleagues had done before in Baghdad, Basista presented this account using comparative means. He published a sequence of four line drawings that showed the changing reality around the mosque, juxtaposed with the shifting approach of Miastoprojekt's planners (fig 11.4).[46]

Basista's claims were consistent with the account of Iraqi architectural historian Ihsan Fethi, who showed that the transformations of Kadhemiya resulted from a confusing negotiation between various actors in Baghdad, among whom Miastoprojekt planners rarely had the last word.[47] But this controversy also testifies to something else. Basista was invited to Cambridge to participate in the 1982 conference, but he was prevented from traveling to the United States—and from making his voice heard—because of martial law that began in Poland

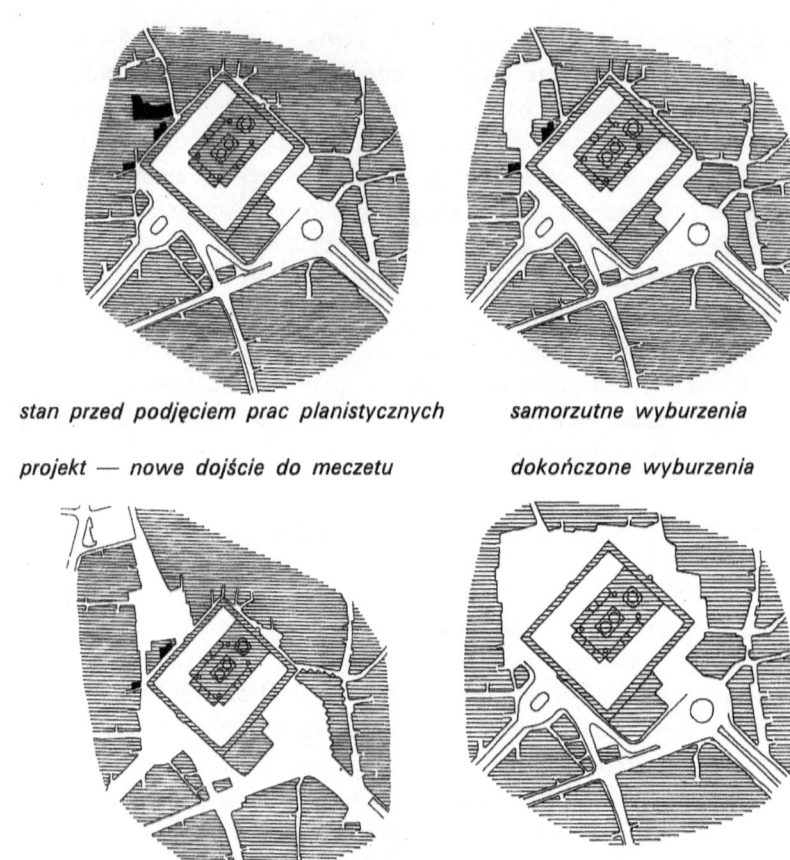

11.4. Kadhemiya, 1972–1973. Top: "Condition before the planning work began" and "Illegal demolitions." Bottom: "Design: new approach to the mosque" and "Finished demolitions." From Andrzej Basista, *Opowieści budynków: Architektura czterech kultur* (Warsaw and Kraków: PWN, 1995), 367.

in December 1981.[48] His letter to Warren and Worskett remained unanswered, and, unsurprisingly, his drawings from the Polish-language publication remained unacknowledged.[49]

Just as Cold War geopolitics and its political economy conditioned the possibility of the co-production of comparative knowledge between the second and the third worlds, so too did they facilitate the active forgetting of this knowledge in the "first" world. During the Cold War, Western access to this knowledge was often filtered, and by the 1990s the active forgetting of it had been reinforced by the "creative destruction" of research institutions in postsocialist Eastern Europe and by their destruction *sans phrase* in Iraq after the US-led invasion in 2003 (in which Poland participated). This forgetting was not just a result of the isolation of Eastern Europe or its particular languages but also the consequence of a systematic devaluation of knowledge production in socialist countries that had taken place in the Cold War, when Western scholarship increasingly saw this knowledge as ideological and unreliable.[50]

This devaluation was rarely revised after the fall of the Berlin Wall. While this particular architectural event has been celebrated as indicative of the elimination of Cold War barriers, these barriers were disappearing in a highly selective and asymmetrical manner. A case in point would be the vibrant debates in "new comparative urbanism" that envisage "new geographies of imagination and epistemology in the production of urban and regional theory."[51] This was how, in the wake of the Cold War, Ananya Roy, Jennifer Robinson, and others challenged the universalistic assumptions of concepts derived from Western debates, experiences, and imaginations and called for cities of the Global South to become sites for theoretical production.[52] For Robinson, there are no privileged sites for theory-building, and any city could be thought "through" any other city in an instance of "experimental comparison."[53]

When envisioning a plan for Baghdad through the lens of Warsaw, as well as Kabul through Tashkent, Algiers through Bucharest, and Conakry through Zagreb, architects, planners, and scholars from socialist Eastern Europe and their counterparts in postindependence Asia and Africa had been performing such experimental comparison. Accordingly, one possible conclusion from this chapter would be to extend the pedigree of new comparative urbanism. The work of Miastoprojekt in Baghdad would be just one example among many, in addition to studies of architecture and urbanization in the Global South by Soviet planners and historians who tapped into the Soviet experiences of Central Asia.[54] Other examples include the comparison between the Eastern European and West African countryside by Hungarian architects, as well as comparative studies by Ghanaian and Eastern European regional planners, to mention just a few.[55] This work also included dissertation research by South American, African, and Asian scholars about urbanization in their countries—research that was carried out at Eastern European institutions or those newly established in the Global South—as well as a reverse movement of ideas, such as attempts at implementing the Chinese experience of laying out special economic zones in Eastern Europe in the 1980s.[56]

However, in spite of the continuities between these experiences and the current comparative debates, their differences are more striking. This chapter has suggested two of them. First, it pointed out the comparative agency of local professionals and decision-makers, who juxtaposed and assessed expertise coming from various centers and applied it to the tasks at hand. In other words, whether "Baghdad was like Warsaw" was not up to the Polish planners to decide; rather, this decision was part of a politics of comparison that was negotiated by Iraqi actors. Second, this agency was informed by knowledge produced beyond former imperial centers in Western Europe. New sites of knowledge production were established in the socialist countries and in the Global South, including the Department of Architecture at the University of Baghdad. Their geography was facilitated by the geopolitics of the Cold War and its political economy, and it contrasts with the geography of the new comparative urbanism. The latter's proponents offer to dislocate the candidates of comparison beyond London, Paris, Toronto, New York, and Los Angeles while at the same time stabilizing these very cities as centers of comparative knowledge. Just as the protagonists of this chapter made strategic use of their distance from the world capitalist system in order to produce a new type of knowledge about Baghdad, so too is the gap between their experience and current comparative debates an opportunity for historicizing the political economy of comparative urbanism, old and new.

12

Forensic Architecture as Symptom

ANDREW HERSCHER

I see our architecture graduates entering all the fields . . . including the hated field of forensic architecture. —Roger Montgomery

Forensics helps widen architecture's mission. —Headline of *New York Times* article by Michael Kimmelman

In 2008, McGraw-Hill Professional Press published *Architectural Forensics*, a book by the architect Sam A. A. Kubba; in 2010, the journal *Radical Philosophy* published "Forensic Architecture: Only the Criminal Can Solve the Crime," an essay by the architect Eyal Weizman.[1] Each text—the first a handbook for aspiring professional practitioners and the second a historical and theoretical exegesis—staged itself as an introduction to "forensic architecture." Yet each was concerned with a rather different subject.

In Kubba's book, "forensic architecture" is practiced within insurance claim assessment, facilities management, and contract disputes.[2] In Weizman's essay, forensics acquires "an architectural dimension" when, in the context of investigations of international humanitarian law and human rights violations, ruins created in the course of violent conflicts are transformed from the simple evidence of violence into "material witnesses"—sources of knowledge about that violence.[3]

Kubba describes *Architectural Forensics* as "a unique handbook in that it deals with virtually all of the topics needed to enter the forensic architecture profession"; it is one of a large number of volumes that Kubba has authored on "professional practice" in architecture.[4] Weizman's essay was part of a larger investigation of contemporary forensic practices in human rights and humanitarian contexts that subsequently yielded an interdisciplinary doctoral research program, exhibitions, and numerous collaborations with scholars, artists, and architects, as well as a nomination for the 2018 Turner Prize, the most prestigious award for contemporary British visual artists. Weizman also included a modified version of the essay in his 2012 book, *The Least of All Possible Evils: Humanitarian Violence from Arendt to Gaza*.[5]

Despite their very different genres and ambitions, however, it may still be somewhat surprising that these parallel expositions of "forensic architecture" had so very little in common. In the years before publishing *Architectural Forensics*, Kubba—CEO of the Iraqi American Chamber of Commerce—worked as a consultant to the United Nations Office for Project Services in Iraq and could have easily encountered scenes of urbanized conflict of the kind that Weizman's forensic architecture has documented and analyzed.[6] Reciprocally, in the article "Forensic Architecture," Weizman provides a historicization of forensic architecture that could have easily noted its emergence and development within insurance claim assessment, facilities management, and contract disputation as described by Kubba. And yet, neither of these texts on "forensic architecture" paid attention to the "forensic architecture" of concern to the other.

In 2017, after a proliferation of publications on what Weizman "would like to refer to as a 'forensic architecture'," he published perhaps his summa on the subject: *Forensic Architecture: Violence at the Threshold of Detectability*.[7] Here, Weizman for the first time noted the existence of a forensic architecture that preceded and in some way paralleled his own practice of the same: those *other* forensic architects, he writes, referring to Sam Kubba's *Architectural Forensics* and another introductory text, "deal with 'the application of architectural facts to legal problems.' ... The legal context is most often an insurance dispute, for which forensic architects provide reports or testimonies under oath."[8] Weizman now posed his project as an "expansion" of a preexisting forensic architecture: "Forensic architecture can exit the specialized framework of insurance disputes and extend the lines of causality originating from architectural failure. One of the most important contexts in which an expansion of the terms of forensic architecture is relevant and urgent is that of armed conflict."[9]

Trading on normative concepts of humanitarian and human rights law as moral structures, Weizman reframes forensic architecture as a protagonist in international courts and tribunals "imbued with the power to imprison violators of war crimes, and to prosecute crimes against humanity and genocide."[10]

Law and its protocols of judgment have historically furnished historiographic models; describing the relationship between history and law, Carlo Ginzburg notes that "since the beginnings in ancient Greece of the literary genre we call 'history,' the relationship between history and law has been very close."[11] Figured in relation to "law," Ginzburg suggests, historical evidence is approached as potential "proof": "a transparent medium ... an open window that gives us direct access to reality."[12] Similarly, Hayden White has argued that this desire for historical truth places historical narrative in relation to legal narrative, each structured by presumptions of moral authority and demands for moral meaning.[13]

Law's bearing on history has only weakened as, under the influence of poststructuralism, postcolonialism, feminism, and other anti-essentializing projects, historiography turned away from positivist attempts to ascertain objective truth and moved instead toward various sorts of situated knowledge. The historiographic turn away from law as a model for history, then, historically preceded forensic architecture's turn toward humanitarian and human rights law as its model for architecture. In the context of this turn, Weizman's project recuperated law—but architecturally instead of historiographically. What does this recuperation reveal about architecture as the basis for legal evidence and narrative? What does it reveal about "law" as differentiated between the nation-state and the international order? What do the seemingly different identities of the two versions of forensic architecture in architecture—as discipline, discourse, or profession—reveal about architecture itself as a structure for evidentiary and narrative protocols? The following will address, albeit briefly, these questions.

Insurance Liability, Expert Witnessing, and the Emergence of Forensic Architecture

Chicago, 1892: after the city's rapid reconstruction in the wake of the great fire of 1871, new buildings began to collapse. When the seven-story Young Building fell less than a year after its completion, killing seven people and injuring many others—the "Pearce Street catastrophe," according to the *Chicago Daily Tribune*—the city coroner held an inquest to determine the cause of the building's failure. Present along with the coroner were the former Cook County architect, the city building commissioner and several of his building inspectors, the owner of the building and his lawyer, the building's contractors and some of their employees, several US government weather observers, relatives of the victims, and, according to the *Tribune*, "many who had come out of the building alive . . . known by their bandages and bruises."[14]

The inquest's jurors were initially told that they would have to decide whether the building collapse was due to a cyclone or faulty construction. After a government weather observer testified that the storm on the day of the building's collapse did not reach cyclone levels, however, two other witnesses were brought to the stand—a Mrs. Weynn and her daughter. Each testified that the building was struck by lightning, putting "faulty construction entirely out of the way of one of the causes of the collapse."[15]

Then, however, "sensational evidence" emerged: people residing near the collapsed building testified that the building had begun to fall apart even before the storm had reached full strength. The next day, according to the *Tribune*'s account, all sorts of building detritus was shown in court, including bricks that were "ham-shaped and egg-shaped, and of other designs greatly out of line for brick." The newspaper's account indicated that "if they [the odd bricks] were used, as the jurors seemed to think, the wonder is how the masons were able to build at all" (fig. 12.1).[16]

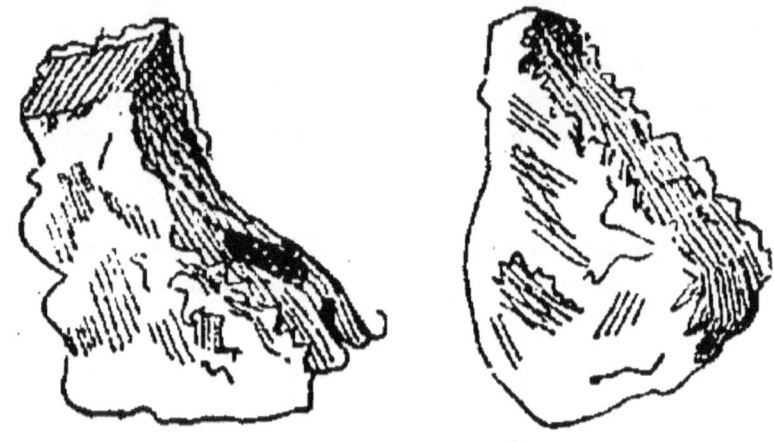

> **Examining the Witnesses.**
>
> The first witness called at the morning session was P. J. Miniter, contractor, of No. 43 Pearce street. He said he had twenty years' experience in building, and that he had ex-
>
> TWO SPECIMEN BRICKS.
>
> amined the ruins of the Young building. The mortar, he thought, was as good as was used for laying common brick in the average building.

12.1. "Curious Bricks." From "Afraid of Its Wall: Witnesses Saw Cracks in the Young Building," *Chicago Daily Tribune,* April 10, 1892, 1.

The jurors then called a series of expert witnesses to interpret the building's construction and collected debris. P. J. Miniter, a contractor who had examined the ruins, noted the adequacy of mortar, brick anchors, and girder strapping but then explained that the mortar had not had time to set properly, causing structural vulnerability to wind and rain.

By contrast, A. W. Rycroft, a bricklayer employed on the building's construction, testified that the brick used was of good quality, as were other building materials. John Vanderpool, a metal contractor on the building, testified that there were no lug bolts to hold girders together on column caps and corporals. A neighbor testified that he saw "the walls spread between the second and third floors" as the building collapsed. Other neighbors testified to seeing jagged cracks on the building's façade as soon as it was completed. Two others testified to seeing a lightning flash—but one saw the flash before the building began to collapse and another saw it after the collapse.

It was the next testimony, by bricklaying contractor John Conway, that was decisive. Conway pointed out numerous flaws in the building's construction; the *Tribune*'s account narrates what followed:

> Juror Hall rose solemnly. He held in his hand a large charred substance, knotty and much warped. "Was this brick struck by lightning?" he asked slowly. Until then few persons in the room knew that the substance referred to was a brick. "O, no," replied the witness, after examining it, "that is a brick which was at the bottom of the kiln. You see that it has been warped from burning. Such bricks are of no use and are thrown away." Mr. Conway did not think any contractor would use such material in building; he knew he wouldn't. When he was informed that the "brick" he had examined had been picked up from a great pile of similar ones in the debris of the wrecked house he exhibited his surprise.[17]

The scene that coalesced around the presentation of what the *Tribune* called the Young Building's "curious brick" could be placed within a genealogy of either Kubba's or Weizman's forensic architecture: it took place not only as an examination of what Kubba called "non-conformity with design expectations" but also as an examination of the ruins, which Weizman called a "source of knowledge . . . of the events that lead to a building's destruction."[18] As such, the scene offers a vivid example of the recruitment of architects and other participants in the building industry as expert interpreters of architecture in juridical contexts at the end of the nineteenth century in the United States. This was the threshold of the "liability century," the era in which insurance and legal liability would increasingly come to mediate the risks and threats of a newly urbanized, mechanized, and industrialized society.[19]

Architectural history has tended to register the emergence and development of the insurance industry implicitly, tracking, for example, the buildings that insurance companies were commissioning architects to design in the early twentieth century as precursors to the skyscraper.[20] But multistory buildings, along with machines, railroads, and then automobiles, were also sites of public danger in the liability century, and part of the expertise of emerging professions like architecture was to protect against this danger. For example, equipment for circulation, from elevators to stair treads to flooring, was advertised and specified in terms of its safety and thus its ability to protect building owners against damage suits.[21] Yet architects were not only involved in preventing injury and damage; they also became involved in testifying to their causes. By the

1890s, then, legal discussion of expert witness testimony included architects as building experts, along with the mechanical experts, railroad experts, insurance experts, patent experts, and other authorities who professed upon the injuries and damages inflicted in and by the modern built environment.[22]

Within architectural discourse, professional journals like the *American Architect and Building News* explicitly pursued the task of educating architects as "expert witnesses" in the course of scripting the forms and processes of architectural professionalization.[23] By 1909, according to the *American Architect*, "expert testimony by architects has become quite frequent of late in our courts" as "few building controversies are disposed of without the giving of more [or] less evidence by members of the profession who qualify as experts."[24]

The type and number of building controversies that found their way to courts vastly expanded with the increase in architects' exposure to legal liability. When architecture became a profession at the end of the nineteenth century in the United States, the legal liability of architects was limited to contractual fraud under the doctrine of "privity of contract."[25] The key development in the emergence of the architect's liability was the understanding of the "building"—the outcome of the work of an architect—as a "product" whose defects rendered the responsible parties liable to suits brought by those injured by these defects. In the words of a classic legal textbook on torts, "there is no visible reason for any distinction between the liability of one who supplies a chattel and who erects a structure."[26]

It took several decades for the architectural implications of this logic to develop, and when it unfolded in the 1950s, architects began to find themselves liable to various "third parties" who claimed damages caused by the architect's negligence.[27] Law reviews began to instruct lawyers on how to define architectural liability, and consumer advocates began to explore the extension of product liability claims to architecture. For example, after the release of his influential 1965 book, *Unsafe at Any Speed: The Designed-In Dangers of the American Automobile*, Ralph Nader began to argue that the architects of slum housing and other forms of inadequate dwelling space ought to be liable for the personal and social damages they caused.[28]

In response, the AIA began to offer liability insurance to its members in 1957, and professional architectural discourse then became increasingly preoccupied with questions of insurance coverage, the responsibilities of insurers, and the drafting of contracts.[29] At the same time, the expert testimony of architects was increasingly solicited in insurance claims and legal cases revolving around architectural negligence (fig. 12.2). As one account of this development pointed out, "the paths of professional glory lead but to liability."[30]

The advent of facilities management in the 1960s and 1970s provided another impetus for the development of forensic architecture. As Robert Gutman pointed out in his landmark exploration of professional practice, *Architectural*

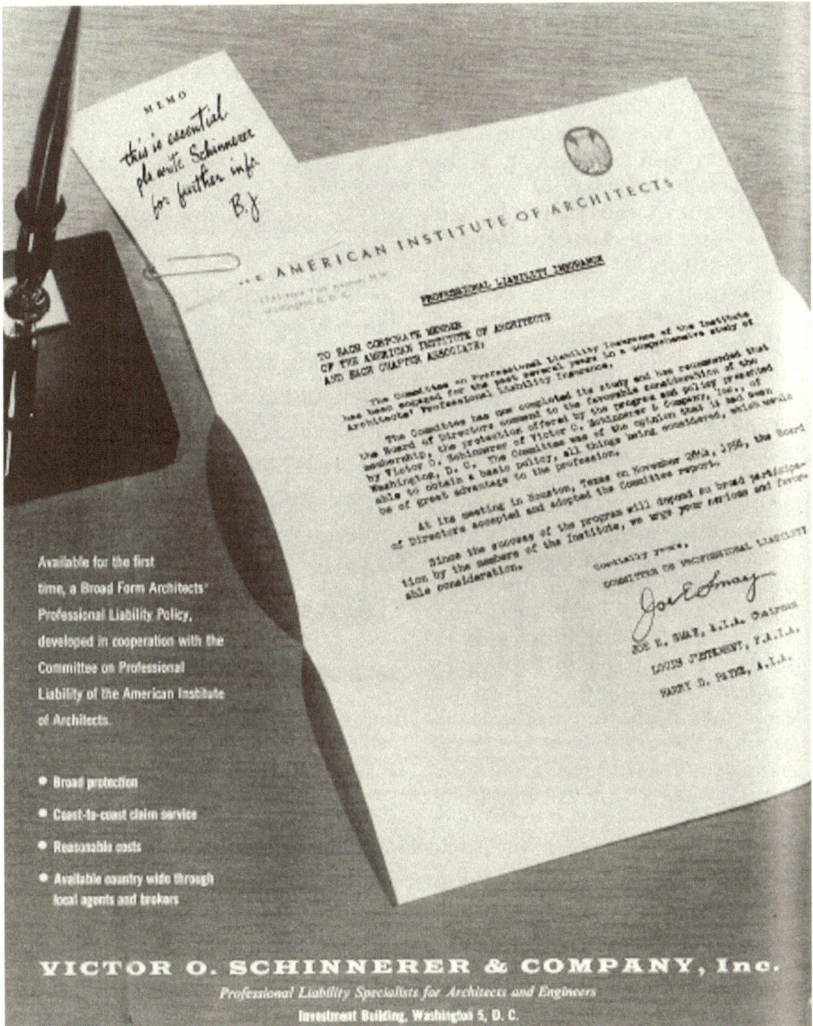

12.2. Advertisement introducing professional liability insurance to architects. *Journal of the American Institute of Architects*, March 1958.

Practice: A Critical View, "because [facilities managers] overlap with architects in design and supervisory roles, and at the same time often perform with the functions of a client, facilities managers represent an especially unsettling and threatening contender for the architect's authority."[31] As a response, Gutman pointed out, some large architecture firms began to claim expertise in facilities management. Another response, however, was to develop architectural expertise of use to facilities managers; as Kubba's handbook pointed out, "forensic architecture" was also a name for this expertise.

CONSULTATION AND POSITION WANTED

Architect, registered, with legal education and training, available for immediate consultation and position in architect-legal specialty of forensic architecture and planning. Age 39. Corporate Member, American Institute of Architects, with seven years experience as principal of firm of architects, engineers, appraisers, and planners. Expert witness in local trial and federal jurisdictions. Prepare trial demonstration media: drawings, perspective renderings, scale models, topography, photographs, reports, appraisals, and feasibility studies for client and corporate requirements applicable to valuation, feasibility, purchase, construction performance relative to merger, expansion, insurance, taxation, planning, zoning, and eminent domain. Resume on request. Reply J. Norman Stark, AIA, 614 The Arcade, Cleveland, Ohio 44114. Tel.: 216/696-2390.

12.3. Advertisement for architect seeking employment in "forensic architecture and planning." *Ohio State Bar Association Report*, August 1968.

As "forensic architects," architects recuperated some of the capital and authority that their profession had been losing to the insurance industry. Forensic architecture also recuperated some of the professional agency that architecture had been losing to the legal profession. The development of forensic architecture allowed architects to regain agency in a realm that was hollowing out the design-based agency they already had; the forensic architect was particularly qualified to serve as an expert witness in a court of law.

Advertisements for "forensic architects" began to appear in law journals in the 1960s, and they soon began to appear in professional architectural journals as well. In these advertisements, the skills of the forensic architect are described as being focused on the preparation of visual media for use in legal proceedings, including perspective renderings, scale models, topographic maps, and photographs, as well as reports, appraisals and feasibility studies in connection with the valuation and purchase of real estate, mergers and expansion, and insurance, taxation, planning, zoning, and eminent domain cases (fig. 12.3).

In the early nineteenth century, architecture in the United States was formulated as a profession that focused on the design skills of the architect, and, even as the work of the architect would change in many ways, architecture's ideological payoffs would continue to be primarily brokered through design.[32] The split between architecture's disciplinary self-consciousness, in the form of professional literature, pedagogy, history and theory, and criticism, and architectural practice was only accelerated and magnified by increasing professional investments in insurance liability, facilities maintenance, and related matters. Among the many outcomes of this split was the abjection of non-design-related practices like forensic architecture and non-design-related concerns like liability insurance and facilities maintenance. Insurance premiums and facilities maintenance were considered problems to solve rather than objects to study, and this rendered expert witnessing, as well as the forensic architecture practiced by the expert architectural witness, inadequate or anxiety-producing substitutes for the profession's single and central object of identification.[33]

In 1991, the newly established Center for the Study of the Practice of Architecture (CSPA) at the University of Cincinnati hosted a symposium, "Emerging Forms of Architectural Practice," as a means to remedy a perceived ongoing disciplinary neglect of practice, but, in so doing, the symposium produced a situation in which forensic architecture's abjection would be at once represented and advanced. Roger Montgomery, dean of the College of Environmental Design at the University of California, Berkeley, reported on the symposium for the *Journal of Architectural Education*. He began his report by lauding the CSPA for inaugurating "a new era concerned with producing empirically based knowledge about what architects actually do."[34] And yet, when faced with one particular aspect of "what architects actually do," Montgomery's attempt at an epistemology of practice abruptly vanished.

Commenting on a discussion after the first panel on the variety of modes of practice, from design-only commissions to construction management, Montgomery mentioned parenthetically that "I'm glad . . . [no] participant took time out to dwell on the ultimate—that is final—mode: that of the forensic architect, a field only too well developed in my adopted state of California."[35] Notably, in the course of a focused inquiry into "what architects actually do," Montgomery could not accommodate an inquiry into a field of practice that he acknowledged was "only too well developed"—forensic architecture.

Even while calling for an expanded perspective on the discipline of architecture, Montgomery still decried forensic architecture as a "hated field," acknowledging the practice only to condemn it. His response was utterly typical. Nowhere in architecture's historical or theoretical reflection on itself has forensic architecture been anything other than ignored or dismissed, leaving it to develop in purely technical terms. Kubba's *Architectural Forensics* is but one of the latest outcomes of forensic architecture's unhistoricized history and untheorized theory.

Political Violence, Humanitarian Law, and the Emergence of Forensic Architecture

Yet another outcome is the appearance of forensic architecture to architectural imagination in the context of international humanitarian and human rights tribunals. Indeed, at precisely the same moment in global history when the Center for the Study of Practice in Architecture was fending off awareness of forensic architectural practice, political violence in Yugoslavia was leading to the formation of the International Criminal Tribunal for the Former Yugoslavia (known as ICTY)—one of the forums, Weizman writes, where political violence became the object of forensic architectural examination.

The practice of forensic architecture at the ICTY, however, can be understood not as the emergence of a new evidentiary mode but rather as a bifurcation in an existing form of architectural practice—an instance when forensic architecture's banalized context of US civil courts, insurance claims, and facilities maintenance came to be paralleled by the valorized context of international tribunals, war crimes, and human rights. While the first context solicited a professional architect, capable of testifying to building failures due to the unprofessional labor of architects, contractors, and others involved in the building industry, the second context solicited an expert capable of testifying to building failures due to bombs, artillery, and other military means.

The historical moment when this bifurcation in forensic architecture appeared in practice can be precisely pinpointed; it occurred in the ICTY's trial of Slobodan Milošević, during Milošević's cross-examination of András Riedlmayer, who testified as an expert witness on the destruction of architecture during the Kosovo conflict. Riedlmayer was presenting evidence from the report he had coauthored with me; documenting architectural destruction during the 1998–1999 Kosovo conflict, this report was entered as evidence in the indictment and trial of Milošević at the ICTY. Riedlmayer was presented to the court as an "art documentation specialist" whose expertise lay in the "research and study of the destruction of cultural heritage"; Riedlmayer presented my qualifications to the court as those of a "trained architect" with degrees in architecture from Princeton and Harvard and a doctorate in progress in architectural history, theory, and criticism.[36]

For the ICTY, interpellated by a deep humanist history of architecture as art, heritage, and culture, our qualifications meant that we could ably document architectural destruction and that Riedlmayer could testify about this destruction.[37] Milošević, however, was not interpellated by this history; when Riedlmayer testified about destruction in Kosovo in the Milošević trial, Milošević argued that this destruction was caused by *military means* and the situation thus called for a *military expert* to interpret.[38] In his cross-examination of Riedlmayer, Milošević thereby explained Riedlmayer's failure to attribute the destruction of buildings in Kosovo to NATO aerial bombardment or rockets (instead of to Serb forces) to Riedlmayer's lack of military knowledge and experience.

One example emerged in a discussion of the destruction of the League of Prizren building—an Ottoman-era building used by the Albanian League of Prizren between 1878 and 1881 and destroyed in March 1999. Milošević claimed that this destruction was due to a NATO rocket, and he used two photographs of the destroyed building as evidence of this claim (fig. 12.4). Discussing these photographs, Milošević argued that "we can see that it was hit from above.... It could not have been destroyed from the ground, as you are claiming."[39]

Riedlmayer, also referring to the photographs of the building, responded that the photographs showed how the building was actually destroyed by fire: "If this

12.4. Photograph of damaged League of Prizren building used as exhibit in the trial of Slobodan Milošević. Photograph from *NATO Crimes in Yugoslavia: Documentary Evidence, 24 March–24 April 1999* (Belgrade: Federal Ministry of Foreign Affairs, 1999), 228.

building had been hit by something with a heavy explosive charge, you wouldn't see this much of it remaining. What I can see here is very typical of a number of other buildings we saw elsewhere in Kosovo, which were clearly burned down, often in an even tighter urban context, with undamaged buildings less than two meters away. So I would rather doubt that this was hit."[40]

For Milošević, this answer presupposed a military expertise that Riedlmayer did not possess:

> MILOŠEVIĆ: Mr. Riedlmayer, NATO hit my house with three rockets. Twelve meters from the house, not a single pane of a glass was broken, a building twelve meters away from the same garden. Are you a ballistics expert?
> RIEDLMAYER: I do not claim to be. I'm simply stating what I saw.[41]

In his further cross-examination of Riedlmayer, Milošević repeatedly brought up the need for what he called a "ballistics expert" to interpret the damage and destruction discussed by Riedlmayer. Milošević's cross-examination of Riedlmayer may be understood as the historical moment when "forensic architecture" began to fissure into two trajectories—one produced through traditional architectural expertise and the other anticipated in Milošević's calls for "ballistics experts." The ICTY endowed an art documentation specialist and architect with capacity to interpret damage and destruction inflicted in political violence; this endowment was comprehensible according to the received/abjected version of forensic architecture, in which architects and experts in related fields possess the relevant expert knowledge. Yet pointing out that Riedlmayer testified to damage and destruction authored by military forces, Milošević claimed that the interpretation of this damage and destruction called for an expert not in architecture but in ballistics.

The ICTY was not convinced by Milošević's argument and in subsequent trials continued to rely on Riedlmayer as an expert witness for architectural destruction. Like Milošević, however, the defendants in these cases continued to challenge his expertise. In rejecting these challenges, the ICTY in effect created a new field of professional expertise called "cultural destruction," positioning Riedlmayer as an expert in a field the ICTY itself had created—a fully proleptic act. But beyond the ICTY, in the trajectory charted, if not authored, by Weizman, other experts began to appear in the settings where damage and destruction to architecture inflicted during political violence were documented, interpreted, and judged—precisely the sort of military experts that Milošević called for to assess violence against architecture in Kosovo.

This was a history in which, as Weizman puts it in his "Forensic Architecture" essay, "only the criminal can solve the crime." Thus, for Weizman, the key figure in the emergence of forensic architecture is Marc Garlasco, former intelligence analyst in the US Defense Intelligence Agency and then military and forensic analyst for Human Rights Watch. Garlasco's shift—from the military to human rights advocacy, made possible by the emergence of forensic architecture in the latter—represents, for Weizman, how "the practice of 'forensic architecture' relies upon the very technologies of bombing they came to monitor."[42]

Symptomatizing Forensic Architecture

How are we to assess the split in forensic architecture between a banal and mundane subfield of professional architectural practice and political advocacy carried out by human rights and humanitarian organizations? To the extent that forensic architecture is only recognized in its human rights and humanitarian guises, architecture and its history implicitly keep faith with an ideological construction of architecture as politically relevant and historically causal, even as they seem to do precisely the opposite by moving from the study of architecture as intentionally authored work to architecture as social object circulating through fields and networks far beyond the profession and discipline of architecture.

"Building," however it has been defined, has traditionally been the vehicle for architecture's relevance, authority, and prestige; in such guises as functionalist object, social condenser, and public housing, "building" was the form in which modernism's social critique was manifested. In the wake of that critique's dissolution through historical accounts of its apparent failure or theoretical accounts of its apparent inadequacy, architecture has been offered a possibility to re-endow itself with some of the relevance, authority, and prestige it seems to have lost as a profession and discipline through what Weizman so compellingly frames as "a constantly transforming, mutating, and vibrant materiality" against which "any reading of an event must therefore be undertaken."[43]

An activist forensic architecture, in other words, offers architecture's disciplinary imagination a seeming opportunity to recuperate the social agency that this imagination has presented as lost—*seeming* because the forensic architecture of humanitarianism and human rights tribunals, circulating amid and between juridical culture and displays of contemporary art and architecture, is even less imbricated in material reality than its mundane counterpart. In this sense, the bifurcation in the genealogy of forensic architecture is an architectural symptom—it assumes and reproduces the abjection of forensic architecture qua banal professional subfield while registering the appearance of forensic architecture at the forefront of what Weizman terms "an emergent object-oriented juridical culture."[44]

Weizman convincingly concludes "Forensic Architecture" by arguing that Marc Garlasco did not cross a line when he moved from the Pentagon to Human Rights Watch, from targeting aerial strikes to examining the violence of those strikes through forensic architecture. But what if architecture also did not cross a line when Garlasco examined ruins as forensic evidence? What if architecture's forensic identity was already long established when Garlasco was recruited as an expert interpreter of the ruins produced in Israel's incursion in Gaza? What if a forensic architecture oriented around humanitarianism and human rights actually extends architecture's long-standing status as evidence—a status that has not only unfolded legally, in the forensic architecture of insurance claims and contract disputes, but even more so historiographically, in architecture's very identity as a phenomenon that can be historicized? And so, what if a forensic architecture of humanitarianism and human rights has arrogated from historian to architect the position of judge and the narrative as judgment?

Michel de Certeau once figured the historian as a judge who "has received from society an exorcist's task . . . to eliminate the danger of the *other*."[45] For Certeau, the work of the critical historian was to historicize and therefore reconceptualize this danger; history was therefore a "heterology," a science of the "other" along with such disciplines as ethnography and psychoanalysis.[46] While a heterological forensic architecture would de-valorize the forensic architect and reframe the relevance, authority, and prestige with which the discipline of architecture has been endowed, it might thereby invite the discipline of architecture to engage in or with a forensics of itself: a forensics of architecture that would at once displace, rename, and possibly also animate its historicization.

13

Architectural History after Sebald's *Austerlitz*
A Squirrel's Hoard, a Curved Road

■

DANIEL M. ABRAMSON

Toward the end of W. G. Sebald's celebrated book *Austerlitz* (2001), the title character's governess relates an anecdote that epitomizes the protagonist's quest into the past. Every time his Czech governess read to the child, named Austerlitz, a picture book about winter, the child "would look up at her and ask: But if it's all white, how do the squirrels know where they've buried their hoard? *Ale když všechno zakryje sníh, jak veverky najdou to místo, kde si schovaly zásoby?* Those were your very words, the question which constantly troubled you. How indeed do the squirrels know, what do we know ourselves, how do we remember, and what is it we find in the end?"[1] This question—how are plain nuts recovered as treasured nourishment?—we might rephrase as a metaphor for history writing itself. How is material from the past recovered as meaningful evidence and narrative, as sustenance for the present and future?

Austerlitz veritably invites architectural historians to plumb its depths. Its title character is, in fact, an architectural historian. Jacques Austerlitz expounds on European architectural history in conversations with the book's unnamed narrator, who sketchily resembles the author Sebald, a German-born writer living in East Anglia. Central to the book, Austerlitz reveals, is his troubled life story as an orphaned Nazi refugee who gradually in midlife rediscovers his origins. Exploring issues of European memory and identity, *Austerlitz* is the last of four "prose fiction" works written in German by Sebald.[2] He might have earned a Nobel Prize, many believe, if he had not died at age fifty-seven in a car accident the year *Austerlitz* was published.[3]

All of Sebald's prose fiction is characterized by a creative amalgamation of genres. These include travelogue and memoir, history and pure invention. Sebald's prose fiction also features numerous architectural citations, from eighteenth-century French architecture to Victorian British country houses and resorts.[4] *Austerlitz* is Sebald's most architectural book. It includes references to the architecture of Prague, Nuremberg, Antwerp, and Marienbad, plus model workers' towns, as well as extended discourses on train stations and fortifications, the Palace of Justice in Brussels, and the Bibliothèque Nationale in Paris. This chapter poses two principal questions about *Austerlitz*: Why, of all occupations, would Sebald choose an architectural historian to explore issues of identity, memory, and history? And how might architectural historians think differently about evidence and narrative after *Austerlitz*, in imitation and in its wake?

The question of why the character Austerlitz is an architectural historian is barely addressed in the Sebald literature.[5] Commentators seemingly content themselves with the account offered by Sebald in a 2001 interview. The author claimed the model for Austerlitz was "a colleague of mine, a scholar, who like my hero, was an architectural historian [*Baugeschichtler*] and taught in London. This was a somewhat eccentric man, who retired early ... and got into a deep life crisis. He began exploring his own origins as best he could at the age of 60."[6] This individual's identity remains unknown. Indeed, he might be Sebald's invention.[7] In fact, the dramatic aspects of Austerlitz's life story, Sebald admitted, were inspired by a true-life story he saw in a 1991 BBC television program about a Briton named Susi Bechhöfer. Like the character Jacques Austerlitz, Bechhöfer had been sent out of Central Europe on a *kindertransport* and was subsequently renamed and raised by a childless Welsh minister. Like Austerlitz, Bechhöfer learned her real name by accident as an adolescent and in midlife researched her origins with the help of a childhood governess.[8] It would seem insufficient then to ascribe Austerlitz's profession to Sebald's claimed acquaintance with a possibly fictional individual of the same vocation who traversed a vaguely similar midlife crisis. Accepting Sebald's explanation, commentators are excused from having to think more deeply about what the *choice*, rather than the supposed happenstance of Austerlitz's profession, offers Sebald. Why do architecture and its history matter to Sebald in telling Austerlitz's story?

Simply put, it allowed Sebald to write more about architecture, which appears for him to provide special access to evidence of the past. In Sebald's prose fiction, the material presence of buildings embodies the identities and motivations of their makers (not their designers).[9] In Paris, the Bibliothèque Nationale's "monumental dimensions ... were evidently inspired by the late President's wish to perpetuate his memory" (276). Austerlitz the architectural historian's most abiding subject is the "architectural style of the capitalist era." In the nineteenth century's institutional building types—from law courts to lunatic asylums to railway stations—he discerns a unifying "compulsive sense of order and the tendency towards monumentalism" (33). But it is not just through the professional architectural historian's visual tools of formal stylistic and typological analysis that the evidence of buildings conveys the past's collective meanings. Intimate, bodily encounters with the Belgian fortress-prison of Breendonk by the book's unnamed narrator frame *Austerlitz* and underscore architecture's capacity to embody individual subjectivity as well. The narrator first experiences Breendonk viscerally, through smell, word association, nausea, and "black striations. . . . before my eyes" (25), as sensorial confirmation of the architecture as "a monolithic, monstrous incarnation of ugliness and blind violence" (21).

Different from conventional pictorial and textual evidence—visually, figuratively, and rationally accessible—architecture as a material, abstract, sensorial, more mute form of evidence provokes in *Austerlitz* deeper, imaginative, subjective connections to the past. The character Austerlitz, for example, anthropomorphizes a train station column as a vessel of his lost memories: "This cast-iron column, which with its scaly surface seemed almost to approach the nature of a living being, might remember me and was, if I may so put it, said Austerlitz, a witness to what I could no longer recollect for myself" (221). Architecture ultimately is the crucial mnemonic device that catalyzes Austerlitz's decisive return of childhood remembrance in the experience of London's Liverpool Street station, which "contained all the hours of my past life" (136).

Architecture conveys both collective historical identity and individual personal subjectivity. Austerlitz metaphorizes his mind architecturally as the "four burnt-out walls of my brain" (230); his memory is spatialized as "all interlocking like the labyrinthine vaults" (136) of the Liverpool Street station. A story about an old paper mill, told to Austerlitz by Marie de Verneuil, his companion and fellow architectural historian, powerfully expresses her identity: "Everything Marie meant to me from then on, said Austerlitz, was summed up in this tale of the paper mill in which, without speaking of herself, she revealed her inner being to me" (263). Above all, Austerlitz's subjectivity and his practice as an architectural historian are intimately joined. His choice of scholarly subjects and evidence is deeply personal. The "obsession with railway stations" (34) and their domed vaults reenacts his primal childhood train journey from Prague to London. In method, Austerlitz plays out subconsciously his own repressed search for a familial identity, seeking to identify "the family likeness" among various types of nineteenth-century architecture based upon "an impulse which he himself, to this day, did not really understand" (33). Austerlitz's intellectual blindnesses, the evidence he ignores, derive, too, from his childhood trauma: "I had always avoided learning anything at all about German topography, German history, or modern German life" (222). He relates that "as far as I was concerned the world ended in the late nineteenth century. I dared go no further than that" (139). Ultimately, Austerlitz characterizes his whole professional vocation as a complex "avoidance system" (198), an "accumulation of knowledge which I had pursued for decades, and which served as a substitute or compensatory memory" (140). His experience of a debilitating nervous breakdown, leaving him unable to write or read, is a result, Austerlitz discerns, of his severe "self-censorship of the mind" that "led to the almost total paralysis of my linguistic facilities" (140), his inability to comprehend and form a narrative wholeness. Austerlitz's subjectivity thus both generates and obstructs the performance of his profession.

Yet, architecture and architectural history can be obdurate evidence and narrative—in a manner similar to the nearly one hundred uncredited, uncaptioned images in *Austerlitz*, which defy easy integration with the text.[10] Buildings fail as a mnemonic signaling device. Austerlitz tries in vain to use the domes and vaults of the Prague train station "to think my way back through the decades" (218). For a moment, Austerlitz believes, architectural history might soothe his traumatized psyche. When his companion and colleague Marie tells Austerlitz the story of the Marienbad spa, as they visit it together he feels a "rare sense of happiness . . . the hope that I was now beginning to be cured . . . the belief . . . within me that I had found release at last" (211). But the morning after, "nothing came of it. I woke before dawn with such an abysmal sense of distress" (211). Memory and the past, meaning and wholeness, remain tragically out of reach.

Fiasco, moreover, is inherent to the way architecture and its history function in *Austerlitz* as evidence and narrative for larger collective meanings. Monumentalism in architecture is generally interpreted ironically by Austerlitz the architectural historian not as a sign of strength but, ultimately, of frailty. "We know by instinct that outsize buildings cast the shadow of their own destruction," Austerlitz tells the narrator (19). About fortifications, Austerlitz observes, "it is often our mightiest projects that most obviously betray the degree of our insecurity" (14), noting how the stoutest defensive emplacements simply "drew attention to your weakest point" (16). Austerlitz insists on the conjunction of countervailing qualities in architecture and the ubiquity of unintended consequences. Train stations are "places marked by both blissful happiness and profound misfortune" (34). Model nineteenth-century towns built for workers "inadvertently changed into the practice of accommodating them in barracks," illustrating the general point that "our best laid plans, said Austerlitz, as I still remember, always turn into the exact opposite when they are put into practice" (28).

Irony is a predominant tone toward architecture and architectural history in *Austerlitz*. Outcomes are incongruous and contradictory to intentions. Buildings can embody two opposite meanings at one time. Indeed, irony and doubling are fundamental to the structure of *Austerlitz* in total. The book is self-conscious about translation. Key phrases are repeated in the original language and in translation, as in the parable of the squirrel, pointing to the inevitable gap in re-presentation. There is also the doubling of the book's principal narrators. The first, unnamed, both resembles but is not Sebald. The second narrator, Austerlitz, bears two names (adopted and birth names), the latter belonging to both the book and the title character, to a train station in Paris and to a town in the Netherlands, which itself is both a mundane place and world-historical battle.

A multiplicity of denotations for the name "Austerlitz" further offsets the unnamed absence of its near equivalent—Auschwitz. This absence may symbolize Austerlitz the character's traumatic amnesia of the Holocaust experience, which itself may be emblematic for the forgetfulness of perpetrators and victims alike, as well as the past's dialectic of absence and presence in memory and history. Austerlitz himself personifies and suffers this contradiction. For him the past is both ever present and ever missing, the source of his incurable melancholy.

Austerlitz and *Austerlitz* are bifurcated in other ways. The protagonist's split psyche is reflected in the book's very narration, which is itself doubled. The first, framing story is the narrator's lineal account of his meetings and conversations with Austerlitz, which proceeds in time, from 1967 to 1997, and through a clean arc in space, from Belgium to London to Paris and back to Belgium. The second, lengthier, embedded tale is Austerlitz's life story, which, by contrast, zigzags backwards and forwards between 1934 and 1997, also looping constantly in space between Belgium, Britain, Prague, Marienbad, and Paris. The double narratives of *Austerlitz* the book—one straightforward, the other tortuous—reenact Austerlitz the character's own traumatized relationship to time and memory.

There is, additionally, Austerlitz the architectural historian's practice of evidence and narrative, which is also dualistic. It is split between the predictable and the unconventional or, as the narrator describes Austerlitz, "a man locked into the glaring clarity of his logical thinking as inextricably as into his own confused emotions" (41). On the one hand, Austerlitz appears as a conventional professional architectural historian, including in his handling of evidence and narrative. He is academically employed for nearly thirty years, until 1991, as "a lecturer at a London institute of art history . . . in Bloomsbury, not far from the British Museum" (31–32) (an apparent reference to the Warburg Institute and not, as sometimes misidentified, the Courtauld Institute, which lay farther west in Portman Square at this time). Austerlitz gathers textual and visual evidence in the usual ways, too, in libraries and on site. He describes himself as having "devoted most of the whole of his life to the study of books . . . losing myself in the small print of the footnotes" (281–82, 260). Among buildings, he sketches and takes notes and photographs, observes the narrator, who lauds Austerlitz's "astonishing professional expertise" (8). In communicating to the narrator his architectural insights, Austerlitz offers skilled architectural history narratives. His opening discourse on Antwerp's Central Station begins with the building's social context and commissioning, proceeds to formal description, and then moves on to historical and philosophical remarks about capitalism and time. (Admittedly, a social history of capitalist architecture would have been precocious for 1960s–1970s British architectural history, which concerned itself primarily with stylistic, monographic studies. This is perhaps why Sebald appears to affiliate Austerlitz with the Warburg rather than Courtauld Institute, the former more unorthodox in its interdisciplinary, thematic approaches.)

Yet, in equal measure, Austerlitz is an unconventional architectural historian in his approaches both to evidence and to narrative. As evidence, he cites "apocryphal stories," and, the narrator notes as well, "anecdotes in curious contrast to his usual rigorous objectivity" (30–31), including unsubstantiated tales of the Brussels Palace of Justice containing "doorless rooms and halls . . . stairways leading nowhere" (29). Austerlitz incorporates into his discourses evidence that includes not only legends and myths but also emotions and feelings, for example, "the agony of leave-taking and the fear of foreign places, although such ideas were not part of architectural history proper," the scholar admits (14). Additionally, bodily sensation becomes evidence for Austerlitz to access the past, particularly his own: architectural details, "which I could tell, by the prickling of my scalp, it had brought back out of my past" (151). And, coincidence and instinct, the fiction writer's tools rather than the historian's intentionality, drive the narrative forward and impel key evidence-gathering acts. Austerlitz happens to overhear a radio story about *kindertransports* and the ferry *Prague*, which induces him to seek his origins in that city. Then his former governess unearths his childhood photograph merely "by chance" (181). Austerlitz "cannot explain what made me follow" (134) a railway porter into the abandoned "Ladies Waiting Room" of the Liverpool Street station—"a series of coincidences" (138)—where dramatically his memory recovery commences. A "premonition" (291) indicates that Paris's Gare d'Austerlitz is a key site related to his father's fate. And, of course, Austerlitz and the narrator's very acquaintanceship and many subsequent encounters occur purely by accident, as they run into each other by chance across the Continent and Britain, thus precipitating their conversations.

By book's end, Austerlitz has seemingly given up on the historian's conventional sources of evidence, what he calls "processed data" with no "living connection to the past" (286). France's gargantuan new Bibliothèque Nationale, with its vast repository of historical books and records, "proved useless in my search for traces of my father" (282). Professional training, skills, and resources fail Austerlitz in his attempts to access the past's deepest import. Instead, and impulsively, Austerlitz turns from the archive to fiction, to "reading the novels of Balzac," whose "melodramatic aspects" regarding the permeability between life and death prove instructive (283). Then by chance one day at 6:00 p.m., Austerlitz recounts, he happens upon, in "an American architecture journal," a photograph of the modern-day records room at Terezín (Theresienstadt), the Czech ghetto-town where his mother had been interned during the war and whose clock in the photograph also amazingly reads exactly 6:00 p.m. (fig. 13.1). Out of this chain of coincidences, "a kind of *idée fixe* forced itself upon me that, all along, my true place of work should have been there in the little fortress of Terezín, where so many had perished in the cold, damp casemates, and it was my own fault that I had not taken it up" (283). Austerlitz the architectural historian's discovery of "the little fortress of Terezín" as "his true place

13.1. Terezín records room. From *Austerlitz*, 284–85. "Illustrations" from *AUSTERLITZ* by W. G. Sebald, translated by Anthea Bell, translation copyright © 2001 by Anthea Bell. Used by permission of Random House, an imprint and division of Penguin Random House LLC. All rights reserved.

of work" encapsulates *Austerlitz* the book's alternatives to conventional evidence and its gathering. His "true place of work" is discovered by impulse, fiction, and coincidence, rather than intention, documentation, and reason. It lies outside official institutions of "processed data" and offers the researcher seemingly direct, experiential access to a subject and material site that are deeply personal. Austerlitz thus seeks to gather evidence from the past, like the squirrel in his childhood picture book, recovering personal sustenance by instinct and spatially. At the same time, it should be noted the photograph that appears to spur this *idée fixe* is a conventional archive, as illustrated (uncaptioned and uncredited) in a double-page spread in the book.[11] The records room is filled with files from floor to ceiling, around simple wooden tables and chairs. It is openly accessible to historians excavating a shared treasure of evidence, to produce collective meaning from the past. Austerlitz's "true place of work" then is not simply an individual digging up a private trove. Rather, it combines both the subjective *and* the professional.

As with practices of evidence, as well as with narrative, *Austerlitz* is marked by irony and doubling. On the one hand, Austerlitz is a failed architectural historian, unable to turn his decades of research into a conventional monographic publication. Thousands of pages of notes remain "fragmentary studies" (120). At book's end, Austerlitz entrusts the narrator with the keys to his home, to "study the black and white photographs which, one day, would be all that was left of his life" (293)—in effect, to curate the accumulated evidence of Austerlitz's work and life, which the architectural historian has been unable to narrate into text himself. Austerlitz is blocked doubly, by his personal trauma and by architectural history's limitations. Despite promising special access to the past, architectural evidence—material and sensuous, collective and subjective—fails ultimately in *Austerlitz* to recover and reconstruct the past and meanings even, and perhaps especially, via an architectural historian's skilled practices of evidence, analysis, and narration.

Although not a successful writer of architectural history, Austerlitz is a brilliant orator, according to the narrator. Indeed, storytelling is the book's dominant rhetorical mode, often composed of multiple small-scale tales in which personal testimonies enter the past's record, one nested within another—"so Vera recollected, said Austerlitz, Maximilian would tell the tale" (167). At other moments, long, breathless narrations run barely interrupted. The book's opening paragraph extends twenty-four pages (3–27). Austerlitz's inaugural architectural history discourse on Antwerp's Central Station builds seamlessly toward "a kind of historical metaphysic" (13) about capitalism and time, as the narrator puts it, until an abrupt swerve, quoted verbatim in French by the narrator for emphasis: "Combien des ouvriers périrent, lors de la manufacture de tels miroirs, de malignes et funestes affectations à la suite de l'inhalation de vapeurs de mercure et de cyanide" (How many workers died making these mirrors, from the horrible effects of inhaling fumes of mercury and cyanide) (13). It is an ironic descent from metaphysical heights to mundane human tragedy. To Austerlitz, history is neither triumphant nor redemptive. Rather, the next day the architectural historian "spoke at length about the marks of pain which, as he said he well knew, trace countless fine lines through history" (14).

In Sebald's prose fiction generally, history appears as an endless accounting of death and fire, plagues and war—a "chronicle of calamities," to use a phrase from his 1990 work of prose fiction, *Vertigo*.[12] As a "chronicle of calamities," history in Sebald's writing departs from conventional triumphalism as well as from what the philosopher Hayden White has called history's "narrativized" form—stories with a conclusive beginning, end, and plot that subsume evidence to grand, overarching meaning.[13] A chronicle, by contrast, is a list of events that lacks closure and final lessons, White writes, and "throws on the reader the burden for retrospectively reflecting on the linkages between the beginning of the account and its ending."[14] As an architectural historian, Austerlitz abjures the narrativized story. He imagines his grand history of the nineteenth century as a catalog of forms standing beyond explicit human agency, "a type of natural history of architecture," as William Firebrace has perceptively observed.[15] In *Austerlitz* the book, facts and events, too, often appear as in a chronicle, one thing after another, isolated from each other without causal relation.[16] As in a chronicle, the dual narratives of *Austerlitz* begin arbitrarily and end inconclusively. At the outset, the narrator's journeys to Belgium, where he first accidentally meets Austerlitz, occur partly for "reasons which were never entirely clear to me" (3). At the end, Austerlitz the architectural historian announces his intention, open-ended and likely futile, to continue searching for Marie de Verneuil and for his father, who had been transported away from Paris by the Nazis. And, the narrator's account terminates the book in a curiously flat manner. The narrator returns to Breendonk fortress but does not re-encounter the structure as he had initially, tumultuously unprocessed directly through his senses. Rather, this time he keeps his distance. He takes from his rucksack a book given to him by Austerlitz. It is *Heshel's Kingdom* (1998), an actual memoir by the South African author and University of London professor Dan Jacobson about memory, history, and Europe's lost Jewry.

The reader of *Austerlitz* does not learn much about *Heshel's Kingdom*. But if we look at it ourselves, we see its appropriateness as a coda for *Austerlitz*. Jacobson's prologue dramatically metaphorizes the past as an abandoned mine pit into which the author gazes solipsistically: "This is what the past is like: echoless and bottomless . . . a darkness that gives back nothing"—a fitting epigraph for *Austerlitz*.[17] At the book's finale, the narrator sits and reads *Heshel's Kingdom* placidly by the fort's moat. The novel concludes as the narrator "then set out on my way back to Mechelen, reaching the town as evening began to fall" (298). Ironically, in *Austerlitz*, a work of prose fiction replete with dramatic and complex evidentiary and narrative experimentation, it is a traditional form of book-writing and reading of Jacobson's *Heshel's Kingdom* that in the end offers quiet solace.

I conclude by returning to the question at the beginning of this chapter: What might architectural history be after *Austerlitz*, in imitation and in its wake? In imitation of *Austerlitz*, we might openly explore and identify our "true place of work"—how our personal histories help determine our choices of subjects and methods, the evidence we seek, and how we narrate it into meaning. In imitation of *Austerlitz*, we might expand our sources of evidence to incorporate affect, memory, instinct, experience, coincidence, and the obduracy of facts resistant to totalizing narrative, as well as to explore alternate narrative forms to the written, overarching story structure. In the wake of *Austerlitz*, we recognize the parts played by impulse and coincidence in the writing of history, as well as the permeability between genres of history and fiction at play in reconstructions of the past. And in the wake of *Austerlitz*, we might acknowledge the inability of architectural evidence and architectural history writing to sufficiently access and reconstruct the past. Perhaps this is why Sebald made Austerlitz an architectural historian. Even privileged architectural evidence matched to the best professional skills fails to deliver what Austerlitz—and we—seek, need, and desire from the past: its meaningful wholeness and ours as well. That previous commentators failed to even try to wrestle with Austerlitz's profession may underscore architecture's ungraspable qualities, its obduracy, inaccessibility, and opacity, its resistance to easy meaning.

Architectural history after *Austerlitz* might further consider the book's ironic double vision, the capacity to see things one way and also the other. *Austerlitz* casts into sharp relief the privileges and pitfalls of architectural history. On the one hand, architectural historians have the advantage of material, sensual evidence of the past's seemingly unmediated presence in buildings. On the other hand, this strength of presence is a weakness; it obfuscates all that is necessarily absent and mediated about the past, unrecoverable, and out of reach. *Austerlitz* moreover demonstrates architectural history's complex relationship to individual and collective meanings, how the architectural historians' quest is both personal and communal, rooted in direct experience of the object while seeking collective, historical meaning from it. We recognize the value of *Austerlitz*'s ironic doublings, too, seeing in architecture unintended consequences and contrary results, strength and weakness simultaneously. *Austerlitz* may encourage us to work as architectural historians, like Austerlitz, both conventionally and unconventionally, objectively and subjectively. The book's structure is simultaneously symmetric and centered on Austerlitz's midpoint onset of recovered memory, and it is hazily indeterminate, open-ended at the conclusion, and undermotivated at the outset. It combines the textual character of a book with the breathless, oral style of its language. Evidence comes from both unprocessed and processed data, unconventional and conventional sources. And at the end, a traditional form of writing and reading in *Heshel's Kingdom* reassumes its place alongside *Austerlitz*'s other evidentiary and narrative alternatives.

To adopt the ironist's double vision is, lastly, a pose both of hubris and humility, of making little things large and large things little. On the one hand, there is an Olympian detachment in seeing things at a distance, all angles at once, sure of one's method. And, on the other hand, there is the acceptance of difference, opposition, contradiction, and the impossibility of final meaning, which should ultimately be humbling. The parable of the squirrel's hoard illustrates this tension. Does one observe an everyday individual squirrel's hoard and turn it into something profound and communal, a parable of memory and history writing, or does one look at history writing and memory, perceiving it to be as ordinary as an individual squirrel recovering nuts? *Austerlitz* at its conclusion provides clues. The book ends on a mundane and quiet note. The narrator reads *Heshel's Kingdom* and heads back to Mechelen, "reaching the town as evening began to fall." Reference to *Heshel's Kingdom* offers a final hint. This book begins with profundity, self-absorption, and nothingness, metaphorizing the past as a bottomless pit. But it finishes with mundanity, community, and possibility, the humble realization that, as Jacobson writes, "the abyss of the past does not have to be figured for us by bottomless pits.... This will do just as well. These benches and that set of civic buildings; those trees and traffic signs; the curve of this empty road."[18]

Architectural history writing after *Austerlitz* might reach just this realization as well. History's evidence is built on the banal: a squirrel's hoard indeed. But the import of this recovered treasure transcends an individual's dug-up memory. Evidence (and its meaning) is communal—these benches, civic buildings, and traffic signs, in Jacobson's accounting. In *Austerlitz*, the narrator also returns from self-absorption to the social, "reaching the town as evening began to fall." History and its writing, in other words, are shared common spaces—narratives as thoroughfares for collective meanings. But these are neither settled nor transparent. Narrative in *Austerlitz*, and in Jacobson's imagery, is oblique, indeterminate, and inconclusive. It is always out of reach, waiting to be filled, just around the corner. There is for architectural history no straight-path method to an elusive meaning, Sebald's *Austerlitz* teaches. The curve of this empty road indeed.

Part V
Testimony

When the conventional archive is not enough, personal testimony provides evidence of facts and feelings, experiences and meanings associated with the built environment. In the following four chapters, the material for writing architectural history encompasses family stories and oral history, legal evidence and eyewitness testimony, ethnography, and historians' and architects' own biographies. Encompassing testimony stretches architectural history, too, toward topics of migration, displacement, land, and race. In these chapters, the evidence of testimony challenges the architectural historian to acknowledge the fallacies of remembrance, to excavate one's own experience, and to interrogate privileged positions.

14

Failing Memories and Forgotten Histories
The Dispute over the Venetian Church of San Giobbe

■

JANNA ISRAEL

> *If we would have imagined that Your Most Excellent Lords could have such little foresight and awareness, we would request the detainment of that thing, that arose today ipso jure, because we will show to Your Lordships more clearly than the sun, that a different sentence can be obtained. As such, to obtain our reversal, we ask you to detain the sentence that they have obtained, and any action that Your Lordships intend, while we narrate this fact.*

This was the wounded rebuttal issued in 1502 by the administrators of San Giobbe—a small, impoverished hospice located on the outskirts of Venice—during a legal process to determine patronage rights at the site. There is no extant record of a final decision in the dispute, but given the request for a detainment, the adjudicators seem to have transferred patronage rights from the hospice administrators to an order of Franciscan friars in residence at San Giobbe since 1428. The secular administrators vowed to "narrate the fact" of the longevity and primacy of their patronage rights by presenting an argument structured by legal documents. This chapter explores how the value of evidence changed during the fifteenth century and how the legal determination of San Giobbe's patronage rights came to rest not on documentary evidence but on the oral testimony of eyewitnesses, thus bringing to the surface a whole series of evidentiary problems related to memory and veracity, authorship and ownership. At stake were claims of responsibility for alterations and maintenance to architecture, property, and infrastructure against the authority of legal documents. In the larger historical context, the physical interventions at San Giobbe, however well or poorly remembered by eyewitnesses, adhered to a representation of Venice that highlighted the city's topography as both a register of physical transformations to the Venetian landscape and as a backdrop to the republic's history.

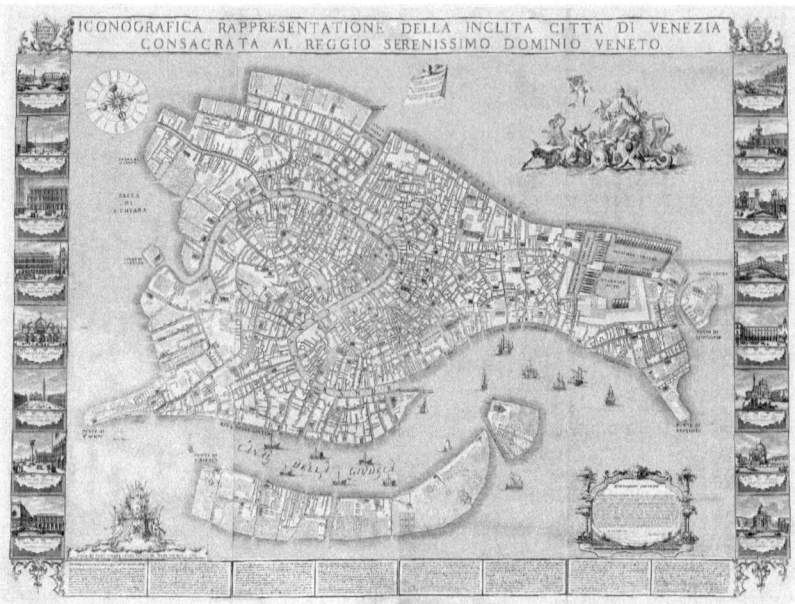

14.1. Ludovico Ughi, *Iconografica rappresentatione della inclita città di Venezia*, 1729. Library of Congress, public domain.

One of the key pieces of evidence submitted to support the patronage rights of the governors at San Giobbe was the testament of the hospice founder, Giovanni Contarini. Composed before his death on September 7, 1407, the testament included instructions for the administration of the hospice that Contarini had established about thirty years earlier to benefit poor sailors. The original site was a largely uninhabited plot of land along the southern embankment of the Canal Regio in the western periphery of Venice (fig. 14.1).[1] Contarini bequeathed his copious landholdings to the hospice to provide a source of revenue under the care of his daughter, Lucia, who shared her legal rights with seven governors, a group comprising relatives, local parish leaders, and allies of her father. Of particular concern for Contarini was the management of a small chapel, built in 1380 to accommodate the spiritual needs of the hospice residents and dedicated to the Old Testament figure Job, whose steadfast faith through prolonged illness and loss would serve as a model for the destitute and sick in residence at the hospice. Contarini obliged the hospice administrators to celebrate mass in the chapel daily and on the Feast of the Annunciation, the day of the mythic founding of the Venetian republic in 421.[2] With the institution of religious rituals that resonated with the civic history of Venice, Contarini expressed allegiance to the foundational narrative of Venice that proclaimed the city a divinely ordained republic.

Contarini insisted that the chapel remain physically separate from the residential and service-oriented areas of the hospice but under the supervision of the administrators who used it. He wrote, "Having erected a chapel near the hospital of San Giobbe, I want and order that this chapel should be divided and separated from the hospital of San Giobbe. I would like, however, that the *ius patronatus*, or legal rights, of the chapel of San Giobbe will always be held by the hospital."[3] Contarini's emphasis on physical divisions and patronage rights suggests that he tried to keep authority in the hands of his secular allies and to harness the potential rise of ecclesiastical power at San Giobbe.[4] However, the separation between the hospice and the chapel mandated by Contarini anticipated arguments about land rights at San Giobbe that would flare up periodically until the suppression of the complex in 1810.[5]

After Contarini's death, the authority that he sought for the hospice governors began to dissolve. In 1428, Lucia Contarini invited an extremely ascetic religious order known as the Observant Franciscans to reside in the cloisters of San Giobbe. Because they deemed the possession of property a violation of their vows of poverty, Observant friars obtained permission from the pope to inhabit property without ownership. This arrangement—referred to as *usus pauper*—allowed the friars to maintain the semblance of a prelapsarian innocence and separation from the secular trappings of owning property.[6] Within the *usus pauper* system, Pope Martin V granted the Observant friars residence at San Giobbe and use of "the chapel to hear the prayers of the faithful," as well as use of the bell and bell tower, and he allowed for additional construction based on necessity, with the consent of the papacy.[7]

However, if Franciscan property regulations were tacitly accepted in Venice, they were never formally incorporated into civil law, which vested proprietorship with the owner.[8] By insisting on allegiance to an absent pope over the local government, the Franciscan *usus pauper* concession potentially ran afoul of Venetian political and social interests.[9] At San Giobbe, *usus pauper* created a lasting antagonism between the hospice governors and the Franciscans. Conflict first erupted in 1434, after Lucia Contarini renounced her patronage rights over the hospice and the friars petitioned to demolish the chapel, alleging that it was close to ruin.[10] Because the chapel was the burial site of her father, Lucia, before a panel of papal adjudicators, contested the proposal to destroy it, thus asserting the authority of the executors of his will. In 1441, based on evidence presented in Giovanni Contarini's final testament, Pope Nicholas V ruled that Lucia had not ceded her patronage rights at the church, because the mandate lay with her father. The pope obliged the Franciscans to preserve the San Giobbe chapel to honor the memory of Contarini and of the many cardinals who had celebrated mass there.[11] However, soon after Lucia's death the Franciscans defied the order to preserve the chapel, destroyed it, and immediately began to construct a larger church.

Information about the destruction of the chapel at San Giobbe by the Franciscans and the development of the complex during the fifteenth century exists almost exclusively in the evidence generated during the 1502 litigation to determine patronage rights at San Giobbe. The adjudicators reviewed mandates and descriptions of San Giobbe in donations, papal bulls, lease agreements, and testaments to determine which party had agency to modify the facilities and the grounds. Validated with the imprimatur of civic notaries, the paper documents contained the "facts" of ownership that the hospice governors vowed to narrate. The judges filled lacunae regarding the development of San Giobbe by soliciting oral testimonies from neighborhood residents about the transformations, experience, and appearance of the site—the location of Contarini's original chapel, the building chronology, patronage, and the ritual conventions of the chapel. The notarial amanuensis who recorded these subjective experiences of San Giobbe authenticated the testimonies by noting "word for word" correspondences and witnesses with *oculata fede*, a "faithful eye," or an assertion of certainty.[12] However, memory often betrayed the eye; several witnesses forgot the chronology and disposition of San Giobbe as it changed during the fifteenth century. One witness echoed the statements of others: "I can't remember when the old chapel was dismantled, but I watched the friars destroy it."[13] The witness testimonies captured the legal failures, uncertainties, and the rapid fading of the building history from memory.

Despite the errors of memory, the testimonial evidence offers insight into the intensity of renegade behavior and competitive interventions at San Giobbe. Giovanni Contarini had requested that masses be said before his tomb in the chapel that he had commissioned. By destroying the chapel, the friars effaced vestiges of Contarini's patronage and secular authority at the site and would not be obligated to direct their prayers to the founder.[14] One witness noted that the Franciscans prohibited Lucia from worshiping at the chapel and displaying in it any imagery associated with Job, the holy figure selected by her father to represent the spiritual ideals of the hospice.

However, the testimonies that recorded modifications to the site by the Franciscans were not necessarily critical of the religious order. Many witnesses noted that the friars drained marshes, constructed embankments to curtail flooding at San Giobbe and accommodated requests for private devotional space and burials by adding a cemetery next to their new church.[15] The eyewitness accounts registered vignettes of the Franciscan friars' ceremonial life and upkeep of the property. In contrast, one witness in the 1502 litigation remarked that he had never seen any administrator of the hospice "show authority over the friars . . . and that he had no desire to know who governed" the site.[16] Giovanni Contarini had attempted to regulate his legacy at San Giobbe through the orders in his final testament, but his allies were largely confined to the local parish; they seem to have lost authority and motivation at the site by 1502.

During the fifteenth century, Franciscans enjoyed increasing popularity, support, and influence with the papacy. At San Giobbe, the friars attracted the patronage of one of the most powerful people in Venice, Doge Cristoforo Moro (1390–1471), who was among the elected leaders of the Venetian republic. The witness testimonies suggest that Moro embedded his identity into San Giobbe as Contarini's legacy was dismantled: "First, the bricks and stones from the former Contarini chapel were used to construct the present church. A second phase of building included the construction of the high altar chapel with the smaller side chapel niches to honor the memory of the Serene Prince Cristoforo Moro, while a third phase of building involved lengthening the nave of the church."[17]

Moro's direct support of San Giobbe spanned a twenty-year period that began in 1451, when he accepted a donation of land from Lucia Contarini's daughter, Isabetta, "to enlarge the monastery and church of San Giobbe."[18] After Moro amassed contracts to secure land donations and abandoned property from Contarini's descendants, his patronage at San Giobbe continued after he was elected doge in 1462. It culminated with his 1470 testament, in which he committed the enormous sum of 10,000 ducats for the enlargement of San Giobbe and the completion of the high altar chapel according to previous "orders given."[19] Exerting rigid control over the production of his memory, Moro ordered that his resting place should be in the ground before the high altar, with the stipulation that those committing transgressions against his will should be blinded. Moro converted the high altar chapel into his personal mausoleum, but by requesting a modest floor tomb rather than the ostentatious wall monument used to commemorate other doges, Moro asserted his identity as a pious ruler.

Moro also promoted the spiritual values of the Observant Franciscans. He adopted their habit, maintained a small cell in their friary, and dedicated the high altar of San Giobbe to Saint Bernardino of Siena, an Observant friar who had allegedly predicted Moro's election as doge before his death in 1444.[20] In 1470, Doge Moro named Saint Bernardino a saint protector of the Republic of Venice.[21] The only other saint to hold the title in Venice at that time was Mark the Evangelist, credited with designating Venice as his final resting place. To augment the republic's profile as a maritime power, a dramatic hagiography for Saint Mark developed in Venetian chronicles, histories, and visual imagery centered on the "sacred theft" of Mark's relics from Alexandria by two Venetian merchants.[22] In rendering a parity between Saints Bernardino and Mark in the Venetian pantheon, Moro conferred weight to Saint Bernardino's prediction of his election as doge and labored to align his political trajectory with the city's mythical history. Moro tried to link Saint Bernardino to tropes of ducal power in architecture as well. His tomb in the high altar chapel of San Giobbe was covered with a low, hemispherical dome that echoed the profiles of the domes in the Basilica of San Marco, the civic and religious center of Venice adjacent to the doge's palace. For the San Clemente chapel in San Marco, where the doge sat on ceremonial occasions, Moro commissioned an altar topped by a sculpted Virgin and Child flanked by freestanding statues of Saints Mark and Bernardino.[23]

By appropriating elements of Venetian foundational narratives for his patronage gestures, Moro wove his rule as doge into the fabric of Venetian history. Moro attempted to convert San Giobbe into a site of ducal power through the repetition of visual motifs from San Marco, thus connecting the periphery of Venice (San Giobbe) to the center (San Marco). The links between visual motifs were activated in representations and descriptions of Venice as well as through the numerous civic and religious processions that crossed the city in strictly regulated routes. On various feast days and religious celebrations, devotional confraternities visited the church of San Giobbe to recite prayers before one of the altars, but in the process, visitors to the church became subsumed into the representation of Venice.[24]

Backed by the force of Moro's ducal patronage, the testimonies of 1502 must have carried significant weight as evidence because a day after the last extant testimonies about the site had been gathered, on March 18, 1502, the administrators issued their rebuttal contesting the decision. The judges validated the Franciscan *usus pauper* regulations, which allowed the friars to make modifications, based on their needs, to property that they inhabited. The introduction of subjective testimonies as evidence for the 1502 patronage case suggests that the judicial process was not impartial but that the adjudicators sought to undermine the legal authority of the hospice administrators at San Giobbe. The 1502 ruling at San Giobbe was a referendum not only on who held determination rights at San Giobbe but whose history was authorized as official.

In his final testament, Moro extended his control at San Giobbe by ordering the executors of his estate to replace themselves in perpetuity, so that a continuous line of authority would carry out building projects and protect his interests.[25] The executors of Moro's will, a group comprising his family as well as scholars and politicians, continued to initiate building projects and place the doge's coat of arms around San Giobbe after his death to ensure that the doge's image would prevail in the visual memory of Venice. A few years after Moro's 1471 death, one of the executers of his estate, the political theorist Domenico Morosini, successfully petitioned the Venetian government to replace the wooden bridge that had spanned the large Canal Regio, adjacent to San Giobbe, with a stone bridge, using the funds left by Moro (fig. 14.2). The executors of Moro's testament not only promoted the doge's memory but marshaled it in service of addressing exigencies related to traffic, renewal, and the conservation of Venice's ecosystem.

In 1503, the Franciscan confraternity dedicated to Saint Bernardino located at San Giobbe provided for a loan of ten ducats for the construction of a stone bridge, indicating that the conflict about patronage rights at San Giobbe in 1502 may have been partially motivated by protest against the bridge that would serve

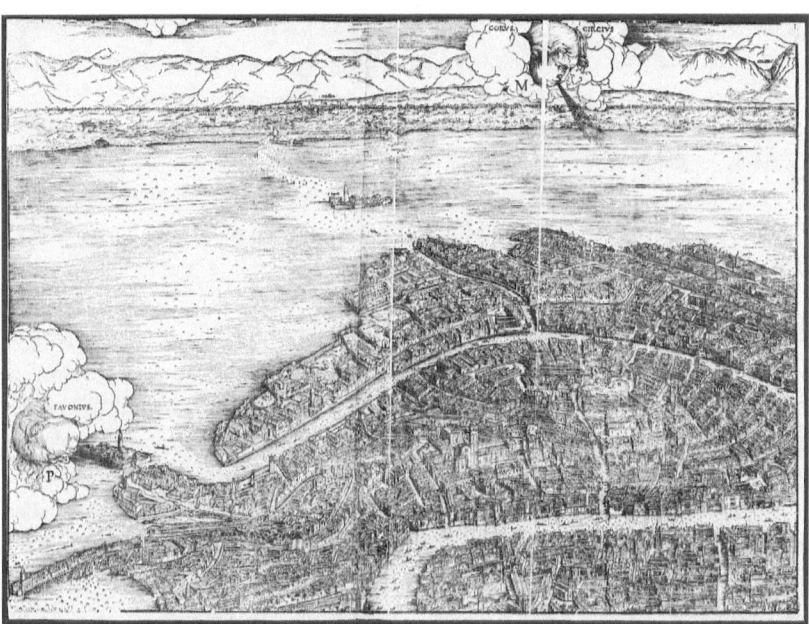

14.2. Detail of San Giobbe. Jacopo de' Barbari, *View of Venice*, 1500, woodcut. National Gallery of Art, Rosenwald Collection, 1950.1.14.

the Franciscans and Moro's confraternity.[26] Doge Moro's estate released funds in 1504 and 1520 for the construction of the bridge, though it would not be realized until 1688 and its construction came without any indication of Moro's patronage. However, in 1475, when the Venetian senate granted permission for the construction of a stone bridge at San Giobbe, its members noted that the bridge would contribute to Doge Moro's "good memory," serve "as an ornament to the neighborhood," and better accommodate visitors to the church.[27]

The commission of a bridge ensured that San Giobbe would strike a more monumental aesthetic in uniting the area to other parts of the city. The bridge became emblematic of civic renewal and ritual. In his 1494 description of Venice, the diarist Marino Sanudo noted that stone bridges had started to replace wooden bridges, likely funded by a special tax that had been instituted in 1490 to help offset new stone bridge construction costs.[28] Morosini had tracked other bridge projects through his diplomatic work, expressing admiration for Pope Sixtus IV's construction of the Ponte Sisto, the first bridge in Rome since antiquity initiated by the pope as part of a project to rebuild the "dilapidated city."[29] Sixtus had been motivated to fix Roman infrastructure to prepare for the Jubilee in 1475, when Morosini petitioned the senate for the stone bridge at San Giobbe. In 1504, Morosini requested that the republic appoint the engineer Giovanni Giocondo to design a new Rialto Bridge based on the success of his bridge over the Seine in Paris.[30] Sanudo dismissed Giocondo's designs and claimed he did not understand Venice's open geography, unencumbered by heavy tectonics and defensive walls.

Despite their disagreements about design, both Morosini and Sanudo highlight the growing importance of infrastructure to communicate ideas about the republic. In approving construction of the stone bridge, the senate drew on theories that celebrated monuments and urban renewal projects as "ornaments," a physical reflection of the quality of the city's governance and its institutional health. This Platonic rendering of a republic promoted beauty in design to foster civic and moral virtue. The first official history of Venice, written by Marc'Antonio Sabellico in 1487, incorporated descriptions of Venetian topography and monuments into the narrative, noting that they shape civic ritual and customs.[31] Sabellico credited those men of the "highest quality" who had founded Venice with suffusing their building campaigns with the principles of liberty and justice.[32]

Domenico Morosini, who petitioned the senate to build the stone bridge in Moro's name, expanded the notion of an ornament as an essential form of communication for the state. In his political tract *De Bene Instituta Re Publica*, written around 1497, Morosini wrote that "the state cannot be established without a decent standard of ornament."[33] Morosini even recommended that Venice adopt a symmetrical and uniform design to increase legibility and facilitate the government's control over the city. He advocated for marshaling Venice's organic layout into a standardized plan through vigorous measurement: "Private dwellings . . . extending beyond the correct measure should be brought into uniformity with the others. Crooked streets should be straightened, narrow ones widened . . . for such diligence requires no great labor and shows off the ornament and decoration of the city."[34]

In a city shaped piecemeal by reclamation and landfill, calls for topographical uniformity are impossible, but they are part of an ideal for urban design that developed in response to pragmatic land management concerns in Venice. Many areas of Venice faced problems with flooding, unclear property borders, and buildings in various states of disrepair. The area around San Giobbe had been subject to flooding due to the flow of the Brenta River and silting in the canals of the northern lagoon area. Throughout the fifteenth century, engineers and civic officials proposed and implemented projects to redirect the flow of the Brenta and the canal system of the northern lagoon area to divert water to the Adriatic rather than toward Venice.[35]

In addition, haphazard construction and land reclamation projects throughout Venice made it difficult to gain purchase over the contours of the lagoon and to levy appropriate property taxes. For example, to circumvent the bureaucracy of land improvements, private citizens often eliminated marshes on their property to create more land for gardens and residential structures through the illicit purchase of sediment dredged from canals.[36] The republic had tried to regulate free-form property interventions though its public works commission. In 1459, officials commissioned a survey of the size and condition of buildings and infrastructure in Venice to assign property tax.[37] In 1485, the Savi Alle Acque—the oversight committee formed to manage waterworks, including the canals, fresh water, and the excessive silting that plagued the Venetian lagoon—began to document property in a land census referred to as the "Book of Measurements."[38] Territorial accounting structured many efforts by city officials to supervise the resolution of property boundaries and the levying of taxes across the lagoon area.

Periodic calls for a land survey point to the difficulty in accurately recording data. In April 1502, the Savi passed legislation ordering a new census to collect data about property in Venice and use that compilation of data to replace the missing Book of Measurements. Unauthorized property modifications would be subjected to a heavy fine of 100 ducats, and there would be penalties for other transgressions as well. An addendum to the 1502 census legislation offered a penalty exception to ecclesiastical institutions like San Giobbe that were subject to flooding from the Brenta and subsidiary waterways in the northern part of the lagoon. The addendum referenced a lost map that demarcated the many sites that could claim an exception.[39]

Land management concerns likely gave weight to the discursive testimonies about San Giobbe property and the active engagement by the Franciscans in contrast to the static contracts and documents submitted as evidence by the hospice administrators. The Commissioners of the Commune who oversaw the Savi and other public works in Venice also adjudicated the 1502 trial at San Giobbe.[40] The overlap in bureaucratic duties suggests that during the 1502 interrogation process at San Giobbe the questions posed about the appearance and upkeep of property, as well as the nature of activity at the complex, paralleled the data collected during the land census that the commissioners requisitioned a month later.

As state operators, the commissioners enacted a tacit agenda related to upkeep and renewal. The 1502 verdict at San Giobbe in favor of the Franciscans seemed to hinge on the success of a legal narrative that adhered to the larger image of the republic at the time—a focus on producing data about the topography and improvements to urban design and planning. In 1487, the Venetian senate offered the first copyright for a history of the republic to Marc'Antonio Sabellico for his thirty-three-volume *Decades rerum Venetarum*.[41] Chronicles and histories of the city had been written before, but with the privilege granted to Sabellico the state validated the projection of its image and left room to prosecute divergent narratives. The state also issued privileges to produce city views. In 1498, the Venetian senate issued a privilege to Giovanni Biondo to amass measurements for a printed view of the city, allegedly already in production.[42] There are no extant copies of this view of Venice, but Biondo alluded to

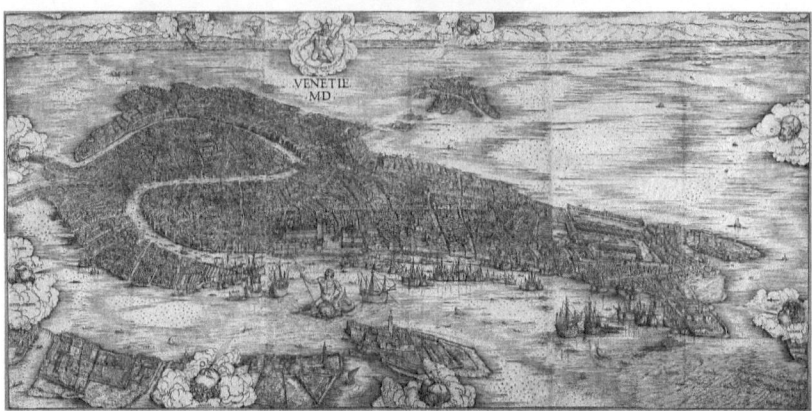

14.3. Jacopo de' Barbari, *View of Venice*, 1500, woodcut. National Gallery of Art, Rosenwald Collection, 1950.1.14–19.

competition in his petition to the senate, suggesting that, at the time, the artist Jacopo de' Barbari was measuring distances on the ground and angles between the rooftops from the bell tower at San Giorgio in the southern lagoon so that he could engrave a view of Venice onto six woodblocks (fig. 14.3). Produced with a license from the Venetian senate, every wave, structure, canal, and line etched into Barbari's woodblocks served as a state apparatus.

In Barbari's image, Venice is enveloped by mountains and winds. He captured the variations between the calm lagoons, the mountainous waves carrying rowers participating in a regatta, and the water patterns and fluctuating depth as the canals linking landmasses in the city empty silt and water into the lagoon. The map drew heavily on contemporary descriptions of Venice, as Patricia Fortini Brown has argued.[43] Barbari draws explicitly from descriptions of Venice by Sabellico, who promised a descriptive representation of Venice from multiple perspectives. Sabellico records the distant Alps at the northern border of the republic with a description of multidirectional winds, then describes the city in detail through its infrastructure and buildings, "as if depicted on a panel."[44] Sabellico even described the god Neptune watching over the city's naval fleet, as can be seen at the bottom of the Barbari view. That Sabellico and Barbari each received licenses from the republic to produce their descriptions of Venice points to an authorized set of criteria that anchored textual and visual representations, delineating the scope of Venetian territory and distributing people traveling through the city or constructing it.

Barbari did not reconstruct Venice precisely, but the print, in its proliferation of details about the physical fabric of Venice, records a city undergoing a transformation, with a developing network of access and movement across the lagoon. The section of the print depicting San Giobbe captures the layers of construction. The small Rio San Giobbe divided the hospice buildings that extended to the western edge of Venice from the church and Franciscan friary. Although the church is now vaulted with stone, Barbari shows that its long aisleless space had been covered by a wooden truss roof during the fifteenth century. In the view, the double ogival windows that had lined the north side of the nave of the church were already blocked to accommodate additional altars and the double-storied loggia in the cloister, to house the friars. Barbari even depicts armatures behind the apse of the church, suggesting that the construction of the long choir that now extends from the high altar chapel was in progress.

Barbari registered dynamic transformations into his static representation of the city to show that the scenography of Venice had a narrative of development. Barbari depicted several wooden bridges over many canals outside the city center, while stone bridges span the canals in the foreground, framing the ceremonial entryway to Venice—the recently paved piazza San Marco. Sanudo and his contemporaries described the constant driving of piles, with fantastic engineering mechanisms used to stabilize the ground for new building. Barbari depicted a scene in which workers strengthen the northern embankment of Venice through pile driving. The view compressed several moments of Venetian engineering into a unified image.

It is worth noting that in 1536 the publisher of Barbari's view, Antonio Kolb, sought a patent for machines that he developed to dredge the canals and drive pilings to secure the coasts and embankments of Venice.[45] Kolb's later inventions suggest that his participation in publishing the woodcut view by Barbari served several agendas. Kolb and Barbari not only created an image of Venice for profit but capitalized on emerging technologies related to printing, land surveying, and hydraulics to contribute to maintaining the Venetian hydraulic system and Venice's image as an orderly maritime and mercantile power during a period of great geopolitical strife. The Barbari view offers a representation of Venice that is fueled not by etiological myths like the relics of Saint Mark the Evangelist arriving in Venice but by the city's infrastructure, maritime power, and mercantile economy. The physical city became an essential armature of representation: Barbari presented the landscape as a miraculous icon of engineering of Venetian history, enlivened by civic and ritual activity and urban renewal. In the 1502 trial at San Giobbe, Franciscan *usus pauper* was privileged as an investment in the experience of the site. Like the proliferation of views, censuses, histories, and guides related to land management in Venice, the testimonies closed the gap between evidence and narrative, as topographic systems became a protagonist in the history of Venice.

15

Settling Imaginations
Between Dust and Silt

■

IJLAL MUZAFFAR

Can memories be evidence? Can their shifting landscapes reveal maps we can trust? In the long history of the Western Enlightenment, maps and memories have stood as opposites, with modernity often seen as a quest for objectivity and fact.[1] Yet, no matter how abstract a map, it is never able to get rid of the ghost of the subjective, the mythical.

I grew up with stories in which these two dimensions—the objective and subjective, the mythic and the factual, the imaginative and the cartographic—seem to forever overlap in dust. My father was born in a small village called Deh 22, deep in the desert of Sindh, now in Pakistan. These villages, with numbers instead of names, were settled by the British to jumpstart a cotton supply chain in the aftermath of the 1867 "Lancashire cotton famine" caused by the American Civil War. Dust, in all its forms, settled on the plans and imaginations of all who took part in this global endeavor. Great canals, carefully laid out by Scottish engineers across the desert, became clogged with silt. Charging horsemen, rebelling against the expansion, emerged out of dust clouds at night. Seen through the squinted eyes of those men pointing rifles in the dark, dust shaped the perception of self and other, friend and enemy. It is as if dust were the minuscule layer in which the cartographic and imaginative were forever locked in battle.[2]

I, too, have pieced these stories together through imagination, both mine and others'. When I look up Deh 22 on Google Maps, instead of an "objective" view from above, I see a turmoil of conflicting narratives: I can see the expanses surveyed by my father on foot on his first job as a young engineer for an equally young Water and Power Development Authority of Pakistan. The irrigation canals cut as a result of those surveys tried to push back the desert just as the ambitious colonial-era canals had tried to do. I can also see the undefeated desert

15.1. Land in its various forms: dust, silt, and mud in and around a tertiary canal near Deh 22. Photograph by Ijlal Muzaffar, 2018.

returning with a vengeance, to demand its place on the map. I see indigenous villages displaced by those canals, and the property holders displaced once again by new dams trying in vain to buy time against the inevitable. I see a map that is simultaneously a palimpsest of testimonies, family lore, lived experience, and archival documents. Can a map ever be read, or made, without imagination?

Imagination is shaped by materiality. Dust and darkness, land and water, all have material dimensions that interrupt testimonies, creasing the perception of space and time along specific folds. By my estimate, it must have been in the late 1920s when my grandfather received two shotguns of unspecified make from the district commission's office. These, and four other pairs like them, were distributed in the village, as I had heard while growing up, to defend against the elusive Hurs, followers of the Sufi saint Pir Pagaro, who had mounted an armed rebellion against the British. I now know that the Pir's name was Sibghatullah Shah Rashidi II, the sixth descendant in a lineage of Pir Pagaros famously known by their title (*Pir* from the Persian word for saint and *Pagaro* from the Sindhi word for a chieftain's turban).[3] The rebellion against the British was initially started by Rashidi's father in the 1890s, when he saw his dominion shrinking. Hurs (their name coming from the Arabic word for freedom) were being scattered by British reorganization of the scant agricultural and pastoral lands. The younger Pir, anointed at the age of twelve in 1921, turned the rebellion into armed struggle. Decentralized from the beginning, the resistance was carried out by independent gangs that sought both strategic targets as well as retribution against any villages allied with the colonial government. The new villages with numbers for names fell into this group, my grandfather recalled, unless they proved otherwise by paying the Hurs for protection. The government had issued the shotguns to the villagers to prevent them from taking that path.

Whenever I visited my grandparents, I never missed the opportunity to take the shotguns from one of the bedroom closets, where they lay behind clothes like forgotten laundry. Their steel barrels felt cold in my hands on hot days. Their beaten wood grips and shoulder stocks smelled musty and battle worn. I could imagine my grandfather as a young man standing at the village edge pointing them at the charging horsemen.[4] That never happened, even in my grandfather's countless retellings. Those tales were about waiting, at night, wondering if and when the Hurs would strike. Each night he picked up his shotgun countless times and aimed it at the darkness beyond the faint glow of the torch. As the nights passed, his fears of rape, plunder, murder, and fire rose to a shrieking pitch in his mind. In these stories the Hurs were transformed into specters that were to come from the darkness and disappear into it without a trace. Where did they reside? he wondered. They were said to have a base in the Makhi Dhand, the jungle that surrounded the wetland of an expansive seasonal lake some ten miles northeast of the village. But that was too far away from the village to enable them to stage an attack in one night. Did that mean the Hurs walked among the settlers during the day, laboring as fieldworkers on the very land and waterways they destroyed at night? Were they avenging a settlement they saw as unjust or squaring grievances from past centuries? All this would remain uncertain in his mind.[5]

To me, too, Hurs have appeared as ghosts, not because they appeared from the darkness and dust that surrounded this land but because the darkness, and the dust, harbored seams in time. The dust that blew up at night to shroud the light of the torch also reflected one's knowledge back on itself. Out there, the land was both native and foreign, the villagers' home and a war zone, both comforting and deathly. Muted red shadows conveyed an altered existence, alien histories, spirits in the jungle, all threatening to erupt into life and consume it. Dust was the irreducible dimension of land that escaped its transformation into property. It could be neither bought nor sold nor controlled through strategy or force. It was the milieu of the rebel, the material trace of resistance.

Perhaps that is why the shroud of dust engendered in those who stood guard through it, night after night, a sense of responsibility that was equally opaque and dispersed. Even during the day, the settlers who guarded the village at night seem to have searched in the dark. Days were passed wandering farther afield along the bank of the nearby canal. Someone on a bridge would throw a brick into a canal and challenge the others to dive into the muddy water to retrieve it. Holding his breath, the diver would descend to a depth of sixteen to

15.2. Jamrao Canal near Jhol, Sanghar District, Sindh. The muddy waters show the immense amount of silt in the canal, thus necessitating yearly cleaning of the waterway. Photograph by Ijlal Muzaffar, 2018.

twenty feet, where he would prod the bed of the canal, his fingers seeking the brick in the darkness (fig. 15.2).

As a child, I visited my grandparents' home with my family on the two Eids, the celebrations for the day after the Hajj in Mecca and the day after the fasting of Ramadan. In those days in the early 1980s, the Eid would arrive during the summer, a period of blistering heat in the desert. (Eids are based on the lunar calendar and rotate about 10 days off from the 365-day solar calendar each year.) With other kids from the village, my brother and I would venture to canals not as deep as the divers' canals for a cool swim on scalding afternoons. If you put your head underwater and opened your eyes, even when the sun was blazing bright overhead, the water in the six- to eight-feet-deep smaller canals would appear blood red, like looking at the sun with eyes closed. And if you opened your eyes while submerged in this muddy water, it was like looking inside your own body, seeing only flickering shades of brownish red light without any sense of nearness or depth.

The murky depths of the bigger canals, where my grandfather went diving with his fellow guardsmen, would have been even darker. I imagine him urgently tapping the deep bed of the canal, searching for a brick as his lungs pressed for air with every passing second. His fingers would have stirred up the silt, making the muddy water even muddier with every urgent tap. Did he ever open his eyes to see this view into his own soul? I wonder if he saw what I imagine: this muted darkness, in a world turned inside out, upside down, the disturbed silt appearing like dust clouds of Hur horsemen approaching as he looked out into the dusty darkness at the village's edge every night. Why did this story, of diving into the darkness of the canal, looking for a brick, a baked and hardened piece of land among the minuscule and emulous particles of land, the submerged desert of silt, form a part of his story of earning the right to settle?

I am pressed to think of the link between the two. Between the darkness of the desert night and the darkness of the muddy water, the two environments were tied together through land in contrasting forms—dust and silt. There, where vision takes a backseat, one fumbles with one's fingers on the trigger and on the canal bed to gain one's bearings, only to realize one's precarious and vulnerable existence in the face of the unknown. This haptic interaction with land, silt, brick, is not metaphorical; it is the currency, the habitus, both epistemological and literal, on which legitimacy is claimed and assigned.[6] Looking out from the tradition of the Enlightenment, we have come to understand darkness as a scene of ignorance. But in this place, darkness, dust, silt, all figure as forms of inhabiting the land between knowing and un-knowing. Dust endarkens, if you will, one's experience to make it not only bearable, possible, plausible, but to coexist with its opposite. It is only when mediated by dust that both the elusive Hurs and the settlers waiting for them through the night with a loaded gun can simultaneously occupy the land.

The Darkened Horsemen

It is this dusted darkness that prevented my grandfather, Abdul Qadir, from knowing that the elusive Hurs he waited for were the very reason he was given the chance to settle on this land in the first place. The land bound their fates together in an ironic union, one in which each was made possible by the other but also pitted against it.

The Hur was a figure etched in darkness, even when he walked the land during the day (fig. 15.3). Hurs moved from village to village through a surreptitious network of informants and spies who looked ahead for police officers and soldiers, while keeping themselves invisible even in the daytime. This cartography of invisibility nevertheless produced a confrontation. For the Hurs, every mile of the new canals was an erasure of the social, religious, and political system of inhabiting land on which they relied.[7]

The British had absorbed Sind into the Bombay Presidency in 1843, in a summary war after extended deception and double crossings. Although the wars at Miani and Hyderabad were easily won, the costs of assimilation became apparent as Hur villages started to resist the expansion of irrigation works and had to be continuously suppressed by force. As arrests and killings by the police widened, the Hur rebellion took up arms in the 1890s. As Sarah Ansari

15.3. The Hur was a figure etched in darkness, even when he walked the land during the day. Photograph taken by Terry Ruff, crew member of RAF No. 357 Squadron, a special operations unit that operated over Burma, Malaya, and Sumatra in the early 1940s. Courtesy of J. Rickard, Hurs of the Sindh Desert, March 18, 2017, http://www.historyofwar.org/Pictures/pictures_hurs_sindh.html.

has argued, the British applied pressure to the then newly anointed Pir Pagaro, Ali Gohar, to maintain "law and order." But the administration also became increasingly anxious to rely on one figure for control.[8]

Contrary to British assumptions, however, the Hurs too controlled the Pir's behavior, by holding him to imagined standards of spiritual leadership. The Pir's resistance and Hurs' intransigence compounded the problem, giving the rebellion new vigor in the 1890s. According to Ansari, when the British administration saw that diplomacy was not producing desired results, it decided to send in the army, generating a manifold increase in the violence.[9] The Hurs had already been declared a "criminal tribe."[10] Now they were to be shot on sight or if under any suspicion. The rebellion continued throughout the 1890s, but by the 1900s the Hur clans had been decimated.[11] Most villages were turned into prison camps with walls and sentry towers, turning what was by all accounts a self-sufficient, if highly political, population of inundation farmers and pasture herders into a community on the verge of famine.

Greater Games

Pir Ali Gohar Shah II's death in 1896 preceded by a decade the death of my great-grandfather's grandfather, Pir Baksh (who shared with Ali Gohar the prenom Pir, or saint, but didn't inspire an armed following).[12] Pir Baksh had been a small farmer in the village of Pilore, near Jalandhar in northern Punjab. Small landholdings had become smaller over the generations, with less than an acre of land for most families. Pir Baksh was more fortunate than most, but he foresaw the inevitable division that was coming to his lot. His relatives had already left for settler colonies in Punjab. Their relative success appeared enviable from Pilore.[13] Pir Baksh decided to remedy the situation by taking the British offer for more land in Sindh. In the official papers, he would be documented as literate, giving him the title of *sufaid posh*, or one who wore white. The reference to white clothes referred to the privilege of receiving five blocks of land (a block held sixteen acres) that would entitle him to hire others to till the land. Those who were to work their own land and were not entitled to keep their clothes at a distance from the dirt were given two blocks.

But titles in an unknown place didn't mean much. Pir Baksh knew very well that his clothes would not remain white. He would till his land for at least a generation and needed all the help he could get from his family. His son was reluctant to follow him. Traveling to Sindh was a one-way journey. Already an old man in 1898, Pir Baksh was desperate. He convinced his grandson, Abdul Haque, to accompany him and migrate to Sindh. Although by the 1900s the memory of the Hur rebellion was still fresh in Hur villages, their circumspection had successfully turned it into only a rumor for those planning to migrate. Although their clan, the Arains, were known to be expert farmers, they had little knowledge of the flora and fauna of southwestern Sindh. To Pir Baksh and his grandson, the south appeared vacant, the land idle.

Little did they know that their knowledge, as well as nonknowledge, of local conditions was an asset for the British enterprise and part of a greater colonial game in which canals functioned as material and epistemological weapons. Benjamin Weil has shown how an engineering-driven approach to river management in the second half of the nineteenth century marginalized social and political understanding of water control.[14] In the narratives of settlement and displacement I have assembled, the engineering of water doesn't function as its de-politicization—if that's ever possible—but rather its re-politicization on a different register. The new canals formed material and epistemological weapons that diluted the Pir's power with water. They turned desert land, no matter how useful and fertile for its inhabitants, into irrigated land, land that was provided with water all year long, land that was held by its inhabitants as property, not as customary possession by religious right. Canals replaced the hierarchies of responsibility allocated by religious and political power with a new hierarchy of landholding, responsibility for paying taxes, management of water quotas, and the sowing and reaping of crops on fixed cycles.

Little did they also know that this game was part of an even larger contest in which the empire itself had been played. That game had come about with the outbreak of the American Civil War in 1861. The American South's plantations stopped sending cheap cotton, grown with slave labor, to the mills in Manchester. The cotton shortage, and the shock, has come to be known as the

Cotton Famine of 1862–1863.¹⁵ The empire attempted to remedy the situation by making inroads in Africa. But there, it had to constantly negotiate with competing colonial powers. The new settler villages in Sindh growing cotton emerged at the same time to provide a safety net if imperial competition undermined similar efforts elsewhere. Little did the settlers and the Hurs know that their transformed fate resulted from being written into this imperial insurance policy.

Of Erasure and Existence

But if Pir Baksh and Pir Ali Gohar's fates were intertwined, they existed in two parallel worlds from the perspective of the colonial administration. The stakes involved in keeping separate the two systems—the two temporalities, the two modes of inhabiting land—would become apparent in 1918. One day Sher Khan, a *hari* (land worker hired on the basis of crop sharing), knocked on Abdul Haque's door. He asked if the *sufaid posh* (white wearer) could come see his guests, who had fallen sick with high fevers soon after their arrival. Abdul Haque kept some basic medicines at home and was often called upon to perform the role of village doctor. Sher Khan's grandson would recall many years later to my father, Abdul Haque's grandson, that he remembered this *barha chaudary* (elder landholder) coming to their hut in the fields wearing a white turban and white *kurta*, riding his white horse, appearing to the young boy as an incarnation of his title, *sufaid posh*, from his clothing to his transport.

But whatever medicine Abdul Haque dispensed to Sher Khan's guests must not have worked, for they were not suffering from travel exhaustion but plague. In 1918, India, situated at the crossroads of colonial trade, was stricken with a plague epidemic.¹⁶ Two days later Abdul Haque, too, developed a fever, one that he wouldn't outlast. Within a month a household of seven was reduced to three. Dying with Abdul Haque were his three young daughters, all under the age of nine, whose names now no one seems to remember. Their only mark on the land that they briefly inhabited are three little graves next to their father's. Abdul Haque's wife, Mariam Bibi, survived him with their three remaining children, two sons and a daughter. The oldest one was my grandfather, who was eight at the time the plague came.

But for Mariam the trouble had only begun. She would later recount that soon after his own grandfather's death in 1906, Abdul Haque had felt overwhelmed by the task of preparing the land for crops he was charged with growing. He wrote a letter to his brother, a police station house officer (SHO) in Punjab, to come help him. The brother, holding what was a post of enviable power in the newly settled canal colonies still rife with disputes over land and property, never arrived. But now, upon hearing of the death of his brother, the SHO held up the letter as a declaration of Abdul Haque's intent to pass the land on to him, and he then arrived with his family to claim what he believed was his due.

Under British common law, Mariam did not possess any rights of inheritance, even from her husband. The land was to be passed on to male heirs or, in their absence, to male siblings. Under Anglo-Muslim law, Mariam and her daughter could inherit only half the share of the male heirs, including her sons and her husband's brother. In this case, this came out to only one-eighth of the property. Whether the SHO filed a claim with the *tehsildar* in Sinjhoro, the seat of all records of land settlement in the area, to confirm that there were no surviving male heirs to the property, or whether he was able to suspend their claims with the sheer weight of his title, I don't know, at least yet. What I know from her and her children's testimonies is that their existence was erased from the world of land settlement, ironically making them akin to the Hurs they had come to displace.

All seemed to have been lost for Mariam, but she refused to leave the village and ensconced herself and her three officially nonexisting children in a mud room with dirt floors at the edge of the compound allotted to her husband and his grandfather. Perhaps her persistence gave her father, a *numberdar* (a revenue collector) in a village in Punjab, the imagination to try the improbable: writing a letter to the king's Privy Council, the advising body to George V, the king of England. After detailing the plight of his daughter, he sent the letter. A year passed, then another. Mariam and the children continued to live invisible lives.

I do not know this for certain, but this must have happened: one day in 1921 the letter was read in the Privy Council. An order was issued. Great injustice had transpired under the British rule and the situation must be corrected. What must be done? Dispatch a magistrate to the village immediately to find out if indeed Mariam still had a living male child who was heir to their father's settlement. But, because the plaintiff was a Muslim widow, she might not be willing to talk to a male officer of the Crown, the council feared. To respect the Muslim family's custom, the council thought to send a woman magistrate, one who could meet the widow in person and verify with her own eyes whether a male child existed.

I know this not because I have found the legendary letter in the Privy Council archives, though I have tried. A large portion of the archives from Sindh still sits, I was told by archivists at the British Library in London, in the basement of 11 Downing Street, next to the famous number 10. Perhaps one day the dust covering these archives will reveal this fate-changing piece of paper. But the missing letter will only document on one epistemological register what I know on another: Mariam, her children, her neighbors, other villagers who were there that day in Deh 22, all testified to this: one day in 1921 four horses surrounded by an entourage of guards pulled a carriage in front of Mariam's compound. A white woman stepped out. She was the special magistrate whom the British government went to great trouble to send because the council had found, to its dismay, that there was no woman magistrate in the entire Bombay Presidency, the administrative province that included Sindh, its canals, its settlers, and their land. The magistrate had taken a ship from Britain, which passed through the Suez Canal and landed in Karachi. From there, she took the train to Nawabshah, the junction some thirty miles from Mariam's village. Since this was no ordinary visit, the deputy commissioner had been notified of her arrival. A carriage awaited her at the station to take her to Sinjhoro, where the records of land settlement resided in the *tehsildar*'s office. Not satisfied with merely retrieving the requisite information, she took the *tehsildar* with her to the village. And now there she was outside Mariam's hut.

The news of her arrival had already reached the surviving members of the family. The children sat on both sides of their mother on the dirt floor, awaiting judgment on their claim to privilege. The magistrate sat on a low stool, with the *tehsildar* beside her, serving as the translator (the Privy Council's fears that Mariam would refuse to meet a male officer of the Crown, the very reason for sending a special female magistrate from England, proved unfounded in the end). The magistrate took the family's statements, confirmed their names, verified the existence of Mariam's children, both male and female, dead and alive, and rendered a decision on the spot. The land would be put in the government's custody and the family would be issued a stipend until my grandfather, Abdul Qadir, came of age. He would then retain the land and the title of *sufaid posh*, the white wearer, ironically the very privilege that had led his father to his death.

I wonder if it felt like a collapse of space and time to an eight-year-old. Who was this white woman in front of him asking if he was dead or alive or whether he even existed? What gave her the power to un-erase his existence, his family's existence, and etch it back onto the map of settlement?

But whereas the woman magistrate's presence might have appeared troubling to my grandfather, his mother, Mariam Bibi, never questioned the authority of the judgment. They were impressed by the surreal unlikelihood of the event but didn't attribute it to the efficiency of the empire. It was their due, an outcome of their steadfastness, their prayers answered.

But if we attribute their acceptance of the event to their religious devotion, how do we explain the king's Privy Council's devotion to heroic action? The king of course led the Church of England, but to which god did the imperial bureaucracy pray?[17] Why did a letter from a *numberdar*, an ordinary revenue collection agent in Punjab, pleading the case of his daughter, become the example on which the credibility of the British Empire itself was imagined to rest? It was not as if every cry of injustice from the colonies was answered. There might not have been many fathers who thought of directly approaching the king of England. But why was this particular letter read and an unlikely agent of the empire then dispatched across a great span of space and time?

Machines of Time

I would venture that the unlikely had to be made likely because at stake was a conflict between a system that imagined the relationship with land as mechanical and a system that imagined it as a set of social and religious obligations. In the mechanical worldview, a measure of land needed a specific amount of seed. This much seed needed this much water, which produced this much crop, which produced this much revenue. Turn the handles on the canal gates to match the input, and you should get the projected output. The settlers, too, were a cog in the machine. Their responsibility was to themselves. To survive, they needed to perform their part. And if they cultivated what was made possible by the system, the rest of the parts turned, each according to its own logic. The *numberdar*s for each village (when not busy writing letters to the British king) would come to demand revenue from settlers according to the water given to them, the crops they had sown, the land they had irrigated.

This system of mechanical relationships demanded visibility, and within it the Hurs' occupation of land on their terms amounted to an insistence on invisibility. A state, a colonial state, could not be administered through invisible actors. The Hurs' only visible node was their Pir. To rely on one man's goodwill for the administration of a vast territory was a risk too high to be tolerated.

This confrontation was also a conflict between multiple temporalities and different scales of understanding land. For British Colonial Office planners, starting a new cotton belt halfway across the world was part of a calculus of space and time that saw the land only as cartography, every node, every coordinate, every boundary of which was saturated with strategic decisions of imperial competition and power. In this calculus, land appeared in quantifiable terms of addition and subtraction. How much investment in canals would produce how much taxation and how much cotton and wheat?[18] For the Hur followers of the Pir, the land did not appear as a cartographic entity, a world that existed in statistical tables, bureaucratic procedures, administrative arrangements, and parliamentary debates. They had a calculus, but it was not of addition and subtraction. For them the parts added up to more than a sum. What they grew, what they consumed, and what they paid as *nazrana* (devotional contribution) to the Pir were investments on many other registers, from spiritual to material to political. Gayatri Spivak has described the divergence between such points of view as the irreducible difference between seeing the world as a globe or as a planet and seeing it being driven by globalization or by planetarity.[19]

The Planet Returns

Are the globe and the planet mutually exclusive? Is land always more and less than its encapsulation in the space of maps, the calculus of investments, and

15.4. Salinized land around Deh 22, with a large tract to the north. The now submerged Makhi Dhand (the historic hideout of the Hurs) and the encroaching desert beyond are also visible to the right. Courtesy of Google Maps, 2019.

the strategies of rule? In chasing ghosts across the land, the colonizers and the settlers missed the inexorable enemy that was rising saliently in their midst. My grandfather had seen it without seeing and touched it without touching when he prodded the dark depths of the canal looking for a tossed brick. The darkness might have reminded him of the Hur horsemen he heard when looking out from the village edge at night. But this wasn't an enemy shrouded in the darkness. It was the darkness itself, the silty water brought against all odds to this land, the water that he himself was pouring into the land to grow what hadn't grown on it before: cotton, sugarcane, wheat—all crops that demanded flood irrigation. This water had nowhere to go. It was not long before it started accumulating below the crops, making its head visible at first in the lower lands, turning them into blackened stretches strewn with lines of evaporated salt that looked like large discarded snakeskins.

Ironically, it is this rising water that would kill the last stronghold of the Hurs as well. After their attacks on the army, or on villages they suspected were allied with it, the Hur gangs hid in the notorious Makhi Dhand, so dense with thorny shrubs and trees that the British Indian army didn't deem entering it worth the effort. In the late 1990s, the Water and Power Development Authority, a federal engineering authority (for which, incidentally, my father also worked his entire professional life), advised by the World Bank's Sustainable Environmental Program, set its eyes on the *dhand*. Its low-lying shrubbery and depressions appear as contours of a future lake that could absorb the flood runs and extend the inevitable perhaps for another half a century.

The *dhand*, however, was never empty. The Hurs disappeared into its depths not because the thorns were too sharp for the army horses; they disappeared into it because it was dotted by Hur villages. The villagers survived by fishing in seasonal lakes and rearing animals. As the reservoir was flooded by a new dam, some 993 families, from 47 villages, lost their homes and their land in exchange for almost nothing.[20] Since they were never property holders, what they got in return for their eviction was not enough to sustain a new life.

When I type "Deh 22 Sanghar Pakistan" in Google Maps, I can see my grandfather's village and the expanse of crops pocked by rising salinity (fig. 15.4). When I zoom out a bit to the northeast I see a dark emerald lake, carving long jagged edges into the desert beyond. This is where the *dhand* used to be. It is now called the Makhi lake. Here, the ghost that my grandfather might have seen in the depth of the canal stares back at me.

16

Dadaab Is a Place on Earth
Land and the Migrant Archive

■

ANOORADHA IYER SIDDIQI

The terms "migrant" and "refugee" carry with them a fiction of the landed, settled figure (fig. 16.1). This fiction has sprung from treasuries and repositories that suggest that legitimate communities have been those not only anchored in the land but fixed in space. This concept of fixity is well guarded, militaristically so.

The migrant or refugee violates that fixity. The refugee's spatial strategy—migration—transgresses territorial formations. While that transgression is most often recognized as a disruption of space, it is less understood as an interruption of time. This figure is cut off from normative temporality and historicity. She is granted only a fraught present and future, without access to a narrative of the past.

What if, instead, the landed archive did not merely represent states and empires but retained a place for the migrant? What histories might that archive privilege? Through one site, this chapter reflects on land and the migrant archive.

Seeing Dadaab

In 1991, the Kenyan government and the United Nations High Commissioner for Refugees (UNHCR) established a refugee camp near the town of Dadaab.[1] This inaugurated a process on the border of Somalia that would concentrate people in settlements at this site for several years (fig. 16.2). Due to state-imposed restrictions on refugees' mobility, the complex of settlements has grown to a size exceeded in Kenya only by that of Nairobi or Mombasa, eventually becoming the largest ever to be administered by the UNHCR, even as it remained absent from ordinary maps.[2] Many people have been born, have died, or have lived in Dadaab.

16.1. M. Saddiq Hassan, in the garden she designed and cultivated in Dagaheley refugee camp, Dadaab, Kenya, 2011. Photograph by Anooradha Iyer Siddiqi.

16.2. Block in Ifo refugee camp, Dadaab, Kenya, 2011. Photograph by Anooradha Iyer Siddiqi.

Dadaab is most often described in blighted terms of political insecurity and economic informality, yet for those confined here it has constituted a world. Even if temporary, it has served as a home for a worldwide diaspora of people from Somalia and elsewhere in Africa who have passed through, as well as many in the Kenyan and international humanitarian relief workforce. Nevertheless, it has been hard to see, in space as well as in time; its historical record has been scattered, at best.

A refugee camp leaves little historical trace. Field offices might not have the capacity to maintain recordkeeping in situ or to archive materials in regional or global headquarters. Humanitarian field stations are often sited in environments in which the preservation of paper documents is impossible. Aid workers vacating a post during an emergency might abandon documents. Filed documents may be limited to "sitreps," or situation reports, a military form of reporting providing no more than priority details, which narrowly convey events, reflect national biases, and limit historical or aesthetic texture.[3] Undertaking nonoperational research or critical inquiry may be difficult or even life-threatening, as refugee camps are sites in which populations are being policed, their public health managed, and their international migration restricted.[4] In Africa, where most of world's refugee hosting takes place, governments have regularly located camps adjacent to the theaters of war that posed the crisis initiating the humanitarian intervention, where struggle continues. Security restrictions, interior containment, and surveillance are regular responses to paramilitary activity, affecting not only refugees and aid workers but also "nonessential personnel" such as researchers who might seek to build solidarities with people living in these zones, to amplify their concerns, and to invite their narratives into scholarship.

Dadaab presents such conditions, and others as well. It has no doubt been silenced. Records belonging to the Department of Refugee Affairs in Kenya have not been publicly accessible.[5] Political instability in Somalia has often limited the access scholars might gain, as well as possibilities for publication.[6] The UNHCR has classified records for much of the duration of the site's existence, per the agency's protocols to protect fleeing individuals.[7] This policy has inevitably exacted a toll on collective and community histories by limiting those that might draw from conventional archival approaches or whose aims do not directly relate to the practice or policy of national security or relief and development operations. However, with careful work, records may be gathered. Official documents of the site are contained within the substantial holdings of the UNHCR and other governmental archives, as well as the collections of local and international nongovernmental humanitarian organizations, academic and cultural institutions, and individuals around the world. A gray literature has been produced since the early 1990s by aid providers; economic, political, and human rights advocates; and technical professionals (from architects to aerial cartographers), as well as journalists and refugees. Residents, neighbors, visitors, resettled refugees, and members of the refugee diaspora, Somalis and others, have left a record in the public domain. Scholars in more than one discipline have studied Dadaab. In doctoral dissertations, books, and articles, they have described and interpreted the site at multiple moments since it was established, building primary knowledge as they contributed to a body of secondary research. Dadaab is thus a muted yet affective object for an architectural and historical study.

Notwithstanding, it is difficult to write a history of Dadaab that seeks meaning in architecture beyond militarism. Although refugee camps are rarely documented in ways that promote seeing them and understanding their pasts, Dadaab can come into view because it is one of the few refugee environments captured in a range of archival materials, media, and visual and material culture, and also because architects and other spatial practitioners have worked in Dadaab, connecting it to designs, aesthetic practices, and territorial strategies around the world. Nevertheless, to see Dadaab, a theory of listening is needed.[8] Listening to diverse sources builds social and material context that is missing in many of the formal records of the humanitarian intervention, which suffer simultaneously from scarcity and abundance, producing obtuseness on the one hand and incoherence on the other. This expansive historiographic practice sees a colonial archive for the fabrication that it is and instead centers a narrative of people. In Dadaab, this includes people who have worked as architects, without any official license, to build an architecture of modernity without modern design at a site whose history could only be written using precarious evidence.[9] This historiographical expansiveness offers an opposition to militarism, beginning by rejecting abstractions of a refugee camp and instead seeing that Dadaab is a place on earth whose architecture has supported a thriving and complex lifeworld in the East African margins.

Land and Borders

The complex of refugee settlements at Dadaab is a constructed architectural form and also a material remnant of colonial practices of territoriality. Specifically, it inhabits a territory between three colonial frontiers, three nation-states, and multiple contested lands. Records of this territory cannot be consulted within a single country, agency, or institution, nor have they been able to be comparatively triangulated since the breakdown of the government of Somalia in 1991.

This condition is not unusual for histories of Africa, which generally demand complex approaches combining unwritten evidence with a variety of primary source types in historical reconstruction.[10] Historians of Africa have little choice but to work ecumenically, in spite of specialist tendencies, to gather information and knowledge from many seemingly disparate sources, to work from hunches.[11] Furthermore, in many African borderlands, states and institutions have asserted themselves asymmetrically, resulting in uneven archiving of historical records and competing claims to the historical record. Wolfgang Zeller argues that reductive ideas of European territoriality have been replaced by "another highly simplified and static reading of boundary-making in Africa . . . the idea that the famous Organization of African Unity (OAU) decision of 1963–1964, which resulted in the principle of acceptance of Africa's colonial boundaries at independence, somehow represented the end of history regarding this matter."[12] Borderland negotiations telegraph through to the asymmetrical archiving of these lands.

Moreover, to a radical degree, land demarcation itself has been perceived differently across East Africa, where, on the one hand, approximately seventeen major boundaries were drawn between Sudan and Tanzania between 1891 and 1915 and, on the other, transhumant lifestyles have left little in the way of any material or aesthetic footprint of certain communities or of human habitation altogether.[13] As Christopher Clapham observes, "for most colonized African peoples, 'nationalism' involved a recognition of the common fate of those *within* a colonial frontier," but "for the Somalis it directly resulted from the resentments of those who had to move across such a frontier."[14] Ethiopian representatives at the founding summit of the Organization of African Unity in 1963 declared that the Somalis had never formed a united territorial state, "as though that settled the matter," but for Somalis the aim was eradication rather than creation of borders, following the adage, "Wherever the camel goes, that is Somalia."[15] The easternmost region of the Northern Frontier, occupying nearly half the area of the Kenya colony and bordering Somalia, demanded regular negotiation. The Anglo-Italian demarcation of the Kenya-Somalia borderland in 1925 explicitly provided for its fungibility. According to Gilbert M. Khadiagala, "If in certain areas specified in the treaty there existed a shortage of pasture for Somali clans, and if during rainy seasons the pasturage on the Kenya side exceeded local requirements, then those clans might be permitted to cross the boundary."[16] This form of regular compromise produced a highly complex set of identities and politics, along with deep antagonisms over frequently performed tensions.

These ground-level engagements produced the figuration of the Kenya-Somalia borderland, as well as its archive. At Dadaab, the afterlife of such tensions appears in the morphology of Ifo camp (fig. 16.3). The blocks on the west side of the settlement adjacent to the highway were the first to be settled, suggesting that refugees approximated the plots they were assigned. The blocks farther east were settled later, and their patterns follow the humanitarian water distribution grid. The demarcations between and around refugee plots were made of live fencing, quite literally a vertical extension of the land. Mobile structures were clustered within, made of the same material harvested from the ground (fig. 16.4). Elements of the land expected to conform to the grid are paradoxical, as are the clustered dwellings that contradict the pastoral political economy. Indeed, the built form of the refugee settlements presents several such impossibilities—aporias between borders and land.[17] A history of architecture in

16.3. Overhead view of Ifo refugee camp, Dadaab, Kenya, 2009. Courtesy of UNHCR.

16.4. Humanitarian shelters and refugee dwellings, Ifo refugee camp, Dadaab, Kenya, 2011. Photograph by Anooradha Iyer Siddiqi.

Dadaab must then follow this irresolvability. It must be understood precisely as a history of borders, of the ground, of the land. Land itself has been the evidence for history, as well as the basis for historical narrative.

Such a study of architecture is subversive. It relies on the positionality articulated by architecture, acknowledging that seeing architecture—as a method of historical research—enables a situated, qualified history that is more urgent than a universal, imperial history. This method orients the construction of historical evidence toward encounter and immersion, ways of seeing and hearing, which thus reveal the precarious authority, the instability, of archives. It also orients the construction of narrative toward the removal of occlusions, toward clarity, and away from obfuscation. Official archives can obfuscate something direct and clear about land and architecture's relationship to it. At Dadaab, the growing of borders and the dense arrangement of mobile architectures—whether made by pastoralists for migrant living or made by humanitarians for refugee living—suggest histories of transgressions and contestations of land.

Migrant Archive

Sometimes an assertion of incompleteness and leaving behind the assurance of evidence can unsettle hegemonic histories. There are often quiet methods behind such assertions, for example, the labor of listening to people's voices or the observation of architecture in use, as Huda Tayob has gently demonstrated.[18] There can be the dreamed figuration, the "critical fabulation" that Saidiya Hartman advanced in order to see women who do not appear in archives in the usual way.[19] In line with these practices, I observed, listened to, and dreamed with hundreds of refugees, aid workers, officials, planners, mothers, children, architects, academics. They were mostly women and generously contributed to a "migrant archive," a neologism coined here in the spirit of countering expectations and desires that most history writing generates around the fixity and landed wealth of institutional archives.[20] This migrant archive included many conversations that occurred on walks through camps, which offered crucial insights into the history and architecture of Dadaab, its relationship to the colony and the nation-state, and alternate nationalist visions, forms of belonging, and relationships to the land.

The walks, conversations, and insights of this migrant archive were a gift I received while working with the Women's Refugee Commission, an advocacy-based research organization that supported my research and connected me to forces behind the camps, including people living in the Dadaab refugee settlements, contractors responsible for their planning and construction, laborers working in the humanitarian and development system, administrative officials, and members of the regional host community.[21] Working with this organization raised conceptual and methodological problems, and not a small degree of anxiety related to research in military zones, compliance with the police state, the claims and distinctions of feminist theory and praxis, and architecture's collusions with power. Yet, it allowed me to turn to architecture in order to understand history in Dadaab.

Dadaab's ubiquitous architectural form operated as anything but an object, rather, as a thread tying together histories of the land and migration.[22] The *tuqul*, a dwelling covered with woven mats or fabric, illuminated a texture and detail that the documentary materials in the UNHCR archives, for example, did not convey. Its resistance to modernization in the humanitarian setting illustrated its possible behavior in a colonial context, in which African dwellings were to be fixed and taxed. It spoke to solidarities, since hidden, from the days when the first humanitarian camp was established at Dadaab; the aid workers as well as the refugees slept in *tuquls*, nearly in the open air, and sometimes in close proximity with each other, sharing disease and hyena attacks.[23] The *tuquls*, forced together in dense groupings as they never would have been under other conditions, suggested longer histories to be traced in a paradoxically ephemeral yet tethered architecture. They gestured toward other histories of forced sedentarization of pastoral communities. I would later learn that these histories consisted of those of formerly enslaved persons cultivating plots in abolitionist missionary settlements, of freedom fighters held in imperial frontier detention camps, and of secessionists restrained in secured borderland villages.[24] Whispers of these histories emerged from looking closely at an architecture, which might have been dismissed as a vernacular cultural object, a primordial house form. The act of historical assemblage began with seeing this architecture as an archive, as archiving the land, as a migrant archive.

The historian assumes the burden of creating, maintaining, and advocating for such an assemblage, but hopefully this energy is expended to meaningful ends. In the preface to *Differencing the Canon*, Griselda Pollock writes that "the conscious awareness of 'narrative' when we write 'history' has special resonances for feminists in their desire not only to do history differently but to tell tales in such a way as to make a difference in the totality of the spaces we call knowledge."[25] The reflection on what it means to "do history differently" and to "tell tales in such a way as to make a difference" suggests a scope for evidence and narrative, its capacity to make meaning beyond the militarism, division, and violence that architecture may enact or obscure. An immersive encounter with architecture enables seeing it, and in doing so, seeing a fuller history for which it serves not as a remnant but as a chamber.

The seasoned historian will understand Pollock's statement as a retrospective reflection rather than a declaration of foresight. History writing is rarely executed with such formed intention or ambition. In an expansive practice of historiography, her suggestion may be instructive, providing the tools and seeding the terms of the labor to be performed.

17

Learning from Johannesburg
Unpacking Denise Scott Brown's South African View of Las Vegas

■

AYALA LEVIN

"I have an African's view of Las Vegas," Denise Scott Brown stated boldly in an oral history interview she gave in 1990, thus characterizing her years growing up in Johannesburg, South Africa, as the formative experience that shaped her approach in her studio Learning from Las Vegas and the subsequent eponymous book she coauthored with Robert Venturi and Steven Izenour, her studio collaborators.[1] This influential work has been considered not only the origin of the "research studio" that takes the city as its object of study but also a cornerstone of postmodernism for its effacement of the barriers between high culture and consumer culture.[2] These two components of that work—its turn toward architectural observation of the city and its breaking down of the city into semiotic signs—can, this chapter argues, be traced to Denise Scott Brown's South African formation—a source of influence largely ignored in previous literature. What is at stake in understanding Scott Brown's view of Las Vegas through her experience growing up in Johannesburg in the 1930s through the early 1950s?[3] This chapter considers the evidence of Scott Brown's autobiographical testimony and photographs, with which she constructed the narrative of her career, as an opportunity to relocate her work in the social life and forms of observation characteristic of apartheid-era South Africa.

Architectural historian Jonathan Massey situates Robert Venturi's *Complexity and Contradiction*, a work now considered a prelude to *Learning from Las Vegas*, in "a history of privilege that skews architectural knowledge." Massey asks, "How can we intersect Venturi's compositional and stylistic approach with analytics . . . relating to architecture's imbrications with systems of class and labor, gender and sexuality, ethnicity and race?"[4] I would like to answer this question by taking seriously Scott Brown's autobiographical accounts. To neglect this part of her story, I argue, is to overlook how her understanding of the relationship between high and low cultures—a theme central to Learning from Las Vegas—was geographically and racially inscribed. As this chapter demonstrates, Scott Brown's cultural relativism emerged from the social life of South Africa's settler colonialism, which gave rise to apartheid. By foregrounding how the experience of coming of age in Johannesburg influenced her methods and theories, I ask what it meant for Scott Brown to view Las Vegas through the imbrication of race and capitalism under apartheid and how this lens refracted her particular politics of consumption.

To account for Scott Brown's South African perspective as an epistemological position that undergirded her work in the United States, I consider the relationship between Scott Brown's narration of her childhood experiences and the photographs she presents as evidence in explaining how she developed an approach to "landscape" that entails an artistic mode of social observation. Given the centrality of the social sciences, and especially anthropology, in implementing apartheid, I highlight the significance of the ethnographic techniques used to observe urban Black populations in South Africa. To provide a comparative basis for Scott Brown's work, I focus on how such techniques were employed in architectural research in Johannesburg from the 1940s through the 1960s.

Autobiographical Narratives, Photographic Evidence

Scott Brown asserted the influence of her South African background on her work in the United States in retrospect, first articulating it in her 1986 article "Invention and Tradition in the Making of American Place" and reiterating it in an oral history interview she gave in 1990–1991 as well as in an address at Johannesburg's Witwatersrand University (Wits), her alma mater, when she received an honorary degree in 2011.[5] As her personal correspondence with South African architect and historian Clive Chipkin demonstrates, she linked her work to her experience in South Africa as early as 1976, as she prepared for the Signs of Life: Symbols in the American City exhibition at the Smithsonian Institution. This correspondence, in addition to her trip to South Africa with Venturi in 1971, demonstrates that her work in the United States continued to be informed by her past and more recent experiences there.

Often her evocations of South Africa serve as points of reference for parallel phenomena in the United States. In her 1976 correspondence with Chipkin, she articulates one of the key themes of her comparison: "Why do people put eagles over their front doors and wagon wheels on their front lawns? And I don't think it's because the capitalist power structure has coerced them into it. I have somehow parlayed my South African xenophobia into its American equivalent and believe in learning from what's around us."[6] She later refined this point on her "South African xenophobia" in her essay "Invention and Tradition," explaining that "we Americans, like other former colonials, are xenophobes, yet in some areas of life, we clutch the apron strings of our mother cultures. We are proud of our indigenous styles, yet at times we still require European endorsement to validate them in our own eyes."[7] In these two provocative statements, Scott Brown situates cultural production in the United States and South Africa in terms of colonial relations between the settler society and the metropole. Her xenophobia, as she explains in "Invention and Tradition," is the settler's desire for nativism in response to the "homesickness" of settler society, for which the colonial center continues to serve as the ultimate reference point. Bringing her South African background to bear on her understanding of American culture, she sees the hierarchy between high and low cultures in American society in terms of colonial center-periphery relations. By considering the United States a settler-colonial society comparable to that of South Africa, Scott Brown both radically provincializes US cultural production, casting it as continuing to seek approval from Europe or its institutional proxies on the East Coast, and normalizes apartheid South Africa, stripping it of its notorious exceptionality as a political anomaly.

As her correspondence with Chipkin in the immediate aftermath of the Soweto Uprising in 1976 demonstrates, positioning her work in a South African context had political implications that she for the most part elided in her professional publications. What is striking about this personal correspondence as well as "Invention and Tradition," which was published the same year the US Congress passed the Comprehensive Anti-Apartheid Act, is that her criticism is directed at the United States, not South Africa. While her conflicted attitude toward South Africa from her position as an expat is outside the scope of this chapter, she daringly uses South Africa, despite its sordid international standing as a world pariah, to critique the United States. At the Wits address, from the safe distance of almost two decades after the end of apartheid, she utters words she could not have previously: "I am amazed by the apartheid I find everywhere, even today."[8] She had already said as much about the United States in her letter to Chipkin, commenting that it is "in many ways so similar to S. Africa that I feel Americans have little right to criticize." Against the dominant framing of South Africa's apartheid as an aberration, Scott Brown perceived it as a mirror in which social injustices and racial tensions elsewhere could be refracted.[9]

If South Africa gave Scott Brown a reflective mirror, it was a mirror mediated by the figure of the "landscape"—a visual sensibility she had cultivated in her childhood. Two female figures stand out in her recollections. First was her mother, whose love for the landscapes of southern Africa contributed to her "patriotism for local landscapes and cultures"—which she contrasted with what she considered colonial jingoism.[10] Her mother, who grew up in the "wilderness" of Rhodesia, introduced her to what has been theorized as the cult of the veld, a settler-colonial romantic vision of an open frontier that helped white South

Africans attach to the colonial territory and imagine an authentic connection with it.[11] Scott Brown developed a similar appreciation for South African urban-scapes through her art education: her Dutch Jewish art teacher encouraged her to look at her surroundings for inspiration rather than repeating European themes. This influence resulted in her painting "workers sowing grain . . . and lots of African street scenes."[12] Considering labor and street scenes part of the landscape genre, Scott Brown foregrounds landscape as a lens that framed her South African perspective: "It's very picturesque, all of this, and it's left me with the same kind of wilderness and feeling for Africa that I got from my mother. . . . What it comes out to is I think I have an African's view of Las Vegas."[13] Through this representation of her "feeling for Africa," she expresses appreciation for her immediate surroundings—an appreciation ostensibly unburdened of the colonial cultural hierarchy that defined "landscapes" according to the metropole's conventions and norms.[14] Yet when she refers to "African streets scenes," the signified shifts to designate streets inhabited by Black South Africans. Considering Black South Africans part of the "landscape," she naturalizes their otherwise contested presence in the city; I turn to the politics of this in the next section.

Through drives across Johannesburg with her mother, an architecture enthusiast who had also studied the subject at the Wits, Scott Brown saw the veld merged with the built environment to form one continuous landscape. This continuity is evident in the series of photo comparisons that appeared in the 2012 online republication of "Invention and Tradition." Taken by Scott Brown in the 1950s and 1960s, one set of photos compares the Mojave Desert in the United States with the Karoo Desert in South Africa (fig. 17.1), while another set features representative houses of English, Afrikaner (Cape Dutch), and Black South Africans (fig. 17.2).[15] These photos articulate her ideas about "landscape" and point to the direct links she made between South Africa and Las Vegas. Imbued with an anthropological documentary value, the photos also provide a quasi-empirical basis for Scott Brown's African perspective while transforming it from a mere metaphor into an apparatus for framing vision—that is, a medium rather than subject matter.[16]

What does it mean to assert that Scott Brown has "an African's view," especially since she enunciates this as a settler-colonial claim to situated knowledge rather than an indigenous claim? Through this assertion, Scott Brown taps into a history of white South African knowledge production that challenged European scientific authority.[17] This challenge was especially pronounced in field sciences such as anthropology, in which South Africans had a considerable advantage over Europeans due to their proximity to the "field." Photography, in this context, served to connote the immediacy and cultural immersion of the researcher's "embodied observation."[18] Elizabeth Edwards describes the emergence of photography as a disciplinary tool in anthropology at the turn of the twentieth century: "as observation was increasingly focused on the body of the

17.1. South African veld, 1957. Photography by Denise Scott Brown.

17.2. Ndebele houses, Mapoch, South Africa, 1957. Photography by Denise Scott Brown.

17.3. Rural general store with goods from England, Eastern Europe, Japan, and America; ads from three continents; and signs in five languages, Natal, 1957. Photography by Denise Scott Brown.

fieldworker, photography becomes, not a mediation of the scientific experience, but an extension, a prosthesis of the fieldwork persona, as an integrated and multilayered system of document which is 'at once an ethnographic object, an analytical category, and a methodological orientation.'"[19] As a multilayered system of signification in which the subjectivity of the researcher plays a role, the anthropological photographic document is also subject to aesthetic choices. In this regard, it is important to note that Scott Brown did not consider her photographs in purely scientific terms. For her, aesthetic conventions worked in parallel with scientific ones in the landscape genre, helping to communicate colonial knowledge to the center and validate it there. In order to make peripheral landscapes visible to metropolitan culture, she argues, emigrant groups artistically re-create landscapes by putting "descriptions in ways that scholarly and artistic people can see them and understand them as part of a culture."[20] For the architect working in the periphery, she seems to imply, the authority of "being in the field" has to be supplemented by an artistic savvy that can make that work legible in the center. "We did it for Las Vegas," she stated boldly.[21]

Scott Brown's ability to take a South African view of Las Vegas importantly demonstrates that this form of situated knowledge was not limited to the locale from which it originated. African perspectives were not bound to African landscapes. "When, in the late 1960s, Robert Venturi and I tried to do something similar in Las Vegas, it was relatively easy to transfer my African attitude to an

American one, suggesting that for the sake of cultural relevance and artistic vitality, American architects look at the landscape around them and learn."[22] An example that presses us to reconsider the Las Vegas study vis-à-vis Scott Brown's South African perspective is a photo from the 1950s that accompanied the published version of the Wits lecture. It shows the façade of a shop named Kwa Adam (Adam's place) decorated with ads; the most prominent one is in isiZulu, indicating the shop's nonwhite clientele (fig. 17.3).[23] Alluding perhaps in retrospect to Las Vegas's billboards, the journal in which it appeared titled this photo *African Pop Culture*. As Scott Brown put it to the Wits audience, what was considered "'debased' African folk pop-art was an inspiration for our study of roadside America."[24] This "African push-back," she explained, "was a factor in my attempt to develop a more inclusive architectural aesthetic."[25] What did she mean by "African push-back," and how did it relate to housing and consumption—the subjects of the photos she presented as evidence of her African view? In the last section of this chapter, I consider these themes through the lens of the social sciences in South Africa and how these informed architectural research practices in the early years of apartheid consolidation.

The Ethnographic Gaze and Its Limits

In his comprehensive study of *Learning from Las Vegas*, Martino Stierli writes, "It was this childhood experience that allowed Scott Brown to understand the *relative validity of cultural norms and values* and to apply this understanding to her practice."[26] But if knowledge can be situated, so can cultural relativism. Scott Brown's cultural relativism was deeply embedded in South African sociality, which used it to justify the apartheid theory of "separate development." Its main proponent was Hendrik Verwoerd, a social psychologist who, before becoming prime minister in 1958, served as minister of native affairs. The "separate development" theory legitimized apartheid—and the displacement of Black South Africans from urban centers to far removed "locations"—by insisting that each "national" group had its own differentiated path to development.[27]

Let us turn, then, from how the artistic genre of landscape mediated Scott Brown's understanding of her "African's view" to how observational practices from the social sciences were entangled with the social life of apartheid. These practices, I argue, shaped Scott Brown's experience and framed her vision. The discourse underlying Verwoerd's thinking can be traced to the field of social anthropology in Afrikaans-speaking universities, which supported and justified segregation.[28] While anthropologists at English-speaking universities argued that European interventions in African societies had affected both groups so much that integration was inevitable, leading Afrikaner ethnologists supported segregation as a means to preserve ethnic-cultural identities. This divide also shaped their research methods. While by midcentury participant observation had become the norm in ethnographic fieldwork, it "required an intimacy of living" that Afrikaner ethnologists, according to Adam Kuper, "found uncomfortable, preferring to rely on formal interviews with authority figures."[29] Such views were in place prior to the consolidation of apartheid in 1948, and the divide between anthropologists at English- and Afrikaans-speaking universities reflected major debates in South African society that extended beyond the narrow domain of academic research, including into investigations of the architecture and lives of Black South Africans.

Architectural observation of the Black South African built environment in the years preceding apartheid can also be divided into two roughly corresponding trends: reformist critique of urban slums and appreciation of traditional aesthetics in rural areas. Both trends involved photographic documentation, either by urban anthropologists or by artists and architects. The first, dating back to the early twentieth century, continued vigorously with architectural and town planning research on "native townships" from the late 1930s to the early 1950s.[30] It responded to studies of African urban slums, such as those pioneered by Ellen Hellmann.[31] As Kuper notes, these studies "must be seen not only as examples of a classic reformist genre of 'social problems,' or even as adaptations of the urban studies of the Chicago school, but perhaps above all as attempts to direct attention to the life of the so-called 'detribalised natives,' the bane of the segregationists."[32] In the 1940s, the second trend was spurred by the work of photographer Constance Stuart Larrabee and publications, such as "Native Architecture" by Betty Spence, that used photography as a form of architectural ethnography.[33]

Scott Brown took her photo of the architecture of the Ndebele village commonly named Mapoch when she returned from her education and travels in Europe in 1957, after the village had become a popular subject for architectural publications by Spence and others.[34] Architectural tourism to the village was in vogue due to its proximity to Pretoria and the stark, colorful geometric images that adorned the local façades.[35] Scott Brown's photo, depicting rows of gates painted with an imaginative array of architectural forms, is reminiscent of photos taken by Larrabee and Spence. Produced as commentary on the effects of intercultural encounter, these 1940s–1950s photographs often lamented the impending loss of an ostensibly authentic African culture even while they obfuscated its modernity.[36] Like Larrabee's famous photo of Ndebele children in traditional garb playing in front of a wall featuring Mr. Peanut, the Planters brand snack-food logo, Scott Brown's photo, showing rows of gates painted with various abstract forms and architectural façades, remarks on the entanglement of the domestic with commodity culture, a theme that she would later develop in the Levittown studio and the *Signs of Life* exhibition in collaboration with Venturi. Yet, rather than lamenting the encounter, as Larrabee and Spence did, Scott Brown's image celebrates the cultural production that results from it. Instead of highlighting the relationship between the human figures and the built environment, the photo is determined by the scale of the architectural ensemble. Featuring a long-shot and wide-angled framing, it captures the ensemble as a whole and takes pleasure in its symmetrical cohesiveness.

While the plethora of Ndebele village photos that circulated in 1940s–1950s South Africa quite starkly presented the entanglement of the domestic (standing for tradition) with the commodity (representing modernity or its corrosive effects), the urban "native township" of "detribalizing" Africans was the primary site for this negotiation. In 1950, Spence published an article titled "How Our Urban Natives Live" on housing in Orlando East, a Johannesburg township. Funded by the National Building Research Institute of South Africa, which conducted research on affordable housing for "nonwhites," it combined tables of numerical data with some rudimentary architectural sketches of furniture and housing plans that replaced the melancholic aura of her Ndebele photographic documentation with matter-of-fact descriptions. Based on a master's thesis by Jacqueline L. Eberhardt (who would later become a prominent anthropologist in France, known as Jacqueline Roumeguère-Eberhardt), the study filled the need for baseline data for township housing planning.[37]

In her opening remarks, Spence pointed out the lack of knowledge about urban Africans' ways of life: "guesses . . . range the full gamut from those which assume that the Native is completely Europeanised to those which consider that locations should be built up in tribal tradition."[38] Spence's survey, which also included a study of furniture purchasing habits in the township, is reminiscent of the burgeoning market research on African consumers at the time. As Deborah Posel has observed, the consolidation of apartheid was concurrent with the advent of mass consumerism in South Africa, and the two were entangled in uneasy ways. The "discovery" of the African market in the mid-1950s led researchers to actively "pursue a degree and form of cross-racial familiarity within the interstices of apartheid segregation, sufficient to open up the 'tastes, desires and habits' of African consumers to commercial scrutiny and to breach the hegemony of everyday racial incomprehension."[39] This production of knowledge about the inner emotional lives of African consumers necessitated using methods akin to urban ethnography in the townships, where white persons would typically not venture. Spence, who had probably not set foot in Orlando East, was assisted by Anna Mokhetle, a social worker who was a "native woman, married with three children."[40] Arguing that "it was probably an advantage to have a woman to discuss the domestic problems concerned, and one not so young or sophisticated as to appear precocious to the inhabitants," Spence neglected to mention the palpable advantage of having a Black African—like the Black "gurus" who played a similar role in consumer research in native townships—to build trust among the research subjects.[41]

The production of the urban African as consumer challenged apartheid's underlying precepts. Analyzing African consumption in terms of status, gender, and generation rather than exclusively in racial terms, such consumer research diverged from apartheid's conception of the "African as primordially an ethnic being, for whom the temptations of 'western' material consumption were suspect and corrosive."[42] It also conflicted with restrictions on African earning and purchasing power, as well as the prohibition on locating in the townships any shopping facilities beyond small grocery stores.[43] In this context, family photos of Black South Africans in their formal sitting rooms with modern furnishings and accessories, such as those taken by father and son photographers Roland Ngilima and Torrance Ngilima, could be interpreted as a form of resistance, since even "the aspiration to luxury—let alone its performance—was a racial offense."[44] This form of subversive mimicry helps us understand what Scott Brown meant by "African push-back." It also helps us complicate her interest in the aesthetics of Las Vegas billboards and lower- and middle-class homeowners in Levittown, Pennsylvania, suggesting a politics of consumption that is just as subversive as it is affirmative—a point that her critics have completely missed.[45]

As opposed to the intimacy and ease conveyed by the Ngilimas' photos, or to Hellmann's underhanded snapshots of street life in a Johannesburg township, Scott Brown's photo of a roadside shop probably located on the outskirts of a township is defined by what Posel describes as "the dialectic of proximity and distance" that "governed the economic and social realities of apartheid."[46] On the one hand, by identifying a form of Black South African cultural production in commercial signs that had no ethnographic value, Scott Brown's photo transgressed the disjointed spatiality of apartheid, where racial groups were brought together, in the words of Okwui Enwezor, "in a gesture of tearing apart, thus deforming any sense of shared space and common values, abrogating all protocols of mutual recognition."[47] On the other hand, however, it was taken from the safe distance of a car, like most of the photos in *Learning from Las Vegas*. Yet while driving in a car afforded the optimal vantage point for taking in American sprawl, in South Africa, where access to cars was racialized, the car functioned as a privileged site from which one could experience proximity without intimacy. Comparing this photo with that of the Ndebele structure makes the limits of this gaze apparent. Like her image of the shop façade, Scott Brown's photo of the Ndebele structure takes only one frontal viewpoint, in marked contrast to her various perspectival viewpoints of the Cape Dutch and English houses. In light of this difference, it is reasonable to assume that the multiple gates, rather than the house behind them, became the subject of the photo because of her limited view.

Scott Brown's characterization of the shop's façade as "African folk pop-art" is reminiscent of Julian Beinart's study of township façades in Johannesburg in the early 1960s. After studying under György Kepes and Kevin Lynch at MIT, Beinart conducted a comprehensive survey of some two thousand homes in the Western Native Township (WNT). As with Scott Brown's billboards and house façades, Beinart's research focused on street views of houses whose individual decoration he interpreted as media. Following Kepes's interest in modern folk art as it emerged from advertising, Beinart emphasized how township residents borrowed forms like commercial logos and magazine advertisements from the urban context in which they lived and worked. Like Scott Brown, Beinart did not perceive this imagery as contaminated by Western mass culture but instead considered it new folk art and a form of "detribalization."[48] With its emphasis on the urban rather than tribal origins of the signs that decorated house façades, along with their ambiguous rather than clear-cut symbolism, Beinart's project challenged apartheid's dependence on signs and markers such as skin tone, clothing, and means of transportation to quickly and transparently communicate racial identity.[49] In this, Beinart's work contrasts with Scott Brown's analysis of how the architecture of the American strip functions as immediate communication, as well as with her emphasis on how Levittown inhabitants conveyed their cultural identity through their house decoration.[50]

Beinart observed that residents of WNT's rudimentary houses transformed them according to aesthetic codes identified with the white middle class, surrounding them "with gardens, paving and pergolas," in addition to "hedges, gates, and sculptured gateposts cum letter-boxes." In other words, residents drew on the same aesthetic codes that the township planners had intended for the houses.[51] Scott Brown originally had doubts about the approach of these planners, who argued, according to her, that "a house with its own front yard and peach tree is the South African way of life. If we want it for ourselves, why wouldn't we want it for them?" Yet upon her return to Soweto in 1971, she saw "cared-for houses, and the two peach trees that came with each house thriving in tended landscapes."[52] While Scott Brown seems to attribute the success of Soweto housing to the planners, invoking the many residential structures that South Africa built before and during apartheid to criticize the United States for its inadequate provision of public housing, Beinart attributed the beautification of houses in the WNT to the residents, interpreting it as a form of resistance and a claim for equal rights to the city.[53]

Closing Remarks

Unlike previous accounts of direct educational or disciplinary influences on Scott Brown, which for the most part have downplayed her own statements about her African perspective, this chapter has traced her "African's view" to visualization practices in South Africa, particularly as they were employed in ethnographic observation, and how these came to bear on architecture. To be sure, this study does not wish to reduce Scott Brown's professional career to her country of origin. Rather, by exploring her South African formation, I have aimed to highlight the southern settler-colonial origins of what became a key text and standard practice in architectural education. Although Scott Brown's South African perspective, situated as it was in settler-colonial conditions, cannot be used to mobilize a radical claim for decolonizing knowledge, its situatedness nevertheless shows how hegemonic forms of knowing were inflected by apartheid and how these forms of knowing in turn affected architectural discourse in the center.[54]

In closing, I would like to propose that Denise Scott Brown's South African view of Las Vegas constitutes an incipient "theory from the south."[55] When asking what the south can teach the north, the accuracy of Scott Brown's accounts seems less important than their audacity. Significantly, she uses the putatively anomalous conditions of apartheid South Africa to turn a critical gaze back on the United States. Establishing common ground through photographs and visual narration, she provokes the historian to see the unthinkable—that is, comparable histories of settler colonialism, capitalism, and racism—and interrogate the unacknowledged similarities between apartheid South Africa and democratic America. Her "African's view" can serve as evidence, then, for architectural historians seeking to overcome the taboos that still dominate the field, including failure to consider Scott Brown's own self-asserted South African positionality.

Scott Brown's and Venturi's iconic self-portraits against Las Vegas's skyline speak to the possibilities and limitations of thinking of the city as a "field" ready and waiting for the architect doubling-as-anthropologist to interpret its visual signs. Inserting themselves into the photographic plane among their inanimate subjects so that their bodies match the scale of the buildings, they literalize the metaphoric dialectic of the researcher's proximity and distance. In contrast to Venturi, whose back faces the camera so that he becomes a generic white male gazing toward the receding horizon of his purportedly available universal knowledge, Scott Brown faces the camera, assertively positioning herself in the landscape and actively acknowledging her situatedness. Like a totem, she stares back at us, marking not only the limits of our gaze but also its critical possibilities.[56]

Part VI

Retrials

In this final section, "Retrials," three chapters feature architectural evidence from the law as productive material for architectural history's reevaluation of icons of the field: a building (Seagram), an architect (Richard Morris Hunt), a concept (space). The law seeks and uses evidence and constructs narrative differently than architectural history does when, for example, rendering value, discerning truth, or achieving justice. The roles of evidence gathering and narration, which are combined in the architectural historian, can be separated in the law, when police and forensic scientists gather facts and prosecutors and jurors narrate and interpret them. In these chapters it is from legal perspectives that there emerge counternarratives for familiar subjects, topics, and concepts, along with opportunities to reorient architectural history's conceptions of value, authorship, labor, and geography. Retried, too, are architectural history's practices of evidence and narrative, when judged against another field's operations.

18

Architectural Narratives of Habeas Corpus on the High Seas
Charles Frederick Lees versus the Crown
■

LISA HABER-THOMSON

The Testimony

July 11, 1856. 5:30 p.m. At sea. Latitude 27°55' S. Longitude 4°35' E. A fight broke out onboard the merchant vessel *Senator*, en route from Bombay to Liverpool.[1] The crew had been disorderly and mutinous, or so the resident master of marine, Charles Frederick Lees, claimed. The ship's log records what would later be presented in support of his testimony: "I went on deck and found the sails wanted trimming. Being the 2nd mate's (Burch) watch on deck at the time, I told him to get a pull on the lee fore brace. He turned round to me with a *sneering* laugh, and asked me if he should slack the weather ones?"[2] The argument escalates; the two men exchange blows. They return to their quarters, but Lees finds he has been so disfigured by the fight that he decides to send Burch to the forecastle. He takes his pistol with him. The log continues:

> [I] went towards the second mate's room—he was sitting at the door. I told him to go forward, out of that, or I would blow his brains out. He went, I thought no more about it, but / It being dark, and some sails in the way, I slipt down, and the pistol went off, and the ball entered the 2nd mate's right side, and I will be upon my oath that it was accidentally, and not intentionally. That I will swear.
> The second mate replied that he did not turn round with a sneering laugh, and that the yards did not want to be trimmed.[3]

It was the "accidental" nature of this shooting that would become subject to legal interrogation three months later. The untrustworthiness of Lees's account, in the eyes of his jury, would lead to his indictment and eventual conviction by the Supreme Court of St. Helena on a charge of shooting with intent to do grievous bodily harm. However, in his ship's log Lees has recorded the perfect testimony: an illustration that allows us to clearly picture the scene.

Earlier entries in the log provide further context, though we scarcely need it. The crew have been onboard since they embarked at Liverpool nine months prior; they reached the port of Bombay to load cargo and then, more briefly, the port of Aden to replenish supplies. The final stretch homeward was approaching. All necessary details regarding the act in question are provided by Lees himself. It's early evening (five thirty); the wind shifts (the sails need to be trimmed). There is insubordination on deck (a *sneering* laugh). Regarding the shooting, Lees does not deny that his pistol went off nor does he deny his anger (*I would blow his brains out*). He denies simply that his act was intentional. It's his only option, really, as there were witnesses to that act. But as intention is notoriously difficult to prove, Lees aims for plausible deniability—not for committing the act but rather for the intentionality of his actions.

Note here the space of the ship—crucial as a framing device for Lees's testimony in this regard, a cascade of uncontestable particulars. The deck, quarters down below, the forecastle: a mobile geography of the merchant vessel. Within this space, we are able to map out the characters and their actions. The second mate, Burch, at his door. Darkness. Errant sails, in the way. Lees, slipping down. The pistol in his hand. The reliability of this space is further emphasized by Burch's own testimony, which does not aim to contest the setting of the scene itself. His retort challenges the signs that were fleeting, clues that might have been interpreted otherwise. *He did not turn round with a sneering laugh. . . . The yards did not want to be trimmed.* As in all good testimonies, Lees provides a vivid depiction that allows his audience to project themselves back to the eve of the act, even a century and a half later. The scene is set for a judgment to be made—for the interpretation of evidence, in other words; for the crafting of narrative.

But my focus here is not on this little drama at sea or, at least, not the initial telling of it, which ultimately failed to prevent Lees's conviction. On October 2, 1856, a criminal quarter session (QS) at James Town on the island of St. Helena found Lees guilty of a felonious wounding and sentenced him to serve three years in jail.[4] Case closed, it seems. Two years into this sentence, however, a packet ship delivered a message that would require that same scene to be interpreted once again. "VICTORIA *by the grace of God of the United Kingdom of Great Britain and Ireland Queen defender of the Faith*," the message began. And in faithful rendition of a well-used script, the writ continued, "TO THE SHERIFF of the Island of St. HELENA and to the keeper of the gaol at St. Helena GREETING. WE COMMAND YOU that you have in our court before us at Westminster Hall in the County of Middlesex on the second day of November next the body of CHARLES

FREDERICK LEES."⁵ On January 15, 1859, Lees, having been removed from the jail at St. Helena, was duly brought before the court of the Queen's Bench, together with the jailer's return of a writ of habeas corpus.⁶

The Common Law Writ of Habeas Corpus

The prerogative writ of *habeas corpus ad subjiciendum et recipiendum* is a remedy for unlawful imprisonment that continues to operate throughout the Anglo-American legal world.⁷ Today we might colloquially understand habeas corpus as a demand of release from imprisonment. This is not quite so. While it is set in motion by prisoners whose objective is their own release, the immediate aim of the writ is to verify the integrity of the judicial system itself, and in particular, the way that prisons and jails are used in law. The writ is directed toward someone or some agency holding a prisoner and commands that this prisoner, along with the cause behind that detention, be brought at a specified time to a specified court. The prisoner is either released or bailed, if the reasons for detention are insufficient, or remanded, if they are sufficient.

My interest in habeas corpus, for architectural history, begins in a quite literal reading of the writ's text, as its formula has remained remarkably consistent over the last four hundred years or so. It is a command from one party to another, as it concerns a third: *Rex vicecomiti salutem. Habeas corpus* (King to the sheriff, greetings. [We command] that you have the body). So begins the writ in its generic form. Issued in the name of a sovereign legal authority, directed toward a lesser authority holding a prisoner in custody, the writ commands that the body of this prisoner be brought to court in order that reasons for the detention are verified as being in accordance with the law. The writ thus outlines a cast of characters and defines certain relationships among them: an authority who is sovereign yet lacks insight into local practice; an authority who is subordinate in the overall scheme of the law yet who maintains a local power to detain; the prisoner, who is helpless in the face of this physical detention yet has the ability to petition for release. By providing an avenue for judicial review, the writ thus confirms interpersonal relationships between sovereign, subject, and the law's administrators.

But if the writ evokes this constellation of characters, it also necessarily produces a certain kind of legal space. As the merchant ship *Senator*'s dark corridor provided the necessary backdrop for one kind of legal narrative, the writ's legal space quietly provides the necessary backdrop for another. Each writ of habeas corpus, if it is returned correctly, describes its own narrative that follows a formulaic script: a series of actions that must unfold sequentially across a specific geography. The script—the words of the writ itself—needs to be enacted. The body of the prisoner must be brought to the courthouse from the jail where they had been detained. The writ therefore always implicates a spatial configuration of detention. Importantly, this carceral space is not located solely within the walls of the jail. The writ implies that any detention must be demonstrably lawful to an authority located at a geographic distance. I argue that habeas thus provides a useful framework for understanding a relational geography of the prison building.

The space of law is typically understood in terms of containers assumed to be self-evident, which can be more or less easily mapped onto corresponding architectural forms: the space of the crime (as we saw above), the courtroom, the prison. These containers signpost, in a way, the narrative form of criminal law—from the crime itself, through prosecution, and finally to punishment. While the profession of architecture has, in certain historical periods, been called upon explicitly to articulate these containers, habeas corpus provides a new opportunity for understanding the architectural space of the law. More specifically, an architectural reading of habeas corpus situates the prison building within the process of legal oversight. The writ of habeas corpus requires us to understand the space *of* sovereign law as including not only the crime scene, the court, and the jail but also the spaces *between* them.

An Image of Finality

Penalty, retribution, and rehabilitation are the terms by which we have typically understood the prison in architectural (as well as legal) history. The now-familiar architectural form of the prison building is closely associated with legal reforms that occurred in England roughly between the mid-eighteenth and mid-nineteenth centuries, when the prison sentence emerged as the dominant legal sanction for most criminal infractions.[8] Replacing corporal punishments and transportation to overseas colonies, imprisonment in designated buildings for a fixed term became the norm for a wide range of criminal convictions. Over the course of this transition, carceral space was repositioned with regard to its role in criminal law procedure. Previously an instrument used primarily to detain suspects prior to indictment and trial, the jail—newly rebranded as prison— became an instrument used primarily for the punishment of those convicted. The decades that bracket the turn of the nineteenth century thus saw a decisive shift—both ideologically and in practice—in the ideal form of legal punishment, as well as in the ideal form of the buildings necessary for this punishment. As a result of this shift (so the standard historical narrative goes) the prison building, purpose-built for the fulfillment of this specific judicial sanction, would subsequently be understood solely in terms of its capacity to behave as an instrument of punishment.

By no accident, this view of the prison building closely aligned with those of late eighteenth-century reformers who sought to remove the personal and arbitrary nature of legal punishment that, in their minds, had led to a degradation of English common law. A primary motivator behind the idea of the prison sentence, after all, was that it provided a definitive schedule of punishments that could be clearly understood by prosecutors and judges, as well as by the general public. It was through the geometric form of the prison building itself that this knowledge was, in part, produced.[9] The prison building provided a bounded space that could be understood abstractly (especially as its diagrammatic configuration could easily be read in plan drawings), while, at the same time, its immediate physical instantiation would be an unmistakable symbol of sovereign authority in built form.

That this measured and calibrated sanction was not subject to interpretation was key in representing the ideal end to a criminal prosecution. By any measure, the definitiveness of judgment is crucial in legitimizing legal authority. But at the same time, the interpretation of a sequence of past events through narrative has long been acknowledged as important in producing legal judgment, especially in criminal law.[10] The form of the adversarial criminal trial itself was explicitly seen in this way, and a successful trial relied as much on the rhetorical skills of the pleader in the presentation of bare "facts" as on those facts themselves. In England in particular, the courtroom was seen as providing the primary space in which lawyers summoned evidence in support of or against the accused and where those standing trial aimed to convince their juries of their own innocence. This reconstructed drama in the form of the jury trial, played out within the space of the courtroom, was to reach its conclusion when judgment was handed down in favor of the most convincing narrative. The interpretive aspects of the law—insofar as it was admitted that the law did indeed rely on interpretation—were meant to be confined to the jurors' bench. Once judgment had been made, the ruling was to be indisputable. This finality of judgment was marked by the handing down of the sentence, followed by the punishment itself. Producing a legible image of that finality was thus an important aspect of the work that the prison building needed to accomplish. The prison marked a defined stage in the process of the criminal law, as the convict was quite literally removed from the space of judgment (the court) to the space of sanction.

An idealized condition of finality in judgment, in which a person standing trial was either found guilty or not (and was therefore imprisoned or not), can indeed be read in architectural drawings of prisons, which, in geometric form, represented the proper distribution of convicts' captured bodies in cells and workrooms. In fact, for architectural historians, the invention of the prison sentence as legal sanction required the specific expertise of the professional architect in this regard. In Robin Evans's influential account, the architectural drawing was the primary mechanism that allowed the prison's objective and legible form to be broadly disseminated.[11] Evans saw the architectural plan, more generally, as a primary device with which to read the connection between ideas of human psychology and behavior and the use of architecture as a tool for social reform and power. Here specifically, the geometric arrangements of prisoners' cells, workrooms, corridors, washrooms, chapels, and inspectors' quarters in plan produced a common discourse regarding the prison *building* that could easily be translated to prison *sentence* as punishment and reform. The measured geometry of the prisoner's cell, distinctly bounded within the prison building, was seen as a clear interpretation of the legal sanction. The drawings demonstrated that the prisoners therein, having been convicted, would proceed through the proper stages of punishment and rehabilitation. In other words, the prison buildings, and their drawings, seem to have left us—by design—little room for reinterpretation.

Or have they? The prison building can be read as a static object only if we make the assumption—and, I will argue, a misleading assumption—that the narratives of law are confined to the discrete spaces that have been handed to us by legal doctrine. Evidence pointing to these doctrinal changes—particularly with regard to crime and punishment—has been productively read from the prison drawings of the late eighteenth century. The writ of habeas corpus does not overturn this reading. It does, however, provide an avenue by which we can ask an overlapping set of questions that may still be posed by the space of the prison, as habeas requires us to look at the prison building outside its well-known geometric form. While they certainly reveal doctrinal attitudes about crime and punishment, prison drawings simultaneously concealed the ways in which legal decisions were made and how subsequent convictions were contested. In contrast, habeas reveals the contextual nature of the carceral space and reminds us that the prison building was always situated within a wider political geography.

Reopening the Closed Lees Case

Recall Mr. Lees, convicted of a felonious shooting with intent to do grievous bodily harm and sentenced to serve three years in the jail at St. Helena. A writ of habeas corpus had been issued by the judges of the Queen's Bench on his behalf; he would be brought to Westminster so that the legality of his detention might be reviewed. The writ here, evidently, was working as it was intended: serving as a mechanism by which the Queen's Bench could review an imprisonment ordered by a lesser jurisdiction (in this case, an overseas jurisdiction). How did this mechanism work, and what can it tell us about the space of the prison? Records from the Queen's Bench and correspondence between it, the Privy Council, and the Court of Admiralty allow us to trace the path of the body of Lees through this process. These details reposition the space of the jail as one among several important in the process of criminal law administration, and they show how the jail was important not only in representing the seemingly final stage of judgment but also in providing a space from which a prisoner might rewrite their own role.

Lees had been held in jail for nearly two years before the writ arrived at St. Helena. Custody of Lees was duly transferred by warrant from William Carrol (sheriff of St. Helena) to William Allen of the ship *John McVicar*, departing for London on October 26, 1858.[12] Allen was charged with transporting not only Lees but also the documentation of the proper return to the writ. His ship arrived in London on December 13, 1858; two days later William Allen, in his capacity as temporary custodian of Lees, presented himself at the Crown Office with the writ's return. As the court had recently adjourned for vacation, Allen received an order transferring Lees to Newgate Prison.[13] The jailer at Newgate now had legal custody of Lees and in early January of the following year delivered his charge, along with the documents that consisted of the writ's return, to the Queen's Bench at Westminster.

These documents do not offer further information about the eve of the felonious act itself. By the writ's nature they cannot. Habeas, as a procedural remedy, is concerned strictly with matters of law, not matters of fact.[14] The criminal act itself is not technically the subject of the writ, and thus original evidence pertaining to the act in question (here, the shooting) must be taken at face value. What is permitted, however, are certain additional details regarding the aftermath of the event originally in question, along with the jurisdictional parameters of the court under interrogation. But while ostensibly concerning only legal questions regarding the scope of the courts, the "matters of law" that a habeas case investigates does require facts, of a particular kind. The evidence presented in a habeas return consists of details regarding the legal and quasi-legal actions that produced the detention under investigation. In this case, Lees had to show that he was wrongfully held in jail, while the sheriff of St. Helena had to show that he had proper authority to detain the prisoner. Importantly, each side's argument relied in a different way on a spatial understanding of the events in question and its aftermath. In other words, the "matters of law" under question here could only be answered by understanding clearly the specific political geography that lay *between* St. Helena and Westminster. In this understanding, the architectural scale of the building was a crucial *mediator* between the scale of the prisoner's body and the scale of the sovereign territory.

Lees's primary claim for why his detention should be reviewed by the Queen's Bench was that the trial on St. Helena had been unfair, as it had not proceeded according to the principles of English common law as he understood them. Pertaining to the trial itself, Lees tells us, not a single man learned in law was present apart from the very lawyer who had prepared his indictment and pleaded in support of it. Lees's own witnesses, whom he had called to speak on his behalf, had been removed from the island before they could give their testimony. Prejudiced against him by default, the jurors had necessarily found him guilty. For further proof of the incompetency of the court, Lees was unable to obtain his original indictment, by which he might have appealed, until January 1858, a full eighteen months into his sentence.

This account of the proceedings was, of course, contested by the sheriff of St. Helena, who stated outright that trial had been conducted properly under provisions granted by the Crown. The sheriff's reply put to fore the institutional relationship between Westminster and the colony. This relationship was relatively new, technically speaking. The uninhabited island of St. Helena had been discovered by the Portuguese in the early sixteenth century but not permanently settled until it was annexed by the East India Company in 1659 in order to provide a convenient place for ships en route from East Asia to replenish food and water supplies before heading north.[15] The settlement remained small—its remote location a barrier to attracting a larger population—but continued to operate as an important stop for ships returning to England from eastern routes. Officially established as a Crown colony under a parliamentary act of 1834, St. Helena was granted the authority to conduct criminal trials on behalf of the Crown, as "all forts factories public edifices & hereditaments whatsoever in the said Island are to be used for the service of the Government therefore shall be vested in his Majesty."[16] That Lees's witnesses had left before his trial could not be helped, as under conditions of this same charter the Criminal Sessions were to convene but once per year, on a fixed schedule.

But did the Supreme Court at St. Helena have proper jurisdiction over the dispute in the first place? Lees's account, as recorded in an affidavit presented at the Queen's Bench, picks up three days after the shooting. On July 14, he recounted that, without warning,

> the crew seized said ship, and me, and placed a rope round me, and doubly ironed me, and so kept me for several days until I was taken on shore at St. Helena as afterwards mentioned.
>
> That the said ship was anchored in the open sea about a mile distance from the Shore and Land of St. Helena.
>
> That on the Third day after anchoring and whilst the said ship was in the same position in said Boadstead and open Sea and on the High Seas, I was taken into a Boat in irons, and taken ashore and landed at St. Helena. And then and there for the first time learnt, and was informed, that a charge was made against me.[17]

The times and places of this sequence of events that occurred in the aftermath of the shooting are important. It seems that the crew clearly understood the parameters of the Court of Admiralty, which allowed a warrant of arrest to be served within six months of an infringement, as long as it was served within three miles of the coast.[18] But how did the jurisdiction of Admiralty intersect with that of St Helena? This was the primary legal question that occupied a series of letters between the Colonial Office and the Judicial Committee of the Privy Council. The matter was settled relatively quickly: under the Admiralty Offenses Act (1849), it would seem as though the Supreme Court of St. Helena did have jurisdiction over the case of the shooting. As the act clarified, any person charged in a colony with an offense committed within the jurisdiction of the Admiralty (in this case, on the high seas) could not be removed to England for trial.[19] The work done through the writ confirmed, in other words, the legal relationships between the Supreme Court of St. Helena and the Court of Admiralty, as adjudicated by the Queen's Bench. Indeed, in a final letter sent to the Office of Colonial Affairs from the Treasury secretary, the issue of judicial oversight was explicitly given as the reason for interest in the Lees case, as "the proceedings in question are likely to raise very important questions as to the jurisdiction of colonial courts in criminal matters."[20]

Lees's account of the events following the shooting depicted a sequence of spaces lawfully under one jurisdiction being usurped by another: his ship on the high seas, taken with force by the mutinous crew; the courtroom at St. Helena, operating improperly under the auspices of the Crown. These events, between the shooting and the prison sentence, had played out in an unlawful way such that the verdict reached by the jurors could certainly not be taken as final. For the jurors in the court of St. Helena, of course, the matter of how Lees got to shore in the first place was not their business. They were there to interpret matters of fact, not law, particularly the facts within the immediate vicinity of the shooting itself. This meant that for these jurors, the space of the ship, specifically as it framed the shooting, was the only one that counted in their deliberations. The territorial space of colonial St. Helena, along with the parameters of the Supreme Court of the island and its jail, were not within their purview. The jury's narration of the events in question was ultimately not so different from Lees's original account, though jury members evidently did not accept that the shooting was an accident:

> And the Jurors aforesaid upon their oath Do further present that the said Charles Frederick Lees . . . then and there being did make an assault and a certain pistol then and there loaded with gunpowder and two leaden bullets which said Pistol the said Charles Frederick Lees in his Right hand then and there felonious and unlawfully did shoot with intent . . . to do some grievous bodily harm, against the form of the Statute in such case made and provided, and against the peace of Our Lady the Queen her Crown and Dignity.[21]

Lees was thus convicted and serving his time. Regardless of whether one agrees with the judgment or not, the case was closed. This closure is what we like to believe the law can produce, or perhaps we can even go so far as to say that this is the purpose of the law. It allows for the resolution of disputes to be considered final. The prison building confirms this final resolution by providing a legible image of judgment. But habeas threatens instability because it questions that closure. It draws attention to the parameters of the legal narratives that produce judgment in the first place and calls attention to how these boundaries, which include the relational spaces between judgment and punishment, always matter.

Importantly, while habeas questions the interpretations of legal narratives, in doing so it relies on a certain kind of spatial knowledge. As we have seen, habeas is very much a self-contained legal problem, as its purpose is to interrogate the legality of a detention, not the events that gave rise to the detention in the first place. But this technical legal instrument requires a certain kind of spatial evidence. In order to be set into motion habeas needs the fact of a contained body; it thus requires a prison building. Habeas thus provides a good place to demonstrate the usefulness of interdisciplinarity in writing architectural history. On the one hand, making visible the architectural space implicit in habeas practice allows legal history to take seriously the role of buildings in producing—and also in contesting—doctrinal attitudes toward punishment and judicial oversight.

On the other hand, using the writ of habeas corpus itself—rather than the architectural drawing—as a form of primary evidence in architectural history produces a new reading of the jail outside our standard narrative that might appear to have been closed. It casts the prison as an architectural space that was crucial not for providing the technological apparatus of the legal sanction but for contesting local authority and, in this particular example, confirming legal relationships between the Queen's Bench and the Supreme Court of St. Helena. In this capacity, the primary role of the building was not to punish but rather to stage a political confirmation—an assertion of the institutional and interpersonal relationships between the Crown and an overseas jurisdiction.

If we abide by disciplinary conventions that suggest we give primary weight to evidence revealed in architectural drawings, the jail on St. Helena would be understood primarily by its capacity to operate as a technology suitable for punishment. In the opening passages of his book, Evans precludes an architectural understanding of jails outside this framework by claiming that such buildings exhibit a "geography, but not yet a geometry."[22] To this we can now respond, "Exactly." The jail on St. Helena, as with every other carceral space reached by the writ of habeas corpus, had, in fact, an exact geography. Here we are ready to define an architectural geography made possible by habeas corpus: a place inscribed by a building and holding an imprisoned body, both of which were made legible to political authority by means of a formal written document. Limiting architectural history, in this subject, to questions of geometry at the expense of questions of geography—to the measurement of the earth and not also to the writing of it—obscures architecture's direct role in producing a geography of custody that was integral in establishing legal oversight.

I have attempted to show how a legal object might be a useful tool when thinking about architectural history. In particular, I have made the argument that the writ of habeas corpus, if taken seriously at its word and understood from the vantage of those using it in the practice of law, is a useful framework for developing an expanded architectural history of the jail in Anglo-American jurisdictions. This expanded history might, among other things, allow the discipline to make claims about spaces of incarceration that formerly fell outside our field's dominant narratives, which focus on geometry and drawings. It could draw attention to carceral spaces that might have been dismissed as being illegible on account of a lack of "proper" architectural representation. It might show how buildings were crucial in producing legal narratives, not only for representing the final results of a criminal judgment but also for contesting them later. It shows how imprisonment was useful in laying the claims of sovereign law, not only to punish or produce labor but also to provide an avenue by which a subject might later petition for liberty from another.

And what of those subjects, those who, in the long history of habeas, have inhabited these spaces described by this writ? For the most part, the writs concern ordinary women and men (if such a designation means anything), and in this sense any broader account of habeas is necessarily populated by the obscured lives of those, like Charles Frederick Lees, about whom we would otherwise know very little. But this is not just a history taken from the registers of the convicted. It is a particular subset of them, of those who share in common the desire, and the ability, to petition for relief. Habeas is a record of agency. All writs of habeas are records of persons who know that their original indictments will not be overturned, that they will remain counted as criminals. Despite this, they know that the circumstances in which their stories are retold can provide a different frame for a different kind of verdict. The prisoner's body, brought from prison to courtroom in this context, is now also that of a subject claiming personal liberty.

By questioning the circumstances in which a legal verdict is made, the narratives of habeas by necessity expose the constructed process of the law itself. The prison buildings evoked in these narratives do not provide indices of definitive endings. Rather, the prisons and jails encompassed by habeas reveal the uncomfortable truth that the stories we tell ourselves in the law are just that: stories, which upon retelling have always the capacity to be rendered in a different hue. For architectural history, I take this as an opportunity to retell the history of the prison building: a case once deemed closed.

19

"This Whole Maze of Evidence"
Revisiting Professionalism and Property through *Hunt v. Parmly*

■

ERIK CARVER

> 1. An architect goes to court over his first building. To a large degree, he loses the case. But he wins a moral victory and learns some important lessons along the way.
>
> 2. An architect sues his client for nonpayment. He wins. The victory sets a precedent for American architects to be reimbursed as professionals, with compensation tied to construction costs.

So proceed two interpretations of the 1861 trial, *Richard Morris Hunt versus Eleazer Parmly*, as told by historians Paul R. Baker in 1980 and by Mary Woods in 1999, respectively.[1] These dueling versions of the story demonstrate a clear dissonance between a monograph and a social history of the architectural profession. But the two approaches begin to resonate at deeper levels, manifesting conformities between their ways of knowing and dividing up the world. The ensuing circularities between society and subject raise historical questions: to what degree do the monograph and social history depend on common metanarratives? To tell the story of professionalism has meant to commit to a theory of modernism and to describe the relationship between social structures and a history of ideas and economies. Have professionals been sources of social stability or agents of exploitation? Are they liberators, walking contradictions, or instruments of contingency? Bound up with this is the unresolved question of what we mean by profession in the first place: Is it a social function, an institution, a bundle of traits? Or is it a discourse?

Reviewing histories of professionalization will demonstrate the persistence and suppleness of past narratives as they have informed architects, historians, and social theorists. A proposed counternarrative decenters industrial rationalization and markets as the origin of modern professions and looks instead to earlier imperial appropriations of land, labor, and resources. Less concerned with asking who the professional is, it starts to ask what forms of knowledge and technologies of governance the profession mobilizes. This counternarrative follows evidentiary specimens—in this case, architectural images—as they inform discrete practices of testimony, beginning with those of the aforementioned historians and litigants.

A Question of Authorship

Richard Morris Hunt was the first American-born architect to study at the École des Beaux-Arts in Paris. There he befriended artist Thomas P. Rossiter, whose father-in-law, Dr. Eleazer Parmly, was a dentist and property speculator. Parmly agreed to finance a house for the Rossiters in 1855. Rossiter's Second Empire townhouse would depart from local practice inside and out, featuring a public gallery among its domestic spaces. Six years later, when Hunt and Parmly met before Judge Murray Hoffman in the Superior Court of the City of New York, authorship was the question at hand. Did Hunt design and supervise construction of the house? If so, what was he owed? Or did Hunt merely provide advice? Historians Woods and Baker and the trial transcripts themselves soon spin these queries out into more profound questions of authorship. Could one say that design was invention in 1855? Or was it labor? If a form of invention, to what extent was invention the property of an individual, and what rights would that property accrue? For judge and jury these questions would ultimately require poring over drawings and scrutinizing the testimonies of a cast of characters ranging from architectural luminaries to manual laborers.

Narratives and Evidence

In Baker's account, the trial displays Hunt's youthful inexperience. For Woods it represents conquest by academics, a first beachhead of the Beaux-Arts invasion. Yet these conflicting judgments—momentary failure and initial success—are inflections of broader story arcs. In what Hayden White would label a "Romantic narrative," Baker positions the trial as a test for Hunt on his road to fame, a lesson that he has "much to learn—and possibly to unlearn" as he plants his European expertise in American soil.[2]

For Woods, the trial appears at the midpoint of the tale, a pivotal moment in a gothic horror story marking the onset of a long decline and reincorporation into a two-tiered and two-faced industry that would reach its nadir in the late twentieth century, under the boot of the university and its "young tenured theorists."[3]

19.1. Thomas P. Rossiter house, New York City. From Paul R. Baker, *Richard Morris Hunt* (MIT Press, 1980), 81.

These twin accounts of the trial represent two preferred vehicles of late twentieth-century architectural scholarship: the monograph and social history. Since its appropriation by art history from natural history, the monograph has been haunted by all the tensions inherent in hitching a life to works, and Baker exemplifies this.[4] Specializing in American history, he spent the late 1950s in Italy researching a dissertation on the grand tour and interviewing art historian Bernard Berenson in his Florentine villa. In the 1970s Baker wrote a book on the atomic bomb and followed it up with *Richard Morris Hunt*, which became the definitive monograph on the architect. Like Berenson's *Lorenzo Lotto*, it starts from the eponymous subject's birth and birthplace and ends with his death and legacy.[5] In between, it betrays an appreciation for Hunt's importance more than his skill, but nonetheless it seeks to restore his reputation. Most illustrations are photographs, and Baker's formal analysis, like Hunt's work itself, is thoroughly citational. In the same way, Hunt's significance is that he represents a larger generation of professionals; the book becomes a social monograph. Furthermore, where Berenson strove to create what he called a "composite image" of his subject, *each image* for Baker is a composite, a magnet for psycho-biography and recycled criticism; the early Rossiter house (fig. 19.1) refers back to his work with Hector-Martin Lefuel on the Louvre and is "awkward and restless," for example, while the more mature work of the 1870s in Newport displays "freedom and inventiveness."[6]

However, in the depths of the same archives, Woods discovers deception and exploitation rather than growth and influence. Her book, like other social histories of architecture, weds cultural history to social science in order to present collective narratives. In focusing on the profession, she takes aim squarely at the monograph. Her stated goal is to challenge the myth of the architect as solitary artist. To that end, she foregrounds nineteenth-century architecture's in-

19.2. "Richard M. Hunt, alternative designs for Mrs. Josephine Schmid mansion, New York, 1893?" From Mary N. Woods, *From Craft to Profession: The Practice of Architecture in Nineteenth-Century America* (University of California Press, 1999), 105.

visible technicians and spaces of production. She describes the book as a "challenge to ... 'Roarkism,' our discipline's traditional focus on the architect as solitary creator to the exclusion of other narrators and narratives."[7] Ultimately, Woods emphasizes one narrative in particular, namely, a Weberian theory of market closure.

Woods situates this narrative by weaving in material from the archives of the elite architects and institutions that she seeks to demystify. There is no better resource for this than Hunt, the premier American academic and institution builder of his time. Drawings of the Josephine Schmid mansion of 1893—showing the same configuration in two completely different styles—convey the soullessness behind Hunt's totalizing production (fig. 19.2). Images in Woods's *From Craft to Profession* reflect the dual nature of the professional project: plans and photos of offices displaying the corporate structure of the profession, or renderings and ephemera illustrating cultural ideology.

Metanarrative

Yet, while for Woods, art mystifies exploitation and for Baker it elevates taste, the two ultimately converge on fundamental boundaries between fields like art and craft, society and the state. Economics reshapes the architecture profession through personal connections, whether through what is described as "capitalism, industrialization, and urbanization," manifesting themselves in clients like Dr. Parmly, or by new money and new materials disembarking on the shores of Newport, Rhode Island.[8] Even as the heir of a frontier land speculator takes an urban land speculator to court on the eve of the Civil War, government seems all but absent from the social and technological forces acting upon the litigants, a remarkable fact when considering the central role it plays in canonical studies of the professions by sociologists and historians.[9]

Implied Scales

Woods's and Baker's modes of history-writing complement one another. The monograph provides a phantom theory of the social, and the social history mobilizes ideal types and a virtual world of aesthetics. For Baker, the development of Hunt's career parallels and informs the elevation of American taste; his mansions become a form of elite cultural politics. For Woods, *Hunt v. Parmly* transforms the nature of the architectural transaction. The architect who once delivered drawings as commodities to the client now delivers a service. The implication is that drawings are decommodified as they exceed use value and float free as representations of an idea. This would make them crucial but ambiguous repositories as craft recedes; it suggests drawings become newly ideological and instrumental as the profession is standardized.

But the conspicuous absence of polity from this process and the weight of the implied aesthetic and social spheres point to the limits of social history and the monograph as conventionally understood. In outlining a counternarrative that traverses these limits, it will be helpful to review some of the literature informing the understanding of the professional in these texts.

The Professional

Woods adopts and nuances sociologist Magali Larson's influential "professional project" thesis. In her 1977 book *Rise of Professionalism: A Sociological Analysis*, Larson argues that the professions pursued monopoly control of their industries during an era of corporate capitalism spanning the second half of the nineteenth century. In this pursuit, professions advanced an ideology of individual autonomy that veiled an increasingly organizational and unequal workplace, one for which universities control access and standardize knowledge.[10] Larson's thesis was thus a direct challenge to sociologist Talcott Parsons's canonical formulation of the professions as bulwarks of society that provide counterweights to bureaucracies and markets. Parsons held the physician—as paragon of collegiality, service, and specialized knowledge—to be the paradigmatic professional. Rooted in the long history of the academy and paralleling its rise, the professions in Parsons's view only crystallized with the late nineteenth-century research university; they then ascended to power in the 1920s with the full emergence of managed capitalism.

In opposing Parsons's narrative, Larson argues that this ascension is illusory. She turns to an early synthetic history of the professions, a 1933 report by A. M. Carr-Saunders and P. A. Wilson's aptly titled *The Professions*.[11] Where Parsons upholds the doctor, Carr-Saunders and Wilson nominate the engineer as the quintessential modern professional transmuting science into large-scale industrial organization.[12] Larson adopts Carr-Saunders and Wilson's conception of the industrial revolution as the historical watershed between traditional and modern professions.[13] Doing so dovetails with her use of Karl Polanyi's thesis of the "Great Transformation," which is to say that industrial mechanization necessitated the modern state through its creation of a thoroughgoing and unprecedented "market society."[14] Keeping the engineer at the center but recasting *The Professions*'s Whig narrative in Marxist terms, she depicts modern professions as changing their structure in response to changing modes and stages of production, from feudalism to competitive capitalism to monopoly capitalism, rather than professions resisting bureaucracies and markets. Larson channels Max Weber in showing state bureaucracies as having effectively swallowed professions by the twentieth century, in particular through states' monopolistic control of higher education.[15] Professionalism then becomes largely a form of false consciousness that serves to reconcile educated workers to their actual position of subservience.

Larson's thesis provoked decades of critique and development. Sociologists became attuned to the discursive work that professionalism performed, while at the same time debating the true extent of social closure it achieved.[16] Larson continued to be cited as an authoritative source by sociologists at least through the 1990s and by architectural scholars up to the present day.[17]

A number of academics took a more critical view, holding that the theoretical narrative in *Rise of Professionalism* ignored historical contingency: though historical evidence provided a foundation for Larson's thesis, it did not provide "scaffolding."[18] Some argued the relative importance of culture and status over class and means of production.[19] Historians of Britain in particular made a case for deeper continuities between the nineteenth century and preceding eras. Geoffrey Holmes and Wilfrid Prest maintained that professions were never the small, genteel preserves depicted by the Industrial Revolution narrative; they were in fact comparable to later manifestations in terms of scale and the social classes they drew on and served.[20] This criticism followed definitive rejections of the "Great Transformation" thesis by historians and anthropologists; nineteenth-century markets were neither qualitatively new nor confined to the West.[21]

Michel Foucault's work of the mid- and late 1970s similarly looked beyond the nineteenth century in describing the complicity of professionals with the rise of modern forms of political power. The disciplinary knowledge at the core of professional identity was a direct product of the disciplining of citizens by the state in the eighteenth and nineteenth centuries and was in turn maintained by professionals.[22] In its functionalism and emphasis on knowledge at the core of the professions, this narrative follows Parsons. But rather than providing society with a stable foundation, Foucault's professionals provide it with the Panopticon. *Discipline and Punish* spawned a generation of works emphasizing the instrumentality of professional knowledge for state power. Making direct connections with

French architectural history, Anthony Vidler portrayed the panoptic discourse as uniting the disciplines in service of carceral power.[23] Antoine Picon wrote of Enlightenment architects agonizing over the question of subordination to the state but ultimately choosing a precarious autonomy. This separated them from the engineers, who decisively embraced the state.[24]

Foucault, later developing and revising his argument through the concept of governmentality, repositions the professional to be less a disciplinarian and more a multivalent mediator of power who is working in response to governmental rationality to implement technologies for the cultivation of self-governing subjects.[25] Power operates not through ideology but below it and above it, through coercive material practices and formations of knowledge that exceed any original intent.[26] Mere discussion of the market as autonomous, for example, regardless of one's politics, helped perform that very autonomy.[27]

Parallel to this in the 1970s and 1980s, critical sociologists began to question models of the interface between sociopolitical space and specialized knowledge. They charted the professional's indispensable role in implementing the categories and norms that constitute the apparatuses of governance.[28] Sociologists of knowledge demonstrated that boundaries between domains of knowledge were historically constituted and that power always operated across them in locally specific ways. The principle of symmetry held that social and political contexts don't just distort specialized knowledge, they make it possible.[29] Through this lens then, *Hunt v. Parmly* would not represent the victory of ideology over craft so much as a clash between two models of production, each with its own systems of exploitation and ideation.

The turn away from an abrupt industrial origin to the professions in these accounts finds support in economic histories written in recent decades, as scholars have moved away from seeing markets and machines as the sole motors of industrial capitalism and shifted toward an emphasis on colonial land and resource extraction. Industrialization in this view was made possible by environmental and historical contingencies. Markets were nothing new; to the degree that institutions were factors, it was the sustained project of armed trade and colonization that produced or facilitated the bounty of nineteenth-century industry.[30]

Recent scholarship has helped us appreciate the centrality of these colonial enterprises in shaping modern labor law. For decades historians with otherwise diverse positions shared a common metanarrative when it came to the relationship between the American economy and the law. Perhaps best summarized as a transition "from status to contract," this story held that a stable, communal eighteenth-century legal culture gave way to a nineteenth century of dynamic individualism. As in the sociology of the professions, this chronology emphasized the rise of industry as a constitutive break in American legal history. For these historians, law had been, for better or worse, an effective instrument of economic development.[31]

In challenging "status to contract" with a narrative of "lordship to consensus," Christopher Tomlins emphasizes that what was new in nineteenth-century law was not the contract itself but its mode of enforcement. The property-owning free laborer had been conceived as the protagonist in seventeenth-century schemes for settling America and reforming Britain. Between the seventeenth and nineteenth centuries, liberals developed this project by redesigning the contract in ways that progressively minimized inherited status and distinguished public and private spheres. In the process, the wage labor contract emerged as a public and nominally consensual document.[32]

Intellectual Property

Mid-nineteenth-century American architects sought to adapt to this environment by asking how professional status might be reformulated in terms of property. As secretary of the American Institute of Architects (AIA), Hunt documented the institute's founding in the pages of *The Crayon*, an arts and culture journal founded by American Ruskinians William Stillman and John Durand. In his meeting minutes, Hunt captures the encounter between members' professional aspirations and an ascendant language of freedom and consensus. Member speeches look to medicine, law, and the clergy as models to emulate.[33] Yet President Richard Upjohn clarifies that the institute would not be driven by "illiberal considerations" but rather work to elevate the public taste, even in the face of ignorant "commissioners."[34] These sentiments echo contemporaneous works of social theory that held government officials and their professional adjuncts in increasing contempt. Herbert Spencer's *Social Statics*, for example, had portrayed professionals as venal, statist sinecure seekers.[35] For Spencer and fellow liberals, the proper role of government was to protect not positions but transactions. Appearing on pages increasingly devoted to such critiques, Upjohn's statement then works to position architects' ambitions as focused on the cultural sphere.

At the same time, the group always considered themselves to be professionals; their mission, as announced in *The Crayon*, was neither to achieve nor renounce professional status but to "elevate" it. Elevation would take a number of forms: their constitution envisioned meetings and sociability, public lectures, and a library.[36] Charles Babcock proposed to add education and credentialing to the mission, likening architects to doctors, members of the clergy, and lawyers, given their years of study. But he also looked to other means of elevation. While others might possess intellect, architects as artists needed "powers of genius."[37] Architect Joseph Coleman Hart, in arguing against encyclopedist Joseph Gwilt's definition of architecture as the "art of building," wherein the architect is responsible for the "design and superintendence" of building, countered that an architect who thinks of his superintendence as building makes "the workmen of his building architects." If superintendence was *not* building, on the other hand, then to call architecture the art of building would be nonsensical. Hart's alternative was to invoke sculptor Horatio Greenough's definition of architecture as "the arrangement of spaces and forms to functions and to site . . . color and ornament to be decided, and arranged, and varied by strictly organic laws." Although "verbose, transcendental," and "German," the formulation best captured for Hart the new theoretical foundation upon which the profession would be rebuilt.[38]

How could such arrangement become part of the system of property? Followed by a discussion on the "copyright of Architectural designs," AIA minutes invoke the concept of "intellectual property," complete with its own internal, constitutive distinction between design and utility.[39] Engravings and textile patterns had been protected by copyright in Britain since the eighteenth century. For artists like Hunt's brother, William Morris Hunt, the print market could be far more lucrative than the sale of original works.[40] An 1829 parliamentary commission had interviewed artists and manufacturers on the question of patents; the architects consulted advocated for protecting ornamental sculpture and industrial products from piracy.[41] But architecture proper did not enter into view; architects' concern with their own field was limited to the education of professionals and the public. This would all change a decade later, however, after designers of "ornamental" manufactures—ranging from textile patterns to domestic furnaces—obtained rights covering design broadly conceived, and artists and architects who read *The Crayon* were confronted with the question of whether their work was not also the sort of "braindom" that deserved legal protection.[42]

The Contract

Given the portrayal of *Hunt v. Parmly* as a turning point in professionalization, it is ironic that this case does not fulfill any of the leading criteria appearing in checklists of professionalization: specialized knowledge, controlled access to the occupation, a code of ethics, certification, or connections with schools. In the end, the trial was a dispute over a contract. By intervening in one case, the court established a common law precedent for a standard fee. Nineteenth-century American law drew on the tradition of English equity courts, which had developed methods for calculating awards in cases lacking statutory rates or clear contracts.[43] The fact that this regulation arose from a contract was significant in itself. As Amy Dru Stanley argues, abolitionist discourse had newly valorized the wage contract; such contracts had come to signify the ownership of one's own labor. From the 1830s on, consensual exchange had become a "central part" of the abolitionist project, a sign of self-ownership as the foundation for autonomy.[44] In an 1849 treatise, popular author John Frost exhorts mechanics to pursue a liberal education in their leisure time; American freedom, unencumbered by Europe's hereditary restrictions, which "almost amount to slavery," would allow mechanics to thereby advance as tradesmen and as men.[45]

But what was a contract? Increasingly in these years, this question was answered by legal scholars and judges rather than legislatures and juries. As Federalists and Whigs pushed for standard courts that would protect investments, their populist opponents established local courts and judiciary elections. These competing initiatives, when taken together, had the practical effect of strengthening judicial power. While eighteenth-century juries had ruled on both fact and law, by the early nineteenth century judges had assumed authority over the law, leaving juries to settle the facts.[46] At the same time, as wage labor was becoming the norm, jurisprudence increasingly reimagined and generalized the old law of master and servant to articulate the ostensibly free employment contract. Behind the public law of contracts, a patriarchal law of servitude was resurrected.[47]

The Superior Court of the City of New York, in which *Hunt v. Parmly* landed, was a state civil court, equivalent to the state Supreme Court but with jurisdiction limited to New York City.[48] A prominent legal writer, Judge Murray Hoffman, had published a treatise on the charter of the City of New York specifying the extent to which the powers granted by the city's royal charter persisted in a postrevolutionary era marked by an ascendant state legislature. His solution was to divide the city's grants into public powers, subject to legislative control, and private property, not subject to legislative power.[49] Thus, consistent with Whig principles, Hoffman advanced both the common law and an aggressive reading of property rights understood as contracts.[50]

In *Hunt v. Parmly*, the contract in question did not exist as a singular document; it was actively conjured by the mass of testimony, correspondence, and work presented in court. This formed another intervention on the part of the judge; though beholden to the increasing regularity of the contract as a conceptual norm in 1860, the will of each party—the fine print of the contract—would be interpreted from the evidence.

The Trial

In the transcripts, Hunt builds his case on a wide spectrum of evidence: (1) norms, or his assertion that architects receive a normal fee of 5 percent of construction costs; (2) his ideas, or the "peculiarity" of the house; (3) his labor—the hundreds of drawings, as well as constant visits, meetings, and letters; and (4) his experience, he having worked, for example, on the Louvre as assistant to the "architect of the emperor" (fig. 19.3). Expert witnesses like Richard Upjohn testify to Hunt's stature and explain optimistically with great confidence that 5 percent is indeed standard. Upjohn notably underscores the intellectual nature

19.3. Rendering of Rossiter residence on Thirty-Seventh Street in New York City. Library of Congress Prints and Photographs Division, AIA/AAF Collection, R. M. Hunt Archive, Unprocessed—drawer 16.

of Hunt's contribution. When a defense lawyer questions the concept of paying for an idea, he retorts, "You as a lawyer . . . do not charge for pen, ink and paper, but for your opinion."[51] In addition to norms, ideas, labor, experience, and authorities, Hunt appeals to aesthetics: after he adapted the initial plan by Rossiter, William Thomas, who was Parmly's architect, prepared another set of plans in which the "axes and general lines of the vistas of the house [were]

19.4. Photograph of Rossiter residence, possibly 1876. Library of Congress Prints and Photographs Division, AIA/AAF Collection, R. M. Hunt Archive, Unprocessed—black box, RG 859, series 1, box 1.

spoiled and lost, and that whatever beauty there might have been in the plan[,] it was all gone." This compelled a third round of plans.[52] The editorial accompanying the transcripts in the *Architects' and Mechanics' Journal* casts this point in decidedly Romantic terms, by deriding the artless Parmly as a "clam listening to Beethoven." But it also argues on more corporeal grounds, eulogizing Hunt's labor as "a year's hard coinage of his brains and nerves."[53]

John Thompson, a carpenter called to the stand for the defense, makes his case *against* Hunt's authorship on a similarly wide set of grounds: industry norms, Hunt's incompetence, and Hunt's absence from the job site. He argues that the Rossiter house is as much his own work as it is Hunt's. For Thompson, an architect's labor is extraneous: "There is no use of an architect about a building unless the owner requires it—nor if he does require it . . . there are men who do not profess to be architects, but who are just as good as professional ones."[54] Notably Thompson does not contrast an oral, embodied practice to a literate one. Rather, in a description strikingly reminiscent of Hunt's own design process of consulting architectural books, sketches, and photographs, Thompson describes how an experienced builder can take a simple plan and elevation then "go to a library and take down a book on architecture and ask the owner to select anything he likes and he can put it in."[55] The mechanic can then go to a woodworker, who has his own book of moldings and details, and select as he pleases. In this process, a superintendent manages a sequence of specialists, each responsible for discrete components whose design is based on a publicly circulating inventory of types.

Thompson continues: Hunt may have contributed drawings, he states, but those drawings were not necessarily *used*. The carpenter is quick to point out the serious gaps and oversights in the documentation: the elevations conflicted with the sections, for example, causing extra work. Builders followed a diverse mix of drawings, some from Hunt, some from Thomas, some from Hunt's assistant, Joseph Wells, and others of their own making. Thompson is proud of his contributions: "Mr. Hunt never gave any plan for the inside; I made it myself."[56] Stonecutter Francis Duncan couldn't read Hunt's sketches, so he asked for color coding and changes in scale, producing a kind of coauthored drawing. Finally, all the builders remark on Hunt's general absence from the site, thus directly contradicting the prosecution's testimony.

The Verdict

In briefing the jury, Judge Hoffman asks first, To what extent there was a contract between Hunt and Parmly? Next he asks, To what extent was agreed-upon work indeed carried out? He assembles a timeline of events and then advises the jury to trace through the "whole maze of evidence, through all its obscurity, ambiguity, and . . . contradictions," by drawing upon the types of evidence he describes as, first, a "mass of ambiguous and conflicting testimony," and second, the "enormous mass of plans."[57] Hundreds of drawings, along with one wooden baluster, dance into the courtroom in a parade of exhibits that parallels the verbal testimony. However, as evidence, the drawings are simultaneously less contradictory and more ambiguous. While they help anchor the convoluted history of the house and its complex circuits of responsibility, they do so only through witnesses who can interpret them.

In the end the jury renders a split decision. Hunt receives half the requested fee and credit for design but not supervision. In doing so, a state judge sets a regulatory precedent by acknowledging a customary price for architectural services. This would provide legal legibility to the architect and haunt contracts to come.

Yet to read the judge's charge, to the extent that Hunt prevailed he did so on account not of his brain but of his toil, the "hard coinage" of his nerves, the great mass of plans he brought in. In this sense, Parmly had won. Hunt was neither an author paid for the value of his property in ideas nor a partner profiting from the value of the real property. The jury in the end rewarded Hunt based on the material evidence of his own labor.

His drawings ultimately were never the decommodified smokescreen of gentility that Woods made them out to be. Rather, the percentage fee played this role, its amount an abstraction of the cost of materials and the labor of others. Hunt's drawings instead performed the ongoing re-inscription of the legal and aesthetic boundaries of urban space by a profession itself caught between a public law of contracts and a private law of service. Neither triumphal romance nor hopeless horror story, *Hunt v. Parmly* was one episode in an open-ended, baroque tragedy.

20

"Striking and Imposing Beauty"
On the Evidence of Aesthetic Valuation

■

TIMOTHY HYDE

What is the value of the Seagram Building? In 1964, the answer was variously $17 million or $20.5 million or $36 million, with the range depending less on reasoned mathematical calculation than on theoretical constructions of value presented during appeals made by the Seagram Corporation against what it considered an excessive assessment for property tax. Although the dry concerns and dull processes of real estate taxation stand at a remove from the aesthetic registers of design and interpretation that are the more customary evidentiary horizons of architectural history, the case of the Seagram Building's taxation offers the chance to explore the adjacency of architectural and legal narration and to consider ways in which the evidentiary processes of law might become evidence and evidentiary models for architectural history. This is because the arguments put forward to the courts that heard the case centered upon a question of aesthetic valuation: What measurable value had the Seagram Corporation gained by erecting a building of "striking and imposing beauty?"[1]

Modern law has, in general terms, been reluctant to take up questions that center on aesthetic judgment. Such judgments, seen to reduce unavoidably toward subjectivity, are difficult to reconcile with legal orientations toward objectivity, normativity, and consistency. Justice Oliver Wendell Holmes laid out the difficulty in an opinion written in 1903:

> It would be a dangerous undertaking for persons trained only to the law to constitute themselves final judges of the worth of pictorial illustrations, outside of the narrowest and most obvious limits. At the one extreme, some works of genius would be sure to

miss appreciation. Their very novelty would make them repulsive until the public had learned the new language in which their author spoke. It may be more than doubted, for instance, whether the etchings of Goya or the paintings of Manet would have been sure of protection when seen for the first time. At the other end, copyright would be denied to pictures which appealed to a public less educated than the judge. Yet if they command the interest of any public, they have a commercial value—it would be bold to say that they have not an aesthetic and educational value—and the taste of any public is not to be treated with contempt. It is an ultimate fact for the moment, whatever may be our hopes for a change.[2]

The variability of aesthetic value, from person to person and from moment to moment, renders it all but inaccessible to legal reasoning, which depends on structures of cause and effect, or anticipation and consequence, and seeks for itself the widest range of applicability. Yet despite the caution of Justice Holmes and the circumspection of law in general, aesthetic questions have arisen within legal cases, inevitably perhaps, and not only as peripheral but as central matters of concern. The difficulty has always been the translation of those matters of concern into matters of fact.[3]

In prominent, precedent-establishing cases that have addressed questions pertaining to architecture, the consideration of aesthetic dimensions has emphasized a social dimension, or a conception of the aesthetic as a social condition. In *People v. Stover*, decided in 1963, a state court established that a municipality possessed the right to set ordinances that regulated the outward, public appearance of private properties.[4] Subsequent cases expanded this ruling, incorporating situations involving landscape and natural beauty, as well as historic buildings and neighborhoods, reinforcing the broadened legal determination through a series of what were explicitly aesthetic evaluations. But in these cases relating to land-use laws, zoning laws, and historic districting laws, the aesthetic dimensions under consideration are social in that they involve the aesthetic as a circumstance existing between individuals, groups, or entities outside of the aesthetic objects themselves. *People v. Stover* sought to resolve the social problem of an unsightly yard that was displeasing to neighboring owners and to town authorities.

In contrast to the social orientation apparent in such encounters between law and architecture, a different measure of the aesthetic has developed in encounters between law and art. In some such encounters—most obviously in obscenity cases—the aesthetic measure is similarly construed in social and normative terms. But in other cases involving the valuation of works of art, the type of aesthetic judgment developed is transactional and speculative. Famously, a 1926 case sought to determine whether a bronze sculpture by Constantin Brancusi was subject to import duty as a manufactured metal object or free of duty as a work of art. More pertinent to the examination that will follow here is the case in which the Sonnabend estate contested the assertion of the Internal Revenue Service that one of its artworks, *Canyon*, by Robert Rauschenberg, should be valued for tax purposes at $65 million.[5] The estate declared that the combine (a mixed media work) incorporated a taxidermy American bald eagle, the sale of which under any conditions was prohibited by federal law, and that the market value of *Canyon* was therefore zero. The inquiry into aesthetic consideration here attempted to resolve a difference between an aesthetic evaluation of the object as such with an aesthetic valuation of the object in transactional circumstances, both of which were understood to be speculative in the diverse senses of the word.

The examination that follows focuses on a similar distinction, between two possible valuations, not of a work of art but of a building, with taxation the prompt for a complex juridical and aesthetic inquiry. The aim of this examination is not to resolve the aesthetic question, not to determine the value of the Seagram Building, but to examine the marshaling of evidence and narrative structures employed in attempts to make that determination.

Seagram v. Tax Commission of New York City

In May 1958, as the Seagram Building was being occupied by its first tenants, the corporation requested that the New York City Tax Commission lower its assessment of the building's taxable value. When this application for correction was reviewed by the commission and denied, the Seagram Corporation filed a petition for review of assessments with the Supreme Court of New York County.[6] Unsurprisingly for a building occupying a large plot of land along the lower stretches of Park Avenue, the property tax due each year ran into the millions, but the core of the dispute was that the tax commission set the assessed value of the Seagram Building at $21 million while the owners proposed its value to be $14.4 million.[7]

There were three methods for calculating real estate value in the prevailing frameworks of property tax law at the time, each intended to establish factually the *market value* of a property. The first method was sale price, the price paid by a buyer to a seller when a property changed hands, understandably regarded as the most accurate register of market value because it designated a value obtained in a specific transaction. (A sale price could be qualified by contingencies that suggested a buyer overpaid or underpaid in a given transaction, in which case the sale price would be supplemented by supporting details.) In the case of the Seagram Building, a new construction that had not changed owners, the sale price method was not available. The second method for determining market value was replacement cost, or the cost an owner would pay to reproduce the building as it existed at the moment of determination, which for a recently erected structure like the Seagram Building was the original construction cost minus depreciation. The replacement cost method was less favored, generally used for "specialty buildings," or buildings with a singular use (like the New York Stock Exchange) that made them unlikely to be exchanged in normal real estate transactions and therefore to have distorted sale prices or other complex contingencies. The third and most common means for calculating the market value of commercial buildings with rental space was the income capitalization method, in which the assessment would be based on the rental income derived from the property. As a calculation of a building's market value based on the current financial benefit to its owner, income capitalization was regarded as the most effective basis for assessment in the variable market of speculative commercial real estate.

In the case of *Seagram v. Tax Commission of New York City*, the incompatible determinations of value by the petitioner and the respondent resulted essentially from two different means of calculation. The owner proposed a value of $14.4 million based on income capitalization, and the tax commission proposed a value of $21 million, taking into account replacement cost. Obviously, the city wanted to garner more in tax payments, while the owner wanted to pay less, but these two rival calculations were contained within a larger question: Which method offered better evidence of the value of the Seagram Building? The answer was not at all straightforward, and this uncertainty, more than the disputed numbers themselves, caused the case to proceed through several rounds of legal inquisition, first in the New York Supreme Court, which ruled on the matter in 1963, and then in the New York Court of Appeals, which issued a final decision on the case in 1964.

At the root of the uncertainty lay one piece of evidence that the judges found difficult to account for. According to Justice Aaron Steuer, writing for his colleagues in the New York Supreme Court, "Nowhere in the record is it explained how just two years before the period under review an experienced owner employing a reliable contractor and having the services of outstanding architects put $36,000,000 into a structure that was only worth $17,800,000. Such a startling result requires more than speculation before it can be accepted as fact."[8] The Seagram Building had cost $36 million to build. How could this be reconciled with an income capitalization of $17.8 million? Was the building worth only half as much as the corporation paid to build it? Was its cost two times its value? The discrepancy lay, the parties and judges agreed, in the architectural value of the building, in the merits of its design and its meticulous, lavish construction. The Seagram Corporation had spent money on these aspects of the architecture, deliberately and with the intention of receiving the benefits of what the court of appeals described as an "architecturally superior and well-known building."[9] Should this architectural value be taxed and, if so, how?

Only unsatisfactory answers ensued. The New York Supreme Court justices ruled in favor of the tax commission and affirmed the tax assessment, but they sought to offer alternative calculations that would employ the income capitalization method with modifications taking into account the "prestige value" being gained by the owner of the building.[10] The Seagram Corporation pursued their case to the New York Court of Appeals but there met with a final ruling confirming that it was possible and permissible for tax assessment to account for prestige value.

The Perspective of Architectural History

The Seagram Building has since its inception served as a privileged disciplinary object; for Vincent Scully it is "an aggressive statement of the special talent of its architects" and for Manfredo Tafuri, "the absoluteness of the object is total." For Detlef Mertins, K. Michael Hays, and many other historians, to talk about the Seagram Building is, it seems, self-evidently to talk about architecture.[11] Any of their interpretations reveal dimensions of the narrative predilections of architectural history, but there are three accounts in particular—by Peter Collins, Felicity Scott, and Phyllis Lambert—that address the details of the tax assessment case in relation to their narratives of architectural history.

Phyllis Lambert's account, in her book *Building Seagram*, is the most recent, but of course Lambert herself was one of the protagonists of the building's design and realization, so the book is both testimonial and retrospective in its viewpoint.[12] In the passages that cover the tax assessment case, Lambert interprets the textual evidence of transcripts, legal briefs, and newspaper reports and editorials to contend that the perception of a luxurious excess in the architecture of the Seagram Building was at the core of the legal judgment in favor of the tax commission. Indeed, she goes so far as to narrativize this decision as an intrusion of moral judgment into the matter of the case: "One must assume a certain discrimination against Seagram. . . . The proceedings show evidence of a puritanical posture in the courts' deliberations that could have been allied to opprobrium levied against whisky makers going back to Prohibition."[13] It was this moral posture that, according to Lambert, led the court to disapprove of the relative luxury of an architecture that did not make full commercial use of its plot of land yet employed fine finishes and details: "The court's attitude seems to have been pervaded by a strong puritanical streak. In expressing the court's dismay that the construction cost was materially in excess of utilitarian standards, Judge Steuer was equally irate that a corporation would sacrifice a substantial amount of land that might be built upon with a consequent reduction of rentable space."[14] Perhaps elsewhere in the historical record there may be cause for claiming an opprobrium toward Seagram's product and its business decisions, but the legal proceedings in fact contain no evidence for such an interpretation, and the transcripts contain no prompt for describing either judicial dismay or irateness.

Put simply, the courts inquired into this marked discrepancy between initial cost outlay and subsequent rental return—"$36,000,000 into a structure that was only worth $17,800,000"—because they had been asked to render a judgment on the best means to calculate the assessed value. The New York Supreme Court's purview was actually to evaluate not the fairness of the assessment or its exactitude but only the reasonableness of the method used to obtain it. The court of appeals could rule only on a possible error of law leading to an erroneous method of valuation, not on questions of fact.[15] The attribution of a moral judgment and the depiction of Justice Steuer's response as "irate" come from outside the legal framework that conditioned the case. They are evidentiary supplements, ones that come not from the legal record but from the narrational perspectives of architectural history in which the rhetoric of luxury, excess, essence, and minimum have a prevailing currency (and emphatically so in interpretations of the architecture of Mies van der Rohe).

Historian Felicity Scott also emphasizes the differential of building cost and investment return as a central consideration in her inquiry into the Seagram Building, but in her account it is evidence not of a moral judgment but rather of a moment of transition in socio-architectural paradigms. In her article "An Army of Soldiers or a Meadow," Scott summarizes the contentions of the tax assessment case as a disputation over the terms of cost and value, which signals not the antagonism of judges but the pointed appearance of a shift in the relationship between architecture, its societal obligations, and its corporate patrons. She constructs a narrative in which the Seagram Building becomes "inscribed" within the ever more encompassing framework of the "globalizing networks of capital" and within "the variegated, dispersed, and rapidly transforming logics of regulatory control."[16] The adjudication of real property tax assessment is a crucial manifestation of this larger surrounding, because in Scott's view, by defining the extraneous economic value contained within the Seagram Building as a form of advertising value, the court enclosed the architecture within a predictive economic logic. If by Lambert's narrative the Seagram Building had encountered in the law a hostility, then according to Scott's it encountered something more like indifference. And although authorial perspective, critical intention, and other nuances clearly distinguish the concerns that give rise to Scott's argument from those of Lambert's, they too come from architectural history rather than legal record or the perspective of law. The sense that there is an architectural before and an architectural after—an avant-garde before and a co-opted complicity after—is an established architectural historical narrative of modernism, one that may or may not coordinate with other histories of the twentieth century, such as those rooted in legal history.

The third architectural historian to have taken an interest in the tax status of the Seagram Building, Peter Collins, was explicit about the disciplinary framework of his interest. His book *Architectural Judgement* followed from a year as a research fellow at the Yale Law School, during which he discerned evident "affinities between legal judgement and architectural judgement."[17] These were affinities that might help establish more reasoned methods of architectural judgment. The lack of reasoned methods, and the consequent lack of rational principles for aesthetic value in architecture, was Collins's main concern. To him, the argumentative differentiation of cost and value in the Seagram case indicated the distance between the professional comprehension of architects and that of their clients or of other professions such as law. He chided advocates from the architectural world who criticized the court decision as a "value judgement," noting, with accurate succinctness, that the "plaintiff had specifically asked the Court to determine the building's value, so what else could the Courts do but give a value judgement?"[18] He found the Seagram case instructive in what was to him its clear demonstration of a different paradigm of judgment in which architectural merit was not taken for granted. But Collins's perspective too was shaped by architectural historical narrative, more specifically, by his assessment that architectural history had been consigned by modern architecture to a generalist irrelevance, no longer serving as the basis for specific principles of judgment that were now to be determined scientifically. To this he contrasted law, with its distinctive regard for the instrumentalization of history through the mechanisms of precedent.

The Perspective of Legal History

Peter Collins was surely correct to emphasize the gulf between architectural and legal thinking in the Seagram case, a gulf that was amply exemplified in commentaries at the time. Professional architectural journals were dismayed by the ruling upholding the higher tax assessment, anticipating that such taxation valuations would come to be regarded as a penalty incurred by the cost that thoughtful design attention added to buildings. *Architectural Forum* bluntly forecast that "the power to tax architecture on its quality is the power to prevent it."[19] George Lefcoe, professor of real estate law, challenged the "heroic assumptions" of the architectural journals. In his article "The Real Property Tax and Architecture: A Note on the Seagram Case," Lefcoe argued that critics of the court's decision "must assume either that costly buildings, that is, buildings which do not pay their way in rents or other revenues, are better architecturally or they must assume that good architecture is, on the whole, costly, economically inefficient."[20] He wondered whether the correlation between economic cost and architectural value might be set in a different register: "Good architecture may be economic—expenditures for architecture may be rewarded adequately in the real estate market—but the owners of good buildings may be unable to package and sell all of the value they create. Some of it may accrue to the professional 'good will' of the builder or architect."[21]

The issue was not the appearance of aesthetic judgment within the law; as Lefcoe noted, either the Supreme Court justices would assign a value to the Seagram Building or the tax assessor would do so, but either way an aesthetic decision would be stipulated within the law.[22] If the presence of the aesthetic within the law arises from the circumstances of architecture's inevitable participation in a public realm, in an economic context, then the distinction of aesthetic judgment and legal judgment is of less moment than the acknowledgment of their contingent reciprocities; differentiation, in other words, is less useful than the recognition of evidentiary exchanges that might be possible between the two modes of judgment. The three exemplary architectural historical narratives that discuss the case—by Lambert, Scott, and Collins—seem to rehearse the separation of architectural and legal thinking, each beginning and ending in architectural history, as well as refraining from incorporating a legal historical perspective of the case proceedings. Each one takes the case itself as evidence, but none takes the additional step of incorporating not just the case as evidence but the evidence in the case. The latter possibility, of revealing the evidentiary of process of law as evidence for architectural history, might temper the certainties of disciplinary conviction with more equivocal approaches to interpretation. A further possibility, of exploring the evidentiary processes of law as models for architectural historical narration, arises with the elucidation of two aspects of the evidentiary reasonings of the Seagram proceedings: first, the formulation of value based upon speculative comparisons, and second, the characterization of aesthetic value as transactional.

From the perspective of law, the main difficulty of the Seagram case lay in the sheer novelty of the circumstances: a property taxation levied upon a new building that could not easily be assimilated into existing standards. The courts made repeated reference to the uniqueness of the Seagram Building. Since the building had never changed hands, its market value could not be ascertained through sale price, and since so few of what the court called prestige buildings had been built, the court also lacked a record of comparable sales. The judges anticipated that this difficulty would be resolved in the near future, because they believed the Seagram Building represented an emerging "class" of buildings that would soon be commonplace. As these future prestige office buildings were bought and sold, an empirical record of market value would be established. Pending that future development, the court undertook a process of speculative comparison: hypothesizing either the building that could have been built—the utilitarian building—or the building that would be built—in the class of prestige buildings—and then using these hypothetical buildings as comparative measures to assess the value of the actual Seagram Building. The reasoning here was, in general terms, counterfactual. More specifically, though, it consisted of the constitution of a norm as an evaluative standard. While architectural history has some familiarity with comparative method—the pairing of slides—in this speculative comparison the use of counterfactual reasoning juxtaposes an actuality with a potential. This distinct type of evidentiary reasoning suggests that a framework of speculative possibility can be constructed from evidence to create a measure, in this case, of aesthetic value.

Another obstacle in the Seagram case lay in the difficulty of reconciling the income capitalization method and the replacement cost method. The decision in the case did not require a choice of one over the other. Although the plaintiffs (and some historians) argued that the tax commission was improperly employing replacement cost instead of the accepted income capitalization method, the tax assessor actually used both, adding an increment to the income capitalization to account for the value to the owner that was clearly indicated by the cost of the original construction. Within the judicial opinions, the courts subscribed to this idea of income capitalization with an additional increment. They proposed that this increment might be calculated in a hypothetical rent paid for owner-occupied spaces, the logic being that the owner was accruing prestige value from the aesthetic excellence of the building and would therefore pay more in rent than a normal tenant. The crucial premise here was that the tax assessment should be concerned with value that could be transferred from one owner to another. Any value that accrued to an original owner that could not be transferred to a new one was not subject to real property tax. But the theory offered by the rulings was that some quotient of the architectural excess *was* a transferable value, reflected quantitatively in a hypothetical rent that any owner would pay to obtain prestige value.

The importance here is less the quantification of aesthetic value than the characterization of aesthetic value as *transactional*. Aesthetic value was understood to manifest in and by the mechanisms of transferring a value owned by one party into a value owned by another party through actions of desire, pricing, exchange, and possession, through a process of transaction. This transactional understanding, like that of comparative norms, is propositional and oriented in a future rather than a present tense. The Seagram case is of particular significance to architectural history because of the object around which the dispute was configured, but this transactional and comparative disposition of aesthetic valuation within a legal structure is not unique to the Seagram case. It was apparent also in the more recent case of *Estate of Ileana Sonnabend v. Commissioner of Internal Revenue*, in which the incorporation of a stuffed American bald eagle into Robert Rauschenberg's *Canyon* combine rendered the work by law unsalable. Did that also render the work valueless? That was the estate's contention when calculating the estate tax owed, but the IRS disagreed, basing its calculation of a market value of $65 million on the high auction prices paid for other works by Rauschenberg and works by other important late twentieth-century artists.[23] Here too the crucial question centered upon transaction—How is it possible to sell the work for a fair market value if the work cannot legally be sold? Also crucial was the question of speculative construction of comparative norms—Is the highest price paid at auction for a Warhol work a standard to be used to estimate the price that will paid for a work by Rauschenberg? When architectural history is opened to the perspective of legal history through instances such as these, the challenging aspect of the Seagram case lies in its extensive evidentiary use of standards that did not yet exist and of logics that could not yet be rationalizations. With the evidentiary paradigm thus assembled, with the Seagram Building as its constitutive evidence, the legal proceeding enabled the production of novel forms of value, which in turn enabled the aesthetic valuation of its architecture. In the Seagram case, and others in which legal reasoning has grappled with aesthetic judgment, architectural history may find the provocation of different evidentiary standards, such as the counterfactual and the transactional, applicable to the interpretive work of not only law but history as well.

Disciplinary Skepticism

The appearance of novelty was one point by which the distance between the historical perspectives of architecture and law was subsequently reinforced by the narrative prerogatives of architectural history. Lambert uses phrases such as "new category" and "novel formula" to critique legal proceedings in which she found it "not only a matter of considerable irony but also deeply disturbing that the courts could not agree on the terms and approaches to be applied."[24] Peter Collins, also suspicious of irrational novelty, made much the same point, only his target for that diagnosis of disagreeable confusion was architecture rather than the courts. But it must be recognized that this appearance of novelty is precisely what signaled the productive capacity of evidentiary reasoning—the capacity of evidence to produce narrative rather than confirm it.

The Seagram case, in fact, offers a challenge to disciplinary chauvinism. If legal judgment in the case did in some sense fail to understand architecture, then it is surely equally evident that the architectural-historical judgments of Lambert, Scott, and Collins failed to understand law. And if disciplinary chauvinism were to be replaced with something like a disciplinary skepticism, in which the priority of the disciplinary view is not assumed, other modes of evidence and evidentiary reasoning, other means of making sense of facts, might substantially alter the narratives of architectural history.[25] Just as in legal proceedings processes of evidentiary reasoning such as the counterfactual or the transactional produced novel calibrations of subjectivity and objectivity, they might also in architectural history challenge disciplinary affirmations of value with extradisciplinary productions of valuation. Answering the question "What is the value of the Seagram Building?" may therefore require architectural history to take a skeptical look at its evidence, its evidentiary narratives, itself.

Notes

INTRODUCTION

1. For "a cross section of the ways the field has expanded into new areas" of evidence, see the collection of Field Note essays in *Journal of the Society of Architectural Historians* 76, no. 4 (2017), compiled by editor Patricia Morton (quote from Morton's editorial, "On Evidence," 433), including Michael Osman and Daniel M. Abramson, "Evidence and Narrative " (443–45), as well as Andrew Leach, "Evidence," in *What Is Architectural History?* (Cambridge: Polity, 2010), 77–96. About narrative in architectural history there are no explicit studies.

2. Fernand Braudel, "History and the Social Sciences: The *Longue Durée*" (1959) in *On History*, trans. Sarah Matthews (Chicago: University of Chicago Press, 1980), 27, 33.

3. This approach has proven useful in efforts to understand the history of concepts that have been central to Enlightenment reason: objectivity, proof, fact, and so on. The approach is associated in North America with Ian Hacking, Lorraine Daston, and others in James Chandler, Arnold I. Davidson, and Harry Harootunian, eds., *Questions of Evidence: Proof, Practice, and Persuasion across the Disciplines* (Chicago: University of Chicago Press, 1994). For a general overview, see Uljana Feest and Thomas Sturm, eds., "What (Good) Is Historical Epistemology?," special issue, *Erkenntnis* 75, no. 3 (November 2011): 285–302.

4. For a critique of historical epistemology's relationship to microhistorical studies, see the contribution by Matthew Jones to a collection of essays in response to Lorraine Daston and Peter Galison's *Objectivity* (Cambridge, MA: MIT Press, 2007): Peter Dear, Ian Hacking, Matthew L. Jones, Lorraine Daston, and Peter Galison, "Objectivity in Historical Perspective," *Metascience* 21 (2012): 11–39.

5. See "About Aggregate," http://www.we-aggregate.org/about/group. More than half the contributors to *Writing Architectural History* are Aggregate newcomers, not having previously participated in the group's activities or governance. See the Acknowledgments for mention of some of the project workshops and events.

6. Mark Jarzombek, "The Disciplinary Dislocations of (Architectural) History," *Journal of the Society of Architectural Historians* 58, no. 3 (1999): 489.

7. Mark Crinson and Richard J. Williams, *The Architecture of Art History: A Historiography* (London: Bloomsbury, 2019), 10, 132.

8. See, for example, Federica Goffi, *Time Matter(s): Invention and Re-imagination in Built Conservation: The Unfinished Drawing and Building of St. Peter's, the Vatican* (London: Routledge, 2013); and William Tronzo, ed., *St. Peter's in the Vatican* (Cambridge: Cambridge University Press, 2005).

9. Spiro Kostof, ed., *The Architect: Chapters in the History of the Profession* (New York: Oxford University Press, 1986), vi. The use of the term "profession" in this title deserves scrutiny for its anachronism. For a critique of this assumption, see Peggy Deamer, "Branding the Architectural Author," *Perspecta* 37 (2005): 42–49.

10. Stanford Anderson, "Critical Conventionalism in Architecture," *Assemblage* (October 1986): 6–23.

11. Bruno Latour, *Reassembling the Social: An Introduction to Actor-Network Theory* (Oxford: Oxford University Press, 2005).

12. Michel Foucault, "The Discourse on Language" [L'ordre du discours] (1971), in *The Archaeology of Knowledge*, trans. Alan Sheridan (New York: Pantheon Books, 1972). The English translation by Rupert Swyer was first published in *Social Science Information* 10, no. 2 (1971): 7–30.

13. Daniel Barber, *Modern Architecture and Climate: Design before Air Conditioning* (Princeton: Princeton University Press, 2020), 275.

14. Steven Shapin and Simon Schaffer, *Leviathan and the Air Pump: Hobbes, Boyle, and the Experimental Life* (Princeton: Princeton University Press, 1985), 49.

15. Alexander Gorlin, "Passion Plays," *Metropolis*, April 1, 2006.

16. Gorlin, "Passion Plays."

17. Allan J. Plattus quoted in "Remembrances of Vincent Scully," *Yale News*, December 2, 2017.

18. Hermann Grimm, "Werth der neueren Kunstgeschichte—Eine der wichtigsten historischen Hülfswissenschaften," *Über Künstler und Kunstwerke* 1 (1865): 38.

19. August Schmarsow, *Das Wesen der architektonischen Schöpfung* (Leipzig: Karl W. Hiersemann, 1894), translated as "The Essence of Architectural Creation," in Harry Francis Mallgrave and Eleftherios Ikonomou, intro. and trans., *Empathy, Form, and Space: Problems in German Aesthetics, 1873–1893* (Santa Monica, CA: Getty Center for the History of Art and the Humanities, 1994), 281–97.

20. Erwin Panofsky, "Art as a Humanistic Discipline," in *Meaning in the Visual Arts* (Garden City, NY: Doubleday, 1955), 19.

21. Erwin Panofsky, *Gothic Architecture and Scholasticism* (New York: Meridian, 1957).

22. See his last book, translated as Manfredo Tafuri, *Interpreting the Renaissance: Princes, Cities, Architects*, trans. Daniel Sherer (1992; New Haven: Yale University Press and Harvard Graduate School of Design, 2006).

23. Colin Rowe, "The Mathematics of the Ideal Villa: Palladio and Le Corbusier Compared," *Architectural Review* 101 (1947): 101–4.

24. Peter Eisenman, "The Formal Basis of Modern Architecture" (PhD thesis, University of Cambridge, 1963).

25. Spiro Kostof, *A History of Architecture: Settings and Rituals* (New York: Oxford University Press, 1985). See also the energetic lecturing style of Kostof in the recorded lectures made public by the University of California, Berkeley, at https://guides.lib.berkeley.edu/kostof.

26. Diane Favro, "The City Is a Living Thing: The Performative Role of an Urban Site in

Ancient Rome, the Vallis Murcia," in *The Art of Ancient Spectacle*, ed. Bettina Bergmann and Christine Kondoleon (Washington, DC: National Gallery of Art, 1999), 204–19. See also Favro's UCLA Experiential Technologies Center, http://etc.ucla.edu.

27. Francesco Passanti, review of *The Le Corbusier Archive*, by H. Allen Brooks, *Art Journal* 43, no. 2 (1983): 204.

28. Passanti, review of *The Le Corbusier Archive*, by Brooks, 203.

29. Beatriz Colomina, *Privacy and Publicity: Modern Architecture as Mass Media* (Cambridge, MA: MIT Press, 1994).

30. Colomina, *Privacy and Publicity*, 2.

31. Mabel O. Wilson, "Rosenwald School: Lessons in Progressive Education," in *Frank Lloyd Wright: Unpacking the Archive*, ed. Barry Bergdoll and Jennifer Gray (New York: Museum of Modern Art, 2017), 96–113.

32. Sigfried Giedion, *Mechanization Takes Command: A Contribution to Anonymous History* (New York: Oxford University Press, 1948).

33. Reyner Banham, *Architecture of the Well-Tempered Environment* (London: Architectural Press, 1969).

34. See Michael Osman, "Banham's Historical Ecology," in *Neo-Avant-Garde and Postmodern: Postwar Architecture in Britain and Beyond*, ed. Mark Crinson and Claire Zimmerman (New Haven: Yale University Press, 2010), 231–50.

35. As examples of these approaches, see Dell Upton, *Holy Things and Profane: Anglican Parish Churches in Colonial Virginia* (New York: Architectural History Foundation; and Cambridge, MA: MIT Press, 1986); Leonardo Benevolo, *The Origins of Modern Town Planning* (London: Routledge and Kegan Paul, 1967); and John Harwood, *The Interface: IBM and the Transformation of Corporate Design, 1945–1976* (Minneapolis: University of Minnesota Press, 2011), respectively.

36. See, for example, Eric Mumford, *CIAM Discourse on Urbanism, 1928–1960* (Cambridge, MA: MIT Press, 2000); Alice T. Friedman, *Women and the Making of the Modern House: A Social and Architectural History* (New York: Harry N. Abrams, 1998); Mark Girouard, *Cities and People: A Social and Architectural History* (New Haven: Yale University Press, 1985); Daniel M. Abramson, *Obsolescence: An Architectural History* (Chicago: University of Chicago Press, 2016); and Lucia Allais, *Designs of Destruction: The Making of Monuments in the Twentieth Century* (Chicago: University of Chicago Press, 2018).

37. See, for example, Zeynep Çelik, *Urban Forms and Colonial Confrontations: Algiers under French Rule* (Berkeley: University of California Press, 1997).

38. See Francis D. K. Ching, Mark Jarzombek, and Vikramaditya Prakash, *A Global History of Architecture* (Hoboken, NJ: J. Wiley & Sons, 2007); and the ongoing project Systems and the South, http://we-aggregate.org/project/systems-and-the-south-architecture-in-development.

39. Louis P. Nelson, *Architecture and Empire in Jamaica* (New Haven: Yale University Press, 2016).

40. See Ann Stoler, *Along the Archival Grain: Epistemic Anxieties and Colonial Common Sense* (Princeton: Princeton University Press, 2009).

41. See, for literature, the work of Franco Moretti of the Stanford Literary Lab and his various collaborators, especially his *Distant Reading* (London: Verso, 2013), plus chapter 9, by Paul B. Jaskot and Ivo van der Graaff in this volume.

42. Nikolaus Pevsner, *Pioneers of the Modern Movement: From William Morris to Walter Gropius* (1936; Harmondsworth: Penguin, 1975), 210, 217.

43. Pevsner, *Pioneers of the Modern Movement*, 178.

44. Hayden White, "The Value of Narrativity in the Representation of Reality" (1980),

in *The Content of the Form: Narrative Discourse and Historical Representation* (Baltimore: Johns Hopkins University Press, 1987).

45. White, "Value of Narrativity," 24.

46. White, "Value of Narrativity," 21.

47. Paul Cret, "Modern Architecture," in American Institute of Architects Committee on Education, *The Significance of the Fine Arts* (Boston: Marshall Jones,1923).

48. Feminist Art and Architecture Collaborative, "Counterplanning from the Classroom," *Journal of the Society of Architectural Historians* 76, no. 3 (2017): 277–80.

49. Martin McQuillan, "Introduction: Aporias of Writing; Narrative and Subjectivity," in *The Narrative Reader*, ed. Martin McQuillan (London: Routledge, 2000), 1–34; Ann Rigney, "When the Monograph Is No Longer the Medium: Historical Narrative in the Online Age," *History and Theory* 49, no. 4 (2010): 100–117.

50. Paul B. Jaskot, "Digital Art History as the Social History of Art: Towards the Disciplinary Relevance of Digital Methods," *Visual Resources* 35, no. 1–2 (2019): 21–33; Mario Carpo, "Big Data and the End of History," *International Journal of Digital Art History*, no. 3 (2018): 22–35, first published in *Perspecta* 48 (2015): 46–59; Rigney, "When the Monograph Is No Longer the Medium."

51. Esra Akcan, *Open Architecture: Migration, Citizenship, and the Urban Renewal of Berlin-Kreuzberg by IBA-1984/87* (Basel: Birkhäuser, 2018), 36.

52. Akcan, *Open Architecture*, 37, 6, 48, 96, 368, respectively.

53. See Janina Gosseye, Naomi Stead, and Deborah van der Plaat, eds., *Speaking of Buildings: Oral History in Architectural Research* (New York: Princeton Architectural Press, 2019).

54. Akcan, *Open Architecture*, 37.

55. Joan W. Scott, "A Rejoinder to Thomas C. Holt," in *Questions of Evidence*, ed. Chandler, Davidson, and Harootunian, 398. See also Joan W. Scott, "The Evidence of Experience," in *Questions of Evidence*, ed. Chandler, Davidson, and Harootunian, 363–87.

56. McQuillan, "Introduction," in *Narrative Reader*, 23.

CHAPTER 1. THE FIRES OF SAINT-DOMINGUE, OR, LANDSCAPES OF THE HAITIAN REVOLUTION

1. Louis P. Nelson, *Architecture and Empire in Jamaica* (New Haven: Yale University Press, 2016), 102.

2. David Patrick Geggus, *Haitian Revolutionary Studies* (Bloomington: Indiana University Press, 2002), 75.

3. Alejo Carpentier, *The Kingdom of This World*, trans. Harriet de Onís (New York: Farrar, Straus and Giroux, 2006), originally published as *El reino de este mundo* (Mexico City: EDIAPSA, 1949).

4. M. L. E. Moreau de Saint-Méry, *Description topographique, physique, civile, politique et historique de la partie française de l'isle Saint-Domingue* (Philadelphia: Et s'y trouve chez l'auteur, au coin de Front & de Callow-Hill Streets, 1797).

5. Robin Blackburn, *The Overthrow of Colonial Slavery, 1776–1848* (New York: Verso, 1988), 172–75; C. L. R James, *The Black Jacobins: Toussaint L'Ouverture and the San Domingo Revolution*, 2nd ed. rev. (New York: Vintage Books, 1989), 47.

6. Moreau de Saint-Méry, *Description topographique*, 1:651–53, with the translation of Moreau de Saint-Méry's block quote from David Patrick Geggus, *The Haitian Revolution: A Documentary History* (Indianapolis: Hackett, 2014), 19–20.

7. Anthony Anghie shows the basis of human rights and international law in the institu-

tions of colonialism in his book *Imperialism, Sovereignty, and the Making of International Law* (Cambridge: Cambridge University Press, 2004), while Giorgio Agamben problematizes the notion of the rights of humankind in *Homo Sacer: Sovereign Power and Bare Life*, trans. Daniel Heller-Roazen (Stanford: Stanford University Press, 1998).

8. I take up Stathis Gourgouris's discussion of opposing concepts of the mythic as articulated by Georges Sorel and Carl Schmitt. See his chapter "The Concept of the Mythical," in Stathis Gourgouris, *Does Literature Think? Literature as Theory for an Antimythical Era* (Stanford: Stanford University Press, 2003), 90–115.

9. Georges Sorel, *Reflections on Violence* (Cambridge: Cambridge University Press, 1999), 126–27.

10. Gourgouris, *Does Literature Think?*, 102–3.

11. Nicolas Ponce, *Recueil de vues des lieux principaux de la colonie françoise de Saint-Domingue* (Paris: Chez M. Moreau de Saint-Méry, rue Caumartin, no. 31; [Chez] M. Ponce, rue Saint-Hyacinthe, no. 19; [Chez] M. Phelipeau, rue Saint-Jacques, près celle des Mathurins, no. 45, 1791). Moreau de Saint-Méry was forced into exile by the Montagne in 1794 and could not publish his *Description topographique*, which Ponce's *Recueil de vues* was to accompany, until 1797, in Philadelphia.

12. Geggus, *Haitian Revolutionary Studies*, 77.

13. Geggus, *Haitian Revolutionary Studies*, 76–79.

14. The account of Antoine Dalmas is particularly indicative of this effort. Antoine Dalmas, *Histoire de la révolution de Saint-Domingue* (Paris, 1814), 1:117–18, with the relevant portion discussed in "The Bois Caïman Ceremony," in Geggus, *Haitian Revolution*, 78–79.

15. Michel-Rolph Trouillot, "An Unthinkable History," in *Silencing the Past: Power and the Production of History* (Boston: Beacon Press, 1995), 70–107.

16. Blackburn, *Overthrow of Colonial Slavery*, 215–18.

17. Marcus Rainsford, *An Historical Account of the Black Empire of Hayti* (1805), ed. Paul Youngquist and Grégory Pierrot (London: Duke University Press, 2013).

18. Paul Youngquist and Grégory Pierrot, introduction to Rainsford, *Historical Account of the Black Empire of Hayti*, xxv–xxvii.

19. Rainsford, *Historical Account of the Black Empire of Hayti*, 134.

20. Edmund Burke, *A Philosophical Enquiry into the Origin of Our Ideas of the Sublime and Beautiful*, ed. Adam Phillips (1757; Oxford: Oxford University Press, 2008), 36–37.

21. David Patrick Geggus, "Marronage, Vodou, and the Slave Revolt of 1791," in *Haitian Revolutionary Studies*, 69–80.

22. Marcus Rainsford, *St. Domingo, or an Historical, Political, and Military Sketch of the Black Republic, with a View of the Life and Character of Toussaint L'Ouverture, and the Effects of His Newly Established Dominion in That Part of the World* (London: R. B. Scott, 1802), 34.

23. Manfredo Tafuri, *Architecture and Utopia: Design and Capitalist Development*, trans. Barbara Luigi La Penta (Cambridge, MA: MIT Press, 1976), 1–40.

24. Jacques Rancière, "Does Democracy Mean Something?," in *Dissensus: On Politics and Aesthetics*, ed. and trans. Steven Corcoran (London: Continuum, 2010), 45–61.

25. Blackburn, *Overthrow of Colonial Slavery*, 245–50.

26. Hubert Cole, *Christophe, King of Haiti* (New York: Viking Press, 1967), 87–88.

27. Cole, *Christophe, King of Haiti*, 206.

28. Peter Minosh, "Architectural Remnants and Mythical Traces of the Haitian Revolution: Henri Christophe's Citadelle Laferrière and Sans-Souci Palace," *Journal of the Society of Architectural Historians* 77, no. 4 (2018): 410–27.

29. Cole, *Christophe, King of Haiti*, 192.

30. Carl Ritter, *Naturhistorische Reise nach der westindischen Insel Hayti: Auf Kosten Sr. Majestät des Kaisers von Oesterreich* (1824; Stuttgart: Hallberger, 1835), 76–82.

31. Cole, *Christophe, King of Haiti*, 270–72.

32. Hérard Dumesle, *Voyage dans le nord d'Hayti, ou, Révélations des lieux et des monuments historiques* (Aux Cayes: L'Imprimerie du Gouvernement, 1824), 250.

33. Jacques Rancière, "Ten Theses on Politics," in *Dissensus: On Politics and Aesthetics*, ed. and trans. Steven Corcoran (London: Continuum, 2010), 37.

CHAPTER 2. KNOWN UNKNOWNS

Epigraph: Dennis Kurjack, interview by Eleanor Prescott, June 18, 1970, INDE 57627, Box 2, Ser. I, Independence National Historical Park, Philadelphia, Pennsylvania. All of the archival sources cited below are housed there.

1. George A. Palmer to Robert Venturi, October 20, 1978, INDE 57627, Box 3, Ser. I.

2. Robert Venturi to George A. Palmer, Philadelphia, Pa., December 1, 1978, INDE 57627, Box 3, Ser. I.

3. Wallace Stevens, "incessant new beginnings lead to sterility," cited in Robert Venturi, Denise Scott Brown, and Steven Izenour, *Learning from Las Vegas: The Forgotten Symbolism of Architectural Form*, rev. ed. (Cambridge, MA: MIT Press, 1977), 87.

4. W. K. Wimsatt Jr. and M. C. Beardsley, "The Intentional Fallacy," *Sewanee Review* 54, no. 3 (1946): 477.

5. Frank Lentricchia, "In Place of an Afterword—Someone Reading," in *Critical Terms for Literary Study*, ed. Frank Lentricchia and Thomas McLaughlin (Chicago: University of Chicago Press, 1995), 429.

6. Edward M. Riley, "Franklin's Home," *Transactions of the American Philosophical Society* 43, no. 1 (1953): 153.

7. Riley, "Franklin's Home," 148.

8. Edward M. Riley, Preliminary Historical Report, Franklin Court, Philadelphia, Pennsylvania, March 1950, 20, INDE 77252, Box 21, Ser. III.

9. Riley, "Franklin's Home," 153.

10. Riley, "Franklin's Home," 148.

11. Roy E. Appleman to Joseph M. O'Brien, April 5, 1950, bound with Edward M. Riley, Preliminary Historical Report, INDE 77252, Box 21, Ser. III.

12. Riley, Preliminary Historical Report, 74.

13. Riley, "Franklin's Home," 150.

14. Robert Venturi, "Architects in the Park," Friends of Independence National Historical Park, February 24, 1979, 3–4, INDE 74045, Box 51, Ser. IV.

15. Stanislaus von Moos, *Venturi, Rauch, and Scott Brown Buildings and Projects* (New York: Rizzoli, 1987), 33.

16. B. Bruce Powell, "Archaeological Data," chap. 3 in Interim Historic Structures Report, Part I on Franklin's House, Independence National Historical Park, November 1960, §1, p. 1, INDE 77252, Folder 9, Box 21, Ser. III.

17. B. Bruce Powell, "Problems of Urban Archaeology," *American Antiquity* 27, no. 4 (1962): 581.

18. Riley, Preliminary Historical Report, 18.

19. John Platt, Franklin Court Historic Structure Report, November 1969, INDE 77252, Folder 14, Box 21, Ser. III.

20. Platt, Franklin Court Historic Structure Report.

21. Constance M. Greiff, *Independence: The Creation of a National Park* (Philadelphia: University of Pennsylvania Press, 1987), 381. Greiff's research files deposited at INHP form the documentary basis of the present study.

22. Greiff, *Independence*, 381.

23. Greiff, *Independence*, 381.

24. Greiff, *Independence*, 198.

25. Robert D. Crompton, "Franklin's House off High Street: The Search for a Missing Watercolor," *Magazine Antiques* 102, no. 4 (1972): 680.

26. Carl M. Williams to Dennis C. Kurjack, New York, November 8, 1961, INDE 57627, Box 3, Ser. I.

27. "Antique Dealer Gets 2 ½ Years in City Archives Theft," *Philadelphia Inquirer*, March 20, 1959, 9.

28. Carl M. Williams, *Silversmiths of New Jersey, 1700–1825* (Philadelphia: MacManus, 1949), 16; "Bridgeton Historian Held on Fraud Charge," *Camden (NJ) Morning Post*, February 21, 1936, 9.

29. *Camden Morning Post*, November 28, 1936, 8.

30. "History Fancier Denied Bail in Rare Will Thefts," *Philadelphia Inquirer*, March 27, 1958, 25.

31. Williams to Kurjack, November 8, 1961.

32. Compare Aron Vinegar, *I Am a Monument: On "Learning from Las Vegas"* (Cambridge, MA: MIT Press, 2008), 98.

33. Penelope Hartshorne Batcheler and Mary Mish, transcript of interview by George A. Palmer, July 6, 1977, INDE 57627, Box 3, Ser. I.

34. Batcheler and Mish interview transcript.

35. Ronald F. Lee to Joseph Brew and Herb Kahler, Philadelphia, March 28, 1969, INDE 104159, Folder 4, Box 19, John Platt Files, Subseries F, Ser. III.

36. Robert M. Utley to John Platt, Washington, DC, April 3, 1969, INDE 104159, Folder 4, Box 19, Platt Files, Subseries F, Ser. III.

37. Utley to Platt.

38. Greiff, *Independence*, 389; Report No. 7 on Franklin Court Study, June 26, 1969, INDE 104159, Folder 4, Box 19, Platt Files, Subseries F, Ser. III.

39. Penelope Hartshorne Batcheler, "An Architectural Summary of Franklin Court and Benjamin Franklin's House," Division of Historical Architecture, Office of Archaeology and Historic Preservation, National Park Service, September 18, 1969, 1, INDE 77252, Box 21, Ser. III (original emphasis).

40. [Benjamin Franklin], "To the Printer from Marcus," *Pennsylvania Gazette*, March 23–30, 1732, quoted in J. A. Leo Lemay, *The Life of Benjamin Franklin*, vol. 1, *Journalist, 1706–1730* (Philadelphia: University of Pennsylvania Press, 2013), 70.

41. Batcheler, "Architectural Summary of Franklin Court and Benjamin Franklin's House," 1. Penelope Hartshorne Batcheler earned a BArch in 1953 from the Illinois Institute of Technology. See Antoinette J. Lee, "An Interview with Penelope Hartshorne Batcheler," *CRM Journal* 2, no. 2 (2005): 41.

42. Batcheler, "Architectural Summary of Franklin Court and Benjamin Franklin's House," 1.

43. John L. Cotter to Superintendent, INDE, Philadelphia, September 19, 1969, INDE 57627, Box 3, Ser. II.

44. Cotter to Superintendent, INDE.

45. Jared Sparks, *The Life of Benjamin Franklin: Containing the Autobiography, with Notes and a Continuation* (Boston: Whittemore, Niles, and Hall, 1856), 106.

46. D. H. Lawrence, *Studies in Classic American Literature* (New York: T. Seltzer, 1923), 15.

47. Ernest Allen Connally to Special Assistant to the Director, Philadelphia, October 2, 1969, INDE 57627, Box 3, Ser. II. Connally concluded that a reconstruction would not be consistent with National Park Service standards, as expressed in *Administrative Policies for Historical Areas: Compilation of the Administrative Policies for the Historical Areas of the National Park System* (Washington, DC: Government Printing Office, 1968), 23.

48. Connally to Special Assistant to the Director.

49. Greiff, *Independence*, 205.

50. Venturi, "Architects in the Park," 4.

51. Venturi, "Architects in the Park," 4.

52. John L. Cotter to Robert Craig, Philadelphia, March 29, 1982, INDE 57627, Box 3, Ser. II.

53. Eric Ekholm and James Deetz, "Wellfleet Tavern," *Natural History* 80, no. 7 (1971): 52.

54. Gérard Genette, *Narrative Discourse Revisited*, trans. Jane E. Lewin (1983; Ithaca: Cornell University Press, 1988), 74.

55. Cotter to Craig, March 29, 1982; Constance M. Greiff Administrative History Project Working Files, 1939–1985, INDE 57627, Box 3, Ser. I.

56. Robert Venturi, "Design for Franklin Court," October 16, 1972, INDE 57627, Box 3, Ser. II.

57. James Deetz, "Plymouth Colony Architecture: Archaeological Evidence from the Seventeenth Century," in *Architecture in Colonial Massachusetts: A Conference Held by the Colonial Society of Massachusetts, September 19 and 20, 1974*, Publications of the Colonial Society of Massachusetts 51 (Boston: Colonial Society of Massachusetts, 1979), 44.

58. *Presidential Design Awards: 1984* (Washington, DC: National Endowment for the Arts, 1985), 16.

59. Venturi, "Architects in the Park," 4.

60. Venturi, "Architects in the Park," 4.

61. Robert Venturi, preface to *Complexity and Contradiction in Architecture*, 2nd ed. (New York: Museum of Modern Art, 1977), 13.

62. Penelope Hartshorne Batcheler, "For the Record: Franklin Court Design," INDE 57627, Box 3, Ser. I.

63. Jack Hurst, "What Did Franklin's House Look Like?," *Philadelphia Inquirer*, October 25, 1972, 21.

64. Donald Janson, "Missing Painting Blocks Franklin House Project," *New York Times*, October 25, 1972, 12.

65. Batcheler and Mish interview transcript.

66. Robert Craig, "Notes Written *after* a Conversation w/ Marty Yoelson," December 17, 1980, INDE 57627, Box 3, Ser. II.

67. Craig, "Notes Written *after* a Conversation w/ Marty Yoelson."

68. Cleanth Brooks, "The New Criticism," *Sewanee Review* 87, no. 4 (1979): 600.

69. Brooks, "New Criticism," 600.

70. "Historic Wills Missing from 'Chaotic' Files," *Philadelphia Inquirer*, August 1, 1957, 1.

CHAPTER 3. VACUUM SUCTION CONVEYANCE, PART II

1. A. E. J. Morris, "The Urban Movement of Goods in Etarea," in *The Urban Movement of Goods: Proceedings of the Third Technology Assessment Review* (Paris: Organisation for Economic Co-operation and Development, 1970).

2. Several recent books have uncovered new narratives about New Towns in Europe. See in particular Rosemary Wakeman, *Practicing Utopia: An Intellectual History of the New Town Movement* (London: University of Chicago Press, 2016). See also Filippo De Pieri, "Reassessing the Legacy of Twentieth-Century New Towns," *Journal of Urban History* 45, no. 1 (2019): 177–87, https://doi.org/10.1177/0096144218806851.

3. Frantisek Vlasák, Oscal Döbert, and Miroslav Hudec were the organizers from the State Technology Commission, and a large team participated in the project. Only two women were acknowledged on the design team: Ludmila Englichová and Ludmila Machová consulted on domestic typologies. The team also included the eminent sociologist and urban theorist Jiří Musil. A full listing appears in Gorazd Čelechovský, *Etarea: Étude du milieu humain dans la ville* (Prague: Institut d'études de la ville de Prague, 1967), 62.

4. Čelechovský, *Etarea*. Three thousand copies of this pamphlet were printed; one ended up in a Cleveland shop selling used books, and I purchased it in 2008.

5. Gorazd Čelechovský, "Man-Made Environment" and "Integration of Shopping Services: Etarea, Prague," appearing together in *Official Architecture and Planning* 31, no. 8 (1968): 1016–29; Margaret Roberts and John Roberts, "Goods Distribution: A New Approach," *Official Architecture and Planning* 33, no. 1 (1970): 35–40.

6. Morris writes that Etarea "was designed for a real site . . . but it was not intended as other than a theoretical study of possibilities." Morris, "Urban Movement of Goods in Etarea," 191.

For a broader take on socialist urbanism in this period, see Ana Miljacki, *The Optimum Imperative: Czech Architecture for the Socialist Lifestyle, 1938–1968* (New York: Routledge, 2017); and Kimberly Zarecor, *Manufacturing a Socialist Modernity: Housing in Czechoslovakia, 1945–1960* (Pittsburgh: University of Pittsburgh Press, 2011).

7. Since I began this research in 2008, other architectural historians have written about Etarea. See note 16 below.

8. Čelechovský, "Man-Made Environment," 228. An abridged version of Gorazd Čelechovský's text on Etarea translated into English makes clear the extent to which he understood Etarea as a technological system that mimicked a biological one. See Gorazd Čelechovský, "Man-Made Environment: Systems in Balance," *Official Architecture and Planning* 33, no. 3 (1970): 228–29. There was also a rather long tradition of biologically inspired planning and architecture work in Prague, especially in the work of Emanuel Hruška, which inspired the planning of Etarea. See Jan Dostalík and Zbyněk Ulčák, "Biologický Universalismus Emanuela Hrušky," *Architektúra a Urbanizmus* 47, no. 1–2 (2013): 52–71.

9. Pneumatic tubes were widely used in banks and for mail delivery in some cities; they were an important early form of high-speed information and goods infrastructure. For other histories of pneumatic conveyance systems in this time period, see Juliette Spertus, *Fast Trash: Roosevelt Island's Pneumatic Tubes and the Future of Cities*, http://fasttrash.org. See also Ernest George Phillips, *Pneumatic Conveying: A Concise Treatment of the Principles, Methods and Applications of Pneumatic Conveyance of Materials, with Special Reference to the Conveying and Elevating of Heavy Solid Materials for Engineers, Works Managers, and Students* (New York: Sir I. Pitman & Sons, 1921); H. A. Stoess, *Pneumatic Conveying* (New York: Wiley-Interscience, 1970); and Wendy A. Thornton, *The Pneumatic Transport of Solids in Pipes: A Bibliography* (Cranfield: British Hydromechanics Research Association, 1972).

10. The Pražská Potrubní Pošta opened in 1899 and remained in use until severe flooding occurred in 2002.

11. Věra Chytilová, *Daisies* (Janus Films, 1966). An "automatic film" was also shown in the Czech Pavilion at Expo '67, emphasizing the extent to which that exposition was focused on ideas about automation. See Marina Hassapopoulou, "Interactive Cinema from Vending Machine to Database Narrative: The Case of Kinoautomat," *Screening the Past*, no. 37 (January 1, 2013). For more on this pavilion at Expo '67, see Terezie Nekvindová and Daniela Kramerová, eds., *Automat na výstavu: Československý pavilon na Expo 67 v Montrealu* (Prague: Akademie výtarných umění v Praze, 2017).

12. I am grateful to Julieanna Preston, who reminded me that Věra's fantasy of feminist conduits could be related to Luce Irigaray's feminist theories of fluid dynamics. See Luce Irigaray, "The 'Mechanics' of Fluids," in *The Sex Which Is Not One*, trans. Catherine Porter (Ithaca: Cornell University Press, 1985), 106–18.

13. Věra and I have a longer conversation about everyday life in Etarea in my forthcoming book, *Cities without Commerce*.

14. Daniel M. Abramson, "Stakes of the Unbuilt," *The Aggregate Website*, February 10, 2014, http://we-aggregate.org/piece/stakes-of-the-unbuilt.

15. Aaron Bastani, Ash Sarkar, and James Butler, "Fully Automated Luxury Communism" (podcast), Novarra Media, June 19, 2015, https://soundcloud.com/novaramedia/fully-automated-luxury-communism. See also Brian Merchant, "Fully Automated Luxury Communism," *The Guardian*, March 18, 2015, https://www.theguardian.com/sustainable-business/2015/mar/18/fully-automated-luxury-communism-robots-employment.

16. J. Skalický, J. Večeř, and K. Bělohlavý, "Etarea—sen o bydlení" (video), *Zašlapané projekty*, Ceska Televize, December 17, 2009, https://www.ceskatelevize.cz/porady/10209988352-zaslapane-projekty/409235100061041-etarea-sen-o-bydleni. After this text was written, I met Zarecor, Kulić, and Krivý; I am very grateful to them for helpful conversations. Krivý's article "Automation or Meaning? Socialism, Humanism and Cybernetics in Etarea," *Architectural Histories* 7, no. 1 (April 15, 2019): 3, published after I wrote this chapter but before it went to press, supports some of my and Věra's interpretations of the town and makes many suggestive interpretations about the importance of Etarea to cybernetic discourse. Jan Dostalík's recent publications on Etarea have also been illuminating, but unfortunately his brief biography of Gorazd Čelechovský makes no mention of Věra. See Jan Dostalík, "Gorazd Čelechovský: Města jako systémy," Katedra Environmentálních Studií, Masarykova Univerzita, 2015, https://humenv.fss.muni.cz/vyzkum/envirostudovna/clanky/gorazd-celechovsky-mesta-jako-systemy.

17. Abramson, "Stakes of the Unbuilt."

18. Arlette Farge, *Le goût de l'archive* (Paris: Editions du Seuil, 1989).

19. See, for instance, Kenny Cupers, ed., *Use Matters: An Alternative History of Architecture* (New York: Routledge, 2013); and also the essays by Siddiqi and Muzaffar in this collection.

CHAPTER 4. TALKATIVE TIMBERS

Epigraph: Don DeLillo, *Point Omega* (New York: Scribner, 2010), 87.

1. A. E. Douglass, *Dating Pueblo Bonito and Other Ruins of the Southwest* (Washington, DC: National Geographic Society, 1935).

2. Clark Wissler, "The New Archaeology," *American Museum Journal* 17, no. 2 (1917): 100–102.

3. See Ernst Hollstein, *Mitteleuropäische Eichenchronologie: Trierer Dendrochronologische Forschungen zur Archäologie und Kunstgeschichte* (Mainz: P. von Zabern, 1980). For the relation of dendrochronology studies to scholarship on Palladian villas, see, among others, Martin Kubelik, "Palladio's Villas in the Tradition of the Veneto Farm," *Assemblage* 1 (October 1986): 90–115. For Byzantine churches, see, for example, P. I. Kuniholm, "Dendrochronology and the Architectural History of the Church of the Holy Apostles in Thessaloniki," *Architectura: Zeitschrift für Geschichte der Baukunst*, no. 20 (1990): 1–2.

4. Lorraine Daston and Peter Galison, *Objectivity* (New York: Zone Books, 2010).

5. Percival Lowell, *Mars and Its Canals* (New York: Macmillan, 1906), 175.

6. For this reason, Peter Galison has cited Lowell's research method as a clear example of the movement of scientific inquiry in the nineteenth century toward an often unachievable ideal of "mechanical objectivity." Peter Galison, "Judgment against Objectivity," in *Picturing Science, Producing Art* (New York: Routledge, 1998), 327–59. See also Daston and Galison, *Objectivity*.

7. This is the broader version of Lowell's comment: "To one standing on the summit of the San Francisco peaks and gazing off from that isolated height upon this other isolation of aridity, the resemblance of its lambent saffron to the telescopic tints of the Martian globe is strikingly impressive. . . . Even in its mottlings the one expanse recalls the other." Lowell, *Mars and Its Canals*, 149.

8. A. E. Douglass, "Tree-Rings and Climatic Cycles," *Phi Kappa Phi Journal* (September 1944): 83.

9. Daston and Galison, *Objectivity*, 17.

10. For Douglass's description of these devices, see A. E. Douglass, "A Photographic Periodogram of the Sun-Spot Numbers," *Astrophysical Journal* 40, no. 3 (1914): 326–31; and A. E. Douglass, "An Optical Periodograph," *Astrophysical Journal* 41, no. 3 (1915): 173–86.

11. Douglass, "Photographic Periodogram," 330. After years of refinement, it should be noted, the periodograms yielded little of scientific value. Such was their inscrutability, in fact, that in at least one of Douglass's technical papers, a figure was unknowingly published upside down.

12. A. E. Douglass, "The Secret of the Southwest Solved by Talkative Tree Rings," *National Geographic Magazine* 56, no. 6 (1929): 741.

13. Douglass, "Secret of the Southwest," 741.

14. Douglass, "Secret of the Southwest," 741.

15. Simon Schaffer, "Self Evidence," *Critical Inquiry* 18, no. 2 (1992): 327–62.

16. Schaffer, "Self Evidence," 330.

17. Douglass, *Dating Pueblo Bonito and Other Ruins*, 7.

18. Douglass, *Dating Pueblo Bonito and Other Ruins*, 19.

19. Douglass, "Secret of the Southwest" 753.

20. Douglass, "Secret of the Southwest," 737.

21. Douglass, *Dating Pueblo Bonito and Other Ruins*, 39.

22. See A. E. Douglass, "Evidence of Climatic Effects in the Annual Rings of Trees," *Ecology* 1, no. 1 (1920): 24–32.

23. See, for example, Ellsworth Huntington, *The Climatic Factor as Illustrated in Arid America* (Washington, DC: Carnegie Institution of Washington, 1914).

24. Douglass, *Dating Pueblo Bonito and Other Ruins*, 49.

25. Douglass, "Secret of the Southwest," 755.

26. Douglass, *Dating Pueblo Bonito and Other Ruins*, 49.

27. Douglass. *Dating Pueblo Bonito and Other Ruins*, 50.

28. For some authors, these readings provide basic coordinates for defining the contours of the Anthropocene. See Simon L. Lewis and Mark A. Maslin, "Defining the Anthropocene," *Nature*, no. 519 (March 12, 2015): 171–80.

29. Robin Kelsey, "Ecology, Sustainability, and Historical Interpretation," *American Art* 28, no. 3 (2014): 9.

CHAPTER 5. CONCRETE IS ONE HUNDRED YEARS OLD

The authors would like to acknowledge the contribution of a team of researchers, including Dorit Aviv, Michael Bozlar, Michael Faciejew, Ryan Hughes, Midori Kawaue, Ingrid Lao, Joon Ma, Clelia Pozzi, Sonya Ralston, Carly Richman, Martina Russo, François Sabourin, Frances Steere, and Urvashi Divia Uberoy. Research and financial support was provided by the Princeton Mellon Initiative in Architecture, Urbanism, and the Humanities, the Council for Science and Technology, the Metropolis Project, and the Humanities Council at Princeton University.

1. See Ian Hacking, *Historical Ontology* (Cambridge, MA: Harvard University Press, 2004); Theodore M. Porter, *Trust in Numbers: In Pursuit of Objectivity in Science and Public Life* (Princeton: Princeton University Press, 1995), viii; and Lorraine Daston, "Science Studies and the History of Science," *Critical Inquiry* 35, no. 4 (2009): 798–813.

2. One example of large-scale equation sharing is the Intergovernmental Panel on Climate Change, an agency that compiles equations pertaining to climate change. On the rise of the engineer's profile, see Matthew Wisnioski, "How the Industrial Scientist Got His Groove," in *Groovy Science: Knowledge, Innovation, and American Counterculture*, ed. David Kaiser and W. Patrick McCray (Chicago: University of Chicago Press, 2016), 337–65. On notable equations as poetry, see Graham Farmelo, ed., *It Must Be Beautiful* (London: Granta, 2002).

3. Dipesh Chakrabarty, "The Climate of History: Four Theses," *Critical Inquiry* 35, no. 2 (2009): 200.

4. Reinhold Martin, "Visualizing Change: The Line of the Anthropocene," in *Energy Accounts: Architectural Representations of Energy, Climate, and the Future*, ed. Dan Willis, William W. Braham, Katsuhiko Muramoto, and Daniel A. Barber (London: Routledge, 2017), 42–47.

5. C. N. Waters and J. Zalasiewicz, "Concrete: The Most Abundant Novel Rock Type of the Anthropocene," in *Encyclopedia of the Anthropocene: Volume 1, Geologic History and Energy*, ed. Dominick A. DellaSala and Michael I. Goldstein (Oxford: Elsevier, 2018), 75–85; Kai Gong and Claire E. White, "Nanoscale Chemical Degradation Mechanisms of Sulfate Attack in Alkali-Activated Slag," *Journal of Physical Chemistry* 122, no. 11 (2018): 5992–6004.

6. Minoru Hamada, "Neutralization (Carbonation) of Concrete and Corrosion of Reinforcing Steel," *Proceedings of the Fifth International Symposium on the Chemistry of Cement Tokyo, 1968*, part 3 (Tokyo: Cement Association of Japan, 1969), 343–69.

7. Guy Keulemans, "The Problem with Reinforced Concrete," *The Conversation*, June 7, 2016, https://theconversation.com/the-problem-with-reinforced-concrete-56078.

8. Minoru Hamada and Uchikazu [Yoshikazu] Uchida, "Durability Test of Concrete," *Journal of Architecture and Building Science* 12, no. 516 (1928): 1287–1303; Kyösti Tuutti, *Corrosion of Steel in Concrete* (Stockholm: Swedish Cement and Concrete Research Institute, 1982).

9. Vaclav Smil, *Making the Modern World: Materials and Dematerialization* (Chichester: John Wiley & Sons, 2014), 36–37 (quote); J. Francis Young et al., *The Science and Technology of Civil Engineering Materials* (n.p.: Prentice Hall, 1998), chap. 11.

10. Adrian Forty, "Natural and Unnatural," in *Concrete and Culture: A Material History* (London: Reaktion, 2016), 43–77.

11. Forty, "Natural and Unnatural"; Cyrille Simonnet, "The Origins of Reinforced Concrete," in *Early Reinforced Concrete*, ed. Frank Newby (London: Ashgate, 2000): 97–134; Michael Osman, "The Managerial Aesthetics of Concrete," *Perspecta* 45 (2012): 67–76; Amy Slaton, *Reinforced Concrete and the Modernization of American Building, 1900–1930* (Baltimore: Johns Hopkins University Press, 2003).

12. Sigfried Giedion, *Building in France, Building in Iron, Building in Ferro-Concrete* (Santa Monica, CA: Getty Center for the History of Art and the Humanities, 1995).

13. The American Concrete Institute was created in 1905; the French had founded the Commission du Ciment Armé in 1900, after a reinforced concrete overpass at that year's Paris Exposition collapsed.

14. Reinhardt Koselleck, *Futures Past: On the Semantics of Historical Time* (New York: Columbia University Press, 2004), 222–48.

15. Peter Collins, *Concrete: The Vision of a New Architecture*, 2nd ed. (Montreal: McGill-Queen's University Press, 2004), 181.

16. *The Durability of Reinforced Concrete in Buildings*, National Building Studies Special Report No. 25 (1956).

17. "Editorial: Corrosion of Steel in Concrete," *Indian Concrete Journal* 47, no. 9 (1973): 217–18.

18. For a critique of monopoly capital in the concrete industry, see Pollux [Georges Baehler], "The Cement Trust in Switzerland," trans. Sarah Nicholls and Lucia Allais, *Grey Room*, no. 71 (Spring 2018): 138–40.

19. Jan A. Wium, Johan Verster Retief, and Celeste Barnardo Viljoen, "Lessons from Development of Design Standards in South Africa," *IABSE Symposium Report* 102, no. 3 (2014): 3198–3205.

20. Jack C. McCormac, *Design of Reinforced Concrete*, 2nd ed. (n.p.: Longman Higher Education, 1986).

21. "Esperienze sull'aderenza del cemento con il ferro," *Il Monitore Tecnico* 35 (1917): 31–32.

22. See for instance "Über Riss und Rostbildung bei Eisenbetonbrücken," *Schweizerische Bauzeitung* 17, no. 12 (1917): 153–54.

23. In a remarkably accurate early guess, an 1893 Norwegian textbook ventured that "the reasons that iron does not rust in cement are . . . that air cannot penetrate to the iron and . . . the iron cannot take the oxygen from the water," but the author still recommended cement as "the best protection against oxidation." Edvard Kolderup, *Monitor Konstruktionerne*, trans. Ueli Angst (n.p.: H. Aschenrug, 1893), 8.

24. Adolf Fick, "Über diffusion," *Philosophical Magazine and Journal of Science* 10, no. 10 (1855): 30; Bernadette Bensaude-Vincent, *Chemistry: The Impure Science* (London: Imperial College, 2008), 185–200.

25. Von A. Bäumel, "Die Auswirkung von Betonzusatzmitteln auf das Korrosionsverhalten von Stahl in Beton." *Zement-Kalk-Gips* 7 (1959): 294–305. D. A. Hausmann, "Steel Corrosion in Concrete: How Does It Occur?," *Materials Protection* (November 1967): 19, described how carbonation reduced pH "but only to a depth of a few millimeters in sound concrete," explicitly ignoring that CO_2 diffusion is continuous.

26. Hamada used the term "neutralization" instead of "passivation." "It was readily assumable," he wrote, "that the alkali of the concrete would gradually be neutralized." Hamada, "Neutralization (Carbonation) of Concrete and Corrosion of Reinforcing Steel," 344.

27. L. Czarnecki and P. Woyciechowski, "Modelling of Concrete Carbonation: Is It a

Process Unlimited in Time and Restricted in Space?," *Bulletin of the Polish Academy of Technical Sciences* 63, no. 1 (2015): 43–54. See also W. P. S. Dias, "Factors Influencing the Service Life of Buildings," *Engineer: Journal of the Institution of Engineers, Sri Lanka* 46, no. 4 (2013): 1–7. For a literature review, see Amin Jamali, Ueli Angst, Bryan Adey, and Bernhard Elsener, "Modeling of Corrosion-Induced Concrete Cover Cracking," *Construction and Building Materials* 42 (May 2013): 225–37.

28. See, for example, the slogan "Make Concrete Last Forever. Do It Now," on the website of Markham Distributing Ltd., accessed December 20, 2020, https://www.markham-global.com.

29. M. G. Stewart, and J. Peng, "Life-Cycle Cost Assessment of Climate Change Adaptation Measures to Minimise Carbonation-Induced Corrosion Risks," *International Journal of Engineering under Uncertainty* 2, no. 1–2 (2010): 35–46; Claus Pade and Maria Guimaraes, "The CO2 Uptake of Concrete in a 100 Year Perspective," in *Cement and Concrete Research* 37, no. 9 (2007): 1348–56.

30. Christophe Bonneuil and Jean-Baptiste Fressoz, *The Shock of the Anthropocene* (London: Verso, 2016).

31. Dirk E. Hebel et al., "Constructing with Engineered Bamboo," in *Cultivated Building Materials: Industrialized Natural Resources for Architecture and Construction*, ed. Dirk E. Hebel and Felix Heisel (Basel: Birkhäuser, 2017), 58–71.

32. "Concrete Studies Continue," *Middle East Construction*, July 1986, 32–33; *Proceedings of the First International Conference on Deterioration and Repair of Reinforced Concrete in the Arabian Gulf, October 26–29, 1985* (Manama: Bahrain Society of Engineers and the Concrete Society, 1985).

33. Christophe Bonneuil, "The Geological Turn: Narratives of the Anthropocene," in *The Anthropocene and the Global Environmental Crisis: Rethinking Modernity in a New Epoch*, ed. Clive Hamilton, Christophe Bonneuil, and François Gemenne (London: Taylor & Francis, 2015), 17–31.

34. Toshiki Sano, "The First Report of the Steel Material Decay Experiment," *Prevention of Earthquake Disaster Research*, Report No. 74 (1911): 25–41. See also Akihiko Yoda, "Predicting the Neutralization and the Age of Buildings Made of Reinforced Concrete," *Materiaru Raifu Gakkaishi* 17, no. 1–2 (January 2005); and M. Kanematsu, "Researches on the Durability of Concrete—Works by Toshikata Sano, Dr. Yoshikazu Uchida and Dr. Minoru Hamada," *Concrete Journal* 51, no. 9 (2013): 716–20.

35. Minoru Hamada, Koichi Kishitani, and Masaji Ikeda, "Influence of Cement Content and Molding Pressure on the Qualities (Specific Gravity, Strength, Water Absorption and Fire Resistance) of Durisol," *Fire Prevention Society of Japan* 8, no. 2 (March 1959): 47–51; "Study of Prevention of Breakage in Asphalt Waterproofing," trans. H. J. Kondo, *Proceedings of the Architectural Institute of Japan*, part 1, 63 (1959): 41–48, and part 2, 66 (1960): 21–24.

36. Kyösti Tuutti, "The Progress of Corrosion for Steel in Uncracked Concrete: A Hypothesis" (doctoral diss., Cement och Betong Institutet, Stockholm, 1977).

37. Carina Gråbacke and Jan Jörnmark, "The Political Construction of the 'Million Housing Programme,'" in *Science for Welfare and Warfare: Technology and State Initiative in Cold War Sweden*, ed. Per Lundin, Niklas Stenlås, and Johan Gribbe (Sagamore Beach, MA: Science History, 2010), 233–50; Frida Rosenberg, "The Construction of Construction" (doctoral diss., KTH Royal Institute of Technology, 2018).

38. See Ralph P. Andrew, "The Swedish Cement and Concrete Research Institute," *Magazine of Concrete Research* 4, no. 10 (July 1952): 29–39; and *Report of Activities 1980–*

1981 (Stockholm: Cement och Betong Institutet, 1981). On fears of the end of the welfare state, see Marten Lagergren, Lena Lundh, Minga Orkan, and Christer Sanne, *Time to Care: A Report Prepared for the Swedish Secretariat for Future Studies* (Oxford: Pergamon, 1984). On conservation and "energy transition," see Mattias Legnér and Gustaf Leijonhufvud, "A Legacy of Energy Saving: The Discussion on Heritage Values in the First Programme on Energy Efficiency in Buildings in Sweden, c. 1974–1984," in *Historic Environment: Policy and Practice* 10, no. 1 (2019): 40–57.

39. Bernadette Bensaude-Vincent, "The Construction of a Discipline: Materials Science in the United States," *Historical Studies in the Physical and Biological Sciences* 31, no. 2 (2001): 223–48; Robert Cahn, *The Coming of Materials Science* (Oxford: Elsevier, 2001).

40. Thomas Heine, "Grand Challenges in Computational Materials Science: From Description to Prediction at All Scales," *Frontiers in Materials* 1, no. 7 (2014), https://www.frontiersin.org/articles/10.3389/fmats.2014.00007/full.

41. Claire White et al., "Investigating Permeability and Carbonation Behavior of Sustainable Cements," *AGU Fall Meeting Abstracts* (N.p., 2015).

42. George Scherer, "Predicting Durability of Novel Cement-Based Materials," *Journal of the Chinese Ceramic Society* 40, no. 7 (July 2012): 1071–80.

43. For a case study of the layer of earth produced by industrialization around the Parisian metropole, see Mathieu Fernandez, Corinne Blanquart, and Éric Verdeil, "La terre et le béton: Le projet d'urbanisme considéré sous l'angle du métabolisme territorial," *VertigO—la revue électronique en sciences de l'environnement* (online), 18, no. 3 (2018), https://journals.openedition.org/vertigo/23302.

44. Jane Jacobs, *The Life and Death of Great American Cities* (New York: Random House, 1961).

CHAPTER 6. MEDIEVAL AND RENAISSANCE MONEY

1. For commentary on the canto, see Sally A. Mussetter, "'Inferno' XXX: Dante's Counterfeit Adam," *Traditio* 34 (1978): 427–35. Maestro Adamo is conventionally identified as Adam of Brescia, employed by the counts of Romena to issue debased coins (428). For alternative identifications, see Giovanni Livi, "Un personaggio dantesco," *Giornale Dantesco* 24 (1921): 265–70; and Gianfranco Contini, "Sul XXX dell'Inferno," *Paragone* 44 (1953): 3–13.

2. Dante Alighieri, *La Commedia secondo l'antica vulgata*, vol. 2, *Inferno*, ed. Giorgio Petrocci (Florence: Casa editrice Le lettere, 1994), line 69.

3. For commentary, see Mark Musa, ed., *Dante's "Inferno": The Indiana Critical Edition* (Bloomington: Indiana University Press, 1995), 221–22.

4. Mussetter, "'Inferno' XXX," 431–32.

5. Dante Alighieri, *La Commedia*, lines 91–92 (emphasis added).

6. Carlo Ginzburg, "Checking the Evidence: The Judge and the Historian," *Critical Inquiry* 18, no. 1 (1991): 84.

7. Peter Parshall and Rainer Schoch, *Origins of European Printmaking: Fifteenth-Century Woodcuts and Their Public* (New Haven: National Gallery of Art, Washington, and the Germanisches Nationalmuseum, Nuremberg, in association with Yale University Press, 2005), 218.

8. For the Trial of the Pyx, see J. G. Noppen, *Chapter House and Pyx Chamber: Westminster Abbey* (London: His Majesty's Stationery Office, 1935); 221–22; John Craig, "Trial of the Pyx," *Canadian Numismatic Journal* 1, no. 11 (1956); Carroll G. Hughes, "Notes on the Trial of the Pyx," *Numismatist* 27, no. 11 (1959); S. E. Rigold, *The Chapter House and the Pyx Chamber, Westminster Abbey* (London: Her Majesty's Stationery Office, 1976); Tom DeLorey,

"The Trial of the Pyx," *COINage* 32, no. 8 (1996). On Henry III and the rebuilding of Westminster Abbey, see Suzanne Lewis, "Henry III and the Gothic Rebuilding of Westminster Abbey: The Problematics of Context," *Traditio* 50 (1995): 129–72.

9. Noppen, *Chapter House and Pyx Chamber*, 5–6; "Westminster Abbey Exhibition: The Trial of the Pyx," *Coins and Medals* 3, no. 8 (1966): 487.

10. Arne R. Flaten, "Identity and the Display of *medaglie* in Renaissance and Baroque Europe," *Word and Image* 19, no. 1–2 (2003): 60. See also Martha McCrory, "Medaglie, monete e gemme: Etimologia e simbolismo nella cultura del tardo Rinascimento italiano," in *La tradizione classica nella medaglia d'arte dal Rinascimento al neoclassico*, ed. Maurizio Buora (Udine: Civici Musei e Gallerie di Storia e Arte Udine, Gabinetto Numismatico, 1999), 39–52.

11. Flaten, "Identity and the Display of *medaglie*," 64.

12. Minou Schraven, "Out of Sight, Yet Still in Place: On the Use of Italian Renaissance Portrait Medals as Building Deposits," *RES: Anthropology and Aesthetics* 55–56 (Spring–Autumn 2009): 185.

13. Stephen K. Scher, *The Currency of Fame: Portrait Medals of the Renaissance* (New York: Harry N. Abrams in association with the Frick Collection, 1994), 19.

14. Luke Syson, "Holes and Loops: The Display and Collection of Medals in Renaissance Italy," *Journal of Design History* 15, no. 4 (2002): 230.

15. Anthony Hobson, *Humanists and Bookbinders: The Origins and Diffusion of Humanistic Bookbinding, 1459–1559; With a Census of Historiated Plaquette and Medallion Bindings of the Renaissance* (1929; Cambridge: Cambridge University Press, 1989), 92. See also Joachim Menzhausen, *Das Grüne Gewölbe* (Berlin: Rembrandt, 1968), table 10; or the English translation, Menzhausen, *The Green Vault: An Introduction* (Dresden: Staatliche Kunstsammlungen Dresden, 1989), 20, 21.

16. Roberto Weiss, *The Medals of Pope Sixtus IV (1471–1484)* (Rome: Edizioni di storia e letteratura, 1961), fig. 26. A portrait of Paul II decorated the original binding of Vatican Library, Vat. Lat. 8913: Vatican exhibition, 1977, no. 12, tavv. XII–XIII.

17. John Spencer, "Filarete, the Medallist of the Roman Emperors," *Art Bulletin* 61, no. 4 (1979): 552.

18. The obverse of the medal declares, ANTNIUS [sic]+PETRI+DE+FloRenTIA+FECIT+MCCCCXLV. The reverse inscription reads, OPV/S/ANTO/NII.

19. Mesticanza di Paolo di Liello Petrone, in *Rerum Italicarum Scriptores*, vol. 24, ed. Ludovico Muratori (1738), col. 1128; Spencer, "Filarete, the Medallist," 553.

20. Andrew Burnett and Richard Schofield, "An Introduction to the Portrait Medals on the Certosa di Pavia," in *The Image of the Individual: Portraits in the Renaissance*, ed. Nicholas Mann and Luke Syson (London: British Museum Press, 1998), 62.

21. Andrew Burnett and Richard Schofield, "The Decoration of the Colleoni Chapel," *Arte Lombarda* n.s. 126, no. 2 (1999): 61.

22. Burnett and Schofield, "Decoration of the Colleoni Chapel," 67.

23. Burnett and Schofield, "Decoration of the Colleoni Chapel," 67.

24. Burnett and Schofield, "Decoration of the Colleoni Chapel," 68.

25. Authorship of the portraits is debated. It could be that they were the work of Cristoforo Solari, Amadeo, Tamagnino, and Benedetto Briosco, although different hands might have been involved. See Burnett and Schofield, "Introduction to the Portrait Medals," 55.

26. Burnett and Schofield, "Introduction to the Portrait Medals," 56.

27. Burnett and Schofield, "Introduction to the Portrait Medals," 57–58.

28. See Burnett and Schofield, "Introduction to the Portrait Medals," 62.

29. Burnett and Schofield, "Introduction to the Portrait Medals," 59, 61.
30. Burnett and Schofield, "Introduction to the Portrait Medals," 59–61.
31. Aldo Foratti, "I tondi nel cortile del Palazzo Riccardi," L'Arte 20 (1917): 20.
32. Martha Levine Dunkelman, "From Microcosm to Macrocosm: Michelangelo and Ancient Gems," Zeitschrift für Kunstgeschichte 73, no. 3 (2010): 366.
33. Catherine Gallagher and Stephen Greenblatt, Practicing New Historicism (Chicago: University of Chicago Press, 2000), 31.

CHAPTER 7. FROM TRUTH TO PROOF

1. Geheimes Staatsarchiv preussischer Kulturbesitz (GStA PK) I. HA Rep. 93B, Nr. 1004, 1. The quote is from Adler's letter of March 6, 1858, enclosed with a proposal from the publishers Ernst and Korn for an advance purchase of four hundred copies of the anticipated architectural history report (to facilitate production), as well as a letter of support by August Stüler, architect of the king, who would ultimately approve the funds. It should be noted that "fatherland" in this context refers to the Prussian and not the German kingdom.
2. Architektur Verein zu Berlin, "Die Baubehörden des Preußischen Staates," Berlin und seine Bauten (Berlin, 1896), 6. The restoration of medieval architecture had been one of the kingdom's central cultural agendas in the face of French occupation between 1806 and 1814.
3. Scholarly precedents included essays by the first state director of conservation, Ferdinand von Quast, Zur Charakteristik des älteren Ziegelbaues in der Mark Brandenburg, mit besonderer Rücksicht auf die Klosterkirche zu Jerichow (Berlin: Unger, 1850), as well as his Denkmale der Baukunst in Preussen (Berlin, 1852), and a book by the first director of the German National Museum, August Essenwein's Norddeutschlands Backsteinbau im Mittelalter (Karlsruhe: Veith, 1855).
4. Friedrich Adler, Mittelalterliche Backstein-Bauwerke des preussischen Staates, vol. 1 (Berlin: Ernst & Korn, 1862), 76. It was the art historian Wilhelm Lübke who had described August Stüler's nineteenth-century addition to the Tangermünde town hall as a masterful example of the medieval Gothic. I am indebted to Michael Gnehm for pointing out this detail.
5. Adler, Mittelalterliche Backstein-Bauwerke, foreword.
6. This criticism was most loudly voiced by editor K. E. O Fritsch in the pages of the Deutsche Bauzeitung. Peter Lemburg, "Leben und Werk des gelehrten Berliner Architekten Friedrich Adler: 1827–1908" (doctoral diss., Freie Universität, Berlin, 1989), 102–3.
7. Paul Frankl, "The Scientific Trend," in The Gothic: Literary Sources and Interpretations through Eight Centuries (Princeton: Princeton University Press, 1960), 491–525.
8. Rhona Richman Kenneally, "Empirical Underpinnings: Ecclesiology, the Excursion and Church Schemes, 1830s–1850s," Ecclesiology Today 15 (January 1998): 14. Thanks go to Joshua Mardell for helping me discover this project.
9. Johann Wolfgang von Goethe, Von deutscher Baukunst (n.p., 1773).
10. Hayden White, Metahistory: The Historical Imagination in Nineteenth-Century Europe (1973; Baltimore: Johns Hopkins University Press, 1980), 164–65.
11. Theodor Fontane's diary states that he, Ranke, Adler, and others dined together on the evening of March 18, 1872, at the house of Auguste Sophie von Meding. Roland Berbig, Theodor Fontane: Chronik (Berlin: De Gruyter, 2010), 1780.
12. GStA PK, I. HA Rep. 93B, Nr. 1004, 19.
13. Some regions, such as Arnsberg, Erfurt, and Oppeln, had little to offer. In areas where sandstone or limestone had historically been the building material of choice or where the Thirty Years' War had raged, all evidence of medieval structures had disappeared.

14. GStA PK, I. HA Rep. 93B, Nr. 1004, 317.

15. GStA PK, I. HA Rep. 93B, Nr. 1004, 3–6.

16. Carl Schnaase, "Mittelalterliche Backsteinbauwerke des preußischen Staates," *Zentralblatt der Bauverwaltung* 9 (1859): 123–34.

17. Christian Scholl, "Friedrich Gilly und die Entdeckung der Marienburg als Bau-Denkmal," in *Gilly—Weinbrenner—Schinkel: Baukunst auf Papier zwischen Gotik und Klassizismus*, ed. Marion Hilliges and Christian Scholl (Göttingen: Universitätsverlag, 2016), 34; Marvin Barner, Ines Barchewicz, Christian Scholl, and Verena Suchy, "Friedrich Frick nach Friedrich Gilly und anderen: Schloss Marienburg in Preußen," in *Gilly—Weinbrenner—Schinkel*, ed. Hilliges and Scholl, 102; Felix Saure, *Karl Friedrich Schinkel: Ein deutscher Idealist zwischen "Klassik" und "Gotik"* (Hannover: Wehrhahn Verlag, 2010), 208–13. Saure discusses the drawings that Schinkel made during a journey to Italy (1803–1805) in which he removed all baroque details from the Gothic churches of Schöngrabern, Abruzzo, and Palermo.

18. Adler, *Mittelalterliche Backstein-Bauwerke*, foreword.

19. Lorraine Daston and Peter Galison, "The Image of Objectivity," *Representations* 40 (Autumn 1992): 84–85.

20. In its breakdown of the surveyed structures by geographic area and the attribution of a region's architectural idiosyncrasies to causal dependence on its geographical environment and local history, the project report reflected a style of writing common in art geography circles and one that would later develop in Germany. See Thomas DaCosta Kaufmann, *Toward a Geography of Art* (Chicago: University of Chicago Press, 2004), 43–67.

21. Hayden White, "The Value of Narrativity in the Representation of Reality," *Critical Inquiry* 7, no. 1 (1980): 17. Among Adler's "distractions" was his simultaneous job of leading the excavations at Olympia under Ernst Curtius for the German Archaeological Institute.

22. Adler, *Mittelalterliche Backstein-Bauwerke*, 1. The (political) history of Brandenburg that Adler utilized was already well documented, and the empirical evidence he produced mapped onto this preestablished narrative. Adler's historical material draws considerably upon Adolph Friedrich Johann Riedel's *Codex diplomaticus Brandenburgensis*, begun in 1838, and would confirm, albeit in greater detail and with local adaptations, the popularized account of the founding myth of Brandenburg in Theodor Fontane's *Wanderungen durch die Mark Brandenburg* (1862–1889). On transitional motifs, see White, *Metahistory*, 6.

23. This quote has long been attributed to Napoleon Bonaparte.

24. The House of Hohenzollern originated in Swabia. In 1411, Frederick VI, burgrave of Nuremberg, was appointed governor of Brandenburg, and in 1415 he was elevated to elector and margrave. However, German origins in the region date back to Albrecht the Bear—the Saxon who was the first margrave of Brandenburg, a rank he held from 1157 until his death. Instead of celebrating the Hohenzollern dynasty, narratives after German unification in 1871 conflate these two stories on the basis of the continuous occupation of Brandenburg.

25. Heinrich Hübsch proposed in his work *In welchem Style sollen wir bauen?* (1828) that the *Rundbogenstil*, the early Gothic style, would be the most appropriate choice.

26. GStA PK, I. HA Rep. 93B, Nr. 1004, 19.

27. GStA PK, I. HA Rep. 93B, Nr. 1004, 19.

28. GStA PK, I. HA Rep. 93B, Nr. 1004, 20.

29. See the panels in volumes 1 (1862) and 2 (1898) of Adler, *Mittelalterliche Backstein-Bauwerke*.

30. This moment of architectural homage symbolically came to a close with Paul Wallot's neo-Renaissance design for the Reichstag, completed in 1894.

31. Roland Jaeger, "Monumentales Standardwerk: Das "Handbuch der Architektur" (1880–1943). Verlagsgeschichte und Bibliographie," *Aus dem Antiquariat*, no. 5 (2006): 346. Here Jaeger is quoting an article in the *Deutsche Bauzeitung* from 1882.

32. Semper was particularly scathing in his view of Franz Kugler, one of the "fathers" of the Berlin school, with whom he exchanged blows over questions of polychromy.

33. Paul Frankl attributes the success of Goethe's essay about the Strasbourg cathedral not to its being factually correct but to the "total effect" brought about by Goethe's passionate rhetoric. Frankl, *The Gothic*, 417–18.

34. For example, in discussing an architectural survey of German architecture, Paul Jaskot and Ivo van der Graaf write that they planned to address any "new research questions that might arise from the data" and that "the database has also spurred questions that lead us to unexplored areas of art historical research. . . . This drew our attention to Leipzig and, in the process, brought up new building sites that exist at the fringes of architectural historical knowledge." Paul Jaskot and Ivo van der Graaf, "Historical Journals as Digital Sources: Mapping Architecture in Germany, 1914–24," *Journal of the Society of Architectural Historians* 76, no. 4 (2017), https://doi.org/10.1525/jsah.2017.76.4.483. Likewise, Leonardo Impett and Franco Moretti were confronted with a surprising new correlation between their *Pathosformeln* and the "outlier" of Catoni's "desperate woman in motion"—a relationship they would not have found without their operations, which, it has to be said, produced "only" three "useful" or "correct" groupings out of sixteen. Franco Moretti and Leonardo Impett, "Totentanz: Operationalizing Aby Warburg's Pathosformeln," *New Left Review*, no. 107 (September–October 2017).

35. *Zentralblatt der Bauverwaltung*, July 7, 1894.

CHAPTER 8. THE BANISTER FLETCHERS' TABULATIONS

1. In addition to the Fletchers' *A History of Architecture*, which is the focus of this chapter, Banister Fletcher Sr. wrote *Quantities: A Text-Book for Surveyors* (1877), *Model Houses for the Industrial Classes* (1877), *Dilapidations: A Text-Book for Architects and Surveyors in Tabulated Form* (1883), *Arbitrations: A Text-Book for Surveyors in Tabulated Form* (1893), and *Light and Air: A Text-Book for Architects and Surveyors* (1895).

2. Most of Banister Fletcher Jr.'s written output consisted of revising and republishing the work that his father had written alone or with his two sons, including *The London Building Act, 1894, and the Amendment Act, 1898* (1901) and *Valuations and Compensations: A Text-Book on the Practice of Valuing Property and Compensations in Relations Thereto* (1905). Fletcher Jr. also wrote *Andrea Palladio, His Life and Works* (1902) and *The English Home* (1910), as well as the prize-winning *Influence of Material on Architecture* (1897), cited below. Fletcher Jr. did not hold a permanent academic position.

3. The first edition appeared in 1896, and a revised twenty-first edition came out in 2020. Except where noted otherwise, we will be referring in this chapter to the page numbers in Banister Fletcher and Banister F. Fletcher, *A History of Architecture on the Comparative Method for the Student, Craftsmen, and Amateur*, 5th ed. (London: B. T. Batsford, 1905).

4. Murray Fraser, general ed., *Sir Banister Fletcher's Global History of Architecture*, 2 vols. (London: Bloomsbury, 2020).

5. Gülsüm Baydar Nalbantoğlu, "Toward Postcolonial Openings: Rereading Sir Banister Fletcher's 'History of Architecture," *Assemblage* 35 (1998): 8.

6. Kathleen James-Chakraborty, "Response to Murray Fraser," *ABE Journal*, no. 16 (2019). Also see Murray Fraser, "A Global History of Architecture for an Age of Globalisation," *ABE Journal*, no. 14–15 (2019).

7. Fletcher and Fletcher, *History of Architecture*, 4.

8. F. M. L. Thompson, *Chartered Surveyors: The Growth of a Profession* (London: Routledge and Kegan Paul, 1968), 70–78.

9. Linda Clarke, *Building Capitalism: Historical Change and the Labour Process in the Production of the Built Environment* (London: Routledge, 2011), 81.

10. Banister Fletcher [Sr.], *Quantities: A Textbook for Surveyors, in Tabulated Form, Explanatory of the Best Methods Adopted in the Measurement of Builder's Work* . . . (London: B. T. Batsford, 1877). On the history of the profession, see James Nisbet, *A Proper Price: Quantity Surveying in London, 1650 to 1940* (London: Stoke, 1997). Other such efforts came before Fletcher's, and his was far from the last. For example, see John Reid, *The Surveyor's and Builder's Assistant, or, Practical Manual of Mensuration* (London: Cunningham, 1848). After the publication of Fletcher's *Quantities*, John Leaning published a series, "Quantity Surveying," in *The British Architect: A Journal of Architecture and the Accessory Arts* 10–11 (1878–1879); those essays were then collected in *Quantity Surveying: For the Use of Surveyors, Architects, Engineers and Builders* (London: Spon, 1886).

11. Fletcher [Sr.], *Quantities*, 5.

12. On the history of profit, see Jonathan Levy, "Accounting for Profit and the History of Capital," *Critical Historical Studies* 1, no. 2 (2014): 171–214.

13. Banister Fletcher [Sr.], *Arbitrations: A Textbook for Surveyors, in Tabulated Form* (London: E. & F. N. Spon, 1875). These issues are also discussed in Fletcher Sr.'s correspondence in the 1870s and 1890s.

14. Fletcher [Sr.], *Quantities*, 28.

15. For a comparison, see Porter's discussion of accountants in Theodore Porter, *Trust in Numbers: The Pursuit of Objectivity in Science and Public Life* (Princeton: Princeton University Press, 1995).

16. Banister Fletcher [Jr.], General Courses 1 and 2, London University Special Collections, 6B-B0990-S02, University College London.

17. Fletcher and Fletcher, *History of Architecture*, 442.

18. Juxtaposing plans of English Gothic cathedrals on several pages, for example, allowed the reader to quickly compare these buildings' spatial arrangements. Fletcher and Fletcher, *History of Architecture*, 299–303.

19. Fletcher and Fletcher, *History of Architecture*, 115.

20. Fletcher and Fletcher, *History of Architecture*, 4.

21. Fletcher and Fletcher, *History of Architecture*, 117.

22. Fletcher and Fletcher, *History of Architecture*, 15.

23. Levy, "Accounting for Profit and the History of Capital," 173.

24. Levy, "Accounting for Profit and the History of Capital," 175 (emphasis added).

25. Levy, "Accounting for Profit and the History of Capital," 175. Levy builds upon the work of William Sewell. See William H. Sewell Jr., "The Temporalities of Capitalism," *Socio-Economic Review* 6, no. 3 (2008): 517–37.

26. Banister Fletcher [Jr.], *The Influence of Material on Architecture* (London: B. T. Batsford, 1897), 5. Style had been theorized earlier in the century by the likes of Heinrich Hübsch in his 1828 essay "In What Style Should We Build?," reprinted in *In What Style Should We Build? The German Debate on Architectural Style*, intro. and trans. Wolfgang Hermann (Santa Monica, CA: Getty Center for the History of Art and the Humanities, 1992), 63–101.

27. Fletcher [Jr.], *Influence of Material on Architecture*, 6; Gottfried Semper, "Four

Elements" (1851), in *Four Elements of Architecture and Other Writings*, ed. H. F. Mallgrave and Wolfgang Herrmann (Cambridge: Cambridge University Press, 1989), 101–29.

28. The most influential theory of *Stoffwechsel* was developed by Hermann von Helmholtz, who argued in his influential paper "Über die Erhaltung der Kraft" that force (*Kraft*) in the universe was never lost but simply transformed from one form to another. Hermann von Helmholtz, "Über die Erhaltung der Kraft" (1847), in *Wissenschaftliche Abhandlungen*, vol. 1 (Leipzig: Barth, 1882), 12–75, published in English as "On the Application of the Law of the Conservation of Force to Organic Nature," *Proceedings of the Royal Institute* 3 (1861): 347–57; and as "The Application of the Law of the Conservation of Force to Organic Nature," in *Selected Writings of Hermann von Helmholtz*, ed. Russell Kahl (Middletown, CT: Wesleyan University Press, 1971), 109–21.

29. Fletcher [Jr.], *Influence of Material on Architecture*, 22. The assertion appeared in Fletcher and Fletcher, *History of Architecture*, 7. The same trope is also found in Louis Sullivan, *The Autobiography of an Idea* (New York: Press of the American Institute of Architecture, 1924), 249.

30. Fletcher [Jr.], *Influence of Material on Architecture*, 26.

31. Banister Fletcher and Banister F. Fletcher, *A History of Architecture on the Comparative Method for the Student, Craftsmen, and Amateur*, 1st ed. (1896), vii (emphasis added).

32. Fletcher [Jr.], General Course 1.

33. Fletcher and Fletcher, *History of Architecture*, viii (1905).

34. Fletcher and Fletcher, *History of Architecture*, vii (1905).

35. Fletcher [Jr.], General Course 1. This quotation in Fletcher Jr.'s lecture notes comes from Gilbert Scott. See also Sir Banister Fletcher, *Architecture and Its Place in a Liberal Education: A Paper Read before the University Extension Guild* (London: B. T. Batsford, 1905).

CHAPTER 9. EVIDENCE AND NARRATIVE IN DIGITAL ART HISTORY

Our thanks to the volume editors as well as Robert Buerglener, Laila Seewang, and Łukasz Stanek for their critical comments on this chapter.

1. Cameron Blevins, "The Perpetual Sunrise of Methodology" (blog post), January 5, 2015, http://www.cameronblevins.org/posts/perpetual-sunrise-methodology.

2. In this regard, see the articles in the *International Journal of Digital Art History*, many of which tend to reflect that technological focus. Of course, for those of us in the subfield, there is no question that this approach is both useful and critical, however much it may be overlooked by traditional art history. For an excellent overview of key issues, see Allison Langmead, "Art and Architectural History, and the Performative, Mindful Practice of the Digital Humanities," *Journal of Interactive Technology and Pedagogy*, no. 12 (February 21, 2018), https://jitp.commons.gc.cuny.edu/art-and-architectural-history-and-the-performative-mindful-practice-of-the-digital-humanities.

3. Exceptions include, for example, the work of Anne Helmreich and Pamela Fletcher in their use of digital approaches that forcefully engage in art-historical analysis. Pamela Fletcher and Anne Helmreich with David Israel and Seth Erickson, "Local/Global: Mapping Nineteenth-Century London's Art Market," *Nineteenth-Century Art Worldwide* 11, no. 3 (2012), http://www.19thc-artworldwide.org/autumn12/fletcher-helmreich-mapping-the-london-art-market. The emphasis on evidence for evidence's sake is certainly not unique to the digital humanities nor is it new. See, in a different light, the analysis of the faith in a "scientific" approach to architecture in Laila Seewang's contribution to this volume, for example.

4. Willard McCarty, in *Humanist Discussion Group* 29, no. 549 (December 14, 2015), https://dhhumanist.org/Archives/Current/Humanist.vol29.txt.

5. We have argued this morphological function in relation to the use of digital mapping more extensively in Paul B. Jaskot and Ivo van der Graaff, "Historical Journals as Digital Sources: Mapping Architecture in Germany, 1914–24," *Journal of the Society of Architectural Historians* 76, no. 4 (2017): 483–505.

6. This construction, influenced by Fredric Jameson's insights, is derived from the critical investigation of digital humanities in Carolyn Lesjak, "All or Nothing: Reading Franco Moretti Reading," *Historical Materialism* 24, no. 3 (2016): 185–205.

7. For an argument affirming the relationship between digital and social art history, see Paul B. Jaskot, "Digital Art History as the Social History of Art: Towards the Disciplinary Relevance of Digital Methods," *Visual Resources* 35, no. 1–2 (2019): 21–33.

8. To this point, see Jaskot and van der Graaff, "Historical Journals as Digital Sources."

9. Manfred Pohl, *Philipp Holzmann: Geschichte eines Bauunternehmens 1849–1999* (Munich: C. H. Beck, 1999); Manfred Pohl and Birgit Siekmann, *Hochtief and Its History: From the Helfmann Brothers into the 21st Century* (Munich: Piper Verlag, 2001).

10. Knut Stegmann, *Das Bauunternehmen Dyckerhoff & Widmann: Zu den Anfängen des Betonbaus in Deutschland 1865–1918* (Tübingen: Ernst Wasmuth Verlag, 2014). See also the draft of an internal firm history in Deutsches Museum Archiv (DM), FA 010/021, Rudolf Kundigraber, "65 Jahre Beton-Technik," December 1929.

11. As with any archival source, significant problems emerged in terms of ambiguous evidence. It became clear that, as is often the case with large projects, the firm was sometimes only involved in the construction of parts of buildings, such as the erection of a steel frame, the pouring of a concrete foundation, or the renovation of the roof on a station platform. This situation forces a confrontation with the splintered nature of the construction industry, where many subcontractors, ranging from window makers to steel manufacturers, are involved in a single project. In the structuring of the database that Ivo van der Graaff and I managed, we developed a "primary structure" field where we identified through simple yes/no responses whether Dyckerhoff & Widmann was the main contractor of a project. The continued development of such fields and parameters is therefore as much an exercise in foresight as it is adjusting the database and its contents to the nature of the evidence. It also indicates the deeply interpretive nature of using humanist sources for digital work.

12. The structuring and visualization of large datasets—especially bureaucratic and statistical ones—predates, of course, the onset of the digital. For analysis of this history and its particular ideological problems, see, for example, Susan Buck-Morss, "Envisioning Capital: Political Economy on Display," *Critical Inquiry* 21, no. 2 (1995): 434–67.

13. Note that the critical use of typological analysis in social art history is well established. See, for example, such foundational texts as Richard Krautheimer, "The Carolingian Revival of Early Christian Architecture," *Art Bulletin* 24, no. 1 (1942): 1–38.

14. See the Dywidag publication in DM, FA 010/190, sec. III, 1, for the first reference to construction for the Zeiss-Werke, Jena.

15. Joachim Krausse has studied the development of the Jena planetarium and has many strong publications on the topic. Notably, he focuses his work almost exclusively on the planetarium rather than its significance for the construction industry more broadly. See, in particular, Joachim Krausse, "Architektur aus dem Geist der Projektion: Das Zeiss-Planetarium," in *Wissen in Bewegung: 80 Jahre Zeiss-Planetarium Jena*, ed. Hans-Christian von Hermann (Jena: Ernst-Abbe-Stiftung, 2006), 51–85. For an English-language summary of

many of his points, see Joachim Krausse, "The Miracle of Jena," *World Architecture*, no. 20 (November 1992): 46–53.

16. Krausse, "Architektur aus dem Geist der Projektion." See also Adolf Meyer, "Das Zeiss Planetarium," *die form* 1 (1925–1926): 17–19. As Krausse also notes, László Moholy-Nagy would use a photograph of the geodesic framework in later publications, indicating the interest of Bauhaus members in the construction.

17. Dywidag index, DM, FA 010/198: sec. VIII, 6–14. Note that the bibliographies following each section of the index contain nineteen references for this technique, many more than other buildings listed. Dywidag often used its varied construction at the Zeiss-Werke as a significant part of its promotional materials, such as the six volumes (1920) featuring illustrations of Dywidag buildings. The first volume begins with an industrial building and an illustration of the Zeiss-Werke. DM, FA 010/192.

18. For a solid analysis of the significance of concrete, see Adrian Forty, *Concrete and Culture: A Material History* (London: Reaktion Books, 2016).

19. Knut Stegmann makes this point at the end of his overview of Dywidag's development from 1865 to 1918. He critiques architectural historians who focus on the innovative uses of cement by modernists like Le Corbusier while ignoring the decades of development by construction firms. In this sense, the ultimate argument for a history of Dywidag is that it does not so much tell us about how architects pushed for new uses of materials but rather indicates that a major impulse for the expressive use of cement came from the building firm looking for clients: "Entwicklung der innovativen Bauweisen war nicht . . . die Suche von Architekten oder Bauingenieuren nach einem Baustoff für eine Bauaufgabe, sondern die Suche der Portlandzementindustrie nach neuen Absatzmöglichkeiten" (The development of innovative building techniques was not [grounded in] the search for architects or engineers for a building material to meet a building task but rather the search of the Portland cement industry for new [profit-making] possible uses). Stegmann, *Das Bauunternehmen Dyckerhoff & Widmann*, 245.

20. The building does after all earn two paragraphs in an important survey of architecture: Wolfgang Pehnt, *Deutsche Architektur seit 1900* (Munich: Deutsche Verlags Anstalt, 2005).

21. The sources on Mendelsohn's building as well as this moment in astrophysics are extensive. However, the canonical work remains Kathleen James, *Erich Mendelsohn and the Architecture of German Modernism* (Cambridge: Cambridge University Press, 1997), esp. 19–30. Notably, James (now James-Chakraborty) mentions Zeiss and Dywidag but makes little of their participation in the context we have discussed here. See also Ursula Breymayer, "Symbole der 'Kulturstellung Deutschlands': Einstein und der Einstein Turm zwischen Wissenschaftsförderung und nationalem Prestige," in *Ein Turm für Albert Einstein: Potsdam, das Licht und die Erforschung des Himmels*, ed. Hans Wilderotter (Potsdam: Hauses der Brandenburgisch-Preussischne Geschichte, 2005), 57–86.

22. For a comparative analysis of the transfer of architectural ideas and technologies in a different context, see the chapter by Łukasz Stanek in this volume.

23. For an extended overview of Marxism and art history, see Andrew Hemingway, "Marxism and Art," Oxford Bibliographies, accessed March 2, 2021, https://www.oxford-bibliographies.com/view/document/obo-9780199920105/obo-9780199920105-0023.xml. Marx's theory of history was never completely articulated as such. For historical materialism, however, one must point to Karl Marx and Friedrich Engels, *A Critique of the German Ideology*, first published in 1932, as a crucial and influential source. See the Marx/Engels

Internet Archive, accessed August 20, 2018, https://www.marxists.org/archive/marx/works/download/Marx_The_German_Ideology.pdf.

24. In this regard, see Lesjak, "All or Nothing," her exploration of the tensions between history and analysis in the work of the well-known digital humanist Franco Moretti. As the proponent of "distant reading," Moretti has challenged digital humanists to expand their data sample from a small series of canonical case studies to the vast potential of "big data"; see Franco Moretti, *Distant Reading* (London: Verso, 2013). While Moretti himself is a product of the Marxist tradition of literary criticism, Lesjak nevertheless faults him for the undynamic or rather undialectic bifurcation of his work. On the one hand, in some of his work he promotes the large patterns that can be exposed in the visualization of big data; on the other, in other contributions he interrogates class by examining the bourgeois in an analog analysis of specific texts. See especially Lesjak, "All or Nothing," 204.

25. Mark Monmonier, *How to Lie with Maps*, 3rd ed. (Chicago: University of Chicago Press, 2018).

26. For recent work on the need for an expansive methodology for historical analysis beyond GIS, see Alberto Giordano and Tim Cole, "The Limits of GIS: Toward a GIS of Place," *Transactions in GIS* 22, no. 3 (2018): 664–76; and Anne Kelly Knowles, Levi Westerveld, and Laura Strom, "Inductive Visualization: A Humanistic Alternative to GIS," *GeoHumanities* 1, no. 2 (2015): 233–65.

CHAPTER 10. COMPARATIVE ARCHITECTURE AND ITS DISCONTENTS

1. Dominick LaCapra, *History and Criticism* (Ithaca: Cornell University Press, 1985), 41.
2. Paul Masson-Oursel, *Comparative Philosophy* (London: Kegan Paul, 1926), 39.
3. Haun Saussy, "Comparative Literature?," *Publications of the Modern Language Association of America* 118, no. 2 (2003): 339.
4. Francis Goyet, "Comparison," in *Dictionary of Untranslatables: A Philosophical Lexicon*, ed. Barbara Cassin (Princeton: Princeton University Press, 2014), 162.
5. Plutarch, *Plutarch's Lives*, vol. 1 (Boston: Little, Brown, 1910), 1.
6. Hayden White, "The Value of Narrativity in the Representation of Reality," in *The Content of the Form: Narrative Discourse and Historical Representation* (Baltimore: Johns Hopkins University Press, 1987), 24.
7. White, "Value of Narrativity," 2.
8. Edward H. Carr, *What Is History?* (New York: Vintage, 1961), 118.
9. Stanislaus von Moos, "Le Corbusier and Loos," in *Raumplan versus Plan Libre: Adolf Loos / Le Corbusier, 1919–1930*, ed. Max Risselada (Rotterdam: 010 Publishers, 2008), 24.
10. Carr, *What Is History?*, 141.
11. Chaïm Perelman, *The New Rhetoric: A Treatise on Argumentation* (London: University of Notre Dame Press, 1991), 247.
12. LaCapra, *History and Criticism*, 36.
13. Michael Podro, *The Critical Historians of Art* (New Haven: Yale University Press, 1982).
14. Adrian Forty, "Of Cars, Clothes and Carpets: Design Metaphors and Architectural Thought," *Journal of Design History* 2, no. 1 (1989): 6.
15. Jacqueline Lichtenstein, "The Comparison of the Arts," in *Dictionary of Untranslatables: A Philosophical Lexicon*, ed. Barbara Cassin (Princeton: Princeton University Press, 2014), 163.
16. Michel Foucault, *The Order of Things: An Archaeology of the Human Sciences* (New York: Vintage, 1994), 263–77; François Jacob, *The Logic of Life: A History of Heredity* (New York: Pantheon, 1982).

17. On the distinction between type and taxonomy, see Christopher Lueder, "Book-Worlds and Ordering Systems as Sites for Invention," in *The Production Sites of Architecture*, ed. Sophia Psarra (Abingdon: Routledge, 2019), 91–92.

18. Gottfried Semper, *Style in the Technical and Tectonic Arts, or, Practical Aesthetics* (Santa Monica, CA: Getty Research Institute, 2004), 468.

19. Semper, *Style in the Technical and Tectonic Arts*, 470.

20. Alina Payne, "Wölfflin, Architecture and the Problem of Stilwandlung," *Journal of Art Historiography*, no. 7 (2012): 4.

21. Heinrich Wölfflin, *Renaissance and Baroque* (London: Collins, 1964), 37.

22. Marshall Brown, "The Classic Is the Baroque: On the Principle of Wölfflin's Art History," *Critical Inquiry* 9, no. 2 (1982): 385.

23. Heinrich Wölfflin, *The Sense of Form in Art: A Comparative Psychological Study* (New York: Chelsea, 1958), 230.

24. Wölfflin, *Sense of Form in Art*, 4.

25. Heinrich Wölfflin, *Principles of Art History: The Problem of the Development of Style in Later Art* (1915; Mineola, NY: Dover, 1950), 188.

26. Wölfflin, *Principles of Art History*, 161.

27. Wölfflin, *Principles of Art History*, 184.

28. Wölfflin, *Principles of Art History*, 167.

29. Panayotis Tournikiotis, *The Historiography of Modern Architecture* (Cambridge, MA: MIT Press, 1999), 224–31.

30. For a discussion of the problem posed by modernism to historical reflection, see Eric Fernie, *Art History and Its Methods: A Critical Anthology* (London: Phaidon, 1995), 16.

31. Carol Willis, *Form Follows Finance: Skyscrapers and Skylines in New York and Chicago* (New York: Princeton Architectural Press, 1995), 10.

32. Tim May, *Social Research: Issues, Methods and Process*, 4th ed. (Maidenhead: McGraw-Hill, 2011), 249.

33. Jürgen Kocka, "Asymmetrical Historical Comparison: The Case of the German Sonderweg," *History and Theory* 38, no. 1 (1999): 49.

34. Colin Rowe, "The Mathematics of the Ideal Villa," in *The Mathematics of the Ideal Villa and Other Essays* (Cambridge, MA: MIT Press, 1976), 4.

35. Rowe, "Mathematics of the Ideal Villa," 11–12.

36. Goyet, "Comparison," 163.

37. Rowe, "Mathematics of the Ideal Villa," 16.

38. Stanislaus von Moos, *Le Corbusier: Elements of a Synthesis* (Cambridge, MA: MIT Press, 1979), 81. Von Moos slyly alludes to Antonin Planeix's occupation as an entrepreneur dealing in funerary monuments.

39. Von Moos, *Le Corbusier*, 80.

40. Tim Benton, *The Villas of Le Corbusier and Pierre Jeanneret, 1920–1930* (Basel: Birkhäuser, 2007), 34–35.

41. Benton, *Villas of Le Corbusier*, 83.

42. Richard Rose, "Comparing Forms of Comparative Analysis," *Political Studies* 39, no. 3 (1991): 458.

43. Günter Frankenberg, "Critical Comparisons: Re-thinking Comparative Law," *Harvard International Law Journal* 26, no. 2 (1985): 443.

44. For a complementary treatment of pairing comparisons that is focused on Le Cor-

busier, see Roy Kozlovsky, "Pairing Le Corbusier and the Affordances of Comparisons for Architectural History," *Journal of Architecture* 24, no. 4 (2019): 549–70.

45. Max Risselada, introduction to *Raumplan versus Plan Libre: Adolf Loos / Le Corbusier, 1919–1930*, ed. Max Risselada (Rotterdam: 010 Publishers, 2008), 6.

46. For the recognition that Tournikiotis's book prompted a wave of historiographical research into the histories of modern architecture, see Gevork Hartoonian, *Time, History and Architecture: Essays on Critical Historiography* (New York: Routledge, 2018), 8.

47. Tournikiotis, *Historiography of Modern Architecture*, 267–68.

48. Tournikiotis, *Historiography of Modern Architecture*, 258.

49. Foucault, *Order of Things*, xiii.

50. Wölfflin, *Principles of Art History*, 227.

CHAPTER 11. WHEN BAGHDAD WAS LIKE WARSAW

1. Lech Robaczyński, interview by author, Warsaw, June 4, 2013. I would like to thank Daniel M. Abramson, Zeynep Çelik Alexander, Paul Jaskot, and Laila Seewang for their comments on this chapter.

2. Phebe Marr, *The Modern History of Iraq* (Boulder, CO: Westview, 2004); see also Odd Arne Westad, *The Global Cold War: Third World Interventions and the Making of Our Times* (Cambridge: Cambridge University Press, 2005).

3. Łukasz Stanek, *Architecture in Global Socialism: Eastern Europe, West Africa, and the Middle East in the Cold War* (Princeton: Princeton University Press, 2020).

4. Robaczyński interview.

5. Robaczyński interview.

6. Peter H. Christensen, *Germany and the Ottoman Railways: Art, Empire, and Infrastructure* (New Haven: Yale University Press, 2017); Zeynep Çelik, *Empire, Architecture, and the City: French-Ottoman Encounters, 1830–1914* (Seattle: University of Washington Press, 2008).

7. Iain Jackson, "The Architecture of the British Mandate in Iraq: Nation-Building and State Creation," *Journal of Architecture* 21, no. 3 (2016): 375–417; Caecilia Pieri, *Bagdad: La construction d'une capitale moderne, 1914–1960* (Beirut: Ifpo, 2015); Neil Levine, *The Urbanism of Frank Lloyd Wright* (Princeton: Princeton University Press, 2016), 334–84.

8. Camillo Sitte, *The Art of Building Cities: City Building According to Its Artistic Fundamentals* (1889; Westport, CT: Hyperion, 1979); Daniel H. Burnham and Edward H. Bennett, *Plan of Chicago*, ed. Charles Moore (1909; New York: Da Capo, 1970).

9. Burnham and Bennett, *Plan of Chicago*, 27–29.

10. *Town Planning Conference, London, 10–15 October, 1910: Transactions* (London: Royal Institute of British Architects, 1911); Jean Royer, ed., *L'urbanisme aux colonies et dans les pays tropicaux*, vol. 1 (La Charité-sur-Loire: Delayance, 1932).

11. Evelien van Es, Gregor Harbusch, Bruno Maurer, Muriel Pérez, Kees Somer, and Daniel Weiss, eds., *Atlas of the Functional City: CIAM 4 and Comparative Urban Analysis* (Bussum, Netherlands: Thot, 2014).

12. van Es et al., *Atlas of the Functional City*, 134–47, 234–49, 288–94.

13. Mark Crinson, *Modern Architecture and the End of Empire* (Aldershot: Ashgate, 2003), 40–43.

14. Anatolii Nikolaevich Rimsha, *Gorod i zharkii klimat* (Moscow: Stroiizdat, 1975).

15. Stephen Ward, "Transnational Planners in a Postcolonial World," in *Crossing Borders: International Exchange and Planning Practices*, ed. Patsy Healey and Robert Upton (London: Routledge, 2010), 47–72.

16. For Iraqi accounts on modernization in socialist countries, see the articles from the *Iraq Times*: January 28, 1960, 1; February 16, 1960, 7; April 5, 1960, 5; July 23, 1961, 7; and September 8, 1961, 7.

17. "Mezhdunaroden konkurs za sgrada na direktsiiata na osvetlenieto v gr. Bagdad—Irak," *Arkhitektura* 10 (1960): 38–40; see also "Internationaler Wettbewerb für das Direktionsgebäude des Werbe- und Informationszentrums in Bagdad," *Deutsche Architektur* 10 (1961): 562–63.

18. On trade exhibitions of Soviet and Eastern European countries in early 1960s Baghdad, see "Iraq 1960–Jan 1963," Confidential US State Department Central Files, microfilm 2003-8, reel 9, Library of Congress.

19. Stanek, *Architecture in Global Socialism*; see also Elidor Mëhilli, *From Stalin to Mao: Albania and the Socialist World* (Ithaca: Cornell University Press, 2017).

20. Town Planning Office for the Planning of Baghdad, "Master Plan of Baghdad," 1967, vol. 1, 0—2–3, private archive, Kraków, Poland.

21. Miastoprojekt-Kraków, "Report on the Master Plan of Baghdad," n.d., private archive, Kraków, Poland; Sayed S. Shafi, *Urban Planning in Iraq: Problems and Prospects: Final Report* (Baghdad: UNDP, 1972), 55.

22. Shafi, *Urban Planning in Iraq*, 55.

23. 'Aqīl Nūrī Ḥuwysh, *Al-'amārat al-hadithat fi al-'iraq: Taḥlīl moqāran fi handasat al-'amārat w al-takhṭīṭ* (Baghdad: Dār al-Shu'ūn al-Thaqāfiyyat al-'āmat, 1988).

24. Levine, *Urbanism of Frank Lloyd Wright*; Panayiota I. Pyla, "Baghdad's Urban Restructuring, 1958: Aesthetics and Politics of Nation Building," in *Modernism and the Middle East: Architecture and Politics in the Twentieth Century*, ed. Sandy Isenstadt and Kishwar Rizvi (Seattle: University of Washington Press, 2008), 97–115.

25. Kazimierz Bajer, "Sprawozdanie z przygotowań do umowy na opracowanie planu ogólnego Bagdadu oraz z rozmów organizacyjnych z Polservice i Grupą Warszawską," 1964–1965, private archive, Kraków, Poland. For discussion, see Stanek, *Architecture in Global Socialism*, chap. 4

26. Town Planning Office, "Master Plan of Baghdad," vol. 1, III—1–28.

27. Town Planning Office for the Planning of Baghdad, "Comprehensive Development Plan for Baghdad 2000," August 1973, 151–52, 163–64, private archive, Kraków, Poland.

28. Town Planning Office, "Comprehensive Development Plan for Baghdad 2000," 152, 164.

29. Town Planning Office, "Comprehensive Development Plan for Baghdad 2000," 164–65, 304–14.

30. Town Planning Office, "Master Plan of Baghdad," vol. 1B, 2/II.

31. Minoprio and Spencely and P. W. Macfarlane, "The Master Plan for the City of Baghdad: Report" (London: 1956), in "Iraq, 1955–1959," Confidential US State Department Central Files, microfilm 95-4564, reel 11, Library of Congress.

32. Andrzej Jędraszko, "Problemy urbanistyczne Bagdadu," *Miasto* 2 (1962): 9–18; Krystyn Olszewski, "Bagdad—relacja o planie ogólnym," part 1, *Miasto* 11 (1967): 1–8, and part 2, *Miasto* 12 (1967): 1–11.

33. Minoprio et al., "Master Plan," 3, 13; Town Planning Office "Comprehensive Development Plan for Baghdad 2000."

34. Miastoprojekt-Kraków, "Report on the Master Plan of Baghdad," 345.

35. Joachim Rees, "Vergleichende Verfahren—verfahrene Vergleiche: Kunstgeschichte als komparative Kunstwissenschaft: Eine Problemskizze," *Kritische Berichte* 40, no. 2 (2012): 32–47.

36. N. Katherine Hayles, *How We Think: Digital Media and Contemporary Technogenesis* (Chicago: University of Chicago Press, 2012), 194–95; Michael Goodchild, "Combining Space and Time: New Potential for Temporal GIS," in *Placing History: How Maps, Spatial Data, and GIS Are Changing Historical Scholarship*, ed. Anne Kelly Knowles and Amy Hillier (Redlands, CA: ESRI, 2008), 179–98.

37. Willard McCarty, "Modelling the Actual, Simulating the Possible," in *The Shape of Data in Digital Humanities: Modeling Texts and Text-Based Materials*, ed. Julia Flanders and Fotis Jannidis (London: Routledge, 2018), 264–84.

38. Japanese Consortium of Consulting Firms, "The Integrated Capital Development Plan of Baghdad," n.d., private archive, Baghdad, Iraq.

39. Łukasz Stanek, "The Master Plans of Baghdad: Notes on GIS-Based Spatial History," *Jadaliyya*, May 17, 2017, http://www.jadaliyya.com/Details/34289/The-Master-Plans-of-Baghdad-Notes-on-GIS-Based-Spatial-History.

40. McCarty, "Modelling the Actual," 275–76.

41. Goodchild, "Combining Space and Time." See also Henri Lefebvre, *The Production of Space* (1974; London: Blackwell, 1991).

42. David J. Bodenhamer, John Corrigan, and Trevor M. Harris, eds., *The Spatial Humanities: GIS and the Future of Humanities Scholarship* (Bloomington: Indiana University Press, 2010).

43. Alberto Giordano and Tim Cole, "The Limits of GIS: Towards a GIS of Place," *Transactions in GIS* 22, no. 3 (2018): 664–76.

44. John Warren and Roy Worskett, "Conservation and Redevelopment of the Kadhimiyeh Area in Baghdad," in *Adaptive Reuse: Integrating Traditional Areas into the Modern Urban Fabric*, ed. Margaret Bentley Sevcenko (Cambridge, MA: MIT Laboratory of Architecture and Planning, 1983), 32.

45. Andrzej Basista, "Kadhemiya—zespół tradycyjnej zabudowy w Bagdadzie," *Kwartalnik architektury i urbanistyki* 21, no. 3 (1976): 217–37; Andrzej Basista, "Plany przekształcenia Kadhemiyi, zabytkowej dzielnicy Bagdadu," *Kwartalnik architektury i urbanistyki* 21, no. 4 (1976): 337–58.

46. Andrzej Basista, *Opowieści budynków: Architektura czterech kultur* (Warsaw and Kraków: PWN, 1995), 366–68; Andrzej Basista, interview by the author, Kraków, Poland, June 2010.

47. Ihsan Fethi, "Urban Conservation in Iraq: The Case for Protecting the Cultural Heritage of Iraq with Special Reference to Baghdad[,] Including a Comprehensive Inventory of Its Areas and Buildings of Historic or Architectural Interest" (PhD diss., University of Sheffield, 1977). Miastoprojekt's earlier "Outlines for Detailed Plan" from 1967 included a "tentative proposal" to demolish some buildings west of the mosque, thus undermining Basista's claims; see "Kadhemiyah Central District: Outlines for Detailed Plan: Short Report," 1967, private archive, Kraków, Poland.

48. Basista, *Opowieści budynków*, 368.

49. Basista interview.

50. Carl E. Pletsch, "The Three Worlds, or the Division of Social Scientific Labor, circa 1950–1975," *Comparative Studies in Society and History* 23, no. 4 (1981): 565–90.

51. Ananya Roy, "The 21st-Century Metropolis: New Geographies of Theory," *Regional Studies* 43, no. 6 (2009): 819–30.

52. Jennifer Robinson, "Cities in a World of Cities: The Comparative Gesture," *International Journal of Urban and Regional Research* 35, no. 1 (2011): 1–23.

53. Robinson, "Cities in a World of Cities."

54. Rimsha, *Gorod i zharkii klimat*; Veronika Voronina, *Sovremennaia arkhitektura stran tropicheskoi Afriki* (Moscow, 1973).

55. Charles Polónyi, *An Architect-Planner on the Peripheries: The Retrospective Diary of Charles K. Polónyi* (1992; Budapest: Műszaki Könyvkiadó, 2000); Wiktor Richert, *Przestrzenne planowanie regionalne w Ghanie: Zasady i metody, problemy kształcenia, przydatność polskich doświadczeń* (Warsaw: PWN, 1973).

56. Piotr Bujas, Alicja Gzowska, Hou Li, and Łukasz Stanek, "Planning Transition beyond Socialism: From Poland to China and Back," presentation at the International Planning History Society conference, Yokohama, Japan, July 15–19, 2018.

CHAPTER 12. FORENSIC ARCHITECTURE AS SYMPTOM

Epigraphs: Roger Montgomery, "Commentary on CSPA Symposium," *Journal of Architectural Education* 45, no. 4 (1992); Michael Kimmelman, "Forensics Helps Widen Architecture's Mission," *New York Times*, April 6, 2018, https://www.nytimes.com/2018/04/06/arts/design/forensic-architecture-human-rights.html.

1. Sam A. A. Kubba, *Architectural Forensics* (New York: McGraw-Hill Professional, 2008); Eyal Weizman, "Forensic Architecture: Only the Criminal Can Solve the Crime," *Radical Philosophy*, no. 164 (November–December 2010): 9–24.

2. Kubba, *Architectural Forensics*, xv, 1.

3. Weizman, "Forensic Architecture: Only the Criminal Can Solve the Crime," 13.

4. Kubba, *Architectural Forensics*, xvi. See also Sam A. A. Kubba, *Space Planning for Commercial and Residential Interiors* (New York: McGraw-Hill Professional, 2003); Sam A. A. Kubba, *Property Condition Assessment* (New York: McGraw-Hill, 2007); Sam A. A. Kubba, *Blueprint Reading: Construction Drawings for the Building Trade* (New York: McGraw-Hill Professional, 2008); Sam Kubba, *LEED Practices, Certification and Accreditation Handbook* (Oxford: Elsevier, 2010); Sam Kubba, *Green Construction Project Management and Cost Oversight* (Oxford: Elsevier, 2010); and Sam Kubba, *Handbook of Green Building Design and Construction* (Oxford: Elsevier, 2012). Kubba has also authored several books on Mesopotamian and Iraqi architectural history.

5. Eyal Weizman, *Forensic Architecture: Notes from Fields and Forums* (Ostfildern, Germany: Hatje Cantz, 2012); Eyal Weizman, *The Least of All Possible Evils: Humanitarian Violence from Arendt to Gaza* (New York: Verso, 2012); Forensic Architecture, *Forensis: The Architecture of Public Truth* (Berlin: Sternberg Press and Forensic Architecture, 2014).

6. On Kubba's biography, see "Biography of Dr. Sam Kubba," https://enacademic.com/dic.nsf/enwiki/6882482.

7. Eyal Weizman, *Forensic Architecture: Violence at the Threshold of Detectability* (New York: Zone Books, 2017).

8. Weizman, *Forensic Architecture: Violence at the Threshold of Detectability*, 51.

9. Weizman, *Forensic Architecture: Violence at the Threshold of Detectability*, 57.

10. Weizman, "Forensic Architecture: Only the Criminal Can Solve the Crime," 13.

11. Carlo Ginzburg, "Checking the Evidence: The Judge and the Historian," *Critical Inquiry* 18, no. 1 (1991): 79.

12. Ginzburg, "Checking the Evidence," 83.

13. Hayden White, "The Value of Narrativity in the Representation of Reality," in *The Content of the Form: Narrative Discourse and Historical Representation* (Baltimore: Johns Hopkins University Press, 1987), 11.

14. "Afraid of Its Wall: Witnesses Saw Cracks in the Young Building," *Chicago Daily Tribune*, April 10, 1892, 1.

15. "Afraid of Its Wall," 1.

16. "Afraid of Its Wall," 1.

17. "Afraid of Its Wall," 1.

18. See Kubba, *Architectural Forensics*, xvi; and Weizman, "Forensic Architecture: Only the Criminal Can Solve the Crime," 13.

19. See Kenneth S. Abraham, *The Liability Century: Insurance and Tort Law from the Progressive Era to 9/11* (Cambridge, MA: Harvard University Press, 2008).

20. A prominent example of this registration is Rem Koolhaas, *Delirious New York: A Retroactive Manifesto for Manhattan* (New York: Monacelli Press, 1997). For a more recent work, see Elihu Rubin, *Insuring the City: The Prudential Center and the Postwar Urban Landscape* (New Haven: Yale University Press, 2012).

21. H. Weaver Mowery, "The Hazards of Walking," *Journal of the American Institute of Architects* 7, no. 1 (1919): 29–30.

22. Gordon C. Hamilton, "Expert Testimony," *Central Law Journal* 43, no. 16 (1896).

23. See, for example, "The Architect's Authority as an Expert: Extensive Authority of Architect in His Own Province," *American Architect and Building News*, December 5, 1891, 832; as well as *American Architect and Building News*, February 24, 1894, 948; December 7, 1895, 1041; February 1, 1896, 1049; and June 26, 1897, 1122.

24. Howard C. Lake, "The Legal Responsibility of an Architect: The Architect as an Expert Witness," *American Architect*, December 22, 1909, 276.

25. Patterned on British law in this area, US law considered the architect to be an "arbitrator" between the various parties involved in a building project and therefore not liable for negligence or other decisions. See Gibson B. Witherspoon, "When Is an Architect Liable?," *American Bar Association Journal* 48, no. 4 (1962): 321–25.

26. William Prosser, *Handbook of the Law of Torts*, 2nd ed. (St. Paul: West, 1955), 517.

27. The landmark case in this development is usually taken to be *Inman v. Binghamton Housing Authority*, 3 NY2d 137, 143 NE2d 895, 164 NYS2d 699 (1957). See George M. White, "Architects' and Engineers' Third Party Negligence Liability: The Fall of the House of Privity," *Western Reserve Law Review* 10, no. 4 (1959): 563.

28. Ralph Nader, "Nader: From Autos to Architecture," *AIA Journal*, November 1970.

29. T. W. Smay, "A New Look at Professional Liability Insurance," *Journal of the American Institute of Architects*, December 1957; John M. Lake, "Notes on Liability Insurance: Part I," *Progressive Architecture*, November 1960; John M. Lake, "Notes on Liability Insurance: Part II," *Progressive Architecture*, December 1960; Judge Bernard Tomson and Norman Coplan, "The Legal Status of the Architect," *American Institute of Architects Journal*, February 1963; George M. White, "Professional Liability Insurance," *American Institute of Architects Journal*, January 1966.

30. White, "Architects' and Engineers' Third Party Negligence Liability," 574.

31. Robert Gutman, *Architectural Practice: A Critical View* (New York: Princeton Architectural Press, 1988), 52.

32. See Mary Woods, *From Craft to Profession: The Practice of Architecture in Nineteenth-Century America* (Berkeley: University of California Press, 1999), esp. 27–52.

33. See Robert J. Piper and Fredrick Kalivoda, "The Architect as an Expert Witness," *AIA Journal* 39, no. 5 (1963): 67–68; Raymond A. DiPasquale, "Expert Witnessing," *Progressive Architecture* 69, no. 9 (1988): 58; and Richard B. Cook and William F. Dexter, "Expert Witness Services," in *The Architect's Handbook of Professional Practice* (New York: John Wiley and Sons, 2004).

34. Roger Montgomery, "Commentary on CSPA Symposium," *Journal of Architectural Education* 45, no. 4 (1992): 230.

35. Montgomery, "Commentary on CSPA Symposium," 231.

36. Transcript, Prosecutor v. Slobodan Milošević, case no. IT-02-54-T, International Criminal Tribunal for the Former Yugoslavia, April 9, 2002, 2634–37. In fact I had a BA in architecture from Yale, MArch from Harvard, and several years of entry-level experience in commercial architectural firms and was pursuing a doctorate in an interdisciplinary program in architecture, landscape architecture, and urban planning. These distinctions in my educational qualifications were no doubt irrelevant to the court. However, given that my undergraduate liberal arts education in architecture included no professional practice classes and my graduate professional education included only one such class (taught by a lawyer and focused on liability issues), my education was crucial to my noncomprehension of forensic architecture, even as I was in the midst of practicing it. On "sanctioned ignorance," see Gayatri Chakravorty Spivak, "Can the Subaltern Speak?," in *Marxism and the Interpretation of Culture*, ed. Cary Nelson and Lawrence Grossberg (Urbana: University of Illinois Press, 1988), 271–313.

37. The ICTY defined an "expert witness" as a person who "by virtue of some specialized knowledge, skill, or training can assist the trier of fact to understand or determine the issue in dispute." "Decision concerning the Expert Witness Ewa Tabeau and Richard Phillips," Prosecutor v. Stanislav Galić, case. No. IT-98-29-T, International Criminal Tribunal for the Former Yugoslavia, July 3, 2002. In determining whether a witness meets these criteria, the court could assess a witness's former and current professional positions, curriculum vitae, scholarly articles and other publications, and other pertinent information. "Decision on Expert Status of Reynaud Theunens," Prosecutor v. Vojislav Šešelj, case no. IT-03-67-T, International Criminal Tribunal for the Former Yugoslavia, February 12, 2008.

38. Educated at the University of Belgrade's School of Law, Milošević might have been trained in the protocols of expert witnessing. See Adam LeBor, *Milošević: A Biography* (New Haven: Yale University Press, 2004).

39. Transcript, Prosecutor v. Slobodan Milošević, April 9, 2002, 2669. Milošević used photographs of the damaged League of Prizren building from *NATO Crimes in Yugoslavia: Documentary Evidence, 24 March–24 April 1999* (Belgrade: Federal Ministry of Foreign Affairs, 1999), 227, 228.

40. Transcript, Prosecutor v. Slobodan Milošević, April 9, 2002, 2670.

41. Transcript, Prosecutor v. Slobodan Milošević, April 9, 2002, 2672.

42. Weizman, "Forensic Architecture: Only the Criminal Can Solve the Crime," 22.

43. Weizman, "Forensic Architecture: Only the Criminal Can Solve the Crime," 13.

44. Weizman, "Forensic Architecture: Only the Criminal Can Solve the Crime," 14.

45. Michel de Certeau, *The Possession at Loudon*, trans. Michael B. Smith (1970; Chicago: University of Chicago Press, 2000), 227.

46. Michel de Certeau, *Heterologies*, trans. Brian Massumi (Minneapolis: University of Minnesota Press, 1986).

CHAPTER 13. ARCHITECTURAL HISTORY AFTER SEBALD'S *AUSTERLITZ*

1. W. G. Sebald, *Austerlitz* (New York: Modern Library, 2001), 204. All subsequent page citations for *Austerlitz* are in parentheses in the main text.

2. Born in Bavaria, Winfried Georg (Max) Sebald arrived in England in 1966 and was for most of his career an academic specialist in German literature and translation at the

University of East Anglia, publishing his first fiction book, in German, only in 1990 (*Vertigo*, English translation by Michael Hulse [New York: New Directions, 1999]). Next came *The Emigrants* (published in German, 1992; English translation by Michael Hulse [New York: New Directions, 1996]); *The Rings of Saturn* (German, 1995; English translation by Michael Hulse [New York: New Directions, 1998]); and, finally, *Austerlitz* (German, 2001; English translation by Anthea Bell).

3. For Sebald's Nobel prospects, see Jon Cook, ed., *After Sebald: Essays and Illuminations* (Woodbridge, Suffolk: Full Circle Editions, 2014), 19.

4. There are citations and allusions to Claude-Nicolas Ledoux's realized and visionary work at Arc-et-Senans and Chaux, as well as to Étienne-Louis Boullée's unbuilt Cenotaph to Isaac Newton, in *The Emigrants* (44–45) and *Vertigo* (201–3), respectively. *The Rings of Saturn* references numerous buildings in Suffolk. Though knowledgeable, Sebald was not very well read in the field; his library contained numerous topographical works, useful for basic background and descriptions, but minimal architectural history and no theory. There are about a dozen books of architectural history in Sebald's collection with only a handful of them having direct relevance to *Austerlitz*, including a few on Antwerp and Liverpool Street station as well as Paul Jaskot's *The Architecture of Oppression: The SS, Forced Labor, and the Nazi Monumental Building Economy* (2000). Jo Catling, "A Catalogue of W. G. Sebald's Library," in *Saturn's Moons: W. G. Sebald: A Handbook*, ed. Jo Catling and Richard Hibbitt (London: Legenda, 2011), 434, 436–38.

5. Many texts about *Austerlitz* omit the fact that the title character is an architectural historian. Rumiko Handa, "W. G. Sebald's *Austerlitz*: Architecture as a Bridge between the Lost Past and the Present," in *Reading Architecture: Literary Imagination and Architectural Experience*, ed. Angeliki Sioli and Yoonchun Jung (New York: Routledge, 2018); Amir Eshel, "Against the Power of Time: The Poetics of Suspension in W. G. Sebald's *Austerlitz*," *New German Critique* 88 (Winter 2003): 71–96. If mentioned at all, it is parenthetically, without much significance attached. Russell J. A. Kilbourn, "Architecture and Cinema: The Representation of Memory in W. G. Sebald's *Austerlitz*," in *W. G. Sebald—A Critical Companion*, ed. J. J. Long and Anne Whitehead (Seattle: University of Washington Press, 2004), 142; Laura García-Moreno, "Strange Edifices, Counter-Monuments: Rethinking Time and Space in W. G. Sebald's *Austerlitz*," *Critique: Studies in Contemporary Fiction* 54, no. 4 (2013): 360–79; Arne De Boever, "Architectures of Exception in W. G. Sebald's *Austerlitz*," chapter 4 in *States of Exception in the Contemporary Novel: Martel, Eugenides, Coetzee, Sebald* (New York: Continuum, 2012); Wim Peeters, "Architektur," in *W. G. Sebald-Handbuch: Leben-Werk-Wirkung*, ed. Claudia Öhlschläger and Michael Niehaus (Stuttgart: J. B. Metzler, 2017) (thanks to Myriam Walter for translating the Peeters text for me). A few writers even misidentify Austerlitz, for example, as a "lifelong student of architecture." Kurt W. Forster, "Sebald's Burning Train Stations and Monstrous Court Houses," *Log* 32 (Fall 2014): 14; William Firebrace, "Restless Writing: The Work of W. G. Sebald," *AA Files*, no. 45–46 (Winter 2001): 163–73. For other discussion of architecture in Sebald's writing, see Todd Samuel Presner, "Hegel's Philosophy of World History via Sebald's Imaginary of Ruins: A Contrapuntal Critique of the 'New Space' of Modernity," in *Ruins of Modernity*, ed. Julia Hell and Andreas Schönle (Durham: Duke University Press, 2010); Simon Ward, "Ruins and Poetics in the Works of W. G. Sebald," in *W. G. Sebald—A Critical Companion*, ed. J. J. Long and Anne Whitehead (Seattle: University of Washington Press, 2004); Michael Niehaus, "No Foothold: Institutions and Buildings in W. G. Sebald's Prose," in *W. G. Sebald: History, Memory, Trauma*, ed. Scott D. Denham and Mark Richard McCulloh (Berlin: De Gruyter, 2006), 315–34.

6. W. G. Sebald, "Ich fürchte das Melodramatishce" (interview), *Der Spiegel*, December

3, 2001, 228. Sebald asserted, too, that the book's cover photo of the young boy Austerlitz was an authentic childhood photograph of this unnamed "London architectural historian."

7. The profile of a London-based architectural historian who took early retirement in the 1990s and explored his roots does not readily conform to a particular individual. To supplement my own knowledge as a specialist in British architectural history, with wide contacts in the field dating to the late 1980s, I consulted with one of Sebald's University of East Anglia colleagues, the architectural historian Stefan Muthesius, about the apparent inspiration for Austerlitz, as well as the London-based architectural historian Andrew Saint, who also queried the architectural writer Gillian Darley. None could offer any firm insights. Darley speculated Sebald's story might be a fiction. Stefan Muthesius, email to author, July 21, 2018; Andrew Saint, email to author, September 1, 2018. I also consulted the online list of correspondence in the Sebald Collection at the Deutsches Literaturarchiv Marbach (http://www.dla-marbach.de/) to see which architectural historians Sebald might have known, and beyond Muthesius, I recognized no other names.

8. Sebald, "Ich fürchte das Melodramatishce"; Jenni Frazer, "Susi Bechhofer: Finding Her Own History," *Jewish Chronicle*, August 21, 2017.

9. The act of designing buildings per se did not interest Sebald. Figures of individual architects almost never appear in his writing. The only time architects appear in Sebald's prose fiction are as a pair of eccentric figures in *Vertigo*: a minor provincial "master builder" and a visionary wheelwright-turned-designer. Sebald, *Vertigo*, 199–202.

10. Sebald explained how these images, collected years before inspiring and being inserted into his prose fiction, serve to "hold up the flow of discourse" and as "tokens to the reader" of his work's ambiguous relations to truth and invention. "W. G. Sebald at 92nd Street Y, October 15, 2001," YouTube, posted July 18, 2018, https://www.youtube.com/watch?v=ccMCGjWLIhY.

11. The "American architectural journal" is apparently *Harvard Design Magazine* No. 9 (Fall 1999), which features the Terezín records room photograph by Dirk Reinartz on its cover and pages four and five. The journal's editor, Nancy Levinson, sent Sebald this very issue when she asked Sebald to make a future contribution to the journal, an invitation Sebald declined. For this information about the *Harvard Design Magazine* source of the Terezín photograph, I am grateful to Andrew Herscher.

12. Sebald, *Vertigo*, 240.

13. Hayden White, "The Value of Narrativity in the Representation of Reality," in *The Content of the Form: Narrative Discourse and Historical Representation* (Baltimore: Johns Hopkins University Press, 1987).

14. White, "Value of Narrativity," 16–17.

15. Firebrace, "Restless Writing," 168.

16. Sebald has described his own narrative process as a type of bricolage, following the anthropologist Claude Lévi-Strauss: "a form of savage work, of pre-rational thought, in which one nuzzles in findings until they somehow make sense." Sebald quoted in Eshel, "Against the Power of Time," 79n20.

17. Dan Jacobson, *Heshel's Kingdom* (London: Hamish Hamilton, 1998), xi.

18. Jacobson, *Heshel's Kingdom*, 208–9.

CHAPTER 14. FAILING MEMORIES AND FORGOTTEN HISTORIES

Epigraph: Archivio di Stato, Venezia (ASV), Provveditori del Comun, B. 86, 38. The original reads, "Non se savemo imaginar Signori Eccellentissimi cui habbi si poco antiveder, ne sì poca Conscientia, che dimanda Incarceration de quella cosa, che Ipso Iure die nascer, perche mostreremo alle Signorie Vostre più chiaro chel sol, che altri che nui tal sententia puol obtener. E però per il converso nostro li dimandemo incarceration de quella sententia loro hanno obtenuto, & azion le Signorie vostre tutto intenda nararemo questo facto."

1. ASV, S. Giobbe, B. 5, xliii, f. 2r; Brian Pullan, *Rich and Poor in Renaissance Venice: The Social Institutions of a Catholic State, to 1620* (Cambridge, MA: Harvard University Press, 1971), 184, 205; Hans Peyer, *Stadt und Stadtpatron im mittelalterlichen Italien* (Zurich: Europa, 1955), 125.

2. ASV, S. Giobbe, B. 5, xliii, ff. 1r–4r; Edward Muir, *Civic Ritual in Renaissance Venice* (Princeton: Princeton University Press, 1981), 70–71.

3. ASV, S. Giobbe, B. 5, xliii, f. 2r. The original reads, "Voglio, et ordeno, che il detto Oratorio, et luogo nel quale è esso Oratorio sia divisi et separato da esso hospedal, et da tutto il sudetto luogo di S. Giobbe di maniera . . . voglio però, che il ius patronato del detto Oratorio di S. Giobbe sia sempre et esser debba del detto hospedal."

4. Enrico Bensa, "Il testamento di Marco Datini," *Archivio Storico Pratese* 5 (1925): 74–78. In his testament of 1410, the merchant Francesco Datini shares similar concerns about rising ecclesiastical power.

5. ASV, S. Giobbe, B. 5; Emmanuele Cicogna, *Delle Inscrizioni Veneziane*, vol. 6 (Venice: Orlandelli, 1853).

6. Virpi Mäkinen, *Property Rights in the Late Medieval Discussion on Franciscan Poverty* (Leuven, Belgium: Peeters, 2001), 148. The papal bull *Quo Elongati*, issued by Gregory IX in 1230, allowed the Franciscans to use but not to own property. In 1279, Pope Nicholas II tried to reinforce *usus pauper* by basing restrictive use on Roman law. John Moorman, *A History of the Franciscan Order from Its Origins to the Year 1517* (Oxford: Clarendon Press, 1968), 50.

7. ASV, San Giobbe, B. 5, xliii, ff. 33r–35r.

8. Vittorio Lazzarini, *Proprietà e feudi, offizi, garzoni, carcerati in antiche leggi veneziane* (Rome: Edizioni di Storia e letteratura, 1960), 62–65.

9. Marino Sanudo, *Le vite dei dogi* (Città di Castello: Lapi, 1900–1911), 365. Taxes became a consistent point of contention between religious groups and the Venetian republic, but authority was also frequently contested. When Pope Sixtus IV excommunicated Venice in 1482 for laying siege to Ferrara, some of the friars refused to say mass in San Giobbe so as to maintain obedience to the pontiff. They were exiled by the Venetian Council of Ten for adhering to the authority of the papacy rather than that of the republic.

10. ASV, San Giobbe, B. 6, f. 6v–r.

11. ASV, San Giobbe, B. 6, f. 6v–r. The papal decision about the fate of San Giobbe reads, "Sentenza difinitiva del sudetto Santo, che conforme Lucia Contarini, non aveva potesta di donare il Juspatronato alli Frati, cosi essi non sanno autorita di distrugger la chiesolla di S: Job e la memoria di quel Ven. Fondatore."

12. ASV, San Giobbe, B. 6, f. 6v–r. The term *oculata fede* appeared in the context of the phrase "con oculate fede vedemmo e spemmo la veritade." Giovanni Villani, *Nuova Cronica* (1348), II.9.58. The term was usually used in a spiritual context, deriving from the belief that Christ's followers had a special ability to see his truth.

13. ASV, San Giobbe, B. 6, f. 6v–r. One witness said, "Non me ricordo el tempo fine gitazoro la chiesa vecchia ma visi ben li frati desfava la Chiesa vecchia e in fra la chiesa vechia. El era un pozzo serado dei frati, e adesso hanno fatto campo santo per sepelir morti."

14. ASV, San Giobbe, B. 5, xliii, ff. 1r–4r. Contarini's tomb slab has been moved. The inscription is no longer legible, but Flaminio Cornaro was able to read it: "Hic Iacet omni

Sanctitate conspicuous Nobilis & Venerabilis Presbyter Joannes Contareno, Quondam Domini Lucae fundator Huius Ecclesie & Loci Sancti Job, qui obit Anno 1407 Die 8 Mensis Septembris." Flaminio Cornaro, *Ecclesiae Venetae antiquis monumentis nunc etiam primum editis illustratae ac in decades distributae* (Venice: Baptistae Pasquali, 1749), 12:78.

15. ASV, San Giobbe, B. 5, xliii, ff. 1r–4r; Richard Goldthwaite, *The Building of Renaissance Florence* (Baltimore: Johns Hopkins University Press, 1980), 12, 98.

16. ASV, San Giobbe, B. 5.

17. ASV, San Giobbe, B. 5.

18. ASV, San Giobbe, B. 5, f. 38. Isabetta's testament states, "Nobilis domina Isabetta relicta viri nobilis Bartholomei Bragadeno . . . donavit inter vivos in perpetuum loco Monasterio se conventu sancti Job, siev spectabili et generoso domino Christophoro Mauro honorando procuratori S. Marci de Ultra."

19. Biblioteca Museo Correr (BMC), Codice Cicogna 3115.12.

20. Cornaro, *Ecclesiae Venetae*, 12:80.

21. BMC, Cod. Cicogna 3287.26.

22. Thomas E. A. Dale, "Inventing a Sacred Past: Pictorial Narratives of St. Mark the Evangelist in Aquileia and Venice, ca. 1000–1300," *Dumbarton Oaks Papers* 48 (1994): 54, 100; Patrick Geary, *Thefts of the Relics in the Central Middle Ages* (Princeton: Princeton University Press, 1978), 88–94.

23. Julia Helen Keydel, *A Group of Altarpieces by Giovanni Bellini* (Cambridge, MA: Harvard University Archives, 1970), 151–62; Andrew Hopkins, "Architecture and Infirmitas: Doge Andrea Gritti and the Chancel of San Marco," *Journal of the Society of Architectural Historians* 57, no. 2 (1998): 185.

24. ASV, Scuole Piccole, B. 261.

25. BMC, Cod. Cicogna 3115.12.

26. ASV, Scuole Piccole, B. 261.

27. ASV, Collegio, R. 12, c. 32v. The senate approved construction of the San Giobbe bridge as follows: "MCCCCLXXV Die xviii November. Supplicantibus nobili viris comissariis bene memorie S.mi Principis Domini christophori mauro posse construi facere pontem lapideum sumptibus commissarit predicte super rivo canalis S. Jeremie per quod acceditor ad ecclesiam S. Job et Bernardin pro comodatate populorum euncium ad visitationem ecclesie ipius . . . Attento quod construtio pontis predicte. Erit ornamento illius contrate . . . Postulante M Dominico Mauroceno consiliario nomine commissarie predicte."

28. Marin Sanudo, *Marin Sanudo, De origine, situ et magistratibus urbis Venetae, ovvero, La Città di Venetia (1493–1530)*, ed. Angela Caracciolo Aricò (Milan: Cisalpino–La Goliardica, 1980), 20–39.

29. Pope Sixtus IV received adulation for his work to restore the infrastructure of Rome, including an encomium from the fifteenth-century poet Pacifico Massimi, who praised his bridge building: "Tu Romanam urbem a magnitudine delapsam restauravisti. Tu pontem tyberium, ab undarum diluvio fluminis multo tempore prerumptum et refecisti:et pontem Sixtum a tuo nomine dictm vocant." Adamo de Montaldo, *De laudibus Syxti*, Biblioteca Apostolica Vaticana, Cod. Vat. Lat. 3568, f. 3v.

30. Vincenzo Fontana, *Fra' Giovanni Giocondo, architetto 1433 c. 1515* (Vicenza: Neri Pozza, 1988); Raffaello Brenzoni, *Fra Giocondo Veronese* (Florence: Olschki, 1960), 26.

31. Sabellico, *Decades rerum Venetarum*, 11. Equating city design with its values, Sabellico wrote, "Situs urbis, viae, templa, areae, rivi, pontes, omniaque aedificia publica et privata, et cum his civium cultus et mores sic habent."

32. Sabellico, *Decades rerum Venetarum*.

33. Domenico Morosini, *De Bene Instituta Re Publica*, ed. Claudio Finzi (Milan: Giuffre, 1969), 214. For information about texts by Giovanni Caldiera, Paolo Morosini, and Lauro Quirini, see Margaret King, *Venetian Humanism in an Age of Patrician Dominance* (Princeton: Princeton University Press, 2016); and Manfredo Tafuri, *Venezia e il Rinascimento* (Turin: Einaudi, 1985), 156–62.

34. "Aedes omnes privatas ad una mensuram in viis porrigere, ultra mensuram porrectos ad aliarum equalitatem referre. Obliquas cales ad rectitudinem adducere, angustas dilatare, areas vero que dant prospectum pulchierimum edibus in urbe et ipsam ameniorem et iucundiorem reddunt sternere et easdem paritate domorum in eas insidentium exornare. Nam hec diligentia non magnam exigit impensam sed magnam prebet civitati ornamentum et decorum." Morosini, *De Bene Instituta Re Publica*, 82–84.

35. Marco Cornaro, *Scritture sulla laguna*, Antichi scrittori d'idraulica veneta (Venice: C. Ferrari, 1919), 198.

36. Elizabeth Crouzet-Pavan, "*Sopra le Acque Salse*": *Espaces, pouvoir et société à Vénice a la fin du Moyen Age*, 2 vols. (Rome: École Française de Rome, 1992), 1:319–33; Salvatore Ciriacono, "Scrittori d'idraulica e politica delle acque," in *Storia della cultura veneta: Dal primo Quattrocento al Concilio di Trento*, ed. Girolamo Arnaldi and Manlio Pastore Stocchi (Vicenza: Pozza, 1980), vol. 3, pt. 2, 491–512.

37. Senate, May 31, 1459, f. besta, 1912, 133–34.

38. ASV, Savi Esecutori sopra le Acque, r. 342, f. 70v; Paola Pavanini, "Venezia verso la pianificazione? Bonifiche urbane nel XVI secolo a Venezia," in *D'une ville à l'autre: Structures matérielles et organisation de l'espace dans les villes*, ed. J.-C. Maire Vigueur (Rome: École Française de Rome, 1989), 485–50.

39. ASV, Savi Esecutori sopra le Acque, r. 342, f. 70v.

40. James Shaw, *Justice of Venice: Authorities and Liberty in the Urban Economy 1550–1700* (Oxford: Oxford University Press, 2016), 26–27.

41. Felix Gilbert, "Biondo, Sabellico and the Beginnings of Venetian Official Historiography," *Florilegium Historiale: Essays Presented to Wallace K. Ferguson* (Toronto: University of Toronto Press, 1971), 275–93; Agostino Pertusi, *La Storiografia veneziana fino al secolo XVI: Aspetti e problem* (Florence: Olschki, 1970).

42. For Biondo's request and analysis of the Barbari views, see Juergen Schulz, "Jacopo de' Barbari's View of Venice: Map Making, City Views, and Moralized Geography before the Year 1500," *Art Bulletin* 60, no. 3 (1978): 425–74.

43. Patricia Fortini Brown, *Venetian Narrative Painting in the Age of Carpaccio* (New Haven: Yale University Press, 1988), 136–38. Brown noted the chronological proximity between guides to Venice and the publication of the de' Barbari view in 1500.

44. Marc'Antonio Sabellico, *De situ urbis Venetae* (Venice, 1489). Sabellico sought to render his description of Venice and its landscape as though he were describing a painting: "Velut in tabula quadam simillimam illius expressisse imaginem."

45. Marino Sanudo, *I Diarii*, ed. R. Fulin, 54 vols. (Venice, 1879–1902), February 19, 1517, 23:590. The Venetian Council of Ten recommended dredging the Grand Canal with a heavy and powerful apparatus "like that in the new towns on the mainland." Bernardino Zendrini, *Osservazioni sopra l'opera Memorie storiche dello Stato antico e moderno delle lagune di Venezia* (Venice, 1812), 24. Kolb's 1536 patent application demonstrates that he engineered dredging and pile-driving machines suited to tackling Venice's particular infrastructure: "Antonio Colb Tedesco e Giovanni Belloni Modanese nel 1536 portarono machine

per cavar fanghi e batter pali sopra i lidi." Cicogna, *Delle inscrizioni veneziane*, vol. 4 (Venice: Presso Giuseppe Picotti, 1834), 701.

CHAPTER 15. SETTLING IMAGINATIONS

1. Lorraine Daston and Peter Galison have shown how this quest harbored its own myths. See their *Objectivity* (New York: Zone Books, 2007).

2. For a history of colonial infrastructure in Sindh, see Benjamin Weil, "The Rivers Come: Colonial Flood Control and Knowledge Systems in the Indus Basin, 1840s–1930s," *Environment and History* 12, no. 1 (2006): 3–29. For a detailed history of canalization in Punjab, see David Gilmartin, *Blood and Water: Indus River Basin in Modern History* (Oakland: University of California Press, 2015).

3. The displacement and criminalization of followers of the Pir Pagaro has been charted in detail in Sarah Ansari, *Sufi Saints and State Power: The Pirs of Sindh* (Cambridge: Cambridge University Press, 2009). The younger Pir's rebellion came to a head in 1943, when the British accused the Hurs of attacking a Royal Mail train, damaging canals, and attacking settler villages along the canals. The British imposed martial law and armed its settlers. The contours of freedom and revenge blurred. When British artillery bombarded the Pir's village itself, the Pir was captured and sent first to prison and then to be hanged in Hyderabad Central Jail, some fifty miles from where his ancestors had had a following for three centuries. For the history of violence against the Hurs, see Nasir Aijaz, *Hur the Freedom Fighter* (Karachi: Culture and Tourism Department, Government of Sindh, 2015); Mohammad Laiq Zardari, *History of Sindh, Vol. II: Pakistan Movement* (Islamabad: National Institute of Historical and Cultural Research, 1996); and Wisal Muhammad Khan, "Hurs Operations in Sindh," *Sindh Quarterly* 8, no. 1 (1980).

4. In all those interactions, the curious mismatch between these artifacts and the legends behind them never occurred to me. Their 12-gauge shell size resembled that of the common British quail-hunting shotgun, making them scarcely adequate for the purpose now assigned to them. But the strategy of defending the empire with a quail-hunting shotgun was not completely misplaced. The British had learned that Hurs rarely attacked a village in the daytime. The standard issue Lee-Enfield army rifle, even with its multiple rounds, would not have been of much use shooting into the pitch darkness toward the muffled sound of charging horse hooves. A shotgun, with a single cartridge per barrel that fired a shower of pellets at a broad angle, had a higher probability of hitting an unseen rider when the defender is perched on a makeshift sentry post at the village periphery.

5. My grandfather did not have to fire the guns. When the Hurs finally attacked, they came in broad daylight. They didn't kill indiscriminately but were said to have been looking for five people who were involved in spying on them, taking their cattle, and kidnapping a Hur woman. They looked through the houses, the shops, and the mosques. They found the accused and, according to their families, brutally murdered them all—three hacked with axes and two shot point-blank at close range.

6. For a description of habitus as the moment of intersection between personal and social agency, see Pierre Bourdieu, *Distinction: A Social Critique of the Judgement of Taste* (London: Routledge, 1984).

7. See F. W. Woods "Irrigation Enterprise in India," *Journal of the Royal Society of Arts* 70, no. 3642 (September 8, 1922): 719–35.

8. This argument is made at great length in chapter 5 of Ansari, *Sufi Saints and State Power*, 101–28. Ansari documents the communication between district commissioners in Sindh and the governor's office of the Bombay Presidency to chart the sway of force and diplomacy.

9. Ansari, *Sufi Saints and State Power*.

10. On the effects of criminalization, see Rachel J. Tolen, "Colonizing and Transforming the Criminal Tribesman: The Salvation Army in British India," *American Ethnologist* 18, no. 1 (1991): 106–25; Preeti Nijhar, *Law and Imperialism: Criminality and Constitution in Colonial India and Victorian England* (London: Pickering and Chatto, 2009); and Henry Schwarz, *Constructing the Criminal Tribe in Colonial India: Acting like a Thief* (Oxford: Wiley-Blackwell, 2010).

11. See Aftab Nabi, "Policing Insurgency: The Hurs of Sind," *Pakistan Horizon* 61, no. 4 (2008): 27–55. Also see N. Shah and H. Mujtaba, "Raiders of the Past," *Newsline* (Karachi), 6, no. 9 (1995): 69.

12. The chronology of the Pir Pagaro lineage is narrated by Zulfiqar Ali Kalhoro, "Of Turban and Flag: The Roots of Sindh's Popular and Anti-colonial Mystics," in *Friday Times* (Pakistan), March 29, 2019, https://www.thefridaytimes.com/of-turban-and-flag. Also see Ansari, *Sufi Saints and State Power*, 72–75.

13. For the justification of the Punjab Canal Colonies, as they were called, see an early assessment in James M. Douie, "The Punjab Canal Colonies," *Journal of the Royal Society of Arts* 62, no. 3210 (May 29, 1914): 611–23. For a more recent critical assessment of flood irrigation promoted in the Punjab Canal Colonies, see Imran Ali, "Malign Growth? Agricultural Colonization and the Roots of Backwardness in the Punjab," *Past and Present*, no. 114 (February 1987): 110–32.

14. See Benjamin Weil, "The Rivers Come: Colonial Flood Control and Knowledge Systems in the Indus Basin, 1840s–1930s," *Environment and History* 12, no. 1 (2006): 3–29.

15. See Sven Beckert, *Empire of Cotton: A Global History* (New York: Vintage Books, 2015). Also see D. J. Oddy, "Urban Famine in Nineteenth-Century Britain: The Effect of the Lancashire Cotton Famine on Working-Class Diet and Health," *Economic History Review*, n.s., 36, no. 1 (1983): 68–86; and Norman Longmate, *The Hungry Mills: The Story of the Lancashire Cotton Famine 1861–5* (London: Temple Smith, 1978).

16. See I. J. Catanach, "The 'Globalization' of Disease? India and the Plague," *Journal of World History* 12, no. 1 (2001): 131–53; Ira Klein, "Plague, Policy and Popular Unrest in British India," *Modern Asian Studies* 22, no. 4 (1988): 723–55.

17. As Bhavani Raman has argued in *Document Raj*, one of the imperial bureaucracy's gods was the myth of its own procedures. In Deh 22, however, the bureaucracy might appear to have tripped over its own procedures. After all, the point of sending the special magistrate was to highlight an exception. But we must remember that the point of this exception was to validate the norm. Special action taken on one letter, for instance, justified the procedural violence meted out to the Hurs. See Bhavani Raman, *Document Raj: Writing and Scribes in Early Colonial South India* (Chicago: University of Chicago Press, 2012).

18. These discussions of cost and benefits at the provincial level are described in Ansari, *Sufi Saints and State Power*, 75.

19. See Gayatri Chakravorty Spivak, *The Death of a Discipline* (New York: Columbia University Press, 2003).

20. For an in-depth debate over and review of the now broad literature on the derelict environmental and socioeconomic impact of the project, see Habibullah Magsi, André Torre, and Fateh M. Marri, "Impacts of Chotiari Reservoir on Environment and Livelihood of Local Population in Sindh, Pakistan," *Journal of Research in International Business and Management* 3, no. (2013): 20–26.

CHAPTER 16. DADAAB IS A PLACE ON EARTH

1. Anooradha Iyer Siddiqi, "Ephemerality," *Comparative Studies of South Asia, Africa, and the Middle East* 40, no. 1 (2020): 24–34; UNHCR Nairobi to UNHCR Geneva, fax cable, May 8, 1991, Central Registry Project Files, UNHCR archive, Geneva.

2. The UNHCR is the agency designated to protect the displaced. Its census and emergency population counting practices demand critical and scholarly inquiry. Data aggregations drawn from them should invite skepticism.

3. See Jennifer Hyndman, *Managing Displacement: Refugees and the Politics of Humanitarianism* (Minneapolis: University of Minnesota Press, 2007).

4. For a history, see Barbara E. Harrell-Bond and Eftihia Voutira, "In Search of 'Invisible' Actors: Barriers to Access in Refugee Research," *Journal of Refugee Studies* 20, no. 2 (2007): 281–98.

5. This may no longer be so. The condition has been dynamic since the department was dismantled in 2016 and integrated into the Ministry of the Interior.

6. For an example of the challenges in constructing the post-1991 history of Somalia, see Lidwien Kapteijns, *Clan Cleansing in Somalia: The Ruinous Legacy of 1991* (Philadelphia: University of Pennsylvania Press, 2014). See also Lee V. Cassanelli, *The Shaping of Somali Society: Reconstructing the History of a Pastoral People, 1600–1900* (Philadelphia: University of Pennsylvania Press, 1982).

7. The UNHCR restricts access to documents on refugee sites for a duration of twenty years, in order to protect persons fleeing from persecution until the immediate threat has dissipated or a refugee camp has been decommissioned. Most individuals displaced in the past twenty years have remained displaced for most of that time.

8. I am grateful to Esra Akcan for an insightful articulation of a "theory of listening." Columbia University Buell Center dissertation colloquium discussion, May 4, 2019.

9. For example, many of the documents I examined in the UNHCR archive were fax telegrams sent in the early 1990s, printed on paper with an emulsion that could no longer hold ink. I held each page leaf directly up to a lamp to study embossed traces of the printed text. Due to the state of the documents, I may be the last researcher able to make out the words on these pages. This raises enormous problems with regard to access to primary materials, especially among peers who might study the same materials and collectively produce scholarship.

10. These may include African, Arabic, and European documents from colonial, missionary, and other institutional archives or private or cached collections; archaeological and ethnographic forms of evidence; analysis of languages, linguistics, and oral tradition; quantitative and qualitative interpretations of oral history; physical anthropological study; and surveys of botanical or geological data. John Edward Philips, ed., "Part II: Sources of Data," in *Writing African History* (Rochester, NY: University of Rochester Press, 2005), 49–283.

11. Daniel McCall, *Africa in Time Perspective: A Discussion of Historical Reconstruction from Unwritten Sources* (New York: Oxford University Press, 1964); John Edward Philips, ed., *Writing African History* (Rochester, NY: University of Rochester Press, 2005), 20.

12. Wolfgang Zeller, "Special Issue: African Borderlands," *Critical African Studies* 5, no. 1 (2013): 1.

13. Gilbert M. Khadiagala, "Boundaries in Eastern Africa," *Journal of Eastern African Studies* 4, no. 2 (2010): 267.

14. Christopher Clapham, "Boundary and Territory in the Horn of Africa," in *African Boundaries: Barriers, Conduits, and Opportunities*, ed. Paul Nugent and A. I. Asiwaju (London: Pinter, 1996), 240. See also Ian Brownlie, *African Boundaries: A Legal and Diplomatic Encyclo-*

paedia (London: Christopher Hurst, 1979); and John Drysdale, *The Somali Dispute* (London: Pall Mall, 1964).

15. Clapham, "Boundary and Territory in the Horn of Africa," 240. See also Catherine Lowe Besteman and Lee V. Cassanelli, eds., *The Struggle for Land in Southern Somalia: The War behind the War* (London: HAAN, 2000).

16. Khadiagala, "Boundaries in Eastern Africa," 268, citing A. C. McEwen, *International Boundaries of East Africa* (Oxford: Clarendon, 1971), 40.

17. On Dadaab's architecture, visuality, bordering, and heritage, see Siddiqi, "Ephemerality"; Anooradha Iyer Siddiqi, "On Humanitarian Architecture: A Story of a Border," *Humanity* 8, no. 3 (2017); and Anooradha Iyer Siddiqi, "A Shadow Heritage of the Humanitarian Colony," in *Things Don't Really Exist until You Give Them a Name: Unpacking Urban Heritage*, ed. Rachel Lee, Diane Barbé, Anne-Katrin Fenk, and Philipp Misselwitz (Dar es Salaam: Mkuki na Nyota, 2017).

18. Huda Tayob, "Subaltern Architectures: Can Drawing 'Tell' a Different Story?," *Architecture and Culture* 6, no. 1 (2018): 203–22.

19. Saidiya Hartman, "Venus in Two Acts," *Small Axe* 12, no. 2 (2008): 1–14.

20. More women than men live in the Dadaab refugee camps. For UNHCR Kenya demographics, see http://www.unhcr.org/ke/857-statistics.html. See also note 2 above.

21. This chapter distills several years of research in state, academic, cultural, and humanitarian archives; individual and group interviews with approximately five hundred refugees, aid workers, officials, and architects in camps and other contexts; and observation of built environments in refugee contexts in East Africa and South Asia. Many of the interviews were conducted by the author on behalf of the Women's Refugee Commission (a US-based international research and advocacy organization founded by members of the board of the International Rescue Committee) and are held in the Duke University Libraries. Some of these interviews informed the report *Preventing Gender-Based Violence, Building Livelihoods: Guidance and Tools for Improved Programming*, Women's Refugee Commission, October 16, 2012, https://www.womensrefugeecommission.org/research-resources/preventing-gender-based-violence-building-livelihoods-guidance-and-tools-for-improved-programming. The Women's Refugee Commission permitted extensions to interviews related to my scholarship and provided ethical guidelines. My focus on putatively neutral or technical matters of planning and building likely eased tensions in discussions of gender-based violence. Languages I spoke were not the lingua franca in these camps, and I benefited from the expertise, social networks, and protection of interpreters. The International Rescue Committee recommended Somali interpreters who were well known in refugee communities, fluent in Somali, Kiswahili, or Amharic, as well as English. I would like to acknowledge the insights of Najib Khalif, a former and future UNCHR employee involved in registering prima facie refugees in the Jijiga camps in the Somali Region of Ethiopia, as well as Norwegian Refugee Council employee Hashim Keinan, who worked in shelter and latrine construction programs in the Dadaab camps in Kenya.

22. I am grateful to Ijlal Muzaffar for this insightful prompt.

23. Maureen Connelly, former UNHCR Emergency Coordinator at Dadaab, interview by author, Brockenhurst, England, May 3, 2012.

24. See Hannah Whittaker, *Insurgency and Counterinsurgency in Kenya: A Social History of the Shifta Conflict, c. 1963–1968* (Leiden: Brill, 2015).

25. Griselda Pollock, *Differencing the Canon: Feminism and the Writing of Art's Histories* (London: Routledge, 1999), xvi.

CHAPTER 17. LEARNING FROM JOHANNESBURG

The research leading to these results has received funding from the European Research Council under the European Union's Seventh Framework Program (FP/2007–2013) / ERC Grant Agreement no. 615564. I would like to thank Denise Scott Brown for her permission to reproduce her photographic work and for generously sharing with me parts of an unpublished manuscript.

1. Denise Scott Brown, oral history interview, October 25, 1990–November 9, 1991, 2, Archives of American Art, Smithsonian Institution, Washington, DC.

2. Martino Stierli, "Denise Scott Brown and Robert Venturi: 'Learning from Las Vegas' at the Yale School of Architecture," Radical Pedagogies, accessed March 23, 2020, https://radical-pedagogies.com/search-cases/a15-las-vegas-yale-school-architecture.

3. Scott Brown (née Lakofsky) was born in North Rhodesia (today Zambia) in 1931 and grew up in Johannesburg from the age of two. In 1952 she left for London, where she studied at the Architectural Association. In 1957 she returned for a brief sojourn in Johannesburg before leaving permanently when she began her studies at the University of Pennsylvania in 1959.

4. Jonathan Massey, "Review: Power and Privilege," *Journal of the Society of Architectural Historians* 75, no. 4 (2016): 498.

5. Denise Scott Brown, "Invention and Tradition in the Making of American Place (1986)," in *Having Words* (London: Architectural Association, 2009), 5–21; Denise Scott Brown, "To the University of the Witwatersrand, from Denise Scott Brown: 21 July 2011," *Architecture South Africa*, September–October 2011, 10–14; Scott Brown Oral history interview; Denise Scott Brown, interview by Evelina Francia, "Learning from Africa," *Zimbabwean Review*, July 1995, 20–29.

6. Denise Scott Brown to Clive Chipkin, June 27, 1976, Clive Chipkin Collection H/13, Witwatersrand University Architectural Library, Johannesburg (emphasis added).

7. Scott Brown, "Invention and Tradition in the Making of American Place," 8.

8. Scott Brown, "To the University," 10.

9. Scott Brown to Chipkin, June 27, 1976. Although concerned with hegemonic disciplinary formations rather than cultures of resistance, this reading is indebted to a theorization of apartheid's "restless itineraries." See Louise Bethlehem, "Restless Itineraries: Antiapartheid Expressive Culture and Transnational Historiography," *Social Text* 136, no. 3 (2018): 47–69.

10. Scott Brown, "Invention and Tradition in the Making of American Place," 5.

11. Saul Dubow, *A Commonwealth of Knowledge: Science, Sensibility, and White South Africa, 1820–2000* (Oxford: Oxford University Press, 2006), 186. See also Jeremy Foster, *Washed with Sun: Landscape and the Making of White South Africa* (Pittsburgh: University of Pittsburgh Press, 2008), 66–71.

12. Scott Brown oral history interview, 2. See also Scott Brown, "Learning from Africa," 28.

13. Scott Brown oral history interview, 2.

14. Scott Brown, "Invention and Tradition in the Making of American Place," 5.

15. Denise Scott Brown, "Invention and Tradition," *MAS Context* 13 (Spring 2012), http://www.mascontext.com/issues/13-ownership-spring-12/invention-and-tradition.

16. W. J. T. Mitchell, "Imperial Landscape," in *Landscape and Power*, ed. W. J. T. Mitchell (Chicago: University of Chicago Press, 1994), 5–34.

17. Dubow, *Commonwealth of Knowledge*; Hellen Tilley, *Africa as a Living Laboratory: Empire, Development, and the Problem of Scientific Knowledge, 1870–1950* (Chicago: University of Chicago Press, 2011), 314–16.

18. Elizabeth Edwards, "Uncertain Knowledge: Photography and the Turn of the Century Anthropological Document," in *Documenting the World: Film, Photography, and the Scientific Record*, ed. Gregg Mitman and Kelley Wilder (Chicago: University of Chicago Press, 2016), 113.

19. Edwards, "Uncertain Knowledge," 116.

20. Scott Brown oral history interview, 2.

21. Scott Brown oral history interview, 2.

22. Scott Brown, "Invention and Tradition in the Making of American Place," 6.

23. I thank Lael Bethlehem, Nokhanya Mkulisi, and Cullen MacKenzie for their help in deciphering the text in the photo.

24. Scott Brown, "To the University," 10.

25. Scott Brown, "To the University," 10.

26. Martino Stierli, *Las Vegas in the Rearview Mirror: The City in Theory, Photography, and Film*, trans. Elizabeth Tucker (Los Angeles: Getty Research Institute, 2013), 109 (emphasis added).

27. While critical of planning in South Africa under apartheid, Scott Brown did not denounce the notion of "separate development," simply referring to it as a given. Denise Scott Brown, "Natal Plans," *Journal of the American Institute of Planners*, May 1964, 161–66.

28. Verwoerd's key advisor was the anthropologist W. W. M. Eiselen. Both taught at the Afrikaans-speaking University of Stellenbosch. On the imbrication of the field with racial policies and the divide between English and Afrikaaner universities, see Adam Kuper, "South African Anthropology: An Inside Job," *Paideuma*, no. 45 (1999): 83–101. For a critique of Afrikaner anthropology made during apartheid and later refined, see John Sharp, "Two Separate Developments: Anthropology in South Africa," *RAIN* 36 (February 1980): 4–6.

29. Kuper, "South African Anthropology," 95.

30. Nic Coetzer, *Building Apartheid: On Architecture and Order in Imperial Cape Town* (Burlington, VT: Ashgate, 2013); Derek Japha, "The Social Programme of the South African Modern Movement," in *Blank—: Architecture, Apartheid and After*, ed. Hilton Judin and Ivan Vladislavić (Rotterdam: NAi, 1998), 423–37.

31. Andrew Bank, *Pioneers of the Field: South Africa's Women Anthropologists* (Cambridge: Cambridge University Press, 2016), 121–23.

32. Kuper, "South African Anthropology," 88.

33. Elisa Dainese, "Histories of Exchange: Indigenous South Africa in the *South African Architectural Record* and *The Architectural Review*," *Journal of the Society of Architectural Historians* 74, no. 4 (2015): 443–63. Larrabee's work was used as ethnographic evidence in *Natural History*, the magazine of the American Museum of Natural History. See Brenda Danilowitz, "Constance Stuart Larrabee's Photographs of the Ndzundza Ndebele," in *Between Union and Liberation: Women Artists in South Africa 1910–1994*, ed. Marion Arnold and Brenda Schmahmann (Burlington, VT: Ashgate, 2005), 76.

34. Dainese, "Histories of Exchange," 458.

35. John Peffer, *Art and the End of Apartheid* (Minneapolis: University of Minnesota Press, 2009), 15.

36. Peffer, *Art and the End of Apartheid*, 16; Dainese, "Histories of Exchange," 458.

37. Betty Spence, "How Our Urban Natives Live," *South African Architectural Record* 35, no. 10 (1950): 221–36. For how this survey influenced housing design, see Hannah le Roux, "Designing KwaThema: Cultural Inscriptions in the Model Township," *Journal of Southern African Studies* 45, no. 2 (2019): 287–90.

38. Spence, "How Our Urban Natives Live," 221.

39. Deborah Posel, "Getting Inside the Skin of the Consumer: Race, Market Research and the Consumerist Project in Apartheid South Africa," *Itinerario* 42, no. 1 (2018): 123.

40. Spence, "How Our Urban Natives Live," 221.

41. Spence, "How Our Urban Natives Live," 222; Posel, "Getting Inside the Skin of the Consumer," 130–32.

42. Posel, "Getting Inside the Skin of the Consumer," 133.

43. Deborah Posel, "Race to Consume: Revisiting South Africa's History of Race, Consumption and the Struggle for Freedom," *Ethnic and Racial Studies* 33, no. 2 (2010): 169–70.

44. Posel, "Race to Consume," 170; Sophie Feyder, "Lounge Photography and the Politics of Township Interiors: The Representation of the Black South African Home in the Ngilima Photographic Collection, East Rand, 1950s," *Kronos* 38 (November 2012): 131–53.

45. For a discussion of the criticism, see Stierli, *Las Vegas in the Rearview Mirror*, 262–67; and Deborah Fausch, "She Said, He Said: Denise Scott Brown and Kenneth Frampton on Popular Taste," *Footprint* (Spring 2011): 77–90.

46. Posel, "Getting Inside the Skin of the Consumer," 122.

47. Okwui Enwezor, "Rise and Fall of Apartheid: Photography and the Bureaucracy of Everyday Life," in *Rise and Fall of Apartheid: Photography and the Bureaucracy of Everyday Life*, ed. Okwui Enwezor and Rory Bester (New York: International Center of Photography; DelMonico Books/Prestel, 2013), 23.

48. Ayala Levin, "Basic Design and the Semiotics of Citizenship: Julian Beinart's Educational Experiments and Research on Wall Decoration in Early 1960s Nigeria and South Africa," *ABE Journal* (online) 9–10 (2016), https://doi.org/10.4000/abe.3180.

49. Posel, "Race to Consume," 165.

50. On the Levittown studio, see Jessica Lautin, "More Than Ticky Tacky: Venturi, Scott Brown, and Learning from the Levittown Studio," in *Second Suburb: Levittown, Pennsylvania*, ed. Dianne Harris (Pittsburgh: University of Pittsburgh Press, 2010), 314–39; Beatriz Colomina, "Mourning the Suburbs: Learning from Levittown," *Public* 43 (Spring 2011): 86–97.

51. Julian Beinart, "Government-Built Cities and People-Made Places," in *The Growth of Cities*, ed. David Lewis (New York: Wiley-Interscience, 1971), 196.

52. Denise Scott Brown, "From Soane to the Strip: Soane Medal Lecture 2018" and "Influences" (unpublished manuscripts). I thank Scott Brown for providing me access to these manuscripts.

53. Levin, "Basic Design and the Semiotics of Citizenship."

54. Bethlehem, "Restless Itineraries," 50–52.

55. Jean Comaroff and John Comaroff, *Theory from the South, or, How Euro-America Is Evolving toward Africa* (Boulder, CO: Paradigm, 2012).

56. This "totemic" interpretation draws from W. J. T. Mitchell's "Imperial Landscape," 24–27. The evocation of the totem is not foreign to Scott Brown. She named a photo she took of surfboards stuck vertically into the sand *Totemic Surfboards*. Perhaps this leads to further explorations of Scott Brown's complicated relationship to Indigenous cultures, photography, and consumer design. *Totemic Surfboards* appeared in an exhibition of Scott Brown's photos, *Denise Scott Brown: Wayward Eye, Photography of the 1950s and 1960s*, at the Betts Project in London, July 11–October 20, 2018.

CHAPTER 18. ARCHITECTURAL NARRATIVES OF HABEAS CORPUS ON THE HIGH SEAS

1. Documents regarding the case *Lees, a Prisoner v. The Queen*, compiled at the National Archives Kew, Treasury Solicitor Records 18/159 (hereafter TNA TS 18/159/[item]).

2. TNA TS 18/159/Ship's log.

3. TNA TS 18/159/Ship's log.

4. TNA TS 18/159/Habeas return, appendix RR. A QS of "Oyer & Terminer and Gaol Delivery" was a court that convened at regular intervals (in St. Helena, once per year) to hear criminal matters. "Oyer & Terminer" is from the French for "to hear and determine."

5. TNA TS 18/159/Habeas writ (copy), submitted with return.

6. Lees was thus several weeks late for his court date. TNA TS 18/159/Letter accepting return.

7. For an overview of the early history of habeas corpus, see Paul Halliday, *Habeas Corpus: From England to Empire* (Cambridge, MA: Belknap Press of Harvard University Press, 2010).

8. The shift in punishment was famously encapsulated by Michel Foucault's juxtaposition of the torture of Robert-François Damiens in 1757, as punishment for attempted regicide, with Jeremy Bentham's panoptic prison scheme (first published in 1791). Michel Foucault, *Surveiller et punir: Naissance de la prison* (Paris: Gallimard, 1975).

9. For example, see the descriptions of the ideal prison in the Penitentiary Act of 1779 (19 Geo. III c.74), such as the description of a prisoner's measured geometric arrangement of parts.

10. "Law is narrative in the sense that cases, at least, have factual basis in human events that can be rendered in conventional narrative form." Robert Weisberg, "Proclaiming Trials as Narratives," in *Law's Stories: Narrative and Rhetoric in the Law*, ed. Peter Brooks and Paul D. Gewirtz (New Haven: Yale University Press, 1996), 66. See also John Langbein, *The Origins of Adversary Criminal Trial* (Oxford: Oxford University Press, 2002).

11. Robin Evans, *The Fabrication of Virtue: English Prison Architecture, 1750–1840* (Cambridge: Cambridge University Press, 1982).

12. TNA TS 18/159/Warrant transferring custody (LHT doc 6218).

13. TNA TS 18/159/Affidavit Lees.

14. For more on the fact versus law distinction, see Barbara Shapiro, *A Culture of Fact: England, 1550–1720* (Ithaca: Cornell University Press, 2000); and Stephen A. Weiner, "The Civil Jury Trial and the Law-Fact Distinction," *California Law Review* 54, no. 5 (1966).

15. For a good overview of St. Helena's East India Company period, see Stephen Royle, *The Company's Island: St Helena, Company Colonies and the Colonial Endeavour* (London: I. B. Tauris, 2007).

16. TNA TS 18/159/Return of habeas corpus, appendix R.

17. TNA TS 18/159/Lees's Affidavit of Verification ex parte in the Queen's Bench (LHT doc 6211).

18. T. Eustace Smith, *A Summary of the Law and Practice in Admiralty: With an Appendix*, 2nd ed. (London: Stevens and Haynes, 1882). As Lees's affidavit stated, three days after the ship anchored offshore he was placed in custody.

19. 12 and 13 Vic c96 (1849); TNA TS 18/159/Letter of December 21, 1859 (LHT doc 6139.)

20. TNA TS 18/159/Brief of the Crown/Letter by the Secretary of the Treasury to Colonial Office.

21. TNA TS 18/159/Return of habeas corpus.

22. Evans, *Fabrication of Virtue*, 6.

CHAPTER 19. "THIS WHOLE MAZE OF EVIDENCE"

1. Paul R. Baker, *Richard Morris Hunt* (Cambridge, MA: MIT Press, 1980); Mary Woods, *From Craft to Profession: The Practice of Architecture in Nineteenth-Century America* (Berkeley: University of California Press, 1999).

2. Baker, *Richard Morris Hunt*, 87.

3. Romance and "gothic horror" are from Bonnie Honig, *Democracy and the Foreigner* (Princeton: Princeton University Press, 2001), cited in Christopher Tomlins, "American Legal History in Retrospect and Prospect: Reflections on the Twenty-Fifth Anniversary of Morton Horwitz's 'Transformation of American Law,'" *Law and Social Inquiry* 28, no. 4 (2003): 1140. Tomlins introduces tragedy as an alternative.

4. On the monograph, see Gabriele Guercio, *Art as Existence: The Artist's Monograph and Its Project* (Cambridge, MA: MIT Press, 2006).

5. Bernard Berenson, *Lorenzo Lotto* (1916; London: Phaidon Press, 1956).

6. Berenson, *Lorenzo Lotto*, 143; Baker, *Richard Morris Hunt*, 235.

7. Woods, *From Craft to Profession*, 1.

8. Woods, *From Craft to Profession*, 149, 166; Baker, *Richard Morris Hunt*, 235.

9. Woods does mention a brief history of state licensing, which parallels populist repeals of professional licensing but seems to downplay them, perhaps being at odds with her larger narrative. Woods, *From Craft to Profession*, 40–45. On populist licensing repeal, see Magali Sarfatti Larson, *The Rise of Professionalism: A Sociological Analysis* (Berkeley: University of California Press, 1977), 118–19.

10. See also Michael Schudson, review of *The Rise of Professionalism: A Sociological Analysis*, by Magali Sarfatti Larson, *Theory and Society* 9, no. 1 (1980): 215–29; Julia Evetts, "Introduction: Trust and Professionalism; Challenges and Occupational Changes," *Current Sociology* 54, no. 4 (July 1, 2006): 515–31.

11. A. M. Carr-Saunders and P. A. Wilson, *The Professions* (Oxford: Clarendon Press, 1933). Sir Alexander Morris Carr-Saunders (1886–1966) was a leading sociologist and eugenicist, author of *The Population Problem* (1922) and *World Population* (1936), and director of the London School of Economics, and he helped found of a number of universities in British colonies.

12. Carr-Saunders and Wilson, *The Professions*, 297.

13. Also relying on Carr-Saunders and Wilson is Barrington Kaye, *The Development of the Architectural Profession in Britain: A Sociological Study* (London: Allen & Unwin, 1960).

14. Larson, *Rise of Professionalism*, 4, 9.

15. Larson, *Rise of Professionalism*, 18, 190–207.

16. See Eliot Freidson, "Occupational Autonomy and Labor Market Shelters," in *Varieties of Work*, ed. Phyllis L. Stewart and Muriel G. Cantor (Beverly Hills, CA: SAGE, 1982), 39–54.

17. Keith M. Macdonald, *The Sociology of the Professions* (London: SAGE, 1995), cited in Dana Cuff, *Architecture: The Story of Practice* (Cambridge, MA: MIT Press, 1991); Peggy Deamer, "The Sherman Antitrust Act and the Profession of Architecture," *Avery Review*, no. 36 (2019), https://www.averyreview.com/issues/36/sherman-antitrust-act.

18. Michael Schudson, review of *The Rise of Professionalism: A Sociological Analysis*, by Magali Sarfatti Larson, *Theory and Society* 9, no. 1 (1980): 215–29.

19. Burton J. Bledstein, *The Culture of Professionalism: The Middle Class and the Development of Higher Education in America* (New York: Norton, 1976); Samuel Haber, *The Quest for Authority and Honor in the American Professions, 1750–1900* (Chicago: University of Chicago Press, 1991).

20. Geoffrey S. Holmes, *Augustan England: Professions, State and Society, 1680–1730*

(London: Allen & Unwin, 1982); Wilfrid R. Prest, ed., *The Professions in Early Modern England* (London: Croom Helm, 1987).

21. Fernand Braudel, *The Wheels of Commerce* (New York: Harper & Row, 1982) 225–30; Arjun Appadurai, *The Social Life of Things: Commodities in Cultural Perspective* (Cambridge: Cambridge University Press, 1986), 3–58.

22. Michel Foucault, *Discipline and Punish: The Birth of the Prison* (New York: Pantheon Books, 1977). See also Jan Goldstein, "Foucault among the Sociologists: The 'Disciplines' and the History of the Professions," *History and Theory* 23, no. 2 (1984): 170–92.

23. Anthony Vidler, *The Writing of the Walls: Architectural Theory in the Late Enlightenment* (New York: Princeton Architectural Press, 1987).

24. Antoine Picon, *French Architects and Engineers in the Age of Enlightenment* (1988; Cambridge: Cambridge University Press, 1992).

25. Michel Foucault, *The Birth of Biopolitics: Lectures at the Collège de France, 1978–1979* (New York: Picador, 2010).

26. Michel Foucault, "Two Lectures," *Power/Knowledge: Selected Interviews and Other Writings, 1972–1977* (New York: Pantheon Books, 1980), 102.

27. See Thomas Lemke, *Foucault, Governmentality, and Critique* (Boulder: Paradigm, 2011).

28. Terence James Johnson, *Professions and Power* (London: Macmillan, 1972).

29. David Bloor, *Knowledge and Social Imagery* (Boston: Routledge and Kegan Paul, 1976); Steven Shapin, *Leviathan and the Air-Pump* (Princeton: Princeton University Press, 1985).

30. Kenneth Pomeranz, *The Great Divergence* (Princeton: Princeton University Press, 2000); Robert C. Allen, *The British Industrial Revolution in Global Perspective* (New York: Cambridge University Press, 2009). See also Ellen Meiksins Wood, *The Origin of Capitalism: A Longer View* (London: Verso, 2002).

31. Tomlins, "American Legal History," 1135–48.

32. Christopher Tomlins, *Freedom Bound: Law, Labor, and Civic Identity in Colonizing English America, 1580–1865* (New York: Cambridge University Press, 2010).

33. R. M. Hunt, "Architecture," *The Crayon* 4, no. 12 (1857): 371.

34. R. M. Hunt, "Architecture," *The Crayon* 4, no. 6 (1857): 182–83.

35. Herbert Spencer, *Social Statics; or, The Conditions Essential to Human Happiness Specified, and the First of Them Developed* (London: J. Chapman, 1851), 223, 373.

36. R. M. Hunt, "Architecture," *The Crayon* 4, no. 5 (1857): 151.

37. Hunt, "Architecture," *The Crayon* 4, no. 12 (1857): 371.

38. Joseph Coleman Hart, "Unity in Architecture," *The Crayon* 6, no. 3 (1859): 85. (This Hart is not to be confused with the prolific, iconoclastic writer Joseph Coleman Hart.)

39. Richard Morris Hunt et al., "Architecture," *The Crayon* 6, no. 9 (1859): 278–79; Jason Du Mont and Mark Janis, "The Origins of American Design Patent Protection," *Indiana Law Journal* 88, no. 3 (July 1, 2013).

40. See Lionel Bently, "Art and the Making of Modern Copyright Law," in *Dear Images: Art, Copyright and Culture*, ed. Daniel McClean and Karsten Schubert (London: Ridinghouse, 2002).

41. *Report from Select Committee on Arts and Manufactures: Together with the Minutes of Evidence, and Appendix* (London: House of Commons, 1835).

42. The design registry appeared in Britain in 1839, while design patents began in the United States in 1842. *The Crayon* 1, no. 5 (1855): 70; "Artistic Copyright," *The Crayon* 5, no. 10 (1858): 299. Following the report of Charles Lock Eastlake's commission in 1862, paintings, sculptures, and architectural drawings would have copyright protections in Britain. (This was Eastlake the Goethe translator, not the designer.)

43. See Judy Beckner Sloan, "Quantum Meruit: Residual Equity in Law," *DePaul Law Review* 42, no. 1 (1992): 65.

44. Amy Dru Stanley, *From Bondage to Contract: Wage Labor, Marriage, and the Market in the Age of Slave Emancipation* (New York: Cambridge University Press, 1998), 17–22.

45. Thomas Kelt, *The Mechanic's Text-Book and Engineer's Practical Guide* (Boston: Phillips, Sampson, 1849), 232.

46. On courts see Kermit Hall, *The Magic Mirror: Law in American History* (New York: Oxford University Press, 1989).

47. Christopher L. Tomlins, *Law, Labor, and Ideology in the Early American Republic* (New York: Cambridge University Press, 1993).

48. The court had initially been set up to prosecute financial conspiracy cases after the Panic of 1826.

49. See Hendrik Hartog, *Public Property and Private Power: The Corporation of the City of New York in American Law, 1730–1870* (Ithaca: Cornell University Press, 1989), 17. Judge Hoffmann also wrote treatises on Anglican law and the chancery.

50. See Murray Hoffman, *Address to the Graduating Class of the Law School of Columbia College of May, 1861* (New York: John W. Amerman, 1861).

51. "Important Trial: Compensation of Architects; Hunt versus Parmly," *Architects' and Mechanics' Journal* 3, nos. 23–26 (March 9–30, 1861): 222–24, 231–34, 242–45, 252–55; 4, no. 1 (April 6, 1861): 4, 9.

52. "Important Trial," *Architects' and Mechanics' Journal* 3, no. 23 (March 9, 1861): 222.

53. "The Rights of Architects," *Architects' and Mechanics' Journal* 4, no. 1 (April 6, 1861): 1.

54. "Important Trial," *Architects' and Mechanics' Journal* 3, no. 25 (March 23, 1861): 243.

55. "Important Trial," *Architects' and Mechanics' Journal* 3, no. 25 (March 23, 1861): 243.

56. Thompson quoted in "Important Trial," *Architects' and Mechanics' Journal* 3, no. 25 (March 23, 1861): 242.

57. "Important Trial," *Architects' and Mechanics' Journal* 4, no. 1 (April 6, 1861): 9.

CHAPTER 20. "STRIKING AND IMPOSING BEAUTY"

1. *Seagram Sons v. Tax Commission*, 14 N.Y.2d 314, 317 (1964).

2. *Bleistein v. Donaldson Lithographing Co.*, 188 US 239, 251 (1903). The argument in this chapter is focused on the context of US law, though similar concerns arise in other common law contexts.

3. For general considerations of law and aesthetic judgment, see Brian Soucek, "Aesthetic Judgment in Law," *Alabama Law Review* 69 (2017): 381–467; Oren Ben-Dor, ed., *Law and Art: Justice, Ethics and Aesthetics* (London: Routledge, 2011); Christine Haight Farley, "Judging Art," *Tulane Law Review* 79, no. 4 (2005): 805–58; and Costas Douzinas and Lynda Nead, eds., *Law and the Image: The Authority of Art and the Aesthetics of Law* (Chicago: University of Chicago Press, 1999).

4. *People v. Stover*, 12 N.Y.2d 462 (1963).

5. See Charlotte Melbinger, "The Sonnabend Estate and Fair Market Valuation of *Canyon*," *University of Pennsylvania Law Review Online* 163 (2015), https://www.pennlawreview.com/notes/index.php?id=12; and Stéphanie Giry, "An Odd Bird," *Legal Affairs*, September–October 2002, http://www.legalaffairs.org/issues/September-October-2002/story_giry_sepoct2002.msp.

6. The application for correction was heard May 25, 1958, and petition for review was filed September 30, 1958, though not heard by the New York Supreme Court until 1962. For an overview of the sequence of filings and hearings, see Phyllis Lambert, *Building Sea-*

gram (New Haven: Yale University Press, 2013), 196. The court decisions are *Seagram Sons v. Tax Commission* 18 A.D.2d 109 (1963) and 14 N.Y.2d 314 (1964).

7. These are the valuations for the 1961–1962 tax year. The valuations for the preceding years varied, but the difference between the two rival calculations was always several million dollars. Although the exact calculations have an evidentiary claim in themselves, one that could be important within quantitative frameworks of analysis, in the argument that follows it is the methods of calculation, rather than the numbers themselves, that are the primary focus. For clarity, only the calculations and numbers instrumental to the argument will be presented.

8. 18 A.D. 2d 109, 112 (1963). In citing the plaintiff's calculation as $17.8 million, Justice Steuer was using an adjusted calculation of income capitalization, but this number stood in place of the $14.4 million put forward initially by the plaintiffs. The $36 million figure was the cost of constructing the Seagram Building, with no deduction for depreciation.

9. 14 N.Y.2d 314, 320 (1964).

10. 18 A.D.2d 109, 117 (1963).

11. Vincent Scully, "The Death of the Street," in *Modern Architecture and Other Essays* (Princeton: Princeton University Press, 2003), 124; Manfredo Tafuri and Francesco Dal Co, *Modern Architecture* (New York: Harry N. Abrams, 1979), 340.

12. The prologue to *Building Seagram* reveals the particularity of the narrative that follows, signaling the need for a reader to anticipate the shifting perspectives of a protagonist and a historian in the evidentiary positions of the book. See "Prologue: Unlikely Convergences," in Lambert, *Building Seagram*, 1–12.

13. Lambert, *Building Seagram*, 198–99.

14. Lambert, *Building Seagram*, 197.

15. 14 N.Y.2d 314, 317 (1964).

16. Felicity D. Scott, "An Army of Soldiers or a Meadow: The Seagram Building and the 'Art of Modern Architecture,'" *Journal of the Society of Architectural Historians* 70, no. 3 (September 2011): 330–53.

17. Peter Collins, *Architectural Judgement* (Montreal: McGill-Queen's University Press, 1971), 13.

18. Collins, *Architectural Judgement*, 200.

19. "Editorial," *Architectural Forum*, May 1963, 97. See also Judge Bernard Tomson and Norman Coplan, "Aesthetics and the Law: Part 2," *Progressive Architecture*, October 1963, 216.

20. George Lefcoe, "The Real Property Tax and Architecture: A Note on the Seagram Case," *Land Economics* 41, no. 1 (1965): 59.

21. Lefcoe, "Real Property Tax and Architecture," 59.

22. "What the critics are asking the court to do, to impose its aesthetic judgment over the assessor's valuation, they would vigorously oppose in most analogous cases involving aesthetic questions." Lefcoe, "Real Property Tax and Architecture," 61.

23. See Melbinger, "Sonnabend Estate and Fair Market Valuation of *Canyon*." The case was settled by the two parties, and in 2012 the Sonnabend estate donated *Canyon* to the Museum of Modern Art. The estate did not pay estate tax on the value of the work, nor did it claim a charitable deduction for its value.

24. Lambert, *Building Seagram*, 198.

25. Skepticism here does not stand for a neutral objectivity on the part of the historian but for a disciplinary standpoint in which architectural history would not presume that its existing disciplinary methods are the privileged way to understand and interpret a given architectural object or instance of architectural process.

Selected Bibliography

Only works related directly to issues of evidence and narrative are listed here. For other important works, see the endnotes in the introduction. This bibliography does not include sources for chapters' specific subjects; those sources are cited in the chapter endnotes.

Abramson, Daniel. "Stakes of the Unbuilt." *The Aggregate Website*, February 10, 2014. http://we-aggregate.org/piece/stakes-of-the-unbuilt.

Braudel, Fernand. "History and the Social Sciences: The *Longue Durée*." 1959. In *On History*. Translated by Sarah Matthews. Chicago: University of Chicago Press, 1980.

Carpo, Mario. "Big Data and the End of History." *International Journal of Digital Art History*, no. 3 (2018): 22–35. Originally published in *Perspecta* 48 (2015): 46–59.

Chandler, James, Arnold I. Davidson, and Harry Harootunian, eds. *Questions of Evidence: Proof, Practice, and Persuasion across the Disciplines*. Chicago: University of Chicago Press, 1994.

Crinson, Mark, and Richard J. Williams. *The Architecture of Art History: A Historiography*. London: Bloomsbury, 2019.

Daston, Lorraine. "Speechless." In *Things That Talk: Object Lessons from Art and Science*, edited by Lorraine Daston, 9–26. Cambridge, MA: MIT Press, 2008.

Daston, Lorraine, and Peter Galison. *Objectivity*. Cambridge, MA: MIT Press, 2007.

Daston, Lorraine, and Katherine Park. *Wonders and the Order of Nature, 1150–1750*. New York: Zone Books, 1998.

Foucault, Michel. "Nietzsche, Genealogy, History." In *Language, Counter-Memory, Practice*. Ithaca: Cornell University Press, 1980.

Gallagher, Catherine, and Stephen Greenblatt. "The Touch of the Real" and "Counterhistory and the Anecdote." In *Practicing New Historicism*. Chicago: University of Chicago Press, 2000.

Gigerenzer, Gerd, Zeno Swijtink, Theodore Porter, Lorraine Daston, John Beatty, and Lorenz Krüger. *The Empire of Chance: How Probability Changed Science and Everyday Life*. Cambridge: Cambridge University Press, 1989.

Ginzburg, Carlo. "Clues: Roots of an Evidential Paradigm." In *Clues, Myths, and the Historical Method*. Translated by John Tedeschi and Anne C. Tedeschi. Baltimore: Johns Hopkins University Press, 1989.

Ginzburg, Carlo. *The Judge and the Historian: Marginal Notes on a Late-Twentieth-Century Miscarriage of Justice*. Translated by Antony Shugaar. London: Verso, 1999.

Gosseye, Janina, Naomi Stead, and Deborah Van Der Plaat, eds. *Speaking of Buildings: Oral History in Architectural Research.* New York: Princeton Architectural Press, 2019.

Grafton, Anthony. *The Footnote: A Curious History.* Cambridge, MA: Harvard University Press, 1997.

Hacking, Ian. *The Emergence of Probability: A Philosophical Study of Early Ideas about Probability Induction and Statistical Inference.* Cambridge: Cambridge University Press, 1975.

Hacking, Ian. *Historical Ontology.* Cambridge, MA: Harvard University Press, 2002

Hyde, Timothy. "'Well Built, But Poorly Roofed': Notes on the Remains of Architectural History." *Architectural Theory Review* 22, no. 2 (2018): 210–32.

Jarzombek, Mark. "The Disciplinary Dislocations of (Architectural) History." *Journal of the Society of Architectural Historians* 58, no. 3 (1999): 488–93.

Jaskot, Paul B., and Ivo van der Graaff. "Historical Journals as Digital Sources: Mapping Architecture in Germany, 1914–24." *Journal of the Society of Architectural Historians* 76, no. 4 (2017): 483–505.

Kozlovsky, Roy. "Pairing Le Corbusier and the Affordances of Comparisons for Architectural History." *Journal of Architecture* 24, no. 4 (2019): 549–70.

Latour, Bruno. "On the Partial Existence of Existing and Nonexisting Objects." In *Biographies of Scientific Objects*, edited by Lorraine Daston, 247–69. Chicago: University of Chicago Press, 1999.

McQuillan, Martin, ed. *The Narrative Reader.* London: Routledge, 2000.

Morgan, Mary S., and M. Norton Wise, eds. "Special Issue on Narrative Science." *Studies in History and Philosophy of Science* Part A 62 (April 2017).

Morton, Patricia. "On Evidence" (editorial). *Journal of the Society of Architectural Historians* 76, no. 4 (2017): 433–35.

Osman, Michael, and Daniel M. Abramson. "Evidence and Narrative." *Journal of the Society of Architectural Historians* 76, no. 4 (2017): 443–45.

Philips, John Edward, ed. "Part II: Sources of Data." In *Writing African History.* Rochester, NY: University of Rochester Press, 2005.

Poovey, Mary. *A History of the Modern Fact: Problems in the Sciences of Wealth and Society.* Chicago: University of Chicago, 1998.

Porter, Theodore. *The Rise of Statistical Thinking, 1820–1900.* Princeton: Princeton University Press, 1986.

Rigney, Ann. "When the Monograph Is No Longer the Medium: Historical Narrative in the Online Age." *History and Theory* 49, no. 4 (2010): 100–117.

Scott, Joan W. "History-Writing as Critique." In *Manifestos for History*, edited by Keith Jenkins, Sue Morgan, and Alun Munslow, 19–38. London: Routledge, 2007.

Scott, Joan W. "Story-Telling." *History and Theory* 50 (May 2011): 203–9.

Sewell, William H., Jr. "Historical Events as Transformations of Structures: Inventing Revolution at the Bastille." *Theory and Society* 25, no. 6 (1996): 841–81.

Weisberg, Robert. "Proclaiming Trials as Narratives." In *Law's Stories: Narrative and Rhetoric in the Law: Premises and Pretenses*, edited by Peter Brooks and Paul Gewirtz, 61–83. New Haven: Yale University Press, 1998.

Weizman, Eyal. *Forensic Architecture: Violence at the Threshold of Detectability.* New York: Zone Books, 2017.

White, Hayden. "The Value of Narrativity in the Representation of Reality." 1980. In *The Content of the Form: Narrative Discourse and Historical Representation*, 1–25. Baltimore: Johns Hopkins University Press, 1987.

Contributors

Daniel M. Abramson is professor of architectural history at Boston University and the author of three books on architecture, capitalism, and society: *Obsolescence: An Architectural History* (University of Chicago Press, 2016); *Building the Bank of England: Money, Architecture, Society, 1694–1942* (Yale University Press, 2005); and *Skyscraper Rivals: The AIG Building and the Architecture of Wall Street* (Princeton Architectural Press, 2001). He also coedited *Governing by Design: Architecture, Economy, and Politics in the Twentieth Century* (2012) with the Aggregate Architectural History Collaborative. His current work is focused on postwar American government centers.

Zeynep Çelik Alexander teaches in Columbia University's Department of Art History and Archaeology. She is the author of *Kinaesthetic Knowing: Aesthetics, Epistemology, Modern Design* (University of Chicago Press, 2017) and a coeditor of *Design Technics: Archaeologies of Architectural Practice* (University of Minnesota Press, 2020). She has also published in numerous venues, including the *Journal of the Society of Architectural Historians*, *New German Critique*, *Harvard Design Magazine*, *Log*, *e-flux*, *Grey Room*, *Journal of Design History*, and *Centropa* as well as several edited volumes. She is an editor of the journal *Grey Room* and a codirector of Columbia's Center for Comparative Media.

Lucia Allais is a historian of architecture in the modern period. Her work focuses on architecture's role in the global culture industry and in international politics. She also writes on the history of building techniques and on contemporary design. Her first book, *Designs of Destruction: The Making of Monuments in the Twentieth Century* (University of Chicago Press, 2018) traces how international cultural heritage was redefined through the midcentury destructions of war and modernization. Allais studied at Princeton, Harvard, and MIT. She is associate professor of architecture at Columbia University, a founding member of the Aggregate Architectural History Collaborative, and an editor of the journal *Grey Room*.

Erik Carver is a PhD candidate in architectural history at Columbia Graduate School of Architecture, Planning, and Preservation and an instructor at the Rhode Island School of Design. His work focuses on design, technology, and labor in the nineteenth century. He was a researcher at Columbia's Buell Center and coauthored, with Janette Kim, *The Underdome Guide to Energy Reform* (Princeton Architectural Press, 2015), which was supported by awards from the Van Alen Institute and the Graham Foundation. Prior to this, he worked in the architecture profession in New York.

Edward Eigen is senior lecturer in the history of landscape and architecture at Harvard Graduate School of Design. His work focuses on intersections of the human and natural sciences in the long nineteenth century in the European and Anglo-American contexts. His recent publications in American studies include a critical chronology of the JFK Memorial Library, a speculative restoration of an epitaph written for Cotton Mather's slave Onesimus, and a bio-bibliography of the reception of Frederick Jackson Turner's frontier thesis. A proponent of the Montaignian essay tradition, he is the author of *On Accident: Episodes in Architecture and Landscape* (MIT Press, 2018).

Lisa Haber-Thomson is a lecturer at Harvard Graduate School of Design. An architectural historian whose research explores the entanglements between territory, law, and architecture, she is currently at work on a book project that takes a multifaceted approach to the history of carceral architecture in the eighteenth and nineteenth centuries. In parallel, she works on the architectural implications of contemporary law, with topics including federal habeas doctrine and Eighth Amendment conditions of confinement claims.

Andrew Herscher is cofounding member of a series of militant research collaboratives, including the We the People of Detroit Community Research Collective, Detroit Resists, and the Settler Colonial City Project. In his own work, he endeavors to bring research on architecture and cities to bear on struggles for rights, justice, and democracy across a range of global sites. Among his books are *Violence Taking Place: The Architecture of the Kosovo Conflict* (Stanford University Press, 2010), *The Unreal Estate Guide to Detroit* (University of Michigan Press, 2012), and *Displacements: Architecture and Refugee* (Sternberg Press, 2017). He teaches at the Taubman College of Architecture and Urban Planning at the University of Michigan.

Timothy Hyde is associate professor of architectural history and theory at the Massachusetts Institute of Technology. His research examines aspects of the relationship between architecture and law, with aesthetic judgment the subject of his most recent book, *Ugliness and Judgment: On Architecture in the Public Eye* (Princeton University Press, 2019), and constitutionalism the subject of his first book, *Constitutional Modernism: Architecture and Civil Society in Cuba, 1933–1959* (University of Minnesota Press, 2012). His writings have also appeared in numerous journals, including *Perspecta*, *Log*, *El Croquis*, the *Journal of Architecture*, the *Journal of Architectural Education*, *arq*, *Future Anterior*, *Architecture Theory Review*, and *Thresholds*.

Janna Israel is completing her book *"As Though Another Byzantium": Ruins, Artifacts, and Conflict in Renaissance Venice*. Her research has been supported by several organizations, including the National Gallery of Art, the American Academy in Rome, Harvard University, and the National Endowment for the Humanities.

Lauren Jacobi is the Clarence H. Blackall Career Development Associate Professor of Architectural History in the History, Theory + Criticism section of the Department of Architecture, MIT. A scholar of early industrial and early modern Europe, she published *The Architecture of Banking in Renaissance Italy: Constructing the Spaces of Money* (Cambridge University Press, 2019). It probes historical relationships between banks and religious behavior, exploring urban geographies and architectural forms that unveil moral attitudes toward money during the birth of capitalism. She is working on a project, nomos of the sea, in which she studies how spatial practices extended to aquatic realms in the Mediterranean world.

Paul B. Jaskot is professor of art history and the director of the Wired Lab for Digital Art History and Visual Culture at Duke University. His research focuses on the political history of modern German architecture with a specific emphasis on the impact of National Socialist cultural policy. He is currently working on a study of the role of the construction industry in the use of forced labor from World War I through World War II. In 2020–2021, Jaskot was the Ina Levine Invitational Scholar at the Mandel Center for Advanced Holocaust Studies at the US Holocaust Memorial Museum.

Roy Kozlovsky is the chair of the David Azrieli School of Architecture, Tel Aviv University, Israel. He received his PhD in theory and history of architecture at Princeton University in 2008. His academic research interests include postwar architectural environments built for children, comparative architectural historiography, coastal landscape infrastructure, and the techno-politics of crosstown expressways.

Ayala Levin is an associate professor in the Department of Architecture and Urban Design at UCLA. Her research is concerned with north-south and south-south architectural knowledge exchange, with a focus on building and urban planning projects in postindependence African states. Her monograph on the export of Israeli architectural and planning models to Sierra Leone, Nigeria, and Ethiopia in the 1960s and 1970s is forthcoming from Duke University Press.

Forrest Meggers is assistant professor at Princeton University, jointly appointed in the School of Architecture and the Andlinger Center for Energy and the Environment. At Princeton he codirects the PhD track in computation and energy and leads the architecture and engineering program. As director of the CHAOS Lab (Cooling and Heating for Architecturally Optimized Systems), he leads a highly interdisciplinary research group developing new technologies, methods, and forms for building systems. Meggers received his doctorate from ETH Zurich, has published numerous peer-reviewed science papers on applied research, and has also written architectural journal articles and book chapters that present a rethinking of technology in architecture.

Peter Minosh is a historian of architecture, urbanism, and landscape with a focus on the relationship between politics and the built environment. His research considers architecture's modernity within the parallel phenomena of expansions of global capital and the emergences of revolutionary political movements from the eighteenth century to the present. His current project examines architecture, slavery, and colonial revolution in the eighteenth-century Atlantic world. He received his PhD in architectural history and theory from Columbia University.

Ijlal Muzaffar is an associate professor of modern architectural history at the Rhode Island School of Design. He received his PhD from MIT in the history, theory, and criticism of architecture and art. He also holds the MArch degree from Princeton University and a BA in mathematics and physics from Punjab University. His work has appeared widely in edited volumes, exhibition catalogs, and peer-reviewed journals. He is a founding member of Aggregate, the architectural history research collaborative and publishing platform.

Albert Narath is an assistant professor of the built environment in the History of Art and Visual Culture Department at the University of California, Santa Cruz. His research and teaching interests focus on the history of modern architecture and design from the nineteenth century to the present, within the intersection of architectural history, environmental history, and anthropology. His current book project focuses on the reception of Indigenous architecture in the American Southwest following World War II.

Michael Osman is associate professor of architecture and urban design at UCLA, where he directs the MA and PhD programs in architectural history and theory. He is the author of *Modernism's Visible Hand: Architecture and Regulation in America* (University of Minnesota Press, 2018). He has published essays in *Perspecta, Cabinet, Log, Grey Room,* and several edited volumes. Osman is a founding member of the Aggregate Architectural History Collaborative.

Laila Seewang is assistant professor of architecture at Portland State University, where she teaches architecture and urban history, theory, and design studios. Her research uses infrastructure as a lens through which to study environmental and urban design, in particular during the nineteenth century.

Anooradha Iyer Siddiqi is an assistant professor at Barnard College, Columbia University. Her book manuscript "Architecture of Migration: The

Dadaab Refugee Camps and Humanitarian Settlement" analyzes the history, visual rhetoric, and spatial politics of the Dadaab refugee camps in northeastern Kenya as an epistemological vantage point in the African and Islamic world. Her book manuscript "Minnette de Silva and a Modern Architecture of the Past" contends with wartime heritage politics in Sri Lanka by examining the intellectual career of a feminist and environmental activist scholar-practitioner, one of the first women ever to establish a professional architectural practice.

Łukasz Stanek is professor of architectural history at the Manchester School of Architecture, University of Manchester, UK. Stanek authored *Henri Lefebvre on Space: Architecture, Urban Research, and the Production of Theory* (University of Minnesota Press, 2011) and *Architecture in Global Socialism: Eastern Europe, West Africa, and the Middle East in the Cold War* (Princeton University Press, 2020). Currently Stanek studies the Africanization of Ghanaian architecture as part of the Centering Africa Program at the Canadian Center for Architecture. Stanek has also taught at ETH Zurich, Harvard Graduate School of Design, and the University of Michigan.

Meredith TenHoor is an architectural and urban historian and is a professor of architecture at Pratt Institute, where she coordinates courses in architectural history and theory. Her publications focus on the relationships between agriculture, architecture, and cultural and territorial change in twentieth-century France; the intellectual history of architectural theory; and racial capitalism and urban transformation in New York. TenHoor is also editor, a founding board member, and former chair of the Aggregate Architectural History Collaborative.

Ivo van der Graaff is assistant professor of art history at the University of New Hampshire. He received degrees in Mediterranean archaeology from the University of Amsterdam, and his PhD in Greek and Roman art history is from the University of Texas at Austin. He currently focuses on ancient Etruria and the Bay of Naples and serves as the field director of the Oplontis Project, which examines a luxury villa and trade emporium destroyed by the eruption of Vesuvius. His book *The Fortifications of Pompeii and Ancient Italy* examines the social and urban role of defensive circuits in antiquity.

Index

Abdul Haque, 220, 221
Abdul Qadir, 215–16, 221, 223
Abramson, Daniel, 53, 58
Adler, Friedrich: beliefs about ornamentation, 115; conducted survey of brick architecture, 103–6, 113–14; goal of scientific objectivity, 103–6; publication of survey findings, 106–10, 116
Admiralty, 254, 256–57
aesthetic value, 274–76, 280–83
Africa: and comparative urbanism, 175; demarcation of land borders, 230–31. See also Dadaab refugee camp; South Africa
Aggregate, 4–5, 8, 16, 53
AIA (American Institute of Architects), 182–83, 267–68
air-conditioning system, 27
Akcan, Esra, 14–15
Albrecht the Bear, 109
Altichiero da Verona, 95
Amadeo, Giovanni Antonio, 96
American Civil War, 220
American Institute of Architects (AIA), 182–83, 267–68
analogy, 147, 150
anatomy, 150
Anderson, Stanford, 7
anecdotes, 33–35, 44
Anthropocene, 74, 75, 78, 83–85
Antwerp, 194, 197

apartheid, 236, 241–45, 246
Appleman, Roy E., 35–36
archē, 21
archaeology: in the American Southwest, 63–64, 67–72; excavation of Franklin House, 36, 39, 42; at Wellfleet Harbor, 42
architect: archives organized around individual architects, 10–11; challenge to concept of architect as solitary artist, 262–63; definition, 7. See also professionalization
architectural history: collaborative scholarship, 4–5, 13, 16; distinguished from art history, 7; epistemological authority, 8–10, 104–5, 113–14; geographical focus, 12–13; historical vs. scientific writing, 75–76; monographs vs. social histories, 260, 261–62, 264; types of expertise, 6–8. See also digital art history; social art history
architectural value: in Banister Fletcher, 119, 127–32; in quantity surveying, 120–23; of Seagram Building, 274–83
architecture schools: during British imperialism, 164–65; curricula, 10; interdisciplinarity of, 5–6; Prussian Bauakademie, 113, 114
archives: boundaries of, 11; from colonial Sindh, 222; depicted in *Austerlitz*, 196; Dywidag project archive, 136, 137, 142; Farge on materiality of, 58–59; geographical focus, 12; migrant archive, 230, 233–34; organized around individual

341

architects, 10–11; political contexts, 11–12; records of Dadaab refugee camp, 229–30; types of materials included in, 10–11
Argentina, 138
Arizona: astronomical observatories, 65–66; Pueblo architecture, 63–71
astronomy, 65–66. *See also* planetaria
Atwood Celestial Sphere, 140
Auschwitz, 194
Austerlitz: characters' identity expressed in architecture, 192–93; and evidence, 194–97; implications for architectural historians, 198–99; inspirations for main character, 191; irony and doubling, 193–94, 199; and narrative, 197–98; prose fiction style, 190–91
Aztec Pueblo, 67

Babcock, Charles, 267
Baghdad urban planning: British and Greek master plans, 163, 166, 168; during British imperialism, 164–65; comparative knowledge from outside the West, 162–68, 175; compared to Warsaw, 162–63, 168, 175; housing, 172–73; Kadhemiya district, 168, 169, 172, 173–74; Miastoprojekt master plan, 162, 166–73; role of local officials, 166; treatment of mosques, 168, 170–71, 173
Baguio, 164
Baker, Paul R., 260–64
bald eagles, 276, 282
Bandung, 164
Banham, Reyner, 11–12
Banister Fletcher (textbook): on architectural value, 127–32; criticisms of, 117–19; on historical and nonhistorical styles, 117–19, 126, 128, 130, 131; publication and editions, 117, 131; readership, 130–31; referenced in Fletcher Jr.'s lectures, 123; reflects quantity surveying methodology, 127, 129–30; tabulated structure, 126, 131; Tree of Architecture, 119, 127, 130, 132
Barbari, Jacopo de', 212–13
Barber, Daniel, 8
baroque, 31, 153, 155
Basista, Andrzej, 173–74
Batcheler, Penelope Hartshorne, 38–44

Bauakademie, 113, 114
Baubeamte, 104–6, 110
Bauersfeld, Walter, 140
Baümel, Von A., 81
Beam Expeditions: goals, 63–64, 70; methods, 66–69; study of climatology, 70–71
Bechhöfer, Susi, 191
Beinart, Julian, 244–45
Berenson, Bernard, 262
Berg, Max, 136
Berlin: during Cold War, 163; municipal architecture, 110–16; public works ministry, 104, 114; school of art history, 113–16; social housing, 15
Bernardino of Siena, saint, 207–8
Bernini, Gian Lorenzo, 153
Bibliothèque Nationale, 191, 195
Biondo, Giovanni, 211–12
Boldù, Giovanni, 97
Bonneuil, Christophe, 85
Boukman, Dutty, 24
Bramante, Donato, 153
Brancusi, Constantin, 276
Brandenburg, 109, 110
Braudel, Fernand, 4
Breendonk, 192, 198
brick architecture: in Berlin municipal buildings, 115–16; construction techniques, 110, 116; in medieval Prussian structures, 103–9; in Young Building collapse, 179–81
British Empire: government of Iraq, 164–65; settler villages in Sindh, 214, 218–20, 222–24; St. Helena colony, 256–57
Brooks, Cleanth, 35, 44
Burnham, Daniel, 164

Campidoglio, 155
canals, 214–15, 216–18, 220, 225
Canyon, 276, 282
Cap Français: burned during revolution, 25, 28–29; map, 22–24; Temple to Emancipation, 25–28
carbonation equation, 76–78, 81–83, 86–87
Carpentier, Alejo, 19–20
Carr, Robert, 35
Carr-Saunders, A. M., 264–65
cathedrals: Gothic, 9, 105; St. Peter's Basilica, 7, 94; tree-ring analysis of, 64
Čelechovský, Gorazd, 46, 293n8
Čelechovský, Věra, 48–60

Central Station (Antwerp), 194, 197
Certeau, Michel de, 189
Certosa, 96–98
Chaco Canyon, 63, 70–71
Chermayeff, Peter, 40
Chicago. See Young Building
Chile, 138
Chipkin, Clive, 236
Christophe, Henri, 28–32
chronographs, 67–68
churches, 104. See also cathedrals; San Giobbe hospice
Chytilová, Věra, 51
cinquecento, 153
Citadelle Laferrière, 29
climate change: and concrete production, 83–85, 88; hockey stick graph, 72–73, 83; impact on architectural history, 76; and tree-ring analysis, 72
climatology: of American Southwest, 70–72; and tree-ring analysis, 64, 66, 71–72
coherence, 7
coins: authenticated in architectural settings, 91–93, 98; compared to medals, 93; counterfeiters of, 90–91; gave authenticity to architecture, 94–99
Cold War, 163–64, 173–75
Colleoni chapel, 96
Collins, Peter, 279–80, 283
Colomina, Beatriz, 11, 159
colonialism: in American Southwest, 69; British settler villages in Sindh, 214, 218–20, 222–24; demarcation of African land borders, 230–31; and Iraqi urban planning, 164–65; jurisdiction of court on St. Helena, 256–57; and modern labor law, 266–67; and pedagogy, 8; in Saint-Domingue architecture, 20–24, 27; Scott Brown on settler-colonial cultures, 236–38
colossal order, 153, 155
Columbia University, 11
comparative method: category of style, 150–52, 156; creative nature of, 147; criticisms of, 157–60; dialectical method, 152–55; empirical method, 150–52; in legal context, 281–82; limitations of, 156, 161; modern contextual method, 150–51, 155–56; relationship to narrative, 148–50, 160–61
comparison (literary device), 147–49

concrete: spraying technique, 140–41; used in ancient Rome, 78, 127. See also concrete, reinforced
concrete, reinforced: carbonation, 76–78, 81–83, 85–89; and climate change, 83–85, 88; in Dywidag projects, 136, 138; early estimates of lifespan, 80; early research on failure, 80–81; ecological history, 87–89; invention, 78–80
Connally, Ernest Allen, 39, 40, 44
construction firms. See Dywidag; quantity surveying
Contarini, Giovanni, 204–6
Contarini, Lucia, 204–6, 207
contractors, 120–23
contracts: precedent established by Hunt v. Parmly, 272–73; and professionalization, 266–67, 268–69
Conway, John, 181
copyright, 268
Corbusier, Le, 10–11, 156, 158–59
Cotter, John L., 40, 42–43
cotton, 214, 220–21
counterfeiters, 90–91
counternarrative, 13–15, 16
Courtauld Institute, 194
courtrooms, 253
Craig, Robert, 42, 44
The Crayon, 267
Cret, Paul, 14
Czechoslovakia. See Etarea; Prague

Dadaab refugee camp: archival records, 229–30; layout of Ifo camp, 231–32; migrant archive, 230, 233–34; size, 227; *tuqul* dwellings, 234
Dalat, 164
dams, 215, 225–26
Dante, 90
Deetz, James, 42
Deh 22: author's visits to, 217; creation of, 214; fears of Hur attacks, 216; Mariam Bibi's inheritance, 221–23; plague, 221; settled by Pir Baksh, 219–20; surveyed by author's father, 214, 225
dendrochronology. See tree-ring analysis
Dessalines, Jean-Jacques, 29–30
De Stijl, 158–59
Deutsches Museum, 136, 140
digital art history: critical nature of process,

133–35; data analysis techniques, 12–13; expands scale of evidence, 134, 139, 140, 141; GIS shapefiles, 170–73; mapping of Dywidag projects, 136–43; raster graphics, 170; and social art history, 143–44
displacement of Indigenous groups, 214–15, 218, 225–26
dome construction, 140–42
Douglass, Andrew Ellicott: claims of scientific objectivity, 64, 67–68, 71–72; ecological concerns, 70–72; Mars canals dispute, 65–66; tree-ring analysis, 63–64, 66–69
Doxiadis Associates, 166, 168
droughts, 70–72
Duncan, Francis, 272
Durand, Jean-Nicolas-Louis, 150
Durand, John, 267
Dürer, Albrecht, 155
dust, 214, 216, 218
Dyckerhoff & Widmann. See Dywidag
Dywidag, 136–43

Eberhardt, Jacqueline L., 243
École des Beaux-Arts, 261
Ecological Society of America, 71
Egypt, ancient, 128, 151–52
Eid, 217
Einstein Tower, 142
Eisenman, Peter, 10
Eliot, T. S., 35
emperors, Roman, 95–98
Empson, William, 35
England: in Pevsner's account of modernism, 13; prison sentences, 252–53; quantity surveying profession, 120–23, 127, 129–30, 131. See also British Empire
environment: environmental degradation in American Southwest, 70–72; space vs. environment, 12; standards for environmental control, 8. See also climate change; climatology
equations, 75–76, 88–89
Essenwein, August, 301n3
Etarea: advantages for women, 48, 50–51; architectural plans, 46–48, 53; planned layout, 49–50, 52; planned location, 55–57; socialist vision, 48, 49, 54; vacuum suction conveyance, 46–48, 49, 52
Eugenius IV, pope, 94
Evans, Robin, 252–53, 258

expert witness testimony, 178, 180–85, 269–70
Expo '67, 48

facilities managers, 182–83
family history. See Deh 22
Farge, Arlette, 58–59
Favro, Diane, 10
feminism, 51, 234
Feminist Art and Architecture Collaborative, 8, 14
Fethi, Ihsan, 173
Filarete, Antonio, 94
Fischer, Theodor, 136
Fletcher, Banister, Sr., 117, 120–23. See also Banister Fletcher (textbook)
Fletcher, Banister Flight, Jr., 117, 123–25, 129–30. See also Banister Fletcher (textbook)
Fletcher, Pamela, 305n3
flooding, 210, 211
Florence, 91–92
focalization, 42
Fontane, Theodor, 301n11, 302n22
forensic architecture: expert witness testimony, 178, 180–85; facilities managers, 182–83; field split between legal and human rights contexts, 177–79, 188–89; and insurance industry, 181–85; and international humanitarian law, 185–88; legal liability, 181–82; tensions with design-focused broader field, 184–85
form: in comparative histories, 149; Fletcher Jr. on form and value, 129–30; formalism, 9–10
Foucault, Michel, 8, 150, 160, 265–66, 328n8
Franciscans, 205–9, 213
Frankl, Paul, 150, 303n33
Franklin, Benjamin, 40. See also Franklin House
Franklin House: archeological excavation, 36; decision not to reconstruct, 33, 38–43; destruction, 35; limited documentary evidence of, 33, 35–41; search for Thackara drawing, 37–38, 39, 44. See also Ghost House at Franklin Court
French Revolution, 20, 79
Frick, Friedrich, 106–8
Frost, John, 268–69

Galbaud, François-Thomas, 25
gardens, 30–31

INDEX

Garlasco, Marc, 188, 189
Gaza, 189
general contractors, 120–23
Germany: in Pevsner's account of modernism, 13; Weimar period, 135–43. *See also* Berlin; Prussia
Ghost House at Franklin Court, 33, 39–45. *See also* Franklin House
Giedion, Sigfried, 11, 79
Gilly, Friedrich, 106, 108
Ginzburg, Carlo, 178
Giocondo, Giovanni, 209–10
GIS shapefiles, 170–73
Giurgola, Romaldo, 40
Goethe, Wolfgang von, 105, 108, 114
Gonzaga, Francesco, 93
Gothic architecture: adopted by Prussian empire as "German" style, 105, 110, 116; heightened interest starting in eighteenth century, 104; and scholasticism, 9
Goyet, Francis, 157
Great Transformation, 265
Greece, ancient, 151–52
Greenough, Horatio, 268
Greiff, Constance M., 37, 42
Grimm, Hermann, 9
Gropius, Walter, 13, 141
Grosses Schauspielhaus, 139
Gwilt, Joseph, 267

habeas corpus: definition, 251; as form of evidence, 258–59; in Lees case, 250–51, 254–57; and prisoners' agency, 259; requires legal facts, 255; and spaces of imprisonment, 251–52, 258–59
Haiti: plantation agriculture, 31–32; revolution, 24, 28–29; rule of Christophe, 30–32. *See also* Cap Français; Saint-Domingue
Hamada, Minoru, 77, 81–83, 85–87
Hart, Joseph Coleman, 267–68
Hays, K. Michael, 278
Hegel, G. W. F., 114, 152
Hellmann, Ellen, 242, 244
Hennebique system, 80
Heshel's Kingdom, 198
Hoffman, Murray, 269, 272
Hohenzollern dynasty, 109
Hollstein, Ernst, 64
Holmes, Geoffrey, 265
Holmes, Oliver Wendell, 274–75

Holocaust, 194
Hughes, Charles E., Jr., 35
humanitarian aid. *See* Dadaab refugee camp
humanitarian law, 177–79, 185–89
human rights, 27–28, 177, 185–86, 188–89
Hunt, Richard Morris: career, 262–63; documented founding of AIA, 267; Josephine Schmid mansion, 263; Rossiter house trial, 261, 262, 269–73
Hunt, William Morris, 268
Huntington, Ellsworth, 71
Hunt v. Parmly: competing interpretations, 260–62, 266, 273; established precedent for contracts, 272–73; and nature of architectural transaction, 264, 273; trial, 269–72; verdict, 272–73
Hurs, 215–16, 218–19, 220, 224, 225–26, 321n5
Hussein, Saddam, 162, 172
Hyde Expedition, 67
hydria, 151–52

ICTY (International Criminal Tribunal for the Former Yugoslavia), 185–88
Independence National Historical Park (INHP), 33, 35, 36, 39, 42
India, 221
Indigenous peoples: displaced by canals and dams in Sindh, 214–15, 218, 225–26; Pueblo Indians, 8, 69, 70–72
Industrial Revolution, 12, 265
INHP (Independence National Historical Park), 33, 35, 36, 39, 42
intellectual property, 267–68, 269–70
Iraq: during British imperialism, 164–65; collaboration with socialist countries, 162–64, 165–66; coup in 1958, 162, 165; postcolonial comparative environment, 162–63, 165–66; US invasion, 174. *See also* Baghdad urban planning
Izenour, Steven, 235

Jacob, François, 150
Jacobson, Dan, 198
Jahrhunderthalle, 136
Jamaica, 12
Japan: in Banister Fletcher, 119, 126; concrete research in, 85–86
Jarzombek, Mark, 5
Jena, 140

Johannesburg, 238, 243, 244–45. See also townships
juries, 179–81, 253, 255, 257, 269, 272–73

Kadhemiya, 168, 169, 172, 173–74
Kent, William, 27
Kenya, 227, 231. See also Dadaab refugee camp
Kepes, György, 244, 245
kindertransports, 191, 195
Kolb, Antonio, 213
Kosovo conflict, 186–88
Kubba, Sam A. A., 177–78, 185
Kugler, Franz, 303n32
Kunstwissenschaft, 9
Kunstwollen, 7

Laboratory of Tree-Ring Research, 70
LaCapra, Dominick, 147, 149
Lambert, Phyllis, 278–79, 283
landscapes, 237–41
Larkin Administration Building, 11–12
Larrabee, Constance Stuart, 242, 243
Larson, Magali, 264–65
Las Vegas, 235–36, 238, 240–41, 244, 246
Latour, Bruno, 58
Laugier, Marc-Antoine, 129
law: aesthetic judgment vs. legal judgment, 274–75, 280–83; criminal justice, 252–54, 258; and deviant comparisons, 159; evidence in legal context, 280–83; liability, 181–82; as model for historiography, 178–79; narrative in legal context, 178. See also contracts; habeas corpus; *Hunt v. Parmly*; Seagram Building
Lawrence, D. H., 40
League of Prizren building, 186–88
Learning from Las Vegas, 235–36, 244
Leclerc, Charles, 28
Lees, Charles Frederick, 249–51, 254–57
Lefcoe, George, 280
Lefuel, Hector-Martin, 262
Lentricchia, Frank, 34–35
Leonowicz, Władysław, 169
Levittown, 242, 244, 245
Levy, Jonathan, 128–29
liability, 181–82
Linnaeus, 150
literature. See *Austerlitz*; comparison (literary device)

Loos, Adolf, 7, 158–59
Louvre, 262, 269
Lowell, Percival, 65–66, 71
Lowell Observatory, 65–66
Lübke, Wilhelm, 301n4
Lynch, Kevin, 244

Mackandal, François, 19–22
Maestro Adamo, 90
Makhi Dhand, 225–26
Makiya, Mohamed, 165
Manila, 164
Mapoch, 239, 242, 244
Mariam Bibi, 221–23
Marienburg Fortress, 106–8
Mark the Evangelist, saint, 207–8
marronage, 19, 28, 29, 32
Mars, 65–66, 71
Martin V, pope, 205
Marxism, 143, 265
Massey, Jonathan, 235
Materialgerechtigkeit, 115–16
measurers, 120
mechanical systems, 11. See also pneumatic tubes
medals, 91, 93–98
Medieval Brick Architecture of the Prussian States: data collection, 104–6, 113–14; as evidence of Prussian history, 109–10, 113; goal of empirical accuracy, 103–6; impact on Prussian architecture, 110, 113–16; legitimized Gothic architecture as "German," 110, 116; publication, 106–9
Mendelsohn, Erich, 136, 142
Mertins, Detlef, 278
Meyer, Adolf, 141
Miastoprojekt-Kraków: comparative practices, 163, 167–68; comparisons of Baghdad and Warsaw, 162–63, 168, 175; documentation of master plans, 166–68; GIS shapefiles of master plans, 170–73; working style, 166
Michelangelo, 155
Mies van der Rohe, 40, 279. See also Seagram Building
migrant archive, 230, 233–34
military structures: Breendonk, 192, 198; fortifications in Saint-Domingue, 22–24, 29–31; Marienburg, 106–8
Milošević, Slobodan, 186–88

Miniter, P. J., 180
Minoprio, Spencely, Macfarlane, 163, 166, 168
MIT, 5, 173, 244
modernism: and comparative analysis, 156, 158; histories of, 160; Pevsner's account of, 13; sense of "before and after," 279; social critique, 188–89
Moller House, 158–59
money. *See* coins
Montgomery, Roger, 177, 185
Moos, Stanislaus von, 148, 158–59
Moreau de Saint-Méry, Médéric Louis Élie, 20–22
Moretti, Franco, 308n24
Moro, Cristoforo, 207–9
Morosini, Domenico, 208–10
Morris, A. E. J., 47, 50
Morris, William, 13
mosques, 168, 170–71, 173
Munich, 91
Museum of Modern Art, 11, 332n23
myth, 21–22, 32

Nader, Ralph, 182
Nalbantoğlu, Gülsüm Baydar, 117–19
Napoleon, 28
Native Americans. *See* Pueblo Indians
NATO, 186–87
Ndebele architecture, 239, 242, 244
Nelson, Louis P., 12
neoplasticism, 158
New Criticism, 10, 35
New Towns, 46
Ngilima, Roland, 244
Ngilima, Torrance, 244
Nicholas V, pope, 205
Nonnenbrücke (Bamberg), 136
Nowa Huta, 167
numberdars, 222, 224

objectivity: and Douglass's tree-ring analysis, 64, 67–68, 71–72; goal of *Medieval Brick Architecture of the Prussian States*, 103–6
Observant Franciscans, 205–9, 213
observatories, 65–66
Oraibi, 63, 69, 71
oral history, 15. *See also* Deh 22
Orlando East, 243
ornaments, 210
Ottoman architecture, 168, 186

paintings, 153–55
Pakistan. *See* Sindh
Palanti, Mario, 138
Palazzo della Cancelleria, 153
Palazzo Medici, 98
Palazzo Odescalchi, 153
Palazzo Rucellai, 153
Palazzo degli Scaligeri, 95–96
Palladio, Andrea, 156, 158
Palmer, George A., 33, 38–39, 43–44
Panofsky, Erwin, 5, 9
Parmly, Eleazer, 261, 270–71, 273
Parsons, Talcott, 264
Passanti, Francesco, 10–11
Pavia, 96, 98
People v. Stover, 275
Perelman, Chaïm, 149
Pevsner, Nikolaus, 13–15
Philippines, 164
philology, 150
photographs: of destroyed League of Prizren building, 186; as form of evidence, 9–10; inspirations for German concrete architecture, 141; of palaces in Wölfflin's *Principles of Art History*, 153–54; of South African landscapes, 237–39; of South African street scenes, 242, 244; as tools for anthropology, 240
Picon, Antoine, 266
picturesque, 27, 31
Pioneers of the Modern Movement, 13–15
Pir Pagaros, 215–16, 219, 224
Planeix House, 158–59
planetaria, 140–42
planetary interior, 8
plantations, 12, 19, 25–27, 31–32
Platt, John, 37, 39
Plutarch, 147
pneumatic tubes: planned in Etarea, 46–48, 49, 52; in Prague, 50–51
Poelzig, Hans, 139
poetry, 35
Poland. *See* Miastoprojekt-Kraków; Warsaw
Polanyi, Karl, 265
Pollock, Griselda, 234
Polverel, Étienne, 25
Ponce, Nicolas, 22–24
Ponte Sisto, 94, 209
postmodern intellection, 5
Powell, B. Bruce, 36

Prague: biologically inspired architecture, 293n8; pneumatic tube system, 50–51; train stations, 191, 193
Prague Institute of Architectural Design, 46
Prague Spring, 48, 51
Prest, Wilfrid, 265
prestige buildings, 278, 281, 282
prisoners. See habeas corpus
prisons, 252–54, 258. See also Breendonk
Privy Council, 222
professionalization: in Baghdad, 166; and contracts, 266–67, 268–69; and intellectual property, 267–68, 269–70; and modern capitalism, 264–65; sociological history of, 260–61, 264–67. See also Hunt v. Parmly
profit, 128–29
Prussia: adopted Gothic architecture as "German" style, 105, 110, 116; national architectural history narrative, 109–10, 113; public works ministry, 103–6, 110–16
public works ministry: Berlin municipal buildings, 115–16; collected data for *Medieval Brick Architecture of the Prussian States*, 103–6, 110–15
Pueblo Bonito, 63–65, 67, 70–71
Pueblo Indians, 8, 69, 70–72
Punjab, 219, 222

Qasim, Abd al-Karim, 162
quantity surveying, 120–23, 127, 129–30, 131
Quast, Ferdinand von, 301n3
quattrocento, 153
Queen's Bench, 251, 254–57

race: apartheid, 236, 241–45, 246; criticisms of racism in Banister Fletcher, 119; *l'aristocratie de la peau* in Haiti, 20–21; and origin of Haitian revolution, 24; racially segregated cities, 164; Rosenwald School project for Black students, 11. See also Indigenous peoples; slavery
Rainsford, Marcus, 25–28
Ranke, Leopold von, 105
raster graphics, 170
Raumplan versus Plan Libre, 159–60
Rauschenberg, Robert, 276, 282
real estate valuation, 276–78, 282
refugees. See Dadaab refugee camp
Rembrandt, 155

Renaissance: in Banister Fletcher, 125, 129; comparison of palaces and paintings, 153–55; medals and coins, 93–99; organized knowledge by similitude, 150; villas, 156–58. See also San Giobbe hospice; Venice
Riedlmayer, András, 186–88
Riegl, Alois, 7, 150
Riley, Edward M., 35–36
Risselada, Max, 160
Ritter, Carl, 30–31
Robaczyński, Lech, 162
Robinson, Jennifer, 175
Roccatagliata Building, 138
Romanticism, 25, 108, 261, 271–72
Rome, ancient: in Banister Fletcher, 127–28; coins, 94, 95–96; concrete architecture, 78, 127; cultural rituals, 10; emperors depicted in Renaissance art, 95–98
Rosenwald School, 11
Rossiter, Thomas P., 261, 270
Roumeguère-Eberhardt, Jacqueline, 243
Rowe, Colin, 10, 156–58
Roy, Ananya, 175
Rue Franklin Apartments, 80
Ruskin, John, 129
Rycroft, A. W., 180

Saarinen, Eero, 143
Sabellico, Marc'Antonio, 210, 211
Saint-Domingue: colonial economy, 22–24; enslavement in, 19–21, 23, 25, 27–28; plantation agriculture, 19, 25–27. See also Cap Français; Haiti
San Giobbe hospice: construction of bridge, 209–10; depicted in Barbari's woodcut, 213; founding by Contarini, 204–5; legal dispute over patronage rights, 203, 206, 208, 211; modifications by Franciscans, 205–9, 213; Moro's patronage of, 207–9; oral testimony about, 206, 208; vulnerability to flooding, 210, 211
Sano, Toshikata, 85–86
Sans-Souci, 30–32
Sanudo, Marino, 209–10, 213
Schaffer, Simon, 8, 68
Schinkel, Karl Friedrich, 115, 302n17
Schmarsow, August, 9
scholasticism, 9
schools. See architecture schools

Schulman, Edmund, 72
Schultze, Richard, 116
Scott, Felicity, 279, 283
Scott Brown, Denise, 33, 41; African perspective, 235–37, 246; critiques US in comparison to South Africa, 236–37, 246; design of Franklin Ghost House, 33, 41; interest in consumer culture, 241, 242, 244; on landscapes, 237–41; *Learning from Las Vegas*, 235–36, 244; mother's influence, 237–38; self-portrait, 246; on settler-colonial cultures, 236–38
Scully, Vincent, 8–9, 10, 278
Seagram Building: cost to build, 278–79; court case in architectural history narratives, 278–80, 281; lack of comparable buildings, 281–82; methods of calculating taxable value, 274, 276–78, 282; *Seagram v. Tax Commission of New York City*, 276–78; significance for architectural history, 278; and transactional nature of aesthetic value, 282–83
Sebald, W. G. *See Austerlitz*
Semper, Gottfried, 113, 129, 150–52, 155
Senator, 249–50
shapefiles, 170–73
Sher Khan, 221
shotguns, 215–16
silt, 217–18, 225
Sindh: British colonial government, 214, 218–20, 222–24; canals, 214–15, 216–18, 220, 225; conflicting cultural views of land use, 224; cotton industry, 214, 220–21; dams, 215, 225–26; displacement of Indigenous groups, 214–15, 218, 225–26; settler villages, 214, 216, 219–21
Sitte, Camillo, 164
situla, 151–52
Sixtus IV, pope, 94, 209
skyscrapers, 138, 156, 181
slavery: and human rights, 27–28; in Saint-Domingue, 19–21, 23, 25, 27–28
slide projectors, 8–9, 153, 281
social art history, 135, 143–44
socialism: in Arab world, 172; devaluation of knowledge from socialist countries, 174–75; and Iraq, 162–63; in Poland, 162, 166; in vision for Etarea, 48, 49, 54
Somalia, 227, 229, 230, 231
Sonthonax, Léger-Félicité, 25

Sorel, Georges, 21
South Africa: consumer culture, 241, 243–44; landscapes, 237–41; Ndebele architecture, 239, 242, 244; townships during apartheid, 242–45; used by Scott Brown to critique US, 236–37, 246
South America, 138
sovereignty, 27–28
Soviet Union, 48, 162–63, 165
Soweto, 245
Spence, Betty, 242–43
Spencer, Herbert, 267
Springer, Anton, 9
Steuer, Aaron, 277–79
Stevens, Wallace, 34
St. Helena, 250–51, 254–57
Stillman, William, 267
Stoffwechsel, 129
St. Peter's Basilica, 7, 94
Stüler, August, 301n1, 301n4
sufaid posh, 220, 221, 223
sunspots, 66
Superior Court of the City of New York, 269
surveys, 104–6, 113–14
Sweden, 86

Tafuri, Manfredo, 10, 27, 278
taxation, 274, 275–78, 282
tehsildars, 222
Temple of Venus (Versailles), 27
Temple of Virtue (Stowe Gardens), 27
Temple to Emancipation, 25–28
Terezín, 195–96
theaters, 138–39
thermodynamics, laws of, 88
tholos, 25, 27
Thomas, William, 270
Thompson, John, 272
Titian, 153
Tocqueville, Alexis de, 148
Tomlins, Christopher, 267
Tournikiotis, Panayotis, 160
Toussaint Louverture, 25, 28
townships: house façades, 244–45; Orlando East, 243; Soweto, 245; Western Native Township, 245
Tree of Architecture, 119, 127, 130, 132
tree-ring analysis: characterized as objective science, 64–65, 67–68; developed by Douglass, 66–69; and environmental

studies, 71–72; and human-caused climate change, 72–73; of Pueblo Bonito, 63–64; as self-evidence, 67–68, 74
Trial of the Pyx, 91–93
tuquls, 234
Tuutti, Kyösti, 77, 86
typology, 14

unbuilt, 53, 59
UNHCR (United Nations High Commissioner for Refugees), 227, 229
United States: compared to South African apartheid, 236–37, 246. See also Beam Expeditions; *Hunt v. Parmly*; Seagram Building
University of Baghdad, 165, 166
University of Berlin, 9
University of California Berkeley, 10
University of Cincinnati, 185
University of Leipzig, 9
Upjohn, Richard, 267, 269–70
urban planning: and automated retailers, 54; housing design in Johannesburg, 245; land management in Venice, 210–11; new comparative urbanism, 175–76; public works buildings in Berlin, 110–16. See also Baghdad urban planning; Etarea
Uruguay, 138
usus pauper, 205, 208, 213
Utley, Robert M., 39

value. See aesthetic value; architectural value
Vanderpool, John, 180
Velázquez, Diego, 153
Venice: Basilica of San Marco, 207–8; bridge construction, 208–10; conflict between civil and ecclesiastical law, 205; flooding problems, 210, 211; founding myths, 204, 207–8; land management, 210–11; legal dispute over San Giobbe, 203, 206, 208, 211; official topographical images, 211–13; ornaments and ideal of well-ordered republic, 210. See also San Giobbe hospice
Venturi, Robert: collaborations with Scott Brown, 235, 236, 243; design of Franklin Ghost House, 33–35, 39, 41–43; self-portrait, 246

Verona, 95
Versailles, 27
Verwoerd, Hendrik, 241
Vico, Enea, 91, 95
Vidler, Anthony, 266
Villa Garches, 156, 158
Villa Malcontenta, 156, 158
villas, 156–58
violence: and forensic architecture, 185–88; and myth, 21–22, 32
Viollet-le-Duc, Eugène, 129

Walpi, 69, 150
Warburg Institute, 194
war crimes, 186–88
Warren, John, 173
Warsaw, 162–63, 168, 175
Weber, Max, 265
Weimar Germany, 135–43
Weizman, Eyal, 177–78, 188, 189
Wellfleet Harbor, 42
Wells, Joseph, 272
Western Native Township, 245
White, Hayden, 13, 108, 109, 148, 149, 178, 197, 261
Williams, Carl M., 37–38, 39, 44
Willis, Carol, 156
Wilson, Mabel, 11
Wilson, P. A., 264–65
Witwatersrand University (Wits), 236, 238
Wölfflin, Heinrich, 14, 150, 152–55, 158, 160, 161
Women's Refugee Commission, 233
Woods, Mary, 260–64, 273
World War I, 140, 164
World War II, 11, 142
Worskett, Roy, 173
Wright, Frank Lloyd, 11–12

Yale University, 8
Yoelson, Martin, 37, 44
Young Building, 179–81
Yugoslavia, 185

Zeiss-Dywidag System, 140–41
Zeiss firm, 140

www.ingramcontent.com/pod-product-compliance
Lightning Source LLC
Chambersburg PA
CBHW032025290426
44110CB00012B/678